CW00956870

DAVID MARTYN LLOYD-JONES

The First Forty Years 1899–1939

John Kerr

DAVID MARTYN LLOYD-JONES

The First Forty Years 1899–1939

Iain H. Murray

THE BANNER OF TRUTH TRUST

THE BANNER OF TRUTH TRUST
3 Murrayfield Road, Edinburgh EH12 6EL, UK
P.O. Box 621, Carlisle, PA 17013, USA

*

© Iain H. Murray 1982
First published 1982
Reprinted 1983
Reprinted 1998
Reprinted 2002
Reprinted 2008
Reprinted 2012

*

ISBN: 978 0 85151 353 9

*

Typeset in 10 / 12 pt Linotron Sabon

Printed in the USA by
Versa Press, Inc.,
East Peoria, IL

TO MRS D. MARTYN LLOYD-JONES
FOR WHOM GENERATIONS
OF CHRISTIANS ARE
THANKFUL TO GOD

Contents

'The Gospels and the New Testament are not a complete record either of the work of Christ or of his disciples – they merely give us an inkling of what happened. The church of Christ has never kept exhaustive minutes of its meetings, it has had no time to do so. There was so much work to be done and so much to record. . . . Her great idea was to do her appointed work, not to write accounts of that work. Do you wish to find an account of what the gospel has done? Well, you must not turn to books for it. Look rather to the reformed sinners – see the lame walking, and the blind seeing and the deaf hearing. The true history of the church is to be found in the lives of the converts that it has produced. You can never really write an account of the conversion of a sinner, the only true account is the man himself. That is why the church has always relied more upon preaching and public testimony than upon documents and the written word.'

M. L.-J.

in a sermon on Acts 3:6, May 15, 1927

Illustrations

Introduction

It was the hope of many around the world that after his retirement from Westminster Chapel in 1968 Dr Martyn Lloyd-Jones would find time to write an account of his life. There were even occasions when he himself spoke of the possibility, yet, much though some of us shared the hope of seeing an autobiography, we doubted if it would ever be written.

For one thing, it was never Dr Lloyd-Jones' habit to *write* for publication. When his books began to appear regularly (beginning with *Studies in the Sermon on the Mount* in 1959), their contents were very largely transcripts of his pulpit ministry. As he preached from brief notes, rather than from a fully-written manuscript, the books could not have appeared at all had it not been for this procedure.

Dr Lloyd-Jones regarded preparation for the pulpit and the preparation of a manuscript for the press as two different things. So committed was he to the former that literary work as such had no appeal for him. The living voice had priority over the written word. In this respect, as in others, he resembled John Knox who gave all his 'study and travail' to the pulpit and could declare, 'I consider myself rather called by my God to instruct the ignorant, comfort the sorrowful, confirm the weak, and rebuke the proud, by tongue and living voice, in these corrupt days, than to compose books for the age to come.'[1]

When, after his retirement, Dr Lloyd-Jones found more time to think of publications, it was characteristically to the editing of the

---

[1] Knox's *History of the Reformation in Scotland*, C. J. Guthrie's edition, 1898, p. 302. The same was true of another foremost preacher, J. H. Thornwell, cf. *The Life and Letters of James Henry Thornwell*, B. M. Palmer, 1875, reprinted, Banner of Truth Trust 1974, p. 555.

transcripts of his sermons that he turned. First and last, the pulpit ministry was his chief concern.

There was a further consideration which led some of us to regard the appearance of an autobiography as very improbable. By temperament and, even more, by theological conviction, Dr Lloyd-Jones disliked any indulgence in personal publicity on the part of Christians. He viewed the personality-cults evident in some of the churches of the Victorian era as disastrous to the interests of true spirituality. Man-centredness in any form disfigures the kingdom of God. The church at her best is a power in the world not because of what she says about herself but because of what she is by the grace of God.

Dr Lloyd-Jones rarely referred to himself in public. His reluctance to speak of his conversion was as strong as John Calvin's. Personal allusions in his sermons were minimal. On two occasions some years ago when admirers prepared biographies of him, he intervened to prevent their publication.[1] Requests that he might speak on his life and ministry were consistently declined. Of course, in principle he was not against good Christian biographies and autobiographies; on the contrary, he regarded them as most profitable reading. But the factors in his own thinking, above mentioned, may help to explain why an account of his life from his own hand was never written.

In view of these considerations it required no great foresight on the part of anyone near to Dr Lloyd-Jones to anticipate the need for material to be put by so that a record of his life might appear posthumously. Intermittently, over more than twenty years prior to his death, the present writer sought to accumulate information – the most important source being Dr Lloyd-Jones himself. When I hesitantly disclosed this fact to Dr Lloyd-Jones in 1974 he made no response whatsoever. But at least I had not suffered a prohibition!

During 1980 when I wrote drafts of the opening chapters of the present biography, it was clear that the record of a number of things in Dr Lloyd-Jones' life and ministry would be lost unless he became directly involved. I therefore approached him again on the subject, this time supported by Mrs Lloyd-Jones and Lady Catherwood, their

[1] One of these was written by his friend the Reverend Eliseus Howells and we can only regret that its present whereabouts is unknown. The probability is that Howells' manuscript was destroyed with his home in London through bombing in the Second World War. The other unpublished biography was written by a minister who had no personal acquaintance with his subject.

elder daughter, and he consented to give me whatever help he could. His one, oft-repeated, proviso, vehemently expressed both in conversation and in prayer, was that the sole aim of any record should be to advance 'the glory of God'.

This involvement on the part of Dr Lloyd-Jones continued almost until his death on March 1, 1981. It must not, however, be understood as his endorsement of everything which appears in the following pages. All I can say is that a considerable part of the volume was prepared in consultation with him and that the general interpretation which it gives of his career is his own.

This volume would have been immeasurably poorer without the aid of Mrs Lloyd-Jones. Unlike her husband (who kept virtually nothing that could aid a biographer!), Mrs Lloyd-Jones preserved a private store of press-cuttings gathered over more than half-a-century. Of these, as well as of her personal counsel, I have made extensive use in these pages. Her own written accounts of some of the early converts of her husband's ministry, to be published in 1983 in her book *Memories of Sandfields, 1927–1938*, have also provided an invaluable aid.

The single most important literary source for these pages has been the box of Dr Lloyd-Jones' manuscript sermons which have survived from his early ministry. At that period he commonly wrote one sermon in full each week and these manuscripts have thus made it possible for me to give his thinking in his own words, and exactly as it was at a given date. These early sermons possess remarkable features. We do not doubt that the forthcoming volume of them, entitled *Evangelistic Sermons at Aberavon* will be very widely read.

If, as I hope, it will be possible to continue this biography at some future date, I shall seek to give fuller acknowledgement then to many who have assisted with help and information on various parts of Dr Lloyd-Jones' life. I cannot, however, omit mention of three friends at this stage. Mr E. T. Rees, Church Secretary during Dr Lloyd-Jones' first pastorate at Sandfields, Aberavon, deserves the gratitude of posterity for his records and memories of those years. These he has shared with me freely and enthusiastically. Dr Douglas Johnson, another of Dr Lloyd-Jones' surviving friends, has given constant encouragement and been a wise adviser on various points contained in these pages. To Mr Dafydd Ifans of the Department of Manuscripts, The National Library of Wales, Aberystwyth, I am immensely indebted for the translation of a large amount of material in Welsh, bearing upon Dr Lloyd-Jones' life and work. The most important of these Welsh sources was the reminiscences of his childhood, which Dr Lloyd-Jones once gave in Welsh on the radio[1] and which I incorporate fully into the opening chapters of this volume. In addition to the translation of sources already known to us, Mr Ifans traced and translated further materials which would never otherwise have come to my notice.

I am also indebted to Westminster Chapel, London, and to the archivist, Miss Dorothy Thompson in particular, for access to church records and for the use of some of the photographs used in this volume.

I must thank Lady Catherwood, Mr S. M. Houghton (who provided the Index) and my wife, for their careful reading of this volume, first in manuscript and then at proof stage. The editorial assistance of Mrs Guy Finnie and Dr Sinclair B. Ferguson at the publisher's Edinburgh office has been indispensable and I acknowledge my gratitude. Finally, I should add that the extent of my wife's involvement is not revealed by the above reference. I am conscious that the undertaking of this biography would not have been possible had she not gladly borne more than her usual large share of family responsibilities, first in Scotland and then in Australia where these pages were completed. Certainly her own gratitude for the ministry of Dr Lloyd-Jones has made those extra duties lighter.

A considerable amount of material is available for a second, concluding volume of this biography, but the work of writing has scarcely begun. There may well be those who could add to the information which is already to hand. Anyone who has a letter from Dr Lloyd-Jones which extends beyond one or two paragraphs has a rarity and copies of such letters (not the briefer ones) would be of interest to us. We would, in particular, welcome any information from service-men or women who benefited from his ministry during the Second World War, and from any in the United States who can provide details or personal impressions of one or more of his post-war visits to North America. Correspondence addressed to the publisher's Edinburgh office will reach the author.

Those who stood close to Dr Lloyd-Jones and who revered him as a leader, indeed father, in Christ, may well find that these pages give but a faint impression of what he was. It is true to say that his

[1] First published in *Y Llwybrau Gynt* 2, Alun Oldfield-Davies (editor), Llandysul, Gwasg Gomer, 1972, pp. 26–56.

ministry, his friendship, his thought, became part of the very lives of those who knew and loved him. For many he was more than anything which print can convey. I have repeatedly been conscious of that fact in preparing this volume.

The truth is that we have lost a leader who, in our generation at least, cannot be replaced. Sorrow is, however, tempered by the conviction that the message which we heard from him and saw in him is with us still. And the grace which made him what he was remains exceeding abundant. The work of God goes on. Oftentimes at a meeting where the life of some former Christian was being considered Dr Lloyd-Jones would give out T. H. Gill's hymn, 'We come unto our Father's God', and no one joined more fervently than he in singing its closing stanza:

> Ye saints to come, take up the strain
> The same sweet theme endeavour!
> Unbroken be the golden chain
> Keep on the song for ever!
> Safe in the same dear dwelling place
> Rich with the same eternal grace,
> Bless the same boundless Giver!

Iain H. Murray
July 1982

'The Child is father of the Man.'
[WILLIAM WORDSWORTH, from
My heart leaps up]

'The fundamental elements in our personality and temperament
are not changed by conversion and by re-birth. The 'new man'
means the new disposition, the new understanding, the new
orientation, but the man himself, psychologically, is essentially
what he was before.'

M. L.-.J.

I

'A Welshman Now!'

In the spring of the year 1905 a pony and trap brought a family to their new home in the village of Llangeitho, Cardiganshire. They were, Henry Lloyd-Jones, then in his early forties, his wife, Magdalene, and their three boys, Harold, Martyn, and Vincent. Martyn, separated by some two years in each case from his older and younger brothers, was aged five years and three months. He was to remember little of the life which they had left behind in Donald Street, Cardiff, where he had been born on December 20, 1899. A flag hung from one of their windows to celebrate some victory in the Second Boer War, a fall downstairs from top to bottom, and a dancing lesson which he suffered at a small private school in Connaught Road – these things were almost all that he was to recall in later life from the days before he reached Llangeitho.

The Lloyd-Joneses felt no grief in exchanging Wales's largest city and port for the sixty or so houses which made up this village in the upper valley of the Aeron. Both parents were native to Cardiganshire. After only indifferent success with his Cardiff grocery shop, and a growing impression that town life did not suit his health, Henry had determined to move back to the country. When, therefore, a favourable opportunity arose, he sold his business, together with the home that went with it, and removed his family to a near-by boarding house until the general store at Llangeitho came on the market. His offer for the store was accepted and a new chapter in their lives began.

By temperament Henry Lloyd-Jones was an optimist and the soul of honour and uprightness. He was once called 'a proper Mr Micawber', ever waiting for something advantageous to turn up, and undoubtedly he felt that there were reasons for hopefulness in the spring of 1906. Wales herself, it seemed to him and to many others, was awakening after a long winter. Certainly times had changed since the days of his own childhood, spent at Cefn-Ceirw, his parents' farm in the Rhydlewis district of Cardiganshire, where Elizabeth, his strong-minded mother, better known as Betty-Cefn, had been famous for her participation in the 'tithe-wars'. Now, as the landslide victory for the Liberals in the General Election of that same year 1906 demonstrated, the Established Church and the landowners could no longer quieten the people with admonitions to 'know their betters'. New political thinking was stirring, the days of privilege were over and reforms certain. With brilliant eloquence, David Lloyd George, Liberal MP for Caernarvon Boroughs, chastised the forces of tradition which had long ruled Wales on behalf of England, and shortly, as Chancellor of the Exchequer, he was even to turn 11 Downing Street into a kind of Welsh embassy. These were heart-stirring events for such a Liberal and a radical as Henry Lloyd-Jones. Patriot though he was in his allegiance to Britain, both conviction and sturdy Welsh independence led him to endorse his mother's belief that the interests of the common man have precedence over those of his superiors. With just such views the Liberals in Wales assisted their fellows in England to sweep into power.

No doubt comparatively little of the change was being registered in Llangeitho in 1906. As a local centre of the Welsh-speaking farming community, it had long stood aloof from much that was going on elsewhere. Its very name was a reminder of how tradition lingered in inland Cardiganshire for, in truth, it ought not to have been called Llangeitho at all, but Capel Gwynfil. Llangeitho parish actually lay on the other side of the river Aeron. The explanation of the anomaly lay in an occurrence two centuries back. Llangeitho ('church of Ceitho') had no fame in the annals of Welsh history until a certain Daniel Rowland became curate there in the 1730's. Thereafter it was to become the centre of a series of evangelical revivals which transformed large areas of the Principality and brought Calvinistic Methodism to birth. At an open-air communion service in Rowland's remote parish in 1742, George Whitefield believed that he saw 'perhaps ten thousand from different parts'. When the authorities of the Church of England, in an attempt to suppress Calvinistic Methodism, ejected Rowland from the parish church in 1763 a 'new church' (*Yr Eglwys Newydd*) was built for him in Capel Gwynfil and the village, considering itself honoured by such a change, was equally pleased to adopt the name of the old parish itself!

[2]

For the most part, by 1906, religion existed in Llangeitho in tradition only, and though the population continued to clean the road in front of their homes and to scrub the front-door step every Saturday night in preparation for Sunday when all went to the chapel, it was hard indeed to imagine how Calvinistic Methodism had ever given such alarm to the bishops. In some parts of Wales the denomination had been touched afresh by a breath of true revival as recently as 1904–05, but in Llangeitho chapel all was as motionless as the statue of Daniel Rowland which the Lloyd-Jones boys passed each morning on their way to school. Martyn's memories of that state of lifelessness were to remain vivid in later years:

'Our minister was a moral, legalistic man – an old schoolmaster. I do not remember that he ever preached the Gospel, and none of us had any idea of the Gospel. He and the head deacon, John Rowlands, looked upon themselves as scholars. Neither had any sympathy for the Revival of 1904–05, and both of them were not only opposed to any spiritual stress or emphasis, but were equally opposed to every popular innovation. Those who came home for their holidays from Glamorganshire, who spoke of their having been "saved", were regarded as hot-heads and madmen from the South. We did not have annual preaching meetings in our chapel, and the eminent preachers of the day were never invited. We would not have heard Dr John Williams and T. C. Williams of Menai Bridge [two leading Calvinistic Methodists of the time] if it were not for the Association Meeting which was held at Llangeitho in June 1913. The only reason for its coming was that the Association itself had asked to come to Llangeitho to celebrate the bicentenary of the birth of Daniel Rowland. Although there is a statue of Daniel Rowland in the village, his influence had long since disappeared from the place, and "Ichabod" had been written across everything. While large congregations still met to worship on Sundays, morning and evening, it was the strong sense of tradition which accounted for it. Llangeitho had lost the fire and the rejoicing of the Methodist Revival to the same extent as Westminster Abbey had lost the life and vitality of the Early Church – "The glory had departed from Israel".'

It was certainly not the Calvinistic Methodist chapel which drew Henry Lloyd-Jones to Llangeitho. Hitherto his attachment had been with the Congregationalists: he now joined the Calvinistic Methodists because there was no real alternative and it was to suffer rather than to sympathise with what Rowland's old congregation had become. Among the Congregationalists in Rhydlewis he had learned to think that such dullness arose from the dead hand of outworn creeds, and he was a warm advocate of the so-called 'New Theology' of R. J. Campbell (Congregational minister of the City Temple in London) which raised a storm among the orthodox in Wales in 1907. Henry Lloyd-Jones had encountered nothing which led him to question whether the 'new' was better than the old. Rather, like so many others, he had been misled into identifying the lifeless traditionalism of Calvinistic Methodism with the real Christianity which it had once represented, and in his reaction to that kind of formal religion he had come to imagine that Christianity's best work lay in achieving social change through education and political action. He was as committed as was his favourite religious weekly, *The Christian Commonwealth*, to an alliance between Liberal politics and religious Nonconformity. At Westminster, Lloyd George gloried in the claim that one had to go back to Cromwell's day to find a Parliament composed of so many Nonconformists. But Lloyd George knew no more than did Henry Lloyd-Jones about what Nonconformity had once been.

At this point 'Maggie' Lloyd-Jones – as everyone called Henry's wife – was in no position to help her husband. Her step-mother had given her an attachment to the Church of England, but there had been little religion of any kind in her parents' home. In fact, David Evans, Martyn's maternal grandfather, was a thorough pagan who made no secret of his indifference to both church and chapel. In many respects David Evans was a remarkable man, not least in his powers of memory: in any market-day debate among his fellow-farmers none was his equal in recalling with effortless accuracy the details of sales of cattle and horses which others had long-since forgotten. With rising prosperity, he had moved from his farm near Aberystwyth to a rather grander establishment, Llwyncadfor, near the border of south Cardiganshire. In his grandson's first memories of the place, Llwyncadfor, with its big house standing at the junction of three roads, and called after the name of an ancient Welsh prince (*Cadifor*), was virtually a village: four uncles helped to direct the many grooms and farm-hands, while the house itself bustled with aunts, servants and maids.

But to return to Llangeitho, an initial problem for the Lloyd-Jones boys on their arrival was the language. Although their parents spoke nothing but Welsh to each other they had used English only in bringing up the children. The explanation for this lay in their mother's own experience. Magdalene was still a child when her mother died and fourteen when her father, David Evans, married again. His second wife was English and so, thereafter, English was the language which the children of the home always heard from their step-mother. When Maggie later had her own children she simply carried on what she had known at Llwyncadfor. Martyn felt his lack of Welsh keenly and determined to remedy it:

'I well remember, about a year after we moved to Llangeitho, as I was playing with a number of children outside the school, that I begged them not to speak English to me any more, "Speak Welsh to me – I'm a Welshman now!"'

Some two years later the point was well proved when Martyn spoke for the first time in public. One of the old Calvinistic Methodist practices which survived in Llangeitho down to the time of the First World War, was the exercise of catechising on the Sunday School lesson in the chapel. At one such catechising in 1909 the minister, with reference to the resurrection of Lazarus, asked, 'Why did Jesus say, "*Lazarus*, come forth"?' Silence followed until there burst out a reply in Welsh from the second Lloyd-Jones boy which was to be repeated around Cardiganshire. 'In case,' Martyn declared, 'they all came forth!'

Another of Martyn's childhood memories of chapel occurred the next year, on the death of King Edward VII in May 1910. The monarch who was head of the world's greatest Empire possessed no mystic aura in the eyes of the tenant farmers of Cardiganshire. As a service was being held in Llangeitho on the day of the King's funeral it was, however, felt that at least something should be said relative to that event and the duty was left to a ministerial catechist who introduced his remarks – in Welsh – with the words, 'I've been asked to say something about this little king who is being buried today.' Such a comment produced no disturbance in the Aeron valley!

It is interesting at this point to remember that the members of the Chapel at Llangeitho were unanimous in prophesying that Vincent would surely be a minister one day – yes, Vincent! This youngest of the Lloyd-Jones boys loved going to meetings. He never missed one – three on Sunday, with the prayer meeting on one week night and the

'Seiat' on another. Vincent attended each one, sitting and absorbing everything, and they all called him *y blaenor bach* – the little deacon. If his place was ever empty, there would be anxious enquiries made to make sure that no illness or accident had kept him away from his usual seat in the front row. At this time, Martyn was more interested in playing football with the village boys than in anything else!

Under Henry Lloyd-Jones, the General Store at Llangeitho soon developed a retail business with surrounding farms and there was nothing which Martyn enjoyed more in his childhood than to accompany his father on such journeys in the trap, pulled by one of the two horses which they owned. Henry Lloyd-Jones was a cheerful man. As a youth he had competed for the bass solo prize at singing festivals and singing was still one of his favourite recreations. His neighbours knew him as a busy, inventive and honest figure. Many years later Martyn was to speak of his father as 'the best natural man I've ever known and the kindest character I've ever met'. His first memories of his mother were of her charm, her activity and her friendliness. In character she was 'very impulsive, generous, and open-hearted'. She delighted in entertaining visitors, whether invited or uninvited. On some points her judgment was fixed; she remained a churchwoman and a Tory; on others she relied on her not inconsiderable intuition. 'I would say that my mother was highly intelligent but not intellectual, she did not read; she was a very quick thinker and could take up a point at once. She was more intelligent than my father.'

Henry Lloyd-Jones showed great wisdom in bringing up the boys. Martyn's greatest desire in life was to be a man, to be grown-up, and, as one sign of manhood was to smoke, he longed for the day when he could join the older lads in this so manly custom.

One day, his father and mother were to be away for the day, and to Martyn's pride and great delight his father entrusted him with all the keys of the house and business – after all he was the practical one, Harold was always reading, and Vincent was too young. So the honour fell to him and the keys were safe in his pocket. But this temporary freedom from the presence of authority gave him an idea. He would buy a packet of cigarettes! Away he went to the appropriate shop and bought a packet of Woodbines. They were not his first smoke but they were the first packet he ever had of his own and he was full of pride and joy. With the responsibility of the keys and the packet of cigarettes, he had arrived!

The boys were asleep when their parents returned, but their father needed the keys and went to get them from Martyn's pocket where he found the packet of cigarettes with them! Whatever else Martyn might forget, he would never forget his father's arrival in his bedroom the next morning. It was the weight of his words rather than his hand which hurt him. He had, his father said, felt he could trust him. He had thought that he was old enough to take responsibility, that he could be relied upon, and he went on to speak of his own deep hurt and disappointment in such a manner that Martyn could bear no more and wept. 'Now get up and get dressed,' said his father. 'We are going down to the shop.' Down to the cigarette shop they went, where Henry Lloyd-Jones announced his displeasure that the shopkeeper had sold the cigarettes to a young boy, and Martyn handed the packet back!

There was another indelible memory of those early days in Llangeitho. Christmas was coming with all its delights and surprises. The carol-singers were out every night, but the Lloyd-Jones boys were not encouraged in that money-raising activity. One night, however, Martyn could resist the temptation no longer and he attached himself to a group of children on their rounds – singing at one door after the other and collecting and sharing the odd pennies which they received right through the village. He never forgot – not to old age – his feelings, when at the end of the round, he learnt that these poor children were collecting money for their mother's funeral. The wound to his conscience was deep and lasting and meant many sleepless hours until the shock faded somewhat, though never the memory.

Through the outings with their father and sometimes through holiday visits to Aberystwyth and other parts by steam train, the Lloyd-Jones boys soon came to know much of Cardiganshire, from its rugged coast on the west to where its eastern boundaries are lost in the mountains and moors of central Wales. They noted the line, north of Llangeitho, where a difference could still be traced between the districts affected by Calvinistic Methodism and those where the Vikings had once settled, where the Welsh dialect changed, and where superstition and folk-lore remained a force even at the beginning of the twentieth century. People in those parts, for instance, spoke with reverence of a 'seer' or 'wise man' at Llangurig who could remove spells or cast spells of his own, turning cream sour at his will! The story was told of a blacksmith in North Cardiganshire who had to make frequent visits to his medical doctor on account of his health until he was 'cured' by this seer. The seer diagnosed that a spell had been cast on the blacksmith, even describing the person responsible for casting it. His promise was that if the suffering blacksmith wore some signs of the Zodiac stitched in his shirt he would have deliverance. And so it proved. But when the displeased doctor subsequently met his former patient and heard his description of the spell-caster, it was at once apparent to him that the clever seer had merely described the blacksmith himself!

At about the age of eight Martyn made his longest journey with his father on what was to be his first visit to London. In December, every year, there was an agricultural show at the Agricultural Hall, London. When Henry Lloyd-Jones decided to go in 1908 it was only possible for him to take one of his sons with him and yet both Martyn and Harold, his elder brother, were anxious to go. No discussion could settle the problem, so lots had to be drawn and it fell to Martyn to accompany his father. This, his first visit to London, was expected to last from a Monday to a Saturday but in the event its excitement continued longer than was anticipated. On the Friday evening in London, as Mr Lloyd-Jones and his second son prepared to return by train the following day, a local squire from the Llangeitho area called where they were staying to say that he was buying a car the next morning and they would be welcome to return with him. The offer was accepted, but finding a suitable car on the Saturday did not prove a straightforward matter. It was mid-afternoon, at a garage near King's Cross, when the squire became interested in an Italian model, a Darracq, built by Alfa Romeo. To say that it was second-hand would be an understatement; Martyn even heard one onlooker remark, 'I would not go fifty miles into the country in that if you paid me £50.' But the deal was done and the journey home of some 300 miles began at last about 5.30 p.m. Scarcely out of the suburbs of London they were stopped by a puncture and, there being no spare wheel, the youngest passenger was left in front of a blazing fire in a hotel in Uxbridge while it was repaired. After the journey was resumed later in the evening, it was soon realised that punctures were likely to be so frequent that they would have to be ignored, and when the next halt was called in the High Street of Oxford at 7 a.m. on the Sunday morning all four tyres were flat and in need of replacement! There was no alternative but to awaken the young owner of a cycle and tyre shop in High Street by the name of W. R. Morris, an action which he did not appear to resent as business had not been good. Here they bought new tyres and tubes, and then, after breakfast at the Randolph Hotel, set off west on the road through Gloucester. The main problem of the day was the December cold, for the car was entirely open to the elements. Only Martyn, huddled on the floor behind the driver's seat, could find any shelter. Assisting the squire in the front was Idris Jones, a cycle dealer from Lampeter, whose mechanical knowledge had caused the squire to take him with him to London. Abergavenny was reached in time for supper but once more the party decided to press on. Not far behind, at Bwlch, where the Brecon road climbs a high hill, Henry Lloyd-Jones and Martyn had to walk behind to ease the load. While doing so they were startled to see sparks and flames at the rear of their vehicle. A warning shout brought it to a halt and Idris had to attend to a badly over-heated engine. Lampeter was reached on the Monday morning and, although repairs were made during the day, the problem soon recurred when the journey was resumed after tea and Martyn was required to run back for the help of Idris Jones who had left them at his home town!

Meanwhile regular telegrams had kept Mrs Lloyd-Jones informed of their progress and when, at length, they arrived at Llangeitho about 9 p.m. on the Monday, the three weary travellers were met by a crowd of villagers. They had driven without rest for two days, yet only once – when Idris Jones was at the wheel and fell asleep – had the vehicle left the road![1]

Here, in his own words, are some of Martyn's own memories of his Llangeitho childhood:[2]

'Our family life was extremely happy. The clearest recollection I

[1] A sequel to the story occurred in August 1947. At the close of a horse-show, which Martyn Lloyd-Jones had attended in Aberystwyth, he happened to meet Idris Jones who told him that he was the West-Wales agent for the former tyre dealer in Oxford, W. R. Morris, now become Lord Nuffield! At business banquets Idris Jones would be called upon by Nuffield to relate the story of one of his first successes – four tyres and inner tubes sold early one morning in Oxford, 'his biggest single order up-to-date'!
[2] In the pages which follow most of his own recollections of childhood are taken from an account he once gave on Welsh radio and published in Welsh under the title 'Martin Lloyd-Jones' in Y Llwybrau Gynt, ed. Alun Oldfield-Davies, vol. II (Llandyssul: Gwasg Gomer, 1972), pp. 26–56. Other memories were given personally to the author.

have is that of always having a houseful of people. The main reason
for this – apart from the fact that my father and mother were very
pleased to welcome friends and others to the house for a meal and a
chat – was that our house was also a business establishment. Like
other shops in the country areas we used to sell all sorts of goods and
my father was also a pioneer in selling machines such as ploughs,
separators, haymaking machines and binders for the hay. And quite
soon he also began a sort of creamery – a dairy. We had two
manservants who toured the surrounding countryside to collect
unsalted butter. Then it was all mixed together, salt was added, and
finally the butter was placed in boxes and sent to various shops and
co-operatives in Glamorganshire. The butter was sold as "Vale of
Aeron Blend".

'I say this to explain why there were always so many people in our
house. We dealt not only with the farmers of the Llangeitho district
but also with those of Tregaron, Llanddewi Brefi, Penuwch,
Bwlchyllan, Abermeurig, Llwynygroes, and even further. Travellers
selling various goods would also call regularly and everyone who
came had to have tea or supper. There is no need to say that such a
life was exceptionally interesting for children. We took great interest
in the different characters and their peculiarities. I remember how we
looked forward to some of them coming because of their remarkable
sayings. For example, whatever was said, one of these characters
would always reply, "*Be chi'n siarad*" ("You don't say"). Another
one, "*Cerwch ona*" ("Get away with you"). And yet another, "*Fo'lon
marw nawr*" ("I'm willing to die now") as a protestation of the truth
of what he was saying.

'There is nothing more interesting than natural, original characters; unfortunately education has almost wiped them out. One
afternoon I remember being with my father in the pony and trap on
our way to attempt to sell a separator at a farm some six miles from
Llangeitho, in the direction of Mynydd Bach. The two farmers were
bachelors and the elder, naturally, was the master. The master was
more conservative than his brother and was very much opposed to
the new machine, but the other was anxious to obtain it. As we were
leaving the road and turning into the lane which led to the farm, the
younger brother greeted us. He had been expecting us: "Mr Jones," he
said, "there's only one way in which you'll sell that separator here, and
that is for me to talk strongly against it. I was anxious for you not to
misunderstand me when I start to object." Then, he disappeared and

we went on towards the house. The elder brother came out and my father began his business. In about ten minutes' time, when everything appeared hopeless, the other brother came forward with a rather grim look on his face, and his brother asked him, "What do you think of this separator?" And he, according to the plan, started objecting strongly. Needless to say, we sold the separator.

'A subject which was often discussed at home was "politics". My father was a staunch Liberal and in those days he was an avid admirer of Lloyd George, although he turned against him from 1915 onwards. It wasn't often that a Tory would call in, but my mother supported that dogma. When she had some measure of support from a visitor there would be a heated argument. Today it is difficult to realise the faith that our fathers had in politicians. I remember one afternoon immediately after the 1909 Budget when I was in the trap with my father and one of our neighbours. This man had been brought up in central Cardiganshire and was therefore a Unitarian. I still remember the shock that I had when I heard him tell my father that he was certain that Lloyd George would do more good than Jesus Christ, because he had a better chance. I pity them! I have a vivid memory of the two elections in 1910. In one of them – if not both – the man who later became Sir George Fossett Roberts stood for election for the Tories against Mr Vaughan Davies [Lord Ystwyth], our M.P. Mr Roberts was a brewer from Aberystwyth. I remember nothing of the speeches but I remember well that Mr Fossett Roberts was not allowed to speak at all when he came to address the meeting held one evening in the day school. The moment he opened his lips some of the Liberal boys started to sing – and many joined in with them.

> Vaughan Davies is the man, Vaughan Davies is the man,
> Farewell to the man of the barrel,
> Vaughan Davies is the man.

Mr Roberts persevered in his attempt to speak for some twenty minutes and then gave up. I am afraid that I was one of those that followed him, still singing the rhyme until he left the village in his car. I must confess that even the Cardi,[1] undoubtedly the most intelligent of Welsh men, sometimes lapses.

'Llangeitho, like many other villages, was rich in characters. Time will only allow me to mention three of them. One of the most original

[1] Natives of Cardiganshire.

was a shoemaker – or Ianto Crydd ("the boot") as he was known by some. His workshop was always full and that was for several reasons. One reason was that he talked so much that he tended to neglect his work, and the only way to make sure of retrieving one's shoes was to stay in the workshop until he finished the work! The shoemaker was a heavy smoker, and for some reason he had a meerschaum pipe. One of his peculiarities was that he was an artistic spitter. I never saw anyone spit so much – not only the number of spits, but the range of each spit. He used to sit on his bench in the morning – not very early – and light his pipe immediately, then suddenly, a huge spit would fall from the left side of his mouth to the floor on his left. The next would fall a little to the right of the first, and so on, until the last at nightfall would land from the right corner of his mouth, with a perfect pattern of spits on the floor! His main feature as a character was his mischievousness and his sparse, dry humour. He was an ardent speaker and had great pleasure from teasing certain simple country folk – but without one degree of cruelty ever.

'He was a kind creature and dear to many. Here is one sample of his ability. One day a farmer went to the shoemaker in great distress. His eldest daughter had failed an examination at the Tregaron Intermediate School and the poor girl was nearly heart-broken. This wasn't the first time for her to fail, and every time she failed in the same subject, namely, algebra. He, the father, did not understand, and he came to the shoemaker and asked, "What is this algebra that this lass always fails in? What is it?" Immediately the shoemaker began to explain and said, "Oh! algebra! Think now of a train leaving Aberystwyth with thirty passengers on it. It comes to Llanrhystyd Road and two get out and one steps in. On arriving at Llanilar, three get out and no one enters. Tregaron, five get off and six enter. Then from station to station until they arrive at Bronwydd Arms where twelve enter. At last the train reaches Carmarthen. Now this is the problem, this is the question – What was the guard's name?" "Dear me," said the farmer, "no wonder the poor lass fails." And he went home to sympathise with his daughter. The shoemaker was very discerning and he knew his customers inside out.

' "Stifin y Fro" was a totally different man. A quiet man, a little eccentric and subdued, but at the same time he was a bit of a genius. He seldom greeted you if you passed him on the road, but he was a great reader, and when other people failed to give a satisfactory answer in the question time at the end of Sunday School, he always knew the correct answer. When he spoke he could say sharp and catchy things. At one time Stifin had devised that which he called "a kicking crank" – an invention to turn with his feet the circular stone for sharpening knives, so that he could use his two hands to hold the knife or whatever else was being sharpened. Everyone in the village was calling to see the invention and among them was a young man, twenty years of age, a youth very fond of provoking Stifin. This fellow began to deride the invention and the inventor. Old Stifin suffered for some time, but at last he became so agitated that he kicked the derider with his right foot saying, "I'm not a prophet, nor the son of a prophet, but I do have authority to cast out demons – get out."

'But the most likeable character, as far as we boys were concerned, was Rhys Rowlands. He was a bachelor, about sixty years old when we knew him, and lived with his brother John who was a little older. They were farmers, but by our time Rhys was a relieving officer and a registrar. He had left the farm and was living in a house in the village. He was a short man, bald, with a full moustache – one which was longer than average. He was an extremely fast talker and he had the most charming and magical smile. He was the best story-teller that I ever knew. He had perfected his craft over the years and like every true story-teller he had an exceptional memory for detail. Usually there was no point to the story, nor any lesson, he just told of some happening from his past. But his gift was such that he held us mesmerised. Rhys Rowlands would call at our house every Sunday evening except during the month when it was our turn to lodge the visiting preachers (*cadw'r mis*). I can see him now coming in with his hymn-book under his arm and placing his hat – always a bowler hat – on the floor beside him. He was in a hurry, he had no time to stay – just call. I don't remember his ever drinking a cup of tea in our house, not to mention having a meal. He was always a heavy smoker – and an artist in that pastime. His favourite tobacco was "Royal Seal" and after lighting up he would draw the smoke into his mouth with such force that his cheeks nearly burst. Then he would exhale the smoke with the same gusto, waving the pipe in the air at the same time. My father knew very well how to draw him into story-telling and we boys would eagerly await this. It is well nigh impossible to give an idea of his magical gift but let me try: my father would mention someone and ask him if he knew of him. "Yes, wait a minute," Rhys would say, "there must be fifteen years since then, but I remember clearly that I had to go to Tregaron, on a Tuesday in February I think it was. Anyway, I decided to put the little yellow mare that we had at the time in the trap – the foal of the old chestnut mare that we had for years and sired by the hackney stallion that Dafydd had [my grandfather who lived at Llwyncadfor at the time]. What was his name? . . . Anyway, I put her in the trap; and I remember when I was riding up this hill that it was raining a cold drizzle." He would say something like this with such emphasis and feeling that we nearly began to tremble with cold. Then he would go on to mention that he had passed such and such a man. He would describe the pony, or the cob, or the horse that he had, and quite often details as to the creature's pedigree. Following this he would give a quick review of the man's financial situation or would relate a story about his friendship with some girl or other, or something of that sort. This would go on and on literally for an hour or two – and sometimes longer – until at last he had reached Tregaron and met the man mentioned by my father at the start. Then he would describe this man – his looks and his clothes, etc.

'Rhys Rowlands saw everything as being either black or white, especially people. Everyone was either perfect or totally unimportant and worthless. He used to voice his opinion of people in a very extreme way. A man was either one of the greatest or the most insignificant creature that Wales had ever bred. Sometimes, after he had been belittling someone in strong terms, a smile would cover his face and he would look like a guilty child.

'I must relate one story about him because it is literally true. He had been to the Wells, i.e. Llanwrtyd Wells, on holiday one year, and had fallen in love with a girl who lived there. He had been in her company quite a lot and felt sure that she should be his wife. As well as being attractive, she also had a "small pocket" (a wealthy background) as was said. But after returning home Rhys had one difficulty – the question was, how was he to write to her and prolong the friendship. He was not enough of a scholar to write on his own behalf or to do that without estranging the young lady. There was only one thing to be done, and that was to ask his minister and friend to write to her on his behalf and in his name. The minister did so; but after some time, and without Rhys's knowledge, he began writing on his own behalf. The story ends with the minister marrying the girl. By our time, she was a minister's respectable and loving wife. What of poor Rhys? He forgave both of them, and no one in the chapel thought more highly of the minister than he did. The wife died about 1909, and when it was time for the minister to leave this world about 1919, he died in the arms of Rhys Rowlands.

'I must speak of another place which plays a big part in my childhood memories, until I reached my thirteenth birthday – and that is Llwyncadfor. This was the name of my grandfather's home on my mother's side. That is where I would spend all my holidays apart from Christmastime, and nothing gave me greater pleasure than this. Llwyncadfor is a fairly large farm not far from Newcastle Emlyn, but in those days it was not only a farm; Llwyncadfor was a stud farm, i.e. a farm for breeding horses. My grandfather was an expert in this matter, and after starting with the Welsh cob, he began to keep both heavy, or shire, horses and the light, or hackney horses. It was he who was responsible for bringing these two latter breeds into Cardiganshire. There were a number of horses of different breeds at Llwyncadfor, and individual stables called boxes had been built for them here and there along the farmyard and also in the fields near the house. He had bred many horses which were shown in the different shows, some in harness and others under saddle or in hand. By my time there were three or four uncles and four or five aunts too, as well as five or six grooms to care for the horses, not to mention the farm hands who worked on the land. Llwyncadfor indeed looked more like a small village than a farm. I can see the servants sitting round the table in the living room – a whole tableful of them, with the family eating in another dining room and my grandfather eating by himself in the best living room. My inclination and ambition in those days was to become a groom and I spent my time carrying buckets of water and horsemeal. Sometimes I would have the extraordinary pleasure of sitting in the four-wheeler with my uncle Tom as he was training one of the best horses for the big show – the Welsh National or the United Counties in Carmarthen, or the Bath and West of England. I remember often leading some of the quietest horses to Henllan station and putting them in a horsebox to go by rail to one of the larger shows. Llwyncadfor farm staff would hire a train for themselves – because they had so many horses in the competition. And almost without exception they would take the chief prizes in all classes and many other prizes as well.

'At night after supper most of the Llwyncadfor family used to sit in the living room around the open-hearth fire, with the chimney open to the sky. This is when they would tell stories and recount happenings, and often they would sing and entertain themselves in various ways. Then, again, there would always be a number of strangers in the company, because the stallions would travel each year throughout the counties of South Wales, apart from Brecknock and Radnor. The place would be ablaze with interest and to be part of it all was a great experience for a little boy. I remember my breast swelling with pride in shows, say at Aberystwyth or Carmarthen or Newcastle Emlyn, when I saw Llwyncadfor horses win cups and medals, and rosettes being placed on their necks. I remember particularly one hackney stallion which was bred at Llwyncadfor and was called "Emlyn Model", the stud name being "Emlyn". When this foal was born, my grandfather saw, with his usual astuteness, that it had something special about it. The first morning, when he saw it, he said to his son Tom, "We shall call this one 'Model', because we won't get a better one than this." And that's how it was. "Model" never had any prize but a first, not only in Wales, but for two or three consecutive years in the Hackney Society Show in London at the Agricultural Hall. After that they sold it to the Spanish Government for 800 guineas – an exceptionally high price in those days!'

*   *   *

Martyn's childhood in Llangeitho was comparatively uneventful until a night in January 1910 which was to influence the life of the whole family. Early in that month Henry Lloyd-Jones had sent out bills to a number of farmers who came to pay them – in old sovereigns and half-sovereigns – on the evening of Wednesday, January 19. The business was done in the clothing section of the shop where the men stood, talking and smoking. Mrs Lloyd-Jones and the eldest boy, Harold, happened to be away from home. About 1 a.m. the next morning, long after everyone had retired for the night, Martyn and Vincent, who shared a room, were half-aroused from their sleep by the smell of fumes, but sensing no danger they merely pulled the blankets higher over their heads. It seems that tobacco ash which had fallen to the floor of the store below, amidst millinery goods, had smouldered and then ignited. Once the building itself caught alight, the wind blowing that winter's night fanned the fire almost immediately into a terrific blaze. Just in time, the cries of the family's maid and the milliner, and their banging fists, awakened the father – a heavy sleeper – who was able to reach the boys' bedroom. 'I was thrown,' recalled Martyn, 'by my father from one of the upstair windows into the arms of three men who were standing in their nightshirts in the road. Then they got hold of a ladder so that my father and brother could climb down.' They were scarcely out when the floor collapsed behind them and everything went up in flames.

Speaking of that early morning of January 20, 1910, Martyn Lloyd-Jones was later to comment in the memories which he gave on radio:

'Somehow things at Llangeitho were never the same after the fire. Although we built a new home and started living in it within the year [1910] things were different. Certainly as a building the new house was a great improvement on our former home, but there was something missing, and more than anything the feeling of home was lacking. I felt as if I were in a strange house and that living there was a temporary matter. I always prefer old houses, although I appreciate many of the modern amenities.'

In fact the effects of the fire went deeper than those few remarks reveal. For one thing, on the material level it brought his father into great difficulties. When they had gone through the ruin the next morning, Martyn had discovered a cracked and discoloured mug[1] and his father the sovereigns – melted into a solid mass of gold – but otherwise the loss was virtually complete. Thereafter Henry Lloyd-Jones was rarely free of financial problems. These were carefully hidden from the boys until David Evans of Llwyncadfor broke the secret to Martyn in 1911. Well able to rule a farm, under the influence of drink the old man could not always rule himself and there were times when as he drove his gig back to Llwyncadfor, after a convivial meeting, at the end of a market day perhaps, the safest thing to do was to hand the reins over to Martyn. On one such occasion David Evans told his grandson of his father's financial distress and though, when sober the next morning, he sought to whittle down what he had said, the damage was done in the boy's mind: 'It left a deep impression upon me. Before then I used to buy a pennyworth of sweets every week, now I reduced it to a half-penny.

[1] In later years this memento always stood on the mantelpiece of his study.

It was my contribution to the family problem.' For the next three years Martyn was not to share with anyone the burden which this news had laid upon him.

It may well have been the case that the fire of January 1910, and its consequences, also influenced Martyn's attitude to school. Probably Llangeitho school was typical of many a Welsh village school in days before rural depopulation emptied many parts of the countryside. With a headmaster and three lady teachers, education was carried up to grade six. For many it would be all the education they were likely to have and for a while it seemed possible that Martyn would fall into that group. Harold was quiet and studious, but Martyn seemed of a more practical and businesslike bent. Until the age of eleven he had no interest in books. Football and other pursuits possessed far more attraction.

About the year 1910 one of the lady teachers at Llangeitho retired, and her place was taken by a man, and it was this assistant schoolmaster who one day interrupted a game of football in the village square to express his serious concern at Martyn's inattention to his work. Unless he settled down, the teacher warned him, he would never get a scholarship to the County Intermediate School at Tregaron. Knowing his father's financial position, Martyn did not need telling that, if he failed to get a scholarship place in 1911, it might well mean an end to his further education. The warning was heeded and in the scholarship examination of 1911 Martyn Lloyd-Jones took second place, close behind the boy who stood first. This convinced him, for the first time, that he could do something with his mind and securing a place at Tregaron County School also opened the way to a new chapter in his life.

For we are all, like swimmers in the sea,
Pois'd on the top of a huge wave of Fate,
Which hangs uncertain to which side to fall.
And whether it will heave us up to land,
Or whether it will roll us out to sea,
. . .
We know not.
[MATTHEW ARNOLD, from *Sohrab and Rustum*]

Words written by Martyn Lloyd-Jones in the album of his school-friend William Evans at Tregaron, July 1914.

2

Schooldays: Tregaron and London

Only four miles from Llangeitho, Tregaron was nevertheless a different world for an eleven-year-old boy. He would not have agreed with the first part of the description given in one guide-book, 'Tregaron is a comfortable old town with a host of local legends'. The market town, situated at a point where a tributary of the Teifi ceases to be a mountain stream, marks a boundary between the fertile west of Cardiganshire and the wild hinterland of the north and east from whence the wind often blew in winter. But what made Tregaron and its school of 120 pupils so different for him was the fact that it was no longer possible to live at home. At the time of his arrival to join his brother Harold, who was already accustomed to spending Monday to Friday in lodgings, Martyn was the youngest in the school. The effect of this we shall note later in his own words.

William Evans, the distinguished cardiologist, one of their con-temporaries, recalls how, as he finished his two-mile walk from his home to Tregaron on Monday mornings, he would often see Mr Lloyd-Jones with the boys arriving in a 'governess trap'. Speaking of those days Dr Evans writes:

'The Tregaron school recruited its pupils from a rural farming community but the three boys were urbanised in their appearance and bearing. Indeed, they stood apart from the less sophisticated and naturally shy Welsh children. They showed more culture, versatility in company, and more confidence in classes and in debate. Although in this way they stood out, distinctive and distinguished, they were never aloof, and Harold and I formed a warm friendship.

'We had two teachers on the staff, namely, S. M. Powell and Miss John, who befriended those pupils showing special aptitude in their particular speciality and would hold discussions with them outside school hours, Powell in English and History and Miss John in the

Classics. These two teachers drew particularly near to both Harold and Martyn to help them prosper.

'In school we conversed in English, but it is likely that Welsh was the language of the hearth. Martyn, then as now, gave evidence of a ready command of Welsh.'

The greatest influence upon Martyn in the school was undoubtedly S. M. Powell who first awakened his interest in history. As well as being an able teacher, Powell had a shrewd ability at setting the pupils on making their own discoveries. 'Find out the date of the beginning of the "cause" or Chapel where you belong,' would be a typical piece of homework set for the weekend. Or again, 'Find out from the hymns of William Williams of Pantycelyn the profession which he had originally intended to follow.' This latter duty caused considerable dismay when it was given out, for the class knew that, while the author of 'Guide me, O thou great Jehovah' had few hymns translated into English, the prospect of reading through all his Welsh hymnal was daunting! In reality the answer was not hard to find. Williams had been a medical student when the evangelical revival of the 1730's changed the course of his life and led him into the ministry. The love of medicine was supplanted by something higher and his hymns often speak of Christ as the better physician. Even so, that weekend none of the boys came back to school with the right answer.

Outside the classroom Powell was also popular with the boys. Without harshness but with quick repartee or puns he could deal effectively with his pupils as they might require it. On one occasion in a summer term, for instance, Powell evidently shared the class's view that a 'cocky' new boy, freshly arrived from London, required some moderating treatment. Cricket was to be played that afternoon as usual and when the individual concerned arrived at the wicket to bat, full of confidence, he began by enquiring from his teacher (who was umpiring) how many runs he would get if he hit the ball various distances. 'How many if I hit it to the fence?' 'Two!' 'And', pointing in another direction, 'how many to the hedge?' 'Four' replied the umpire. 'What if I put it straight into the road?' 'Six' said Powell, with patience. One last question still occurred to this cricketing tyro. The window of Mr Lewis, the headmaster, was visible from where he stood, and carrying his imagination to its limits, he asked, 'How many if I hit it through Mr Lewis's window?' 'Two shillings and six pence!' replied Powell instantly, to the amusement of the entire class.

Whether the new boy from London retained his enthusiasm for cricket is not known, but it was certainly to endure in the second son of the Lloyd-Jones' home.

Mr Lewis himself had fewer personal dealings with the younger boys although he left an impression of his wisdom by actions which were not always predictable. When Martyn won a prize for Mathematics he was surprised to find himself presented with a book on woodwork, a subject for which he had no aptitude or interest![1] As he later came to see, that was precisely why the old Head had given it to him. It was a first lesson in the need for balance.

We continue with Martyn's own account of this period of his life:

'What shall I say about Tregaron and the time I spent in that school? These are the things which stand out in my memory. The first is an impression of how cold the town was. Tregaron is still to me the coldest place on the face of the earth. This can be attributed to the fact that the town lies between Cors Caron [Tregaron Bog] with its dampness, and the pass of Cwm Berwyn in the mountains, which is like a funnel drawing the cold easterly winds on to the town – all so different from Llangeitho which nestles cosily in the Vale of Aeron with the kind hills sheltering it from nearly all directions. But one has to be fair to Tregaron, although I suffered so much there. To judge from the state of the blood circulation in my body, I am much to be pitied, and as a result I have suffered a great amount of discomfort every year from chilblains for which we had our own local name *maleithe*. If that happened in Llangeitho with all its home comforts, then it was far worse in Tregaron where I stayed in lodgings from Monday morning until teatime on Friday. I can remember now the terrible burning sensation and then the itching which nearly drove me mad, and that happening not only on my hands but also on my toes. I was not able to run or play to lessen the complaint because of the pain; there was nothing to do but to suffer.

'But, in addition to this, I must add that I suffered at the same time from a far greater sickness, and a more painful one, which has remained with me all along life's path – and that was *hiraeth* [longing

---

[1] On one occasion when he was given a block of wood to be planed smooth during a carpentry class, he failed to such an extent that the wood had almost been planed away by the time the master came to inspect it. He could not get it smooth. Thereafter he was excused carpentry, being judged incapable of ever learning the art.

or home-sickness]. I am pleased to tell my friends at Tregaron that I do not hold them or the place responsible for this. What is the reason for it? The psychologists cannot explain it. I believe that this again, like the circulation of the blood, belongs to a man's constitution, and that it is decided in part by the functioning of the ductless glands! Be that as it may, *hiraeth* is an awful thing, as also is the feeling of loneliness, and of being destitute and unhappy which stem from it. It is difficult to define *hiraeth*, but to me it means the consciousness of man being out of his home area and that which is dear to him. That is why it can be felt even among a host of people and amidst nature's beauty.

'My three years in Tregaron County School were very unhappy and that was only because of this longing. I had bosom companions there, like Dai Williams and others, and I enjoyed the lessons . . . but! I remember as if it were yesterday sitting in our pew in chapel at Llangeitho before the service on Sunday night and suddenly being hit by the thought – "This time tomorrow night I shall be in my lodgings in Tregaron" – and all at once I would be down in the depths. And if it was like that on Sunday night, when still able to go home from the service, what about being in Tregaron with the chilblains on top of everything else!

'Every Tuesday a market was held at Tregaron, and once a month the monthly market. This was before the time of marts as such, of course. My father and many of the farmers from the Llangeitho area came to Tregaron therefore nearly every Tuesday. Rather than being any consolation to me, this knowledge merely added to my hurt. I would sometimes go in the pony and trap with my father to Trecefel Bridge, about a mile out of the town, in order to lessen the pain, although I knew, like the poor drunk, that I was making things worse, because I would have to leave him and return by myself. Sometimes I would stand close to the school to see some of the farmers returning home – while I had to remain in Tregaron.

'I suffered in this way for a year without any lessening of the complaint. Through the first two terms of the second year I was also in the same state – indeed in a worse state. And then in the summer term 1913, I persuaded my parents to allow me to return home every night. The journey was only about four and a half miles, and when the weather was fine I would travel on a bicycle. On very wet days I used to walk. This was heavenly for me, and I could reflect on that summer term without a shadow or cloud, apart from the fact that I happened to read *David Copperfield* about the same time. That caused me a great deal of unhappiness, like all the works of Dickens, because of the suffering and the unhappiness, especially among children, which is found in them.

'Well, that's how it was with me. In September 1913 my youngest brother started at Tregaron, and so we were three brothers in the lodgings. But I failed to get over my malady even by this remedy, though it did ease a little of the heartache. At the end of the Christmas term it was customary to perform a play or a cantata in the school, and for about ten days or more before the performances, preparations of various kinds were being made. As a result very few regular lessons were held, and for a few days, no lessons at all. I used to take advantage of this to go home every night, and the last days to stay at home – while both my brothers in Tregaron enjoyed themselves!

'Time does not allow me to talk at length, as I would wish, of Tregaron School, but I would be willing to challenge the world that there were never two such teachers together in the same school as G. T. Lewis, the headmaster, and S. M. Powell, his chief assistant – the first was a "character" verging upon the eccentric, the other was a genius. Both were Welshmen to the core and spoke a great deal of Welsh in the classroom. Mr Lewis would sometimes break out into a sermon in Welsh, and that might happen halfway through a geometry lesson. S. M. Powell was famous for his pioneering work in the field of drama – he wrote many plays himself and was a born actor. I remember his giving us a lesson on the *Merchant of Venice* and taking the part of Shylock himself. I see him now taking a knife from his pocket, opening it and sharpening it on his shoe, declaiming the words "three thousand ducats" and "one pound of flesh", the while.

'Possibly the greatest genius in the school in my time was Tom Hughes Jones who died a short time ago in Wrexham. "Twm Bardd" ("Tom the Poet") was the name we gave him and he was a born poet. Unfortunately he turned to the field of politics after the First World War and tended to ignore his exceptional talent. Tom used to excel in most fields. I remember walking with him to dinner one day before Eastertime in 1913. Someone gave him the programme of an *eisteddfod* which was to be held at Llanddewi Brefi. Tom looked at the list of competitions and he noticed that a prize was being offered for a sentence formed from the letters in the word JERUSALEM. In a few minutes he turned to me and asked – "What about this one: '*Jerusalem Er Rhybuddion Un Sanctaidd A Laddodd Ei Messiah*'?

(Jerusalem in spite of the warnings of a Holy One, killed its Messiah.)

'The mention of 1913 causes me to mention two other providential happenings in my story. The first is that this was the year in which I decided to be a doctor. I am not quite sure what caused me to take this course. The fact that my mother's father's father had been a doctor could be one element in the reason perhaps, but I believe that my admiration for David Davies, Birchill – a local boy who had returned home to practise his profession – was even greater. Whatever lay behind it, it was my personal choice to be a doctor, and I received every support and encouragement from my parents.

'The other truly important event in 1913 was that our Chapel had invited the Summer Association of the Calvinistic Methodists to Llangeitho. As I have already said, the reason for this was the bicentenary of Daniel Rowland's birth. This Association had a deep impact on me. I had never seen or heard open-air preaching before, but because of the number of people expected, the main meetings were held in a field at the bottom of, and to the left side of, the hill which leads down into Llangeitho from the direction of Tregaron. A stage had been erected, with a pulpit at the front for the preacher and seats for the leading ministers behind him. And then the congregation of about four to five thousand sat on benches facing the preacher. I well remember the meeting held to celebrate Daniel Rowland on the Wednesday afternoon, when we had addresses by Dr Thomas Charles Williams, Dr John Morgan Jones, Cardiff (the historian), Dr John Williams, Brynsiencyn, and the Rev. W. E. Prytherch of Swansea. The only thing which I remember from the meeting is an illustration used by Mr Prytherch. He gave us the story of the coming of electric tramcars to Swansea. He described how they placed tracks on the streets, and then raised great posts and connected these with wires. A grand-looking vehicle was then placed on the rails – a vehicle with a number of seats in it both upstairs and downstairs, with room for about forty people to sit. "But", Mr Prytherch said, "although everything was perfect, nothing moved!" But the important opening day arrived and a member of the Royal Family came to Swansea. At the ceremony, all he did was to pull a rope to release a big pole fixed to the top of the vehicle and when the little wheel at the tip of the pole touched a wire, all at once the vehicle began to move. What was the explanation? Oh! the rails and the vehicle were more than ready, and the electric power was flowing strongly in the wires, but they had to be connected before any movement could be got from the vehicle. That's what Daniel Rowland did; he connected the moribund church to the forces of the Holy Spirit.

'I also remember the last preaching meeting on the Thursday night, with Dr T. C. Williams and Dr John Williams preaching in the same service. I had not seen or heard either of them before, and I was entranced by them – not only by the eloquent preaching, but also by their magnificent personalities. Dr T. C. Williams appeared to me to be the most handsome man I had ever seen, and I still say that. For Dr John Williams, there is only one suitable word – aristocratic. I see him now wrinkling his forehead, and I remember his description of how he and some friends climbed to the top of Snowdon to see the break of dawn. When the dawn eventually broke they were filled with a sense of wonder, a friend crying out "magnificent", Dr John Williams adding, in Welsh, "glorious". Then he went on to declaim, in his incomparable manner, a verse of a well-known Welsh hymn by William Williams, beginning *Gwawrddydd, Gwawrddydd*. It may be freely translated thus:

> The dawn, the dawn is everything to me,
> And to catch a glimpse of the dawn means health and life.
> I will wait until it comes,
> And come it will in a little while.
> O come! O come! that I may see
> My native land.

'I, and most others present were deeply moved, although that is all I remember clearly about it. That Association had a deep effect upon me, and possibly the most important thing it did was to create in me an interest in the Calvinistic Methodist Fathers which has lasted until today.'

*　　*　　*

This regular routine of childhood came to a sudden end one Sunday night in January 1914. As the three brothers were sitting reading, as they usually did after supper, their parents came into the room,

'and my father started to say that he had something extremely important to tell us, and that he was sure that we would receive what he had to say like men.

David Martyn Lloyd-Jones

'The message was that we were to leave Llangeitho within a few weeks and that it would be for ever. Difficulties had arisen in the business and there was nothing to do but to sell everything and face a new life. As we look back in the terms of today, I can see clearly that there were two elements in that crisis, over-expansion and under-capitalisation. The business in its varying aspects had grown too big and the machines were expensive and costly. Added to that, our customers were short of money and were very slow in paying their bills. There was no Milk Marketing Board; and no quotas or subsidies in those days. It is obvious that my father was about twenty years and more before his time. He also, on principle, refused to bargain in the usual way – and between everything we were in a crisis and there was nothing for it but to try to collect the debts and to hold an auction. So in February everything was sold during two whole days in the Jubilee Hall – everything, the horses, the contents of the shop, and even the furniture from our home, apart from a few minor items. This came as a great shock to us as boys, but I remember that our main reaction was that we felt a challenge in the situation and that we were willing to do anything in order to help. I remember saying that I would forgo the chance of becoming a doctor, and that I would become a bank clerk when I was old enough.'

The bankruptcy which Martyn had secretly feared for the past three years had become a reality. To some extent it was probably a relief to him, after listening to his father's sad words on that January Sunday evening, to be able to exclaim, 'I knew all about this.' Henry Lloyd-Jones was astonished and very grieved to realise the burden which his second son had been carrying.

The head of the household was not, however, a man to sit down in despair. He meant to find other work, concerned for the best for his family, and also determined that outstanding debts would be repaid. The best course of action, he came to believe, was to emigrate to Canada and to start a new life. But there were practical difficulties. Harold was due to sit the Senior Central Welsh Board examination in June and July of that same year and Martyn's own ability was by now clearly established. His powers of memory – inherited from David Evans – were exceptional. As one of the Tregaron teachers told his father, 'What Martyn knows, he *knows*!' It was important, therefore, that Martyn should sit the Junior Central Welsh Board examination in the summer before leaving the district. Henry

Lloyd-Jones resolved the dilemma by deciding that he would go himself to prepare the way as soon as the auction had taken place and that Maggie and the boys would live in part of a house near the school of Tregaron until July when they also could sail for Canada. Martyn recalled:

'The most heart-breaking moment in the whole process for me was the morning my father bade us all farewell, and began his journey. After that we used to try to imagine what sort of life would be waiting for us in Canada, and we played with various fantasies. But before the end of the three months it became obvious that we were not to go to Canada. My father wrote regularly, about twice a week from Winnipeg, where he was staying with one of my mother's brothers. The refrain in his letter was that he could see clearly that there was no hope for us there. He was by then past fifty years of age and could not find suitable work. His opinion on the situation was: "A wonderful country for young people, and a great chance for the boys, but hopeless for a man of my age."'

By the end of May, Henry Lloyd-Jones had decided to return to Britain and to try to restart life in London. His hope was that Maggie might be able to arrange something through relatives and that meanwhile he would attempt to earn a little by occasional work in Winnipeg. These must have been deeply perplexing months for Mrs Lloyd-Jones, with Harold and Martyn facing important examinations, pressure from creditors in the Llangeitho area, and her husband eagerly awaiting news of some opening in London. All the enquiries she attempted from Tregaron ended in failure. Understandably, Henry Lloyd-Jones was hardly his old buoyant self when on notepaper headed 'Memo. from H. Lloyd-Jones, General Merchant, Albion Stores, Llangeitho', he wrote from Winnipeg on July 1, 1914:

My dear Maggie and Children
I am writing today again. I am doing nothing now and am quite miserable. I very much hope you will be able to hit on something in London very soon, I do not think it is any use thinking of staying here, things are too bad here. I cannot get anything to go on with, the place is so much overdone. I am trying every day but there is nothing to be had. I only want something until you fix in London. We are all of the same opinion that it is safer there than here on the whole. One may have a job here today and be out of it tomorrow, that is the way

of the country. There is no such thing as being given notice here. Please do not lose any time as I am getting so uneasy – spending every day and nothing coming in for me anywhere. Perhaps when the school is broken up for holidays the children can go somewhere for a week or so. Keep it strictly to yourselves about going to London, I hope I shall not be bothered there. We can live there quite as good as here, I mean as private if we only think of it for few years. I am anxiously expecting to hear from you on the matter, all we want is a support for a little while.

I do hope you can get something in London, no doubt we can do well there once we can have a start, and get good posts for the children as well.

I am anxious to know what the children are thinking of it. Do they prefer going to London than coming over here? I am sick of this country on account of its uncertainty, and everyone would come back tomorrow if they could.

Please write me at once. I am quite miserable here now, nothing coming in. I have no news. I have asked Willie for my money back; he cannot pay me now, he said, and I do not know what to do. If I had a month's work at $80 or $100 I could manage it very well without, but I cannot do it as things are now.

Mind to keep everything entirely to yourselves and let me hear from you at once.

No news, only my very best and warmest love to you and children.   Your loving
                                   Dada.

Mrs Lloyd-Jones must have read these lines with a feeling of utter helplessness, but shortly after that, another letter brought the news that her husband was about to begin his return journey and expected to be in London on August 3. No doubt his hope was that Maggie would be there to meet him, with the boys left at Llwyncadfor, until a new home could be found. In the event Mrs Lloyd-Jones made what proved to be a providential decision. Martyn, with his practical skills, would be the best one to help his father look for a business, so on Saturday, August 1, she put him on a train at Tregaron, bound for London, and went herself, with the other two boys, to Llwyncadfor.

There could scarcely have been a more memorable moment to arrive in London than that Bank-holiday weekend. At Paddington station Martyn was met by his mother's brother and as they made their way back to the uncle's home in Bermondsey, the fourteen-year-old boy noticed more than the shops and great buildings, the tram cars and some of the quarter-of-a-million toiling horses still present in the streets of the capital. Tension filled the air. England, which had sent no troops across the English Channel since 1815, was poised ready for the shock of the war against Germany which would be declared the following Tuesday.

On the Monday, which brought a hot, dry morning, Henry Lloyd-Jones' boat was due at the Surrey Docks. But, not wishing to bring a passenger ship through the English Channel because of the international crisis, the shipping company had ended the voyage at Plymouth, and so in the afternoon Martyn was once more back at a railway station to meet his father. In the evening of the same day he walked from Bermondsey to the Elephant and Castle, surveying the crowds of people, many, no doubt, returning from their Bank-holiday outings. Few anticipated the scale of the war that was about to begin, or knew that London's halcyon Edwardian period was at its end. Taking up the story on the day that war broke out, Martyn Lloyd-Jones recalled:

'On Tuesday, August 4, my father took me to Westminster in the morning. We succeeded in joining the crowd which had gathered in Downing Street, and there we stayed for hours watching the various members of the Cabinet going in and out of No. 10. At last the moment we had been waiting for arrived, namely, that of seeing the door of No. 10 opening, and Mr Asquith leaving the house and getting into his car and starting off to Parliament, where he was to hear Sir Edward Grey making his never-to-be-forgotten speech. I remember the thrill I felt to see the man that was so much of a hero to my father, the man of whom I had heard so much. The only disappointment that day was that we had not caught sight, for some reason, of the "little man", Lloyd George.

'Every day, straight after breakfast, we went in the direction of Westminster and stood outside the Palace Yard or Downing Street to catch a glimpse of the giants. And we were particularly fortunate. It is impossible to try to describe the people of London at that time. The fever of war had taken a firm grip of them, and they sang and waved banners both large and small. They possessed a confident spirit, and a certainty that we would conquer the Germans in a short time. We heard somehow that a regiment of our soldiers who were about to cross over to France, were to march through the city, setting out from the Tower. We went there early, and we caught sight of them marching by in their red coats and the band playing "It's a long way to Tipperary". The people nearly lost control of themselves in their enthusiasm, and while most of them were shouting and clapping their hands, others would break into song, and many wept. We saw many young men decide to enlist in the army on the spot and sharing the news with their friends. That was a glance at the "Old Contemptibles". We saw Lord Kitchener more than once, but he, with his stupid face and his sullen bovine eyes, was not a hero in our estimation.

'Strange days, fearful days – nothing was the same after that. I pity my father and his contemporaries with their unfailing loyalty to those political leaders. I'm glad that they are not alive to read the diaries of C. P. Scott, which I read recently, and to realise that their idols had feet of clay.'

*   *   *

For Mr Lloyd-Jones and his second son that first week in August was the beginning of a great trial which had nothing to do with the war. It was not the spirit of sight-seeing which took them up each day into the heart of London but the urgent need to find a small business and a new home. Together they tramped the streets, looked at notices in shop windows, and read the advertisement columns of newspapers. The difficulties were immense, especially his father's lack of money and the unwillingness of relatives and friends to lend him any. Of those days Martyn Lloyd-Jones once said, 'I will never forget the discouragement and the depression. We had endless disappointments. My father and I, to save money, we walked and walked and walked.' On the days when Mr Lloyd-Jones found it necessary to go alone in his search for work he was concerned not to leave Martyn at Bermondsey lest he should be a burden on their none-too-sympathetic relatives. So Martyn recalled how, to fill the time, he 'used to walk from Bermondsey to St James's Park and buy a sandwich at a booth there and a cup of tea'.

There were, however, times when Martyn's uncle did want him at home. Mr Evans carried on a milk and dairy business which enabled him to do well enough without a great deal of personal effort. But during August some of his roundsmen, anxious to be among the victorious troops who were expected to push the Germans back to the Rhine before winter, suddenly joined the army without any warning. Unless milk deliveries were to be curtailed there was no choice but to do a round himself, and to lessen the work he took Martyn with him. A milkman's job in those days was not as simple as it became when milk was bottled. Each roundsman either on a horse-drawn cart, or on a barrow which he pushed, carried a large churn of milk from which, at each household, the correct quantity had to be measured into little cans or jugs which might be brought to him. This was all new to Martyn and it was to prove one of the most valuable lessons of his schooldays.

After many disappointments, by the end of September 1914, Mr Lloyd-Jones was settled in his plans. Another dairy and milk business at 7 Regency Street, Westminster, was on the market and the price asked was extremely attractive. Perhaps, at the time, Henry Lloyd-Jones did not know the reason for the low asking price. The fact was that a fellow-countryman, M. D. Williams, having run this business for a number of years, was alarmed at the possible effects of the war recently declared. Williams remembered that during the Boer War of 1899–1902, when he had contracts with the troops at Chelsea and Wellington barracks, his profits had slumped when most of these men had been sent to South Africa and the barracks left comparatively empty. This time he decided to get out in good time and, to make sure of doing so, he had set the price which attracted the attention of Henry Lloyd-Jones. When all was weighed up, the latter found that he only needed £50 to secure the dairy, with its home above the shop and the business. And yet no such sum could be found in London. His brother-in-law in Bermondsey would not lend a halfpenny. In the end it was a groom at Llwyncadfor, who had long admired Henry Lloyd-Jones, who offered the necessary sum. Thus, after Martyn had spent two months at Bermondsey with his father, the family was again reunited as they set up home in Westminster's Regency Street in October 1914.

Meanwhile, during all the heartache of September, one bright piece of news had arrived from Tregaron via Llwyncadfor. It was in the handwriting of the headmaster of the boys' former school:

> The County School,
> Tregaron
> 14 Sept. 1914

My dear Mr Evans

I do not know where to send the results of the exams which your two grandsons, Harold and Martyn, entered.

Harold is through in all, with conversational power in French. Martyn is through in all, with distinction in arithmetic, maths and chemistry, and conversational power in French. Tell the boys they have done remarkably well – 29 certificates besides 4 supplementary.

You will, I feel sure, be kind enough as to forward this note on to them.

Yours in a hurry

G. T. Lewis

Notwithstanding these results, it was not immediately apparent to Henry and Maggie Lloyd-Jones, in their very straitened circumstances, that Martyn would be able to return to school.[1] His elder brother, Harold, became an articled clerk in a solicitor's office. Some thought that Martyn was the natural lawyer of the three, but for the moment there was talk of his becoming a bank clerk. Meanwhile in the initial days at Regency Street, Martyn's help was invaluable, for (after his experiences at Bermondsey) he was the only one who understood the business of milk rounds. No small part of that work was done before the average person's day had even begun. Between 4.30 and 5 in the morning, milk was delivered to their premises in huge churns by wholesalers. This had then to be divided into the deliveries for the four rounds, a horse-drawn cart for one round and barrows for the remainder. While the driver of the milk-cart arrived regularly every morning, this was by no means the case with the rest of the roundsmen and Martyn would often be required. In his own words: 'I would be sleeping, with my brothers, and suddenly hear my father whistling. That meant a roundsman had not turned up and I had got to do the round – half-past five in the morning!'

The name of the dairy was not immediately changed and as Martyn soon became familiar to customers (who recognised that he was not the usual milkman), he was surprised to be addressed as 'Mr Williams'!

Mr Lloyd-Jones' new business made a successful beginning and the fears of the former owner were never realised. The dairy was to flourish and in due course the debts which had brought such a shadow over the family were all repaid. Perhaps it was because he sensed that relief was in sight that Henry Lloyd-Jones sent Martyn back to school, along with Vincent, in January 1915. In any case,

[1] Not until 1918 was education to the age of fourteen made compulsory: in September 1914 Martyn had already passed the normal school-leaving age.

Martyn could still do a round, if necessary, before leaving for Marylebone Grammar School. Not infrequently it was necessary, and on at least one occasion some confusion at the dairy even led his father to send an urgent message to the school asking that his son be sent home!

*   *   *

The shop at 7 Regency Street brought many interesting customers, among them a near-neighbour by the name of Miss Brandon who enthusiastically proposed her church to the Lloyd-Joneses – Westminster Chapel, in Buckingham Gate – and only a short walk away. When Martyn delivered milk to the Wellington Barracks he passed its imposing Victorian front. For Henry Lloyd-Jones it had recommending features: it was Congregational, for example, and its fifty-one-year-old minister, George Campbell Morgan, was famous for the way in which he had turned a cause which had been the despair of the denomination into the city's foremost Nonconformist pulpit. But the family were already committed to continuing with the Calvinistic Methodists or Welsh Presbyterians (a synonymous term) and had joined one of the oldest and best-known chapels of that denomination, at Charing Cross Road. The ardent Miss Brandon, however, was not to be easily put off and Martyn recalled the day in 1915 when she arrived at their home accompanied by a gentleman of the name of Arthur E. Marsh, 'to try to persuade us as a family to join Westminster Chapel'. In view of subsequent events Marsh warrants more than passing reference. Prior to 1907, when he had gone to Princeton Theological Seminary to study for the ministry, he had been Campbell Morgan's private secretary, but the next year when Morgan had lost his ministerial colleague, Albert Swift, Marsh was called back to become assistant at Westminster. There he was to remain for more than half a century, his squarely-built figure appearing to the last in the same impeccable Edwardian dress which he had worn six years before the First World War.

Arthur Marsh's visit to Regency Street was a failure, and yet, perhaps, not entirely so, for in the course of 1915 Martyn, along with one of his brothers, made one visit to Westminster Chapel. One of Campbell Morgan's friends was Dr Thomas Charles Williams, the great contemporary Welsh preacher, who, as already noticed, had attended the Association at Llangeitho in 1913. He normally

David Martyn Lloyd-Jones

preached at Westminister at least once a year (commonly staying with Lloyd George in Downing Street!) and it was on such an occasion that Martyn made his first visit to Westminster Chapel. After the service the congregation was invited to meet Dr Williams in the large Institute Hall and the two boys were gratified to speak to him in Welsh!

Thereafter, once or twice, Martyn heard sermons by Campbell Morgan. He also tried to go to Westminster Chapel whenever Williams was visiting there, but Charing Cross Chapel was his decided preference. If the Welsh Chapel was not Cardiganshire, at least it provided a cross-section of London's Welsh-speaking community and a centre for both religious and social life. In the fine building erected in 1887 there were Literary and Debating Society meetings on Friday nights in which he was subsequently to join, and on Sundays, besides the usual services, Sunday School for all age groups (in the Welsh tradition) and the practising of hymn tunes at the end of the day. There was no choir, for the whole congregation was expected to sing!

There was much about the minister at Charing Cross, the Reverend Peter Hughes Griffiths, which appealed to Martyn. For one thing, he was an original character and an individualist. With his shock of black, well-groomed hair, his morning coat, his Gladstone collar and flat, black, cravat type of tie with a gold pin in the centre, Griffiths did not look much like the average Welsh minister. Out of doors he wore a silk hat. He certainly did not wear such things out of deference to London's higher circles, for respect for the establishment was an attitude from which the minister of Charing Cross was wholly free. While still at College he had amazed his fellow students by his indifference to the drudgery of Greek syntax, and when examination time came round, instead of giving the required answer, he calmly wrote, 'See *North and Hillard*, page x!' When Martyn, thirty years later, wrote a tribute to his former minister it is clear he had a certain approval for Griffiths' independency:

'He hated anything purely mechanical and abominated rules and regulations, and to be stereotyped was to him to be of necessity useless. He liked spontaneity and freshness. The ordinary way of doing anything was obviously a poor way, and when planners and organisers would try to force that way upon all, whether in education, in church government, or anything else, he literally "saw

[36]

red". He was convinced that genius and originality were being throttled and strangled by the mechanical ideas governing church and state, and he constantly protested against them.'[1]

There was another area in which, temperamentally, Martyn was like Peter Hughes Griffiths. Prior to the War, Griffiths was a pacifist (as were many other Nonconformist ministers): once the conflict 'for King and country' had begun pacifism fell silent, but though having to make some adjustment to the times, Griffiths never shared in the euphoria which led the country to turn every soldier into a hero. He hated the regimentation of armies as he hated conjugating Greek verbs. Campbell Morgan, though another pre-War pacifist, allowed an upsurging patriotism to carry him to the point of saying, 'The sign of the Cross is on every man that marches to his death'. Martyn, like Griffiths, was uncomprehending of that attitude and of the rush to volunteer for the front. He was shocked at the blasé confidence with which troops sang,

> Pack up your troubles in your old kit bag
> And smile, smile, smile!

It is true that at the beginning of the First World War, when county cricket continued as usual, men did not know that it would require five million Britons in arms before it could end, and that the pre-1914 'Pax Britannica' was never to return. Yet even before the slaughter of the Somme and of Passchendaele Martyn's mind was made up:

'Those days were horrific days for me; I was glad that I was young enough not to have to face the situation personally. I have never understood the minds and constitutions of men who see war as a romantic thing and who are anxious to join the forces to have a chance to fight and kill. Maybe the reason for this is the fact that I am almost totally devoid of any physical courage. At the same time, I feel that there is nothing so degrading, and which throws so much disrespect on the human race, as a sergeant-major shouting and screaming at a troop of soldiers. Seeing soldiers doing the "goose-step" is abhorrent to me. The fact that I had started as a medical student at the age of sixteen years was why I was spared the horrible fate. By then there was a scarcity of doctors to such an extent that the boys who had started a course but who had joined the army, were

[1] D. M. Lloyd-Jones in a short tribute to Griffiths published in *Y Ganrif Gyntaf, Eglwys Bresbyteraidd Cymru*, Charing Cross Road, London, *c.* 1950.

David Martyn Lloyd-Jones

being sent back from France to resume their medical studies. I have given thanks a hundredfold that I was never forced to live in a barracks – that would have been even worse than my lodgings at Tregaron.'

One side-effect of the War was to heighten the interest in politics in the Lloyd-Jones' home. Now, however, there was no need to wait for newspapers from London with the latest speeches of the country's leaders, for little more than a quarter of a mile away was the House of Commons itself, and Harold and Martyn were often to be found in the Strangers' Gallery. The Liberals still virtually headed the country in a Coalition government formed in 1915, but their leaders, Asquith (the Prime Minister) and Lloyd George, were plainly divided. In that rivalry, which was to lead to the Welshman's becoming Prime Minister, all the Lloyd-Jones household, except the mother, opposed Martyn's enthusiasm for Lloyd George.

Sometimes, in his keenness, Martyn was at the House of Commons alone of his family, as happened on a memorable Monday night in June 1916. Despite the Great War, the question of Ireland was still a prominent issue, the Irish nationalist M.P.'s at Westminster (led by John Redmond) being dissatisfied with a promise of Home Rule for all Ireland once the European conflict was over. Also in Parliament, and a member of the Coalition government, was Sir Edward Carson who as 'uncrowned king of Ulster' had done so much to thwart the hopes of the Irish nationalists prior to 1914. This was part of the background to what proved to be one of the great debates on the Irish question. Martyn recalled:

'I got in quite accidentally. I was sitting on a bench in the Victoria Tower Gardens, by the House of Lords, revising for the London matric, and suddenly thought, I wonder what is on in the House? One could get in without any trouble in those days – people didn't know about the Strangers' Gallery – so I went in. You had to sign both downstairs and upstairs and the two men on the doors both knew me well. The House was almost empty – McKenna, the Chancellor of the Exchequer, was speaking on the Finance Bill and it was dull and boring. After sitting there for about half-an-hour to three quarters I decided I would go home. As I was reaching down for my hat a man sitting along the bench sidled towards me and said, "Have you got to go?" I replied, "Well, no, I haven't *got* to go."

[38]

"Well, if you are wise," he declared, "you will stay where you are; there is a great debate coming on at 8.15. John Redmond has been questioning the Prime Minister in the question hour, he didn't get satisfaction and brought in a resolution to move the adjournment of the House at 8.15 to debate the Irish question. Stay where you are! It's going to be a great debate." So I put my hat back.

'The members began to come in until the place was literally packed, with members standing, and at 8.15 John Redmond got up to speak. He was followed by Lloyd George who had been in charge of the negotiations to settle the thing. He had, in fact, almost succeeded when Lord Lansdowne threw a spanner into the works at the last moment. Then Sir Edward Carson, John Dillon, who was Redmond's deputy, and finally Asquith. That was the night when not only were the members on their feet but we were allowed to clap our hands in the Strangers' Gallery – I never saw that at any other time. Carson was the most impressive. He set the place on fire with a great emotional appeal, which he could do, for he was an orator as well as a great advocate. He was debating the issue but appealing to John Redmond to come down to the floor of the House to shake him by the hand, to make up their difference and go on. Redmond wouldn't do it.'

It was well past 11 p.m. before Martyn Lloyd-Jones returned home with his school books that June evening. No doubt his parents had guessed where he was. Perhaps they sometimes wondered whether, with all Martyn's keenness for politics, the present emphases of his school work were the best for their son. When he started at Tregaron he had enjoyed History and English, the novels of Sir Walter Scott being special favourites. By this date, however, almost all his attention was given to science and to subjects related to his anticipated career in medicine.

The results of his summer examinations in 1916 were to show that neither the dairy, nor the House of Commons, had distracted him from his main purpose. A Welsh newspaper, under the heading 'Llangeitho', announced that 'an old Llangeitho boy, David Martyn Lloyd-Jones, at the London University Senior School examination, passed in seven subjects and gained distinction in five'. With such results it was probable that he could gain a place for medical training in any of the best teaching hospitals in London. On his own initiative he wrote to several hospitals for information and then made up his own mind to apply to St Bartholomew's. A preliminary examination and an interview with the Dean, proved enough, even at the age of sixteen, to secure him a place among the eighty-two students who began their course on October 6, 1916.

In later years Martyn Lloyd-Jones was never to sympathise with those who looked back to their schooldays as the happiest years of their lives. In his memory the time at Tregaron County School and at Marylebone Grammar School was associated with the family difficulties with which he had felt so closely involved after his grandfather's disturbing disclosure in 1911. After that event he was never the carefree footballer who had so troubled the assistant master at Llangeitho by his lack of application. It was as though he by-passed much that is common to youth, which is what he meant when he sometimes said, 'I was never an adolescent'.

'The fact is that, in Western Europe at least, it was the Church which founded the Hospital . . . I am proud to remember that in 1923 we were celebrating the foundation of the oldest and greatest hospital in London – the Octocentenary of St Bartholomew's. That Hospital was founded in 1123 by a Christian, a monk by the name of Rahere.'

M. L.-J.
in an address *Will Hospital Replace the Church?*
(Christian Medical Fellowship, 1969, p. 4)

3

The World of Medicine

A short walk from St Paul's, from Newgate and Aldersgate Streets, St Bartholomew's Hospital stood in the centre of the old city of London. Within its buildings Cromwell's injured troops had been nursed in the 1640's; outside its walls, at the time of the Reformation, the Protestant martyrs had died in Smithfield, and it was more than a hundred years before that when the hospital first began its work of healing among London's poor. In 1916 the principal part of the hospital, with some 600 beds, still consisted of the four buildings around a square, built in the mid-eighteenth century. To enter its 1702 gateway was to enter a world quite as distinct and influential as that of any ancient university.

But it was Bart's doctors, not mere antiquity, which made the hospital what it had become, with a distinguished line of physicians and surgeons going back to the sixteenth century. John Abernethy was the first to give a regular programme of lectures to students and by the time of his death in 1831 Bart's had the largest Medical School in London. New buildings for the School were put up in 1879–80. Abernethy, and the hospital 'chiefs' who followed him, had airs and habits of pungent speech which placed them rather above the common race of mortals. It was not only students who could receive their summary treatment. Once when the famous Duke of Wellington, intent on seeing Abernethy and arriving at his room unannounced, was asked how he got in, 'By the door,' was the reply. 'Then,' said the doctor, 'I recommend you to make your exit by the same way.' The same man is said to have refused to attend King George IV until he had first delivered a lecture! Both the medical brilliance and the authoritarian manners of the Bart's chiefs contributed in no small measure to the ethos into which each new generation of students entered. The biographer of one of the hospital's chiefs, writing about the period when Lloyd-Jones was a student, says:

'Bart's doctors, like graduates of Trinity College, Cambridge, acquire a feeling that membership of their institution is alone enough to set them somewhat apart, that they are not as other men are; but even allowing for this "consciousness of effortless superiority", the galaxy of medical talent deployed at Bart's during the first forty years of the twentieth century was an exceptionally splendid one.'[1]

Martyn Lloyd-Jones' first impressions of Bart's are unrecorded. Almost all we know is that his friendships made in these early years were warm and lasting, even though opportunities of meeting were later to be few and far between. He was popular among his fellow-students and respected for his undoubted ability. One early photo from this period – hardly printable except in a medical text-book! – shows him at work in the post-mortem room. He clearly imbibed the common Bart's opinion that, in the words of Sir Norman Moore, 'the best physicians were all morbid anatomists, who regarded the post-mortem room as the place from which, after the wards, a physician should fill his mind, and where he should acquire a familiarity with the interpretation of symptoms and the course of diseases'. Even when he was only on the first rungs of the ladder he knew clearly where he wanted to be.

Martyn's commitment to medicine gave him exemption from military service, unlike his elder brother, Harold, who, having begun to study law at Aberystwyth, was called up to join the Royal Welsh Fusiliers. Such was the shortage of doctors that, as Martyn found at Bart's, medical students who had joined the army were being sent back to resume their studies. But to some extent the War itself came to London. He recalled:

'We saw many things happening for the first time ever during the War. One event was seeing the first Zeppelin to attack London. Strangely enough, instead of looking for a hiding place, we all used to run out into the street to stare at the Zeppelin and the searchlights playing on it, making it look like a huge illuminated cigar in the sky. I also remember the first daylight raid by an aeroplane. The first bomb fell on a Saturday morning quite close to St Bartholomew's Hospital where I was a student, and I rushed there to give a helping hand.

[1] Mervyn Horder, *The Little Genius, A Memoir of the First Lord Horder*, 1966, pp. 15–16.

Then there was one memorable Sunday night. We had gone upstairs
to bed when suddenly the Northern sky became as red as a sunset for
some minutes and then the colour faded out. Simultaneously there
was a victorious shout to be heard with people running out into the
streets rejoicing. Lieut. Leif Robinson had managed to shoot down
the first Zeppelin above Cuffley, near Potters Bar.'

Next to home and hospital, the most important thing in his life at this
date was Charing Cross Chapel. It had so happened that on the very
first Sunday that the Lloyd-Jones family came to their new church
they occupied a pew immediately in front of the Phillips family who
were to play such a major part in subsequent events. Dr Tom Phillips
belonged to Newcastle Emlyn, where his father, the Reverend Evan
Phillips, had been the much-esteemed minister of Bethel Calvinistic
Methodist Chapel for more than fifty years and among the foremost
leaders in the 1859 Revival in Wales. By the autumn of 1914 Tom
Phillips had been in London for more than twenty years and had
become a well-known eye specialist. David Lloyd George was one of
his patients. With his wife, their eighteen-year-old son, Ieuan, their
sixteen-year-old daughter, Bethan, and ten-year-old Tomos John,
they were never missing from their seats at Charing Cross, even
though their home at Harrow was some twelve miles out of London.
To this day, Bethan can remember the appearance of the three boys
as the new family arrived in the pew in front of them, Vincent, in the
younger style, wearing his Eton collar outside his jacket. She was
unaware that Martyn had already admired her from a distance at
Newcastle Emlyn. Bethan and Ieuan were often in Newcastle Emlyn,
staying with their relatives; indeed, as far back as 1904–05 when
revival had come to that town, Tom Phillips had sent both children
down by train that something might be imprinted on their memories.[1] It was probably on some market-day at Newcastle Emlyn in his

[1] Hearing news that revival was present in Newcastle Emlyn to a marked
degree, Tom Phillips suddenly decided to send his two eldest Ieuan, eight,
and Bethan, six, to their grandparents (Evan Phillips). To the very natural
remonstrances of their mother that they were at school, he said: 'Nonsense,
they can have school any time, but they may never see another revival'! He
took the two to Paddington and put them on the train and gave half-a-crown
to the guard to remind them to change trains at Carmarthen. Ieuan and
Bethan were ever thankful for the day when their father made such a far-
seeing decision. The third child, Tomos John, who also became an eye
specialist, was a baby at the time – born on March 4, 1904.

early youth, while accompanying his grandfather from Llwyncadfor, that Martyn first saw Bethan Phillips.

Bethan was to start the study of medicine at University College the same day that Martyn started at Bart's in 1916: over the next nine years there were to be periods of friendship and association between them interspersed with considerable intervals. For one thing, despite their initial parity in medicine, it was difficult for her to forget that Martyn was eighteen months her junior. He was to find friendship with Ieuan Phillips an easier proposition and before long the two were to become close friends. In the first instance, however, it was Dr Tom Phillips who was to play a major part in Martyn's life once the young medical student joined his Sunday School class in 1917. Henry Lloyd-Jones had always encouraged his sons to debate public issues amongst themselves in the home and in the open kind of class which Tom Phillips conducted Martyn was soon in his element. Speaking of Dr Phillips' class (in which he was to remain until 1924) he said:

'The arguing was keen and sometimes fierce every Sunday afternoon, and very often he and I were the main speakers. I have argued a lot, and with many men during my lifetime, but I can vouch that I have never seen his like from the point of view of debate and the swiftness of his mind. He, my brother Vincent, and Dr David Phillips of Bala, are the three best debaters that I have ever met and my debt to the first two is very great. There is nothing better for the sharpening of wits and to help a man to think clearly and orderly, than debating, and especially to debate on theological and philosophical topics.'

Sometimes debates became so excited that members from other classes (who were being disturbed) were sent to request a reduction in the noise! Martyn's own growing astuteness in discussion cannot have been unrelated to his continuing attendance at the House of Commons where (as mentioned above) he was to hear some of the most important debates of the War.

'I was there on a Monday night in June 1916 and I heard John Redmond, Lloyd George, Sir Edward Carson, John Dillon and Asquith, discussing the Ireland question in a great debate from 8.15 p.m. until 11 p.m. I was there also on another Monday afternoon in November 1917, to hear a great debate on Lloyd George's plan to establish an international military council at Versailles and to place

Sir Douglas Haig under the authority of Marshal Foch. Many thought that Asquith would be successful but it was not so. I see Lloyd George this minute stretching out his finger at Asquith and saying with a piercing strength: "Speeches are no substitute for shells".'

Before the end of the War the family circle was again complete as Harold had been invalided out of the army on account of a heart condition. His condition soon improved and he looked forward to the legal career upon which he now embarked. Verses from his pen which appeared in the well-known periodical, *John o' London's Weekly*, also revealed his considerable poetical gifts. In his mother's opinion Harold was also the most eloquent of the three sons though an incident which occurred at this date perhaps casts some doubt on the correctness of her judgment. A family friend from Wales, D. J. Williams, was visiting the Lloyd-Joneses and, being a lay-preacher among the Calvinistic Methodists, he had been asked to preach at the Welsh Chapel in Holloway. Harold and Martyn went with him and thus became involved in a service which, before it concluded, was far removed from the denomination's dignity. Before he arrived, apparently, it was rumoured among the congregation that Williams' pacifist leanings made him no supporter of the desperate struggle then going on in France. Not a few at Holloway had sons then serving on the Western Front and when Williams inadvisedly made some reflection in the course of his sermon which seemed to support their suspicions, there was an ugly and tense scene as normally sedate worshippers rose angrily to their feet to protest and to condemn the preacher. Feeling some responsibility for the visiting preacher, Martyn nudged his elder brother and urged him to intervene. But Harold indicated that Martyn would have to do it, and so, losing no time, Martyn stood up to give what was to be his first 'address' in public. 'I said that I actually did not agree with the preacher yet I could vouch for his character – he had offered himself voluntarily to the army at the outbreak of war but had been turned down on account of his eye-sight. I told them that he was a man of integrity and honest opinion, who was prepared to fight for what he believed, and that, in any case, we should be tolerant as we did not all agree about the implications of the gospel.' Listening to these and other words, spoken in Welsh, from the young Lloyd-Jones, the strong feeling subsided and quietness was restored!

David Martyn Lloyd-Jones

Martyn and Harold continued to do a number of things together until a Sunday morning in June 1918 when Martyn awoke to find himself dizzy and unable to stand up. He was a victim of the great 'flu epidemic which was to claim so many lives. On the Tuesday his elder brother went down with the same infection and never recovered. Harold Lloyd-Jones at the age of twenty was buried in a parish graveyard near Llwyncadfor on July 1, 1918. A new grave, that of David Evans, his grandfather, was alongside. The master of Llwyncadfor, with whom the boys had spent so many memorable childhood days, had died the previous year.

A tribute to Harold Lloyd-Jones, written by T. A. Levi, his professor at Aberystwyth, and published by *Y Gorlan* (*The Fold*), the magazine of Charing Cross Chapel, spoke of him as 'one of the best boys I have ever known'.

'He was a Welshman through and through. He joined Aberystwyth College about two years ago intending to study law. When he enquired of me regarding books, he would ask not how many he *had* to read . . . He would ask questions oftener than any of his contemporaries and would prepare them before coming to the class. He would read the Parliamentary Debates fully, and would send the reports to me with comments on them. Harold was very popular with all the students and his influence on them was outstanding.'

Four months later came the end of the War. As soon as Martyn Lloyd-Jones heard of the signing of the Armistice on November 11 he laid aside any more thought of work that day at Bart's:

'I went at once from the hospital in the direction of Westminster. I heard, after arriving there, that the members of the House of Commons intended crossing the road to a short service of thanksgiving in St Margaret's Church. I, like many others, was allowed by a policeman to stand and watch the procession, and at about three o'clock they came, with Lloyd George and Asquith walking together at the front. In December I stood on my feet for about four hours to catch a glimpse of President Woodrow Wilson of the U.S.A. going past in an open carriage with King George V. I was a bit of a hero-worshipper in those days, and I still tend to be so. But alas! the heroes have become scarce.'

That same December of 1918, at Christmas, there was a special

[48]

treat in welcoming Rhys Rowlands, the man who had so often enlivened conversation at Llangeitho, to their home:

'My father persuaded the dear fellow to come to stay with us for a fortnight in London. We had hoped that he would travel in his breeches of black and white check, and so he did. We had a banquet, a feast of stories. One afternoon my brother Vincent and I were trying to show him a little of London. We were opposite Westminster Abbey and were trying to direct his attention to the ancient, world-famous building. But at the same time it happened that a van or cart belonging to a famous brewery and pulled by two large shire horses passed by. The competition was completely unfair, Rhys turned his back on the Abbey and with shining eyes said: "Well indeed, what two smart horses! It was worth my coming to London to see them." I would go much further than from London to Llangeitho to listen to Rhys Rowlands telling a story once again. What is television or radio compared with such talent as that!'

The earliest letter of Martyn's to survive was written to his mother, who was on holiday near Newcastle Emlyn, on July 18, 1919. Its contents are of little moment but they give some idea of the horizons of every-day thought in the life of a medical student:

> St Bartholomew's Hospital
> London, E.C.
> Friday

My dear Mamma

Again I am writing without having much news to give you. I would have written earlier in the week but for the fact that I have been extremely busy. As I think I pointed out before, I was on duty over the weekend so that I was kept very busy until Wednesday. Since then also, I have been very busy with operations to attend etc. Added to these I caught another nasty cold last weekend, so that I have been feeling very tired. However, it is much better by now; with the rest over this week-end, I hope to be all right once more.

I am very glad to hear that you are enjoying yourself so much, and I suppose that you have been to Llangeitho by now.

I do not know exactly how I am going to spend to-morrow. I feel that in view of my cold it would perhaps be advisable for me not to play tennis as it might get worse. At the same time I do not feel like standing in the crowd watching the procession. Of course, the

David Martyn Lloyd-Jones

peace celebrations will not make much difference to you down there.

Well, Harcombe[1] has now left London for good. He was discharged Wednesday morning and went home yesterday. It was very amusing to watch him listening to D. O. Evans[2] speaking on Tuesday night in our house. Of course after D O went, he broke out. The same night Tom Hugh Jones called round. Mary Jane has undergone the operation and is going on all right, but on opening her up they found out that it was not an 'ovarian cyst' at all, but tuberculosis of the peritoneum, which means tuberculosis of the membranous lining of all the viscera. It is a very serious condition although not as serious as tuberculosis of the lung. She will probably have to go to a sanatorium and have the ordinary treatment. It is hard to tell which way it will turn out. She may recover completely, but on the other hand she may die very suddenly. They are worrying terribly about it, and their Doctor has given them to understand that it was absolutely hopeless. However, I have had several cases of it and some of them have done quite well, and got quite all right, and on reading up I find that the text-books say the same thing.

Well, I must stop now if I want to catch this post. I will write to you over the weekend.

With fondest love to you and all down there. I remain
Your loving son
Martyn.

Martyn Lloyd-Jones reached the first goal of his medical studies in 1921 taking his M.R.C.S. and L.R.C.P. degrees in July and his Bachelor of Medicine and Bachelor of Surgery (M.B., B.S.) in October, with distinction in Medicine. There was another reason, besides examinations, which was to make the year 1921 a vital one of his whole medical career. For the first time he began to work under Sir Thomas Horder, a doctor whose name must stand in any list of Bart's most brilliant men.

While still in his thirties, Horder's call to the sickroom of King Edward VII in 1910 had established him as one of the most sought-after men in private practice in Harley Street. This practice he conjoined with duties at Bart's where he became Physician to the Hospital in the same year that Lloyd-Jones qualified. It was, as Horder's biographer says, the entrance to the peak years of his life

[1] Formerly one of the masters at Tregaron County School.
[2] Future M.P. for Cardiganshire.

and work in clinical teaching. Prior to that date the medical student from Regency Street, Westminster, had seen comparatively little of Horder, as he had worked in a different firm from that of which the latter was Chief.

An incident in 1920 first brought Lloyd-Jones to Horder's notice. According to the usual practice Lloyd-Jones had one day examined and made a diagnosis of a patient allocated to him as a student in the out-patient department. The same patient was later seen by Horder on a teaching round with a group of students, and he expressed surprise at the diagnosis which Lloyd-Jones proposed. Its correctness was dependent upon being able to feel the patient's spleen – something which Lloyd-Jones professed to be able to do even when Horder twice failed. Not surprisingly the gathered students supported their chief's judgment, in part, no doubt, because they knew that a mistake could bring down upon them some caustic witticism quite as pungent as anything ever uttered by Abernethy. 'Let me see, Mr Smith,' Horder said one day to a student. 'What is the cause of this disease?' 'Well, sir,' the young man responded, 'I did know but I have forgotten.' 'A pity,' exclaimed the Chief, 'because now no one knows!'[1]

For a different reason Lloyd-Jones had himself had a similar uncomfortable encounter with Horder on an earlier occasion. It was one of those days, which still occurred, when some emergency at the dairy had caused him to rise very early before he went on to Bart's. There one of his first duties was attendance at Horder's out-patients clinic where he arrived half asleep only to be faced with one of the chief's piercing questions which he scarcely heard. To the merriment of his fellow students Horder at once pulled his leg as he hesitated and dithered. It was different, however, on the day to which we are now referring in 1920. In full possession of his senses Lloyd-Jones stood by his diagnosis and when a few days later he was proved correct by the course of the patient's illness Horder's interest in him was established.

[1] On another occasion one of Horder's students was giving a report to his chief in front of other students and was clearly anxious to impress. With a sense of self-importance, and some pomposity, the student related various symptoms of the patient and in beginning to describe how he made his examination he said, 'As I approached the bed I noticed a look of apprehension . . .' 'Stop!' interrupted Horder. 'Because the patient looked apprehensive when *you* approached the bed that is not necessarily a medical symptom!'

David Martyn Lloyd-Jones

In 1921, when it came to the time of making hospital appointments, which was before the results of the October M.B., B.S. examination were known, Horder took the unusual step of going outside his own firm to appoint Lloyd-Jones as his Junior House Physician. Two previous house physicians of Horder's were disappointed that he had overlooked another man whom they had advised him to choose. 'Wouldn't I have looked a fool if I had appointed your man instead of mine,' the Chief told them, once the distinction which Lloyd-Jones had gained in his M.B., B.S. became known.

Lloyd-Jones' subsequent years with Horder were to make a deep impression upon him. After a year as House Physician there followed two years, 1923–24, as Horder's Chief Clinical Assistant, by which time he was also associated with his private practice. In 1924 at Horder's instigation he was the first to benefit from a scholarship from the R. L. St John Harmsworth Memorial Research Fund, in order to undertake important research work on sub-acute bacterial endocarditis, a condition affecting the inner lining of the heart which Sir William Ostler and Horder had first described in 1909. It was this research work[1] which later gave rise to the often repeated misunderstanding that he had been a heart specialist. In fact, like his Chief, it was always his first-love to be a general physician.

Horder's influence upon him lay chiefly in the manner in which he thought and taught. Notwithstanding the number of distinguished men – physicians, surgeons, and professors – whom Dr Lloyd-Jones had met at Bart's it was his opinion that 'Horder was quite on his own'.

'The most astute and clear thinker that I ever knew was my old teacher, Lord Horder. This was the chief element in his outstanding success as a doctor. He was a thorough diagnostician and after he had collected his facts, he would reason until he reached his diagnosis. His method was to work always from first principles, never jumping to conclusions. Having gathered all the data on a patient he would then set up all possible explanations for his illness like a group of skittles. These he proceeded to "knock down" one by one, as objections were applied to them, until there was only one left.'

Often, in dealing with cases, Horder was able to go through this

---

[1] Part of the results of his research was published under the title, 'An Experimental Study of Malignant Endocarditis', as an appendix in *Bacterial Endocarditis*, C. Bruce Perry, 1936.

process with such speed that he became known, in the words of the
poet T. S. Eliot, as 'The Little Genius'. This was the case, for
example, in 1910 when, after one of the royal physicians, Dr Samuel
Jones Gee, had called him in to advise on the chest condition of King
Edward VII, it had seemed as though a mere glance at the King's full
ash-trays had been enough to lead him to identify the cause as
nicotine poisoning. There were far more difficult cases which Lloyd-
Jones was to see his chief deal with effectively. When, for instance,
four or five distinguished specialists had failed to diagnose the
gasping for breath of a rich Welsh coal-owner in 1923, Horder – by
no means universally popular among his colleagues – was called in.
As he arrived to make his examination one of these men was heard to
exclaim with some relish, 'Well, Horder will soon find this is where
he gets off.' Instead within a few minutes, the Bart's physician was
pointing to the evidence for a pleural effusion.

The Chief Assistant, who was frequently with him on such cases,
knew that Horder's success was not the result of any magic. As usual,
Horder was working from first principles. On his teaching rounds
Horder would constantly demonstrate the process with his students
– often 'grooming' them by close questioning in the 'Socratic'
tradition of instruction. He aimed to demonstrate that mastering 'the
elements of precise thinking and precise expression of thought' was
equally important with mastering the elements of clinical medicine.
In the extent to which he did this he exceeded many of his older
colleagues, and it was characteristic of him that one book which he
constantly urged on his students was not a medical text-book but
William Stanley Jevons' *The Principles of Science: a Treatise on
Logic and Scientific Method.*[1] It was a mark of Horder's affection for
Lloyd-Jones that he was to pass on to him his own copy of Jevons,
bought in 1893 and carefully annotated in pencil.

For Dr Lloyd-Jones the benefits of working with Horder abundantly compensated for the excessive demands on junior colleagues
which the Chief could sometimes make. There was one occasion, for
example, when Sir Thomas was so late in preparing the material for
some important public lectures which he was giving, that Lloyd-
Jones and another junior member of staff had to have permission to
remain in the Bart's Library late into the night pursuing quotations
and references which would be needed the next day. The work was

[1] First edition, 2 vols, 1874; 2nd edition, 1 vol., 1877.

not completed before the research colleague collapsed with exhaustion and had to be removed to a ward where Lloyd-Jones revived him with brandy! A considerably larger task Lloyd-Jones had to take on single-handed in 1923 when Horder, now aged fifty-two, found his powerful memory was not always reliable in recalling the names of the patients suffering from the many and varied diseases which he had treated. Hitherto all Horder's case histories were grouped under the patients' names. What he now wished to have was a second classification under the diseases, and many of Lloyd-Jones' evenings and Saturday afternoons were to be given to the work of preparing this second index.

Yet life was not all hard work at this date. Lloyd-Jones could enjoy lunch hour musical recitals at St Sepulchre's Church opposite Bart's, or evening theatre or opera visits. The financial difficulties of earlier years were now behind him – a fact perhaps, which his father had in mind on his death in 1922, when he exhorted his sons 'not to forget the poor'. New avenues of social life were also opened up, as Horder, whose patients included many celebrities and national figures, frequently invited him to join the circle who enjoyed the stimulating conversation and the *bonne vie* of Ashford Chace, his country estate at Petersfield, Hampshire. One of the earliest of those invitations read:

> Ashford Chace
> Petersfield
> August   24,   1924
>
> Dear Lloyd-Jones
>   The time flies away and I must not delay asking you to come to see us for a night, – because I am due to go to Scotland on the night of 28th can you come here on Tuesday evening, to return with us on Wednesday, or, if we are too full in the car, by train? There is a good train leaving Waterloo 4.50 and arriving Petersfield 6.23. I will meet that train in the car if I hear that you can come.
> With best wishes, I am.
>   Yours sincerely,
>   Thomas Horder.

Before Lloyd-Jones took his postgraduate examination for the Membership of the Royal College of Physicians in April 1925, the final examination which it was possible for him to take, his reputation in the medical world was already beginning to be established. Other Bart's chiefs, including Sir Thomas P. Dunhill and Sir Bernard

Spilsbury, took a close interest in his future. Spilsbury, who was Chief Pathologist to the Home Office, sought to draw him into his own private practice. The invitation was declined, though Lloyd-Jones admired the man whom he met so often in the post-mortem room.

'I had, [he recalled] the privilege of knowing and of working together with the famous Sir Bernard Spilsbury. If Thomas Carlyle's definition of genius is correct – "An infinite capacity for taking pains" – then Spilsbury was a genius. He did not have a clear and lively mind as Horder had – his strength was the thoroughness of his researches. Nothing was too much trouble for him and he would not take anything for granted. On top of this, when he was giving evidence in court, not one barrister – not even the famous Marshall Hall – could cause him to become ruffled or confused. He would answer quietly and courteously and would keep to the facts of which he was certain, avoiding any speculation.'

Some of Dr Lloyd-Jones' contemporaries at Bart's, who had distinguished careers before them, and who remain alive to the present, have recorded their memories of his days in medicine. Dr C Langton Hewer, then a junior anaesthetist recalls: 'I got to know Dr Lloyd-Jones as a brilliant scholar and teacher of medicine and also as a music lover. I used to go with him sometimes in the lunch hour to St Sepulchre's church opposite Bart's where they had a first-class organist.' Sir Geoffrey L. Keynes, one of Bart's leading surgeons of the present century, wrote in 1980: 'I was very friendly with Martyn Lloyd-Jones when we were both working as Chief Assistants at St Bartholomew's Hospital in the early 1920's, he on the medical side, I on the surgical. I greatly admired his intellectual approach to Medicine as a profession. I was not the only one of his friends to have these feelings and to appreciate also his humanity as a doctor.'

'The prerequisite of a path is that it leads to a road. I strayed, I got lost and I grew tired on many paths, but I was always aware, as was Francis Thompson, that the "Hound of Heaven" was on my tracks. At last He caught me and led me to the "way that leads to life".'

M. L.-J.

'If you were to ask me to give a definition of a Christian I should say that he is one who, since believing in Christ, feels himself to be the happiest man in the world and longs for everybody else to be equally happy!'

M. L.-J.
on Psalm 34:8, June 28, 1931

4

'All Things New'

Psychology, in which Martyn Lloyd-Jones became interested at Bart's, taught him that the opinions which a man expresses, instead of being purely the results of his voluntary decisions, are rather the consequence of prejudices which arise from previous conditioning factors. Thus in his own case, it might be said, he was ready to argue for Christian opinions because of the formulating influences present throughout his upbringing. In February 1914, at the suggestion of their minister, all three Lloyd-Jones brothers had professed their faith and become communicant members of the Calvinistic Methodist denomination before they left Llangeitho. Once in London, as we have seen, the affiliation was strongly maintained and Martyn, at the unusually early age of eighteen, was Superintendent of the whole Sunday School at Charing Cross Road for one year. He was certainly conditioned to think of himself as a Christian. Of course, neither he, nor his religious teachers, would have expressed this in merely psychological terms. They would have seen it as a God-appointed process in virtue of which we become Christians by family ties and by church connections.

In fact, as Martyn Lloyd-Jones entered his early twenties, he was brought to an entirely new opinion. It was an opinion which owed virtually nothing to the events in his life which we have so far considered. Contrary to the thought of both home and chapel, he was now to come to the belief that so far he had never been a Christian at all. 'For many years I thought I was a Christian when in fact I was not. It was only later that I came to see that I had never been a Christian and became one. But I was a member of a church and attended my church and its services regularly.'[1]

---

[1] *Preaching and Preachers*, 1971, p. 146.

David Martyn Lloyd-Jones

To his contemporaries the conditions producing such a major change of opinion were not easy to see. As we have already said, his spiritual change, far from being the product of his regular religious education was clean contrary to the assumptions which that education had instilled. Peter Hughes Griffiths, the minister at Charing Cross, had more sympathy with evangelical Christianity than the minister of Llangeitho, yet he had the same propensity to treat all his hearers as Christians and in consequence his preaching also made little appeal to the mind or conscience. Instead of theology or exposition, Griffiths supplied an abundance of anecdotes and illustrations. Feeling and sentiment were what he aimed at, and not without effect; as, for example, with such themes as 'A Mother's View of Things' based on Isaiah 66:13 ('As one whom his mother comforteth, so will I comfort you'). On that occasion Martyn Lloyd-Jones saw the whole congregation dissolve into tears. Characteristic of Griffiths' illustrations was the story of how he once had been staying at a farm near Carmarthen when one night most of the family went out to a concert. At length, as the party returned, an orphan boy who belonged to the house came in first. He was asked by the farmer's wife which he enjoyed most, 'The Recitation or the Singing?' 'Oh, the singing,' the boy replied. 'And which song in particular?' '*Home, Sweet Home!*'

Commenting on this situation, Martyn Lloyd-Jones was later to say: 'What I needed was preaching that would convict me of sin and make me see my need, and bring me to repentance and tell me something about regeneration. But I never heard that. The preaching we had was always based on the assumption that we were all Christians, that we would not have been there in the congregation unless we were Christians.' It is clear from the testimony of others that the type of preaching which he heard was very far from being uncommon. One Welsh minister, E. Keri Evans, in his autobiography, reflected on what had become the general characteristics of the Welsh pulpit towards the end of the nineteenth century:

'Although I heard the best-known preachers in Wales of every denomination during these years, I cannot recall that a single one of them touched my conscience. . . . We used to go to the services for enjoyment and eloquence, and if we got these we considered that the object of worship had been attained. But it is beyond doubt also true that the majority of the popular preachers did not aim at convicting

[58]

anybody so much as at discussing the subject in a masterly and an eloquent manner and having a "good time".[1]

If Chapel life does not explain Martyn Lloyd-Jones' spiritual change, far less does any influence which he encountered at Bart's. That he became a Christian while at the hospital, and about the time that he was Horder's Chief Clinical Assistant, was in spite of his location, not because of it. William Hogarth's painting of the pool of Bethesda still adorned the main staircase of the eighteenth-century buildings, but not much of the influence of the Scriptures remained at Bart's in the 1920's. Medicine and biblical Christianity had parted company. None of the chiefs to whom Lloyd-Jones was closest was a Christian. Horder was an avowed rationalist and a vigorous exponent of what would now be called scientific humanism. The common belief was that modern knowledge, not least the recognition of evolution, had made historic Christianity untenable. Even in the Christian Union at Bart's (at that time run by the Student Christian Movement) the concessions made to modern thought were so large that Lloyd-Jones, even before he was a Christian, regarded attendance there as worthless.

It might seem, then, that in Dr Lloyd-Jones' case, the argument that 'belief' is the result of a prior 'conditioning' breaks down. But was this really so? Though his new faith did not come from the areas we have mentioned, yet he was *led* to it. It was no mere voluntary and irrational whim which was to make him different, rather he had been prepared and brought by influences which at length proved irresistible.

The earliest of these 'influences' had to do with the events which even as a child impressed upon him the very uncertain and changing character of life in this world. The home which he saw burned down in the night when he was ten years old was the third in which he had lived, and, not only did he never feel 'settled' in the new house which followed, he became conscious that this world itself can provide 'no continuing city'. After the sudden death of his brother Harold, with whom he had done so much, in 1918, he could say, as Edmund Burke once said in similar circumstances, 'What shadows we are and what shadows we pursue!' The death of his much-loved father, four years later, reinforced the same truth.

[1] *My Spiritual Pilgrimage*, E. Keri Evans (1860–1941), translated from the Welsh by T. Glyn Thomas, 1961, p. 53.

A further powerful factor in his life was an acute awareness, of which he had been conscious from childhood, of 'destiny' standing behind events. Shakespeare's famed axiom, 'There's a divinity that shapes our ends, rough hew them how we will,' he understood, and he could never doubt that his deliverance from the fire of January 1910 was all part of a higher purpose. In the words of a Welsh hymn which he used to sing in Llangeitho chapel,

> There must have been some silent providence . . .

He also began to see this same destiny in past history and especially in the story of the Christian Church. The Llangeitho Association meetings of 1913 first awakened his attention. Just a few weeks after that event, as he had stood in the playground at Tregaron at the end of the summer term, his history master, S. M. Powell, thrust something into his pocket with the abrupt instruction, 'Read that!' It was a penny booklet on the ministry of Howell Harris, one of the foremost figures in the eighteenth-century revival in Wales. This was his first reading in the history of Calvinistic Methodism – a history from which he was to gain a distinct view of the majesty and power of God. This new interest was greatly confirmed when, while reading the Scriptures at the age of seventeen, he came to see the truth of predestination – that doctrine which places all things under the rule of God's eternal throne. Thereafter he was eager to expound his 'discovery' both to his family and in the Sunday School class of Dr Tom Phillips at Charing Cross Chapel, where it often came to be debated. Once, on a holiday with his brother Vincent and a friend at Craven Arms, in the home of an uncle, a discussion on predestination began after lunch one day. It was still continuing when tea was brought in and finally concluded late in the evening, but only after Vincent had lost his voice!

Early in 1923 Dr Lloyd-Jones began to hear sermons which, though not distinctly evangelical, added something to his understanding. This was at Westminster Chapel, the Congregational church on whose behalf Arthur Marsh had unsuccessfully visited the family at Regency Street in 1915. Much had happened at Westminster in the intervening years. Campbell Morgan, the minister at that time, had resigned and gone to America in 1917. His successor John Henry Jowett (1863–1923) struggled with poor health and a declining congregation before preaching for the last time on December 17, 1922. Shortly after that date Martyn Lloyd-Jones made one of his periodic visits to hear Dr T. C. Williams who was again filling the Westminster Chapel pulpit. At this service he was interested to learn of the new minister, a Scot by the name of Dr John A. Hutton, who was due to begin his pastorate on the following Sunday. Martyn again varied his customary church attendance to hear Hutton the next week and he was at once impressed with the fifty-three-year-old Scot – indeed so gripped was the entire congregation that an unintentional wave of the preacher's hand as the sermon closed brought everyone to their feet! 'This man's preaching appealed to me tremendously,' Lloyd-Jones later recalled. 'I often listened to him. I think I listened to him most of the Sunday mornings that he was here.' Hutton's preaching was uneven in effect. He was not expository, and his best efforts were occasional rather than regular; but he added something more to Lloyd-Jones' thinking, 'He impressed me with the power of God to change men's lives.' He believed in rebirth and regeneration. Hutton's young medical hearer already knew that God plans and purposes, he was now becoming aware that He also acts and intervenes. At Westminster Chapel he was aware of a sense of spiritual reality which he missed at Charing Cross.

The most powerful influence of all in Dr Lloyd-Jones' complete change of direction has still to be stated. It was the fact of sin, the evidence that something is profoundly wrong with man himself. He observed it among London's poor with whom he had often to mix while at Bart's. In particular, while undertaking his student training in obstetrics in some of the roughest areas of Islington he met with conditions of ungodliness of which he had no conception in rural Cardiganshire. And yet what he saw in Islington was by no means so decisive in affecting his thinking as was the close contact which he came to have in the 1920's with people at the opposite end of social life. After all, wrong-doing among the poorer classes was, so it was said,readily explicable: it was merely a problem of education, housing and economic improvement. Change their conditions and their environment and all would be well! Precisely the same philosophy, taken up by politicians and by the League of Nations, was going to reconstruct the world and prevent any future war. But if that theory were correct – that is, that man is morally neutral and only needs help and education in order to be good – it ought to have been demonstrated among Horder's patients who often represented the best of the land from among the wealthy and the great. Certainly the patients of the King's physician who came to Horder's rooms at Harley Street were neither deprived nor uneducated. Three Prime Ministers were to be numbered among them, and many of the leading intellectuals, writers and musicians of the day. As Lloyd-Jones moved with his Chief in these circles he found such people altogether as needy as any whom he had seen in Islington. Their basic need was still untreated; for once, Horder's diagnoses did not go far enough. This lesson never came home to Lloyd-Jones more forcefully than it did in 1923 when, as mentioned earlier, he had to spend a number of weeks re-classifying his chief's case histories under their respective diseases. Horder's notes revealed that perhaps as many as 70 per cent of his private cases could not be classified under recognised medical criteria at all. 'Eats too much', 'Drinks too much' and similar comments, pointed to signs and symptoms with origins normally outside the province of medicine. Strange though it may sound, it was in a temple of scientific humanism – Horder's clinic – that Lloyd-Jones was helped to see the fallacy of the argument that modern man is so different from his forebears that historic Christianity is no longer relevant. He discovered that man in his fundamental need of a changed relation to God had not changed at all: 'All the changes about which men boast so much are external,' he observed. 'They are not changes in man himself, but merely in his mode of activity, in his environment.' The real problem which he now saw written large on Horder's case notes was neither medical nor intellectual. It was one of moral emptiness and spiritual hollowness. Horder's card index was to him almost what the vision of a valley of dry bones was to the prophet Ezekiel.

Nor did it escape his attention that nominal religion gave no help to these patients. The idol of his youth, David Lloyd George, had ceased to be Prime Minister in 1922, by which time his faith in him was already dead. Lloyd George was followed in the premiership by Andrew Bonar Law – another of Horder's patients whose very Christian names reflected his upbringing. At the time of his birth in 1858, his mother, the wife of a Free Church of Scotland minister, had been reading Andrew Bonar's *Memoir of R. M. M'Cheyne*. But when, shortly after coming to power, Law lay dying in 1923, his biographer reports that 'there are no signs that he ever sought consolation in the sombre faith of his ancestors. . . . He had too much intelligent integrity to turn in sickness to a creed which had long ceased to carry conviction to him.' Horder's patients indeed

represented the mood of the 1920's. What was lacking, as C. S. Lewis
has written in a criticism of Rudyard Kipling (another of Horder's
circle), was 'a doctrine of Ends'. Life in Kipling's eyes, said Lewis,
had lost all cosmic context. 'He has a reverent Pagan agnosticism
about all ultimates. "When man has come to the turnstiles of Night,"
he says in the preface to *Life's Handicap*, "all the creeds in the world
seem to him wonderfully alike and colourless".'[1]

Parallel with Lloyd-Jones' observance of the world around him,
but ultimately more decisive, was the growing recognition which
came to him of his own sinfulness. He began to recognise that sin was
much more profound than such acts as are commonly recognised as
immoral: there is a wrongness in man's very desires. What the
Apostle Paul calls 'the lusts of the mind' – pride, jealousy, envy,
malice, anger, bitterness – are all part of the very same disease. Even
in the mind, his highest faculty, man has become a fool. As this fact
slowly dawned upon Lloyd-Jones at about the age of twenty-three,
his estimate of his whole life was changed. The very debates which he
had so enjoyed on religious subjects he discovered to be nothing but
evidence of his depravity. Preaching in later years on the 'lusts of the
mind', he made one of his rare personal allusions when he declared:
'As I was preparing this sermon it filled me with a loathing and a
hatred of myself. I look back and I think of the hours I have wasted in
mere talk and argumentation. And it was all with one end only,
simply to gain my point and to show how clever I was.' He was
thinking of the years prior to 1923–24.

But the diagnosis had to go further still. He learned from both
Scripture and his own experience that he was actually dead to God
and opposed to God. He found the ruling principle of self-
centredness and self-interest in his own heart the final proof of his
fallen nature and of his wrong relationship to God. 'Sin is the exact
opposite of the attitude and the life which conform to, "Thou shalt
love the Lord thy God with all thy heart, and with all thy soul, and
with all thy mind, and with all thy strength." If you are not doing that

[1] C. S. Lewis, *Selected Literary Essays*, ed. W. Hooper, 1969, pp. 243–48.
Speaking of Kipling's praise of 'British' virtues Lewis asks, 'How if this
doctrine of work and discipline, which is so clear and earnest and dogmatic
at the periphery, hides at the centre a terrible vagueness, a frivolity or
scepticism?' It was Kipling who, in May 1923, urged Lord Beaverbrook to
get Horder to Paris to examine Bonar Law. Horder diagnosed cancer of the
throat and six months to live.

you are a sinner. It does not matter how respectable you are: if you are not living entirely to the glory of God you are a sinner.' Giving testimony to his own experience of this truth he was to say:

'I am a Christian solely and entirely because of the grace of God and not because of anything that I have thought or said or done. He brought me to know that I was dead, "dead in trespasses and sins", a slave to the world, and the flesh, and the devil, that in me "dwelleth no good thing", and that I was under the wrath of God and heading for eternal punishment.

'He brought me to see that the real cause of all my troubles and ills, and that of all men, was an evil and fallen nature which hated God and loved sin. My trouble was not only that I did things that were wrong, but that I myself was wrong at the very centre of my being.'

In other words, Dr Lloyd-Jones came to see that his outward life had been little more than play-acting: the real truth was that he had been seeking to escape from God.

This knowledge did not come to him in days, nor even weeks. He put no date to his conversion. It was progressive, like the experience described by Francis Thompson in his poem 'The Hound of Heaven'. To the words of that poem Martyn Lloyd-Jones could now readily respond:

> I fled Him down the nights and down the days;
>   I fled Him down the arches of the years;
> I fled Him down the labyrinthine ways
>   Of my own mind; and in the mist of tears
> I hid from Him . . .
>
> In the rash lustihead of my young powers,
>   I shook the pillaring hours
> And pulled my life upon me; grimed with smears,
> I stand amid the dust o' the mounded years –
> My mangled youth lies dead beneath the heap.
> My days have crackled and gone up in smoke,
> Have puffed and burst as sun-starts on a stream . . .
>
> I dimly guess what Time in mists confounds;
> Yet ever and anon a trumpet sounds
> From the hid battlements of Eternity;
> Those shaken mists a space unsettle, then
> Round the half-glimpsèd turrets slowly wash again.

'*All Things New*'

But not ere him who summoneth
I first have seen . . .

Now of that long pursuit
Comes on at hand the bruit;
That Voice is round me like a bursting sea:
'And is thy earth so marred,
Shattered in shard on shard?'
Lo, all things fly thee, for thou fliest Me!

It is possible to trace Lloyd-Jones' growing spiritual awareness and understanding in two addresses which he gave at the Chapel in Charing Cross Road in 1924 and 1925 at the Friday evening meeting of the Literary and Debating Society. He had first spoken at these meetings in 1921 on the subject of Modern Education. The meeting of March 1924 is the first address of which his manuscript survives and it gives us direct access to his thinking at that date. With a title, 'The Signs of the Times', his theme was basically serious, namely, the moral chaos of the times, which he proceeded to illustrate from eight different areas: dress (female and male); bathing ('the modern method of installing a bath in each house is not only a tragedy but has been a real curse to humanity'!); the rage for degrees and diplomas; newspapers and advertising; the wireless craze; the women of today; nationalism; and finally, the position of the church. By any standards it was a scintillating speech, yet despite its general intention there was probably too much of the personal tastes and humour of the young advocate to subdue and convince those who listened. His conservative, old-fashioned sympathies in dress and attitude, with his indifference to such things as London's football finals and tennis championships, were well known among the young people who supported the Literary and Debating Society. Nor was Martyn entirely averse to allowing his dogmatism to add an element of entertainment to their evening. His pronouncements included:

'I cannot possibly understand any man who wears silk stockings or even gaudily coloured socks; rings, wrist-watches, spats, shoes instead of boots, or who carries a cane in his hand.'

'If I had to spend a life-time with a companion who had one bath a day or with one who had one bath a year, I should unhesitatingly choose the latter, because a man's soul is more important than his skin.'[1]

'There was a time when fox-hunting was the greatest sport in this country, but it has long since been replaced by divorce.'

'Horse-racing, football, boxing and tennis – what food for immortal souls! Yet they are things that concern the majority. You really are very old-fashioned if you do not know whether Jack Dempsey beat Joe Beckett, or whether Mlle Lenglen cried or lost her temper, and really it is very important to know whether, three or four generations ago, that capricious young lady's forefathers were English or French.'

'When I enter a house and find that they have a wireless apparatus I know at once that there is something wrong . . . Your five-valve sets may do wonders, they may enable you to hear the voice of America, but believe me, they will never transmit the only Voice that is worth listening to.'

'I would much prefer the young lady of the Victorian era who fainted at the sight of a mouse, to the present modern young lady who says she is afraid of nothing.'

It is understandable that, when the address was over, some of these sentiments rather than his basic theme should have largely occupied subsequent discussions! The message had included an earnest plea for serious thought, and a charge that the degeneration of the pulpit was the real cause of the weakness of the Church, but, spiritually, there was an element of vagueness and indistinctness. The truth seems to be that the young Lloyd-Jones was as yet only half-alert to the message of Scripture. Perhaps, like the blind man at Bethsaida, when partially restored to sight, he might have said, 'I see men as trees, walking' (Mark 8:24). Hesitatingly, it may be, faith was in exercise but was not yet professing with Charles Wesley

> Thou, O Christ, art all I want,
> More than all in Thee I find.

When another eleven months had passed and he spoke again to the

[1] Dr Tom Phillips (who was to be his father-in-law) speaking in total agreement with the serious aspect of the address, brought the house down with a comment, 'Our Bethan is for ever in the bath'!

Literary and Debating Society on February 6, 1925 (shortly after taking the diploma which made him a Member of the Royal College of Physicians), the change was marked. His first intention on this occasion, he told the gathering, had been to give a biblical paper on the subject of predestination, but instead he felt compelled to take up 'The Tragedy of Modern Wales'. The title itself was startling among a people who, as he had alleged the previous year, made such 'great play of nationalism'. The fact was that, in the light of his own spiritual experience, he had gone back to his national history with new insight and was now surer of the message without which Wales, he believed, could not be true to herself. 'It is my love and my devotion to the Wales of the past that makes me talk about the tragedy of Modern Wales.' To give blind praise to Wales and to Welsh virtues might be the habit of politicians but 'to state the truth as it is, is the duty of the true patriot'. Wales' spiritual need, he declared, was his absorbing concern: 'My waking hours are filled with thoughts about her, and in my dreams I cannot escape from her; indeed everything else seems to be relative and subsidiary.'

His starting-point was the piece of sound psychology already noted: a man's opinions and attitudes depend upon the nature of his prejudices, and this he illustrated in one of the few semi-humorous remarks in the address:

'It will be quite obvious to you that I was born with strong prejudices against silk stockings, wireless and excessive bathing. Were I suddenly to start indulging in a daily bath and to install a wireless apparatus at home and come here in silk stockings, it would not be correct to say that I had changed my opinions, because what would have happened would be that I myself would have changed, or rather that something had completely changed my nature and character. One of the great fallacies of the present age is to imagine that a man and his so-called opinions are distinct and separate. What we affirm or deny will depend upon what prejudice we possess.'

Applying this to the subject in hand, he went on:

'The business of preaching is to give us a new prejudice, in fact the only prejudice that counts – the Christian prejudice. . . . If we do not start with the same prejudice, discussion is quite impossible, because virtually we shall be talking different languages. To a man who has the Christian prejudice all other prejudices are worse than useless, they spell damnation; to the man who possesses those other prejudices the Christian prejudice appears to be madness. Lunatics, as you know, generally think that all other people are mad.'

The address contains many of the features which were to become so common in his later public speaking – a unified argument ('Wales is what she is because of the absence of the Christian prejudice'), penetrating analysis and forceful application. He saw six principal signs of his country's degeneration:

1. The tendency to judge a man by his degrees and diplomas rather than by his character. 'What degrees,' he asked, 'had Daniel Rowland (Llangeitho), Howell Harris, William Williams (Pantycelyn), John Elias? Is it not pathetic that the nation which produced such men should be found today worshipping at the altar of degrees? That it should have crept into our chapels is still worse.' Education in Wales had replaced real Christianity:

'For a Welshman to quote the Bible in the same spirit as the Englishman quotes Shakespeare is surely blasphemous, and yet it is an exceptionally common practice. If we do not believe the Bible, then let us at least leave it alone altogether and not regard it as a text-book of history or literature.

'The great struggle in Wales today is the struggle between Education and Religion. If ever a nation was intoxicated with the idea of education, surely we are at the present time. The ironical fact is that we cannot somehow differentiate between culture, and knowledge. The true business of education is to give culture and the only culture that is worth considering is the culture possessed by Christian men and women. Has Wales more of this culture than she used to have in the days before education became so general? I am afraid the answer is definitely in the negative. What has become of those discussions that used to take place in the workshops of the blacksmith and the shoe-maker? They are represented today by the futile arguments as to whether the Bolton Wednesdays beat the Chelsea Saturdays in their latest football match.

'We worship today any man who knows many facts and we despise the man who knows the only thing that is really worth knowing. Because he does not know geometry and algebra, and because he has never heard of Bernard Shaw, he is considered to be narrow and old-fashioned; the truth is that he understands the magic of the sun and the stars in a way that a mere scientist can never hope to do . . .

'What education cannot teach us, death will demonstrate to us. How will all our learning and all our knowledge avail us then? Oh that we may be sobered before it is too late!'

2. The enthronement of financial success as the ultimate goal in life and the love of position and power which is its constant concomitant. 'One of the first remarks you hear these days almost about any man or, at least, one of the first questions asked is, "Is he doing well?" which, being interpreted means, as you well know, "Is he making money?" The respect which we pay to wealthy men, and the almost slavish adoration with which we regard their success, is sure proof of our worship of wealth. I am not at all sure but that we even excel the Jews in this respect – given a little more time we shall soon out-distance them.'

The same attitude showed itself, he argued, in the way the 'Successful' London Welshman is received back home when he returns in his new clothes and motor car, soon to be given a seat in the diaconate of the chapel. In Wales herself, bankers in towns and villages were particularly to be blamed, he believed, for changing attitudes:

'They form a little society of their own and regard all those who work for their living with disdain. . . . One of the greatest glories of the Wales of the past was that we knew of no such things as class distinction. We were all one because we worshipped the same God. The so-called country squires were generally Englishmen. But since the advent of bankers a spurious aristocracy has arisen whose definition of a gentleman is one who wears formal trousers or plus fours. There is one other attribute of these self-styled gentlemen which I had almost forgotten. According to them you are not one of the élite if you believe in Sabbath observance – the Continental Sunday will soon be a notable feature in Welsh life.'

After enlarging on the wider theme of the pursuit of money, he went on:

'Of course, the fallacy which underlies all these things is a very old one – it is that, if you are wealthy, you are happy. Quite by accident, it has been my lot to be able to study a large number of wealthy men at close quarters. The conclusion at which I have arrived concerning them has been that they are intensely miserable people, their misery being exceeded only by those who worship wealth and have it not.'

3. The proneness of the Welsh press to blazon forth 'the smallest achievements'. 'We are all "brilliant", at least so the Welsh newspapers say. The form of the paragraphs is well-known to you and reads somewhat as follows: "His numerous friends will be delighted to hear of the success of Mr Johnny Jones in passing the entrance examination into the London and Wales bank. This brilliant young man, etc., etc." – then follows an almost complete genealogical table of the prodigy.'

Some of the London Welsh, in particular, he blamed for this attitude –the type of man who thinks he is a gentleman because he smokes a cigar and belongs to one of the fashionable clubs 'where men eat and drink like beasts' and try to 'hang around the coat-tails' of the so-called great. 'For myself,' he declared, 'I have no hesitation whatsoever in stating that some of the most intelligent and cultured men whom I have had the privilege of meeting have been farmers in Cardiganshire. You will often hear the club-men speak of a friend in these terms, "He drinks his whisky like a gentleman"! Nature's gentlemen walk with God.' The cult of free-masonry, with its idea of status, received the same castigation: 'Why is it that we avoid the one thing that will give us real status – the status that belongs to those who are brothers of the Prince of princes? Surely this is a real tragedy!'

The speaker then turned, in the fourth and fifth places, to the evidence of national degeneration in the making of public appointments and in the misuse of hymnody. The sanctity of worship, he believed, was disappearing: 'Hymn-singing is to us what a glass of beer is to the Englishman.' Instead of being for God's praise, singing had become an expression of mere sentimentality: 'Is it not time that we sang less and began to think more seriously about life?'

The sixth sign of degeneration he drew from the state of the pulpit, as he had done a year before, but now his words are fuller and stronger:

'A nation given wholly to worldly success cannot possibly produce a great pulpit. Preaching today – again please note the glorious exceptions – has become a profession which is often taken up because of the glut in the other professions. I have already referred to the method adopted in the choice of ministers and we are reaping what we have sown. It is not at all surprising that many of our chapels are half-empty, for it is almost impossible to determine what some of our preachers believe. Another great abomination is the advent of the preacher-politician, that moral-mule who is so much in evidence these days. The harm done to Welsh public life by these monstrosities is incalculable. Their very appearance in public is a jeer at Christianity. Is it surprising that the things I have already mentioned are so flagrant with all these Judases so much in evidence? We get endless sermons on psychology, but amazingly few on Christianity. Our preachers are afraid to preach on the doctrine of the Atonement and on predestination. The great cardinal principles of our belief are scarcely ever mentioned, indeed there is a movement on foot to amend them so as to bring them up-to-date. How on earth can you talk of bringing these eternal truths up to date? They are not only up-to-date, they are and will be ahead of the times to all eternity.'

The address finally concluded:

'We think that we are on the high road of progress and that our future is assured; little do we realise that we are merely treading on the edge of the bottomless pit of destruction and damnation. I cannot prove this to you – you can either see it or you cannot, but the future will show. I find it very difficult to be patient. What is our duty at the present time, what are we to do in the face of the catastrophe that threatens to overwhelm us at any moment? What Wales needs above everything else at the present time is men, men, men; not educated snobs, not bloated plutocrats, not conceited agnostics, but men, real men, "men with vision and the faculty divine"; men who can say, without an apology, with Wordsworth:

> And I have felt
> A presence that disturbs me with the joy
> Of elevated thoughts.[1]

'I am optimistic, I believe that the day is coming when Wales will once more be in the van of the Christian crusade. I feel that our past is a guarantee of our future. Our condition today is remarkably like

[1] 'Lines composed a few miles above Tintern Abbey.'

that of a ship trying to set out to sea. We are rowing as hard as we can, trying our best to get away from our native land. But the sea is angry and we are being tossed and buffeted by the waves. At first it seemed to be rather pleasant, but now there are ominous signs of our approaching ship-wreck. I often wish that I could not see these billows, they frighten me. But when I look back towards the land I see there those great peaks pointing towards Heaven, secure in their solidarity and unshaken by the tempests. Those great peaks are the Methodist Fathers – let us return to them and nestle in their strength. Let us look at them more frequently. If we but did so we should soon return to them, for we should begin to feel that in our present position it is with us as it was with him who sang:

> Dyn diethr y dwyf yma
> Draw mae'm genedigol wlad!'[1]

The speech was followed by loud and prolonged applause. Of the seven speakers who rose to comment only one attempted to criticise. Dr Tom Phillips, with whom Martyn had been known to have many a tussle in the Sunday School, declared that he agreed with every word. Peter Hughes Griffiths, who presided, was not prepared to go just so far, indeed, he disagreed on two points; but he was, he professed, fully in accord with 'the spirit of the address'. For many of the wider audience who, through the columns of the press of South Wales, were to hear of Martyn Lloyd-Jones for the first time, it was a different matter. A reporter had been at the meeting and the result was in the *South Wales News* the next morning, Saturday, February 7, 1925. No sooner had Peter Hughes Griffiths read his copy of the paper than he 'phoned Martyn to make sure he had seen the references. Martyn, in fact, had cast his eye over all the sub-headings of the paper without seeing the least trace of their meeting the night before. On a second look, following the 'phone call, he discovered his mistake. In the same bold heading as was given to another leading article, 'America's Prosperity. Trade Expert's View', and with more space given to it, he read: 'Modern Wales, A Sweeping Indictment, London Welsh Lecture'. Sub-headings read, 'Colleges, Pillars of Hell', and 'Money-Making Mania'. The report commenced: 'A devastating criticism of modern Wales was made by Dr Martin

[1] I am a stranger here
My native land is far away! (Wm. Williams)

[72]

'All Things New'

Lloyd-Jones, M.R.C.S. (formerly of Llangeitho) in an address to a London Welsh audience in London last night, the Rev.'Peter Hughes Griffiths being in the chair.'

Two columns of selections from the address followed. The introduction to his speech with its carefully argued Christian approach was ignored, and full attention was given to all the sentences most likely to be regarded as sensational. This report was followed, in the next issue of the same paper, by a full-length editorial column (Monday, February 9, 1925) headed 'A Critic of Modern Wales'. 'There were one or two minor features in the address of Dr Martin Lloyd-Jones on "The Tragedy of Modern Wales", reported in our issue of Saturday, which may be regarded as fair subjects of criticism,' wrote the Editor. But, he went on to assert, nothing existed to justify 'the wild and indiscriminate abuse of his fellow-countrymen in which he indulged'. He continued:

'Amongst Dr Jones' indefensible assertions were that "Wales has lost her soul", that our people are "treading on the edge of the bottomless pit of destruction and damnation", that our preacher-politicians are "Judases" and "a great abomination", that the Welsh University Colleges are "pillars of hell". Is this really criticism, or only an outbreak of hysteria? We are really amazed that an audience of London Welshmen could tolerate quietly this torrent of unreasoned abuse of their country and its people. . . . What is happening in Wales at the present time, however ignorant Dr Jones may be of the fact, is to the highest credit of the people. Religious effort finds expression in the ardent enterprise of the liberated Episcopal church, the establishment of new bishoprics being one most prominent sign. It has expression also in the sustentation and other funds that the Nonconformists are raising – with a fair measure of success considering the very serious industrial depression. Has Dr Jones never heard of the Welsh Memorial's campaign against consumption; of the great work of the Welfare Fund; of the Prince of Wales Hospital; of the Welsh section of the League of Nations; of Monmouthshire and Sunday Closing? . . . Judged by any recognised criterion of progress – religious, moral, or industrial – Wales and her people occupy a vastly more important place in the world than they could claim fifty, or even ten years ago, and it is monstrous folly to shut one's eyes to the widespread evidence which establishes this fact, and to note only the faults, defects and shortcomings of a comparatively insignificant minority . . .

'Finally, we should like to know where and when has Dr Martin Lloyd-Jones done anything towards delivering Wales from its besetting sins and shortcomings? What has he contributed to our national movements? A critic who claims the right to indict a nation should at least be able to show that he has laboured long and assiduously to save it from itself. But so far as we can discover, this is Dr Jones' first adventure in this field.'

The same theme was carried on another page of the same paper under the heading 'Modern Wales, Doctor's Charges "Scurrilous". Banker's Spirited Reply.' Missing the real point of Dr Lloyd-Jones' criticism of the deference shown to money, Mr L. D. Lewis, 'assistant general manager of one of the Big Five Banks', asked indignantly, 'What is wrong in bank officers wearing flannel trousers and plus fours?' He was sure that the speech of the previous Friday was simply an attempt 'to gain notoriety . . . I would advise Dr Lloyd-Jones, before he again engaged in such diatribes, that he would be good enough to make sure of his case'. In the same column the subject of the speech was pursued, with further extracts given by the paper's London correspondent, but with the misleading caption, 'Dr Jones Returns to his Indictment'. The quotations were introduced by the false assertion that Dr Martyn Lloyd-Jones was 'elaborating his charges against the Welsh people to our London correspondent'. In fact, what followed was not a fresh statement at all, but only additional extracts from the speech which the reporter had failed to quote in Saturday morning's edition.

All this was too much for the Reverend Peter Hughes Griffiths and a long letter from his pen appeared in the Correspondence Columns of the *South Wales News* on Saturday, February 14:

'In your report you found it possible only to give excerpts, omitting altogether the speaker's remarkable brilliant Introduction, as well as many passages – possibly extemporaneous – of rare beauty and exceptional force. The inevitable result is that the symmetry, possibly the soul of the address as delivered, is missing.

'As to its angle of approach and general content the address was indeed startling and new, and I do not for a moment deny that the speaker said some startling things. It is a proverb that you cannot make omelettes without breaking eggs, and Dr Jones would be the last to try. His is too honest and transparent a nature to mince the terms of his message, or to think of dipping his shrapnel in treacle. So it was not a pea-shooting exercise with bank clerks or preachers for target that he gave us, but a diagnosis of the national condition that revealed the enemy within our gates . . .

'It is not easy to bring people to stand at the point of vision. They will remain where they are, self-centred and departmental, as if the universe existed for their very own little shop, and especially for the "tape" in the haberdashery department thereof.

'I do not say I agreed with every point that Dr Jones made, but his address as a whole was magnificent in its appeal. Did he go for degrees? Well here is a young man of 25 years who is M.R.C.S., L.R.C.P., M.D., and M.R.C.P. To be M.D. of London at 23 and M.R.C.P. at 25, and yet make an onslaught on degrees! A mystery surely! But let us pause! Are not the sober leaders of all those agencies that have striven to produce a better world, in trouble to-day? Do they not stand aghast, disillusioned, bewildered, and is not the soul of the human race lean and sad?

'A reviewer points out this week that that once impressive phrase, "Science teaches us", has lost much of its force, and science is busy to-day making inquiry into her own right of tenure. She has been compelled to this: Is she an aspect of reality, or is she outside of it? Why do we remain famished in soul, developing greater and greater tragedies in our relation to one another individually, internationally? Is there a solution to our problem? Dr Martin Lloyd-Jones thinks there is, and that the way *not* to get at it is to lie entrenched in a decorated obscurantism, mis-called learning. We must get back to the soul of things, and therein to the knowledge that will educate education and redeem the world.

'Wales could lead, but she has much nonsense to be got rid of. There was nothing ambiguous about Dr Jones' address. It was the utterance of a modern Judas Maccabaeus trying to save Jerusalem, the Mount of Vision, the City of God.'

Despite this earnest plea, however, the Editor of the *South Wales News* was by no means pacified nor ready to withdraw. Rather, in his editorial columns of the same issue, he gave renewed censure to 'A Critic of Modern Wales', and at some length:

'Much may be forgiven of a young firebrand of twenty-five. But before the young doctor gives another address we hope he will take the trouble to acquaint himself with the facts about the subject that he chooses, and, instead of libelling his fellow-countrymen, and pouring on them barrels of senseless abuse, he will show how they can solve their problems and deliver themselves from the evils of the time. The Rev. Peter Hughes Griffiths does his best, out of the abundant charity of his heart, to whitewash the offender by declaring that our report did not contain some passages in the lecture which were of "rare beauty and exceptional force". Does he expect us to give a verbatim report of every unknown lecturer of twenty-five? We do not feel called upon to deal with the matter further, beyond saying that among the passages of "rare beauty and exceptional force" which we did publish were the unqualified statements that "Wales has lost her soul", that her preacher – politicians are "Judases" and a "great abomination", and the Welsh University Colleges are the "portals of hell". If Dr Martin Lloyd-Jones talks like this at twenty-five, we tremble to think what he will say about us when he is fifty.'[1]

From all these and other press comments it is clear enough that few outside Charing Cross seemed at all sure of the identity of this suddenly famous young medical. Mr Lewis, the spokesman for the insulted bankers, would only go so far as 'venturing to think that Martin Lloyd-Jones belonged to the country which he traduced'. Perhaps he had not actually seen the *South Wales News* which named Llangeitho as the speaker's former home. A correspondent writing to the *Western Mail* (another daily paper and rival of the *South Wales News*) put the record straight: 'The statement that Dr

---

[1] Ironically, this editorial comment is immediately followed by another entitled 'Crisis in Welsh Methodism' in which the Editor approves of the 'present agitation' for the removal of restrictions imposed by the denomination's Confession of Faith. 'Truth is progressive,' he declares, 'the heretics of one generation may be the saints of the next.' He was supplying the very evidence which, he claimed, the 'unknown lecturer' could not give. Unbelief in cardinal Christian doctrines was 'progress'! A move to relax the doctrinal standards of the Church of England was also under discussion in 1925. An Archbishop's Committee calculated that the average age of clergy on the active list was not less than fifty-two and the continuing imposition of the 39 Articles was assumed to be one cause of the shortage of clergy – 'a consciousness of their being largely irrelevant to existing conditions is confined to no particular school of thought', *The Church Times* declared.

Lloyd-Jones is a native of Llangeitho is not correct. . . . he was born in Cardiff, where his father, the late Mr Henry Lloyd-Jones, carried on a grocery business. . . . he is a grandson of the late David Evans, Llwyncadfor Stud Farm, Brongest, near Newcastle Emlyn'.

The *Western Mail* was decidedly more sympathetic to the speaker. After interviewing him and Peter Hughes Griffiths, the *Mail* covered the story under the caption: 'Modern Wales, Dr Jones's Attack. Welsh Congratulations. "Plea For A Return To Christianity".' But the paper's London correspondent could not write without falling at once into one of the very faults about which the speaker had protested:

'Dr Martin Lloyd-Jones, whose criticism of modern Wales has caused a sensation, and who, since his criticism appeared in the *South Wales News* has received a number of telegrams of congratulations and thanks from all over the Principality, is one of the most brilliant Welshmen Wales has sent to London. . . .'

Mr Griffiths, reported the same writer, considers Dr Jones to possess 'one of the most independent minds. He thinks a thing through to the bottom and does not accept surface appearances. His plea for a return to reality was the great thing.'

There was, however, something far more important about this Literary and Debating Society address of February 1925 than anything noticed by the press. Some, at least, who were present could recognise that the lecturer was really preaching and that a living experience lay behind his words. The fact that he was speaking in the basement beneath the church made no difference: there was now a prophetic, authoritative element in his mode of speech which led these hearers to wonder whether the hospital and Harley Street were the right place for him. They did not know that Martyn Lloyd-Jones had already reached a decision upon that subject. A pull far more powerful than that of Medicine had entered his life. God had become real to him. The truths which now thrilled him he had rarely heard preached and yet he knew that the same grace which had come to him could bring people everywhere to real Christianity. 'The Kingdom of God' was in the world in 1925. In the opening words of Francis Thompson's poem which has that title, Martyn Lloyd-Jones could say,

> O world invisible, we view thee,
> O world intangible, we touch thee,

David Martyn Lloyd-Jones
O world unknowable, we know thee,
Inapprehensible, we clutch thee!

The closing verses of the same poem were equally meaningful. Now delivered from his own spiritual blindness, he knew that he could also testify to those around him of the glorious realities to be experienced in the heart of London:

'Tis ye, 'tis your estrangèd faces,
That miss the many-splendoured thing.

But (when so sad thou canst not sadder)
Cry; – and upon thy so sore loss
Shall shine the traffic of Jacob's ladder
Pitched betwixt Heaven and Charing Cross.

Yea, in the night, my Soul, my daughter,
Cry, – clinging Heaven by the hems;
And lo, Christ walking on the water,
Not of Gennesareth, but Thames!

We may best sum up the lesson of Dr Lloyd-Jones' conversion in his own words:

'Many people come to listen to the gospel who have been brought up in a religious atmosphere, in religious homes, who have always gone to church and Sunday School, never missed meetings; yet they may be unregenerate. They need the same salvation as the man who may have come to listen, who has never been inside a House of God before. He may have come out of some moral gutter; it does not matter. It is the same way, the same gospel for both, and both must come in in the same way. Religiosity is of no value; morality does not count; nothing matters. We are all reduced to the same level because it is "by faith", because it is "by grace".'

'A preacher is not a Christian who decides to preach, he does not just decide to do it. It is God who commands preaching, it is God who sends out preachers.'

M. L.-J.

'It is not often that I make any kind of personal reference from this pulpit but I feel this morning that I must speak of an experience which bears on this very subject. When I came here, people said to me: "Why give up good work – a good profession – after all the medical profession, why give that up? If you had been a bookie for instance and wanted to give that up to preach the gospel, we should understand and agree with you and say that you were doing a grand thing. But medicine – a good profession, healing the sick and relieving pain!" One man even said this, "If you were a solicitor and gave it up, I'd give you a pat on the back, but to give up medicine!" "Ah well!" I felt like saying to them, "if you knew more about the work of a doctor you would understand. We but spend most of our time rendering people fit to go back to their sin!" I saw men on their sick beds, I spoke to them of their immortal souls, they promised grand things. Then they got better and back they went to their old sin! I saw I was helping these men to sin and I decided that I would do no more of it. I want to heal souls. If a man has a diseased body and his soul is all right, he is all right to the end; but a man with a healthy body and a diseased soul is all right for sixty years or so and then he has to face an eternity of hell. Ah, yes! we have sometimes to give up those things which are good for that which is the best of all – the joy of salvation and newness of life.'

M. L.-J.
in a sermon on 'Render therefore unto
Caesar the things which are Caesar's;
and unto God the things that are God's'
(Matt. 22:20–21), April 28, 1929

5

The Call to the Ministry

It is by no means unknown that those who become ministers of the gospel should have a sense of that calling given to them before they are converted. Such was the case with Dr Lloyd-Jones. There were times in his youth, and more particularly in his eighteenth and nineteenth years, when he felt a degree of conviction regarding his own future and the work of the Christian ministry. No sooner had he consciously become a Christian than this awareness of a call to a different work reasserted itself, not now in the sense of an occasional premonition but with a compulsion from which he could scarcely escape. During the controversy following his address on 'The Tragedy of Modern Wales' in February 1925, criticism that he was merely interested in his own fame hurt him for, in his conscience, he knew that a higher motivation had led him to speak. On the Tuesday following that lecture he wrote to his older friend, Ieuan Phillips, then studying at Aberystwyth for the ministry of the Calvinistic Methodist Church:

> 7 Regency Street
> Westminster
> London S.W.1
> February 10th, 1925

My dear Ieuan
 You are probably well aware of the fact that I really have a good excuse this time for not answering your exceptionally nice letter long before this. I assume you have seen the *South Wales News* the last few days and can therefore understand that what with people calling and phoning I have had very little time to myself.
 Last week, of course, I was well occupied with my paper and I want to tell you some of the facts.
 I have already made up my mind as to my future, in fact I did it as soon as I finished with the exam, and I have already had one

lesson in Greek. My paper was prepared therefore without any restraint or restriction apart from the fact that I withheld the fact that I intend to practise what I have preached.

It is not for me to say anything about the paper – all I shall say is this. The people who count at Charing Cross all liked it, while I myself was moved to an extent that I have never experienced before. I have visions of a great Wales in the future, Ieuan, and, God-willing I think that you and I will play a part in its coming. However, I must try to keep to the actual details for a while.

Mr Griffiths informed me that he had got a *South Wales Daily News* representative there as he wanted my remarks to have a wider circulation than they had last year. Feeling as I do that I had a real message for Wales I consented to his taking notes and further, when he came to me at the end and asked for my papers I gave them to him so that they might print what I actually said.

Well, next day they published the extracts which you have probably seen. There are numerous mistakes in it, for instance I said 'portals' and not 'pillars' of Hell. Further than that, they have deliberately withheld most of my best sentences and phrases, in which I shewed that I was facing the problem from a Christian stand-point. I dealt at length in my introduction with that point and explained my attitude fully. When you see my paper you will understand how they have deliberately misrepresented what I said, just for the sake of creating a sensation. The London Editor wrote to me asking for permission to give a full publication, but so far they have not done so. If they are honest men they will not hesitate about it. However, I am not worrying at all, because I know that all the people whose opinion I value will understand what I meant. Given even the misrepresentation that has occurred I still think it may do some good. In any case, I have not yet finished with the Tragedy of Modern Wales.

At Charing Cross on Friday, the paper was received extraordinarily well, better than I had anticipated, for I really felt that it did not do justice to my theme and was in any case necessarily incomplete. The whole of my future life will be devoted to its completion and then I shall not have finished.

The criticisms that appeared in yesterday's paper have naturally served to strengthen my belief in what I have done and what I propose to do. Oh that I could see you now and talk to you for several hours. I thought of you several times this evening while I was with Bethan. I really think that she is now about as determined about Wales as I am – Ieuan, she almost makes a vital difference to me and yet when she asked me the other day whether she or Wales came first, I had to say that Wales came first. That was certainly the most awful question I have yet been asked during my life. She was great enough to say that she thought still more of me for saying that.

I am now longing for the time to come so that I may start on the way. The beginning which I had intended to be quiet and unobtrusive has, to say the least, been dramatic, hasn't it? It was the very last thing I wished for – but there you are, I have sufficient faith to believe that it is all for the best. They can heap all the personal abuse they like on me, it will make no difference, but I will not tolerate any misrepresentation of the truth.

I am deeply conscious of the great responsibility that now rests upon me and will rest upon me in the future, to maintain with undiminished energy and vigour, the work which I have begun. At this time, Ieuan, I look to your fellowship and friendship with a love and a longing greater than anything I have ever felt before. I often get glimpses of the future in which I always see us both together. Our friendship, my dear Ieuan, has been meant for some great purpose, that is why it has stood the strain of the past few years. Indeed, our fellowship has been that of those who believe in Him – our work in life should be to shew ourselves worthy of it. As I said on Friday night, I believe that conditions in Wales will have to become still worse before the great dawn appears. That intervening period will be our most trying time, but with faith and love we will be patient, and, when the time comes, let us pray that we shall be ready for it.

We shall have a hard struggle – all the resources of Hell will be against us, but, if I mistake not, and the last few days have given me some experience of it, the effect of the persecution will be to make us feel that what we are now prepared to live for, we shall then be prepared to die for.

Is it not a glorious thing to be able to feel that we are fighting in the Great Cause, in the Great Crusade and that ultimately we shall triumph? We have had some never-to-be-forgotten times together in the past, but they will all be as nothing compared with what is in store for us.

Let us pray for one another, still more than we have ever done in the past.

Oh! how I would like to see you; but we must be patient, the time will soon come. I cannot help feeling that we are on the threshold of great things in the history of Wales – let us be worthy of the trust that has been invested in us.

I must now end with a request. Would you be kind enough to

David Martyn Lloyd-Jones

send to the hospital some of the papers that have been set in the first paper in Greek, in the entrance examination? The man who is coaching me would like to see them.

Good night, Ieuan, and may He who has guarded you and blessed you until this moment, be with you for ever. With fondest love from my mother and myself.

I remain

Yours, in His love

Martyn.

Before long there were a few others at Charing Cross who knew of Martyn's decision to become a preacher. Some rejoiced, as Ieuan Phillips undoubtedly did. One of this number was a man belonging to the congregation who had been blessed in Wales at the time of the 1904 revival and who now ran a small hotel near King's Cross. He was among the first to tell him, 'You have got a message for this generation.' Another encourager was a Miss Ellen Roberts who ran a tumble-down mission hall in Poplar, close to East India docks, in the rough East End of London, for the help of down-and-out Welsh people. It was at Poplar about this date that he preached his first sermon. Shortly afterwards he preached again at the Poplar mission and twice in Welsh in a schoolroom rented in Walthamstow where a Welsh dairy-owner was seeking to start a new cause for his fellow-countrymen. Perhaps the first minister to urge him to preach was the Reverend Joseph Jenkins, one of the outstanding evangelical preachers of the Principality, who shared a service with W. E. Prytherch at Charing Cross in 1925. Dr Lloyd-Jones was to remember that service as 'quite unique, the most remarkable service I was ever in. Jenkins preached first and spoke with such force and conviction on the conversion of Saul of Tarsus that the congregation were utterly unable to give their attention to the popular William Prytherch when he attempted to follow.' It was Jenkins who, after hearing of Martyn's February address, wrote to urge him to accompany him on a preaching campaign through Wales. Other invitations had already arrived from Wales, but Martyn declined them all with the exception of a request that he should address the annual conference of the East Glamorgan section of the Union of Welsh Societies at Pontypridd in April 1925.

His immediate need, as he saw it, was to be clear about his future and with that in view he went, as a prospective student, for an interview at the denomination's Theological College at Aberystwyth in March 1925.[1] Naturally the Principal, Dr Owen Prys, was delighted to see him, but even before Martyn had finished his return railway journey to London he knew that a regular theological training at Aberystwyth was not the right way ahead. Despite the welcome he had received, instinctively he had not felt drawn to that situation.

There were now pressures to face from other directions. His nearest counsellors were not in favour of the radical change which he was proposing. Peter Hughes Griffiths bluntly declared, 'If I had my time again I would be a doctor'! More serious still, his own mother was equally uncomprehending at such an unexpected turn of events. Generally confident that Martyn's judgment was sound, the possibility of his exchanging Harley Street for a pulpit was more than she could accept.

Martyn now found himself in the throes of an intense struggle over whether or not he was right to abandon medicine. It was true he was already established in private practice at Harley Street (with the use of one of Horder's rooms) and he was also still in the midst of important research work at Bart's, the conclusion of which was not in sight. There was also to be considered the Christian influence which he could exercise in the higher ranks of the medical profession open before him. On the other hand, he knew what it was to have experiences which rendered all questions of position and self-interest utterly insignificant. One such experience occurred at Easter 1925 in the small study which he shared with Vincent at their Regency Street home. Alone in that room on that occasion he came to see the love of God expressed in the death of Christ in a way which overwhelmed him. Everything which was happening to him in his new spiritual life was occurring because of what had first happened to Christ. It was solely to that death that he owed his new relationship to God. The truth amazed him and in the light of it he could only say with Isaac Watts,

> Were the whole realm of nature mine,
> That were a present far too small;
> Love so amazing, so divine,
> Demands my soul, my life, my all.

[1] It was in anticipation of taking the entrance examination to this College that he was studying Greek, as mentioned above in his February letter to Ieuan Phillips.

David Martyn Lloyd-Jones

It was in this spirit that he went to the Pontypridd conference of the Union of Welsh Societies on a Saturday in April 1925 to speak on 'The Problem of Modern Wales'. His address – his first in Wales and delivered from the pulpit of the Pontypridd Baptist Tabernacle – was largely a restatement of what he had said at Charing Cross two months earlier, for, as he reminded the Congress at the outset, they had invited him 'to reiterate and to re-emphasise' what he said on that occasion. Before going over his main points, he did, however, comment on three criticisms which had followed his earlier address.

The first concerned the doubts expressed about his patriotism and his alleged incompetence as a resident of London to talk about 'modern Wales'. Responding to these charges he said: 'It is because I love Wales passionately and devotedly, it is because I am proud of her glorious past and jealous of her future, that I talk about the *tragedy* of Modern Wales . . . I am proud of the fact that I was born and bred in Wales, that I attend a Welsh Chapel in London every Sunday and that I spend every holiday in Wales. These are my credentials – I think they entitle me to an opinion.'

The second criticism was one which he was often to hear in later life, namely, an expression of sympathy with his views followed by a complaint that he was 'too negative' in the way in which those views were expressed, 'We quite agree with you in what you say, but we do not agree with your method of redressing the evil.' Addressing himself to this point he told the Congress:

'It is a criticism which I can understand and with which I have a certain amount of sympathy. Indeed it appealed to me to this extent, that I hesitated and pondered over the question for some time before I decided or realised that it also was based on a fallacy. Now what is the fallacy? It is, that people who hold that view no longer remember that conviction of sin is the essential prelude to salvation. In other words I believe that it is one of the most vital functions of all preaching – and incidentally I regard any collection of statements coming from the soul as a sermon – to demonstrate the necessity for that preaching. It is not sufficient merely to tell a man that he is a sinner – you must prove it to him – give him examples and make him think, then there may be some hope for him.

'If a man goes to a doctor with a bad liver as the result of constant drinking of alcoholic beverages and the doctor says to him, "Well, of course, you are an ill man, that is to say, you are not well. I will give you some medicine and then perhaps you will be as well as Mr Davies round the corner", is that man likely to get well? Of course not, because he has not been told the cause of his trouble. He thinks the alcohol is the one thing that keeps him going, especially when he feels faint. The only thing to do with such a man is to tell him plainly that his troubles are all due to the drink and that if he persists in drinking there is no hope for him. Keep on telling him until you make him think, then he will realise the truth and mend his ways. Of course the patient will go home and say, "That doctor is not a sport." He may not be a sport but he is certainly a good doctor, an honest doctor, a doctor who does not merely wish to please his patient at the time, but to save him, whatever the patient may think of him. . . . Our trouble is that we do not realise that there is anything wrong with our national life. It is because I feel that I can see some of the causes of the trouble that I am here tonight.'

The third criticism, he proceeded to remind his hearers, was 'much more serious', namely, that his indictment of Modern Wales was false and his facts untrue. But, he argued, this very criticism proved the main point of his earlier address: his case had been that judgments of this kind were not mere 'opinions', they were the result of a man's whole outlook and prejudices. Without the same prejudices agreement was impossible:

'Now, to me, the only prejudice that really counts is the Christian prejudice, by which I obviously mean that the only thing that really matters is whether a man is, or is not, a Christian. The great characteristic of the Wales of the past was that she was a Christian nation, the majority of her inhabitants had the Christian prejudice. That is the standard which I set for Modern Wales, that is the test which I apply to the conditions of life amongst us at the present hour. . . . Those who have not this prejudice will obviously disagree with what I say, indeed, were they to agree I should have more than a suspicion that I was false to my own case. I was not surprised therefore at his third criticism. But I regret it so deeply that I have come here in the hope that I may kindle into flame a smouldering prejudice for truth in some young heart, and that as young people we may go onwards believing in our cause and fighting with resolution all the forces of sin and corruption that are arrayed against us, until we shall have guaranteed that the Wales of the future will be worthy of the Wales of the past. . . .'

As Lloyd-Jones went on to review the charges which he had made in February, his statements were sharpened rather than moderated. On the move away from the Bible which was becoming increasingly prominent in the education given in the University Colleges of Wales he said:

'Our education may teach us that Hell does not exist, but death is a surer and sterner master. How much will our degrees and diplomas avail us then? My friends, do let us return to the stern realities of life before it is too late.'

Further, he urged that the high regard paid to financial success was evident even in the church itself:

'The possession of wealth counts more even in our chapels these days than does a simple faith in God. If you do not believe me, I ask you all to look in the direction of the *Sêt Fawr*[1] when you are in chapel tomorrow. It has permeated right through our religious system and, speaking of the Calvinistic Methodists to whom I belong, I have no hesitation in saying that, as a financial organisation, it will bear comparison with the Bank of England itself.'

As he had done in London, he treated the state of the church as the ultimate cause of the national degeneration and with the pulpit as supremely at fault. Nonconformity was now in the same kind of mechanical and stereotyped condition as the Church of England was before the Eighteenth-century Revival:

'Preaching has very largely become a profession. Instead of real Christian sermons we are given second-hand expositions of psychology. The preachers say that they give the congregations what they ask for! What a terrible condemnation both of the preachers themselves and their congregations! Daniel Rowland, Llangeitho

---

[1] The 'big seat' or platform beneath the pulpit where the elders sat.

used to preach Hell. Has there been preaching which has had anything like the effect of his preaching since those days? We know quite well that there has not been. I am one of those who believe that until such men rise again in our midst, our condition – far from improving – will continue to deteriorate. Our pulpit today is effete and ineffective. It is the final touch in the tragedy of Modern Wales!'

Before he concluded, Dr Lloyd-Jones boldly introduced one new note, which was not likely to please some of his hearers at this gathering of Welsh Societies. After referring to the inability of all political parties to restore a nation's soul, he spoke specifically of the auspices under which they were gathered:

'This movement is out for Welsh Home Rule and in some cases for a Welsh Republic. It believes that the restoration of the Welsh language as the universal language in Wales is vital, is indeed the most important point of all. If we all speak Welsh we shall all be happy. . . .

'Let us get rid of all injustices by all means, let us fight for the right to manage our own local affairs in our way, but do not let us delude ourselves into believing that we shall be better Christian men and women merely because we speak Welsh and have a parliament of our own. No, what Wales needs above everything today is not a republic but a revival, a revolution in the sense that we turn back to the things, to the one thing that has made us great. By a revival I do not mean a wave of emotionalism, but a great spiritual awakening such as took place in the eighteenth century under the influence and guidance of the Methodist Fathers.'

Once the address was over, it was not only the more ardent Welsh republicans who considered that they had reason to be aggrieved. The twenty-five-year-old speaker had first to listen to some criticism from two members of the conference and then an onslaught from the Reverend W. A. Williams, the pastor of the building in which the conference was meeting. Although Williams had risen to his feet at the chairman's request to second a vote of thanks to Dr Lloyd-Jones that intention was scarcely in his mind. He began by repeating a complaint against the speaker's method which had first been voiced in the influential columns of *The British Weekly* following the controversy in the Welsh press two months earlier over the address

David Martyn Lloyd-Jones

on 'The Tragedy of Modern Wales'. In a column on 'Wales', J. Hugh
Edwards, M.P., had been the first to introduce the name of Dr Lloyd-
Jones to the world-wide readership of the foremost Christian weekly.
Moderate in tone, Edwards had nonetheless approved the rejection of
the young doctor's case by the *South Wales News*, claiming that the
particular instances of degeneration which had been stated were far
too inadequate to warrant the general conclusions which the speaker
had drawn.[1] The pastor of Pontypridd Tabernacle, after repeating
this criticism that Lloyd-Jones' reasoning from the particular to the
general was faulty, went on to deny what he had just heard from his
own pulpit on the alleged state of preaching in Wales. One Welsh
paper, under the heading, 'No Longer a Christian Nation', was to give
full coverage to the collision between the two men:

'A devastating indictment of modern Welsh tendencies was made by
Dr Martin Lloyd-Jones, a young man of penetrating mind and fearless
disposition, hailing from Cardiganshire, but now residing in London.
Against him arose a man of mature years and extensive experience of
life in the industrial districts of Wales, the Reverend W. A. Williams.

'The scene at the close will not soon be forgotten by those who
observed it – the young doctor in the pulpit proclaiming the
degeneration of modern Wales and the grey-haired preacher in the
pew protesting vehemently against what he considered to be a false
view of things. It was not a mere battle of words, but a confident clash
of opinions, representing the struggle between the old and the new in
the Welsh life of today.

'From what he knew of the Welsh pulpit, the Reverend W. A.
Williams declared seriously and sincerely that the speaker's conclusions were wrong. There were as good and honest preachers as Daniel
Rowland in Wales today, but they preached to a different kind of
people and had to face vastly different problems.

'With flashing eye, clenched fist, and upraised voice Mr Williams
asserted that men did not ascend the pulpit in Wales today to preach
things they did not believe. The men of the Welsh pulpit, he went on,
would rather lose their heads or die at the stake than stand between
God and man and preach what they disbelieved.'

There was 'vigorous applause' as Williams at length resumed his
seat and still more as Lloyd-Jones rose to reply. He understood the

[1] *The British Weekly*, Feb. 19, 1925.

The Call to the Ministry

Baptist pastor's standpoint. Williams was suspicious that the young Calvinistic Methodist was merely making a denominational point in praising the Eighteenth-century Revival leaders, and that he was ignoring what Baptists and Independents had done in Wales both before that time and since. This was in no sense the object of his speech, Dr Lloyd-Jones, now reasserted. Far from pointing them to denominations, his whole case was that only the Holy Spirit can change the fundamental prejudices which govern men. He had instanced the Methodist Fathers because their whole ministry illustrated that fact. 'If', as Mr Williams believed, 'there were as good preachers as Daniel Rowland in Wales today where was the effect produced by their preaching?' Before he could continue, Williams was on his feet with the reply, 'Welsh life is not the same today.' But the objection was swept aside: 'It is not a question of changed conditions. The teaching of Jesus Christ does not vary from age to age. Name me one preacher of the standard of Daniel Rowland?' 'There is Evan Roberts,' Williams confidently answered, as he gave the name of the man who had suddenly become famous in the Revival of 1904. Dr Lloyd-Jones' response, 'I would not compare Evan Roberts with Daniel Rowland,' brought interruptions from others and the intervention of an astonished chairman who had to remind the conference that discussion was not in order while the speaker was replying to 'the vote of thanks'. But Dr Lloyd-Jones was not prepared to leave the point at issue and pressed on with his challenge to W. A. Williams. Let him point to a preacher in Wales whose ministry was accompanied by anything like the effect produced by Rowland, Harris, and Williams, Pantycelyn: 'I am surprised,' he went on, 'that a minister of religion should say here seriously that there are men of that type in Wales today. Where are the results? They are not to be seen. The membership of most chapels is dwindling and Sabbath observance is rapidly going out of our lives. We see things today that were unknown in the Wales of the past.'

Some of his hearers were far from pacified. The newspaper account reported that at this point:

'There were more interruptions from several quarters, and the chairman, declaring that the meeting was going out of hand, said he had never been in a meeting, not even a political meeting, where such interruptions had taken place.'

The final newspaper comments illustrate an aspect of Dr Lloyd-Jones to which we shall have occasion to refer again. Disagreeing strongly though he had done with W. A. Williams, and unable to convince him that his judgment of the times was wrong, he had nevertheless won him as a friend: 'Dr Jones and Mr Williams, however, continued the argument privately for some time, but parted very good friends, the minister remarking, "You are welcome to come into my pulpit again."'

Not a few who heard the visitor from London giving his first address in Wales at the Pontypridd meeting of April 1925 must have recognised that his main emphasis came fresh from his own experience. He knew that God himself must bring men to the truth. We are in God's hands: 'You can never reason at Truth, you can never find it by looking for it. Truth is revealed to us, all we do is to reason about it after having seen it.'

*   *   *

If the ability to speak, and the readiness of others to listen, had been all that was needed, Dr Lloyd-Jones would have been confirmed by this time in his decision to leave the medical profession. But his difficulties were much deeper than those considerations. He feared that his initial decision to turn to the ministry had lacked the clear guidance of God. Enough had happened since he had written to Ieuan Phillips on February 10 to give him cause to doubt, and how could doubts be consistent with a divine call? Not without much difficulty, he came to the conclusion that he must remain in his present career. In his own words, 'I went through a great crisis and decided I would not do it. I made a solemn decision to go on with Medicine.'

There were those around him who felt that he was distressing himself needlessly in viewing the future in terms of either Medicine or preaching. The ideal solution, they urged, was to do both; he should remain a physician and preach as opportunities arose. This advice never appealed to him. His view of the ministry was such that he could not conceive of that calling having a second-place in the life of any man. His whole background was against lay-preaching. Calvinistic Methodism had arisen in a generation of men who interpreted literally the apostolic injunction and gave themselves 'continually to prayer and to the ministry of the word'. Whatever he was, he knew he could not be a part-time preacher. Accordingly, the next time he was asked to speak at the Poplar Mission he declined the invitation.

For the greater part of another year, until the early summer of 1926, the issue which he thought was settled in the spring of 1925 would not leave him. In his own words, 'It was a very great struggle, I literally lost over 20 pounds in weight.' Involved in that struggle, and its final outcome, were several incidents of which Dr Lloyd-Jones rarely spoke. Although he was not conscious of it at the time, and despite the spiritual blessing of Easter 1925, an element in his hesitation had come from the degree of attachment which he still felt to the life which he had formerly found so appealing. Experiences through which he had now to pass were to bring home to him yet more powerfully the emptiness of the world's glamour. One of these occurred during a visit of their family friend, D. J. Williams, whose indiscreet remarks had brought Martyn to his defence during the scene at Holloway Welsh Chapel already described. Though now about forty-five, Williams had just married and was busy showing his bride the sights of London. 'One night,' Martyn recalled, 'they wanted to go to a theatre in Leicester Square and they persuaded me to go with them. I have no idea what the play was about at all, but they were very excited about it. What I remember is this: as we came out of the theatre to the blare and glare of Leicester Square, suddenly, a Salvation Army band came along playing some hymn tunes and I knew that *these* were my people. I have never forgotten it. There is a theme in Wagner's opera *Tannhäuser*, the two pulls – the pull of the world and the chorus of the pilgrims – and the contrast between the two. I have very often thought of it. I know exactly what it means. I suppose I had enjoyed the play. When I heard this band and the hymns I said, "These are my people, these are the people I belong to, and I'm going to belong to them."'

But it was in Medicine that Dr Lloyd-Jones had felt the pull of the world most keenly and it was this pull which, in these months of struggle, was finally overcome as he came to see still more clearly the futility of all earthly ambitions. Once more, in this connection, his closeness to Horder was to prove a help. Although the last thing which Sir Thomas intended was to assist Lloyd-Jones spiritually, his actions unintentionally served that end. As Lloyd-Jones explains: 'Horder was very kind to me. He would take me now and again to medical dinners where the top people were present, and I used to hear the mutterings, the criticisms, and the jealousies. It sickened me.' What he saw of life at 'the top' killed any ambition to get there.

There was also an occasion of a different nature, not connected with Horder, which enforced the same lesson. One of the most famous of the Chiefs at Bart's was closely attached to a lady friend on the hospital staff and Lloyd-Jones was one of a small circle aware of their relationship. Then with scarcely any warning the woman died. Shortly afterwards Dr Lloyd-Jones was surprised to find the bereaved chief standing at the door of his research room and asking if he might come in and sit by his fire. Probably it was a corner where he knew he would be undisturbed. For some two hours, without a word, the distraught man stared vacantly into the grate until every aspect of the scene was indelibly fixed upon Lloyd-Jones' memory. In his own words, 'That event had a profound effect upon me. I saw the vanity of all human greatness. Here was a tragedy, a man without any hope at all.'

These experiences did more than mortify ambition; they added to the compassion which he now felt for those around him and for those whom he saw daily as he walked the crowded streets of London. Though he might decline to preach at Poplar or elsewhere, Dr Lloyd-Jones found that, as he worked alone at his research bench, he was often preaching to himself. The Bible itself had come alive and its arguments pursued him. If, as he believed, bodily suffering justifies care for people, what kind of concern is warranted for those who are shut out from the presence of God? However much sickness can be alleviated, men must still die, and die deserving hell, unless they be first reconciled to God through Christ. Possibly he had not yet thought much of the words of the Apostle Paul, 'I am debtor both to the Greeks and to the Barbarians . . .' (Rom. 1:14), but he felt their meaning and the sense of responsibility which they express. 'A debtor,' he once said in a comment on that text, 'is a man who is conscious of certain pressures being brought to bear upon him. He is a man who feels that he has got something to which other people have a right. Paul is a man who has got something to give. He has been given it by the Lord. He has received it; he has got it. It has transformed his life, and he feels that he must give it to others.'

In 1925 Lloyd-Jones knew the same constraint of spirit and it troubled him deeply. A few years later he was to say: 'I used to be struck almost dumb sometimes in London at night when I stood watching the cars passing, taking people to the theatres and other places, with all their talk and excitement, as I suddenly realised that what all this meant was that these people were looking for peace, peace from themselves. . . .' Robert Bruce, a prosperous young Scottish nobleman whom God intended to be the successor to John Knox, once testified, 'I resisted long my calling to the ministry and, during that period, I never leaped on horseback nor alighted, but with a justly accusing conscience.' Dr Lloyd-Jones might have spoken similarly.

The statement already made that Dr Lloyd-Jones had now stopped preaching needs some qualification. He was now teaching a Sunday-school class at Charing Cross, having left Dr Phillips' class with reluctance in 1924. The older adolescents to whom he spoke each Sunday afternoon certainly heard him 'preach'! In the latter part of 1925 he also spoke at a meeting of the Temperance Association at Charing Cross. This address revealed an aspect of his ability as a speaker which was seldom to be prominent again. He was deliberately amusing. At the outset he did not disguise the fact that he had no enthusiasm for the Temperance Association; indeed, previously, he had only been to one of their meetings and that, he confessed, was 'because I was particularly anxious to hear a particular person singing'. Proceeding with this unusual introduction he recalled:

'I listened to one of your members addressing the Sunday School one afternoon, listened nursing a very real grievance that the valuable time of the Sunday School – short as it is – should be taken up in that manner while we in Dr Phillips' class had to bring to a premature conclusion a very important discussion. I expressed my grievance to the lady that night and we naturally had an argument about it, but as usual, in all arguments with ladies, I felt that I was temporarily defeated. . . .'

He went on to explain that, although a total abstainer himself, he disagreed with the narrow definition and objectives of the Temperance movement: 'The intemperance which I most frequently meet as a medical man, the excess which brings patients to me for treatment most frequently is excessive tea-drinking among ladies who belong to "temperance associations". . . . This curious association of tea-drinking with your so-called temperance work is to me most baffling. . . .'

The humour, however, had an end in view which became clear as he proceeded. He wished his hearers to take their Temperance work activities less seriously because he was sure there was a better alternative: there was something far more important than their spending their time and money 'in telling people who are temperate and moderate to be total abstainers'. Men and women needed to become 'temperate', not only with respect to alcohol, but in all matters and 'the only way to do that is to make them Christians'. It was not 'the pledge' but the knowledge of Christ which was needed –and that by so many in the very district around Charing Cross. The gospel had to be taken to them:

'That is a much more difficult task than the one you are engaged in. It demands a divine sympathy, self-sacrifice, and very often suffering. . . . It is not only the great weakness of our churches but also a crying condemnation of them that we all come here from Sunday to Sunday, intent upon saving our own souls and never doing anything to help those who are thirsting for the real life.

'Let us decide here tonight that henceforth we will not spend our energy and time in appealing to one another to avoid a sin of which we are not guilty, and let us at the same time decide that we will go out into the world, singly and in bands to rescue these poor souls who need our help.'

Such was his chief concern when he spoke for the Temperance Association. This same sense of constraint which now interrupted his thoughts was strengthened through another unanticipated occurrence. As already mentioned, it was Dr Lloyd-Jones' custom during these years to go frequently to Westminster Chapel for one service on a Sunday. This he was doing as usual in the summer of 1925, and when Dr Hutton preached for the last time on July 12 before leaving for a preaching tour in the United States, he looked forward to the resumption of his ministry in September. But, to the surprise of all at Westminster Chapel, John Hutton's ministry among them was almost over, because of the death in August of the Editor of *The British Weekly*, the Reverend J. M. E. Ross. The issue of *The British Weekly* for October 8, 1925, announced that Hutton had accepted the editorship and would enter upon his new work the following week.[1] Once more Westminster Chapel was vacant. Dr

[1] It needs to be understood that *The British Weekly* (founded in 1886) still possessed great influence at this date, being read throughout the British Empire. John A. Hutton (1868–1947) was to remain its Editor until 1946.

Lloyd-Jones ceased to attend but his appreciation for Hutton was such that he now became a regular reader of *The British Weekly*, and it was this which brought him to a new area of reading.

He came to this reading, however, not through the principal columns of *The British Weekly*, many of which had little appeal to him, but rather through a few scattered references to the English Puritans which he found in that journal. On the front page of the issue of *The British Weekly* announcing Hutton's appointment was a publisher's advertisement of a new edition of *The Autobiography of Richard Baxter* and this led Dr Lloyd-Jones to read F. J. Powicke's *Life of Richard Baxter 1615–91*. 'The Puritans', wrote Powicke, 'were men sure of God, sure of his will, sure of the absolute duty to act in his sight and for his approval. Nothing else mattered by comparison. Consequences were of no account. Obedience alone held the secret of freedom, courage, peace, power, happiness and salvation. Essentially they were right.' Such was his first introduction to the Puritans and his affinity with them was instant. Baxter's earnestness stirred him deeply and so when Peter Hughes Griffiths asked him to speak again at the final session of the winter meetings of the Literary and Debating Society at Charing Cross in March 1926 he agreed and stated that his subject would be 'Puritanism'. Some of his friends were clearly surprised, a fact which the speaker took into account as he prepared his introduction. When at length the evening came he was ready to justify his selection of a subject with which he was not hitherto known to be familiar:

'I chanced to tell a friend of mine the other day that I was coming here tonight to talk Puritanism. He asked me a question, which has deeply impressed itself on my mind, to this effect, "Surely this has entailed a tremendous amount of reading? Have you gone deeply into seventeenth-century history and literature and have you read the standard works on the subject?" I confessed that I had fallen very far short of his demands and that my acquaintance with the said works was particularly casual and superficial. But I did not stop there. I pointed out that I was not going to talk *about* Puritanism – that I deprecated talking about or around anything, but I was coming here to talk Puritanism.'

Dr Lloyd-Jones proceeded to explain that the Puritanism which he found in Bunyan's *Pilgrim's Progress*, in the lives of Richard Baxter and George Fox (apparently the limit of his seventeenth-century reading!) was nothing other than thorough-going Christianity, and so, he asserted, what was needed to interpret Puritanism was not vast erudition but experimental knowledge:

'If you wish to know what Puritanism really is, don't read large volumes on the subject by men who may be scholars but never were Puritans, but rather read the life-stories of Puritans such as I have named, and pray God to give you light not merely to see what is in print but also to see what is between the lines. The great truth in Bunyan's *Pilgrim's Progress* is not that Christian endured great hardships on his way to the eternal city, but that Christian thought it to be worth his while to endure those hardships. . . .

'The only people who have a right to say anything about Christianity are those who have felt its force in their own lives. . . . I do claim, therefore, with modesty and humility, that I have known something, I believe, of the spirit which animated the old Puritans – the spirit which all Puritans have felt at some time or other. I cannot claim, unfortunately, to be a real Puritan, because an analysis of my life finds me seriously wanting, but there have been moments, unhappily infrequent, when I have felt that I could move mountains. It is with the memory of those moments that I hope to be able to tell you something of what Puritanism means. . . .'

Despite the youthfulness of the speaker, and the small range of his reading, the address contained a number of perceptive thoughts. The Puritan, he argued, is not 'the strong man'. He is: 'a very weak man who has been given strength to realise that he is weak. I would say of all men and women that we are all weak, very weak, the difference being that the sinners do not appreciate the fact that they are weak, whereas the Christians do.'

It was this knowledge of their own frailty, he believed, which made the Puritans careful how they lived and led them to avoid all that is doubtful. 'Soberness and restraint are the key-notes of the character of the Puritans. Have you any objection to them? If you have, you cannot regard yourself as a Christian because these are two essentially Christian virtues.'

But this address on Puritanism in March 1926 is chiefly important as an indication of what was going on in the speaker's own spirit at a time when he was in the midst of his struggle over the question of his life work. Had any stranger dropped into Charing Cross Chapel that Friday evening he could have been forgiven for supposing that the slimly built, dark-haired young man was a preacher rather than a medical doctor. And yet it was not preaching which fitted into any type which was common to the 1920's. The main challenge was for a Christianity which exists not in belief only but in 'vital force'; a Christianity which 'does not merely improve a man but rather completely changes him'. Such Christianity, he argued, is not to be found without 'the baptism of the Holy Spirit' and a personal experience of God.

It is not hard to see an element of autobiography in the closing paragraphs of his address on 'Puritanism'. The Puritan, he declared, is distinct both in his sorrows and in his joys. The knowledge of God prevents him from living as other men do. He has indeed not ceased from sin, yet he cannot sin as an unbeliever does. The known presence of God makes that impossible:

'He sins while God is watching him and in these times God is terrible to him. He wanders abroad to do evil like a fox, conscious of his guilt, but there is one difference between him and the fox, for he knows that "the Hound of Heaven" is on his track. He knows that he is no longer a free agent – he cannot do as he likes because God loves him and God is determined to hold him back from committing evil ... "Why cannot I sin like everyone else?" he demands. "Why must I be followed? Can I never get away from God?"

'John Bunyan is reported to have said that he ran away from the voice of God, but even his fingers stuffed hard in his ears could not save him from hearing. The Christian cannot be round the corner from God. He is never away from home and amongst strangers because God is always following him. . . .

'I have mentioned Baxter, Bunyan and Fox, but if you wish to have the best description of all of what Puritanism means, read the epistles of St Paul. During the air raids many of us, indeed most of us, objected to the restrictions that were imposed upon us by the army commanders. We objected to dark blinds and shaded lights. We objected because we did not realise the danger, we did not realise that we were at the mercy of those powers that were in the air or might be there at any moment. But the army commanders knew and carried out the preparations on our behalf. Sin is ignorance, and we object to the restrictions and the vigour of the Puritan régime, but let me remind you that the Puritans are, and were, the commanders-in-chief of God's garrison upon earth.

'But God does not always appear to the Puritan as the Hound of Heaven. There is another mood, there are occasions when God is love, when God is a gentle Father taking an occasional walk in his garden – the earth on which we dwell. During these days nothing can equal the ecstasy of the Puritan. . . . Richard Baxter felt the gale of the Spirit and bowed his head to it lest the sensation passed. The Immanence of God may be a mystical idea but it is certainly no myth to the Puritan. . . .

'Is it surprising that, to the Puritan, life is a serious matter, demanding the whole of his time and attention? If you have once seen the face of God, there is nothing else worth seeing as far as you are concerned. All these other things merely obscure the vision, therefore they must be swept away. . . . If anything interferes with the worshipping of God it must be destroyed. . . . It is because of these feelings that the Puritan is always a crusader. To him Christianity is a fight, a noble crusade, not merely a defensive action against the principalities and powers, but also a challenge to and an assault upon their fortresses. . . .

'Oh! how far we have wandered from this! "Plain living and high thinking" are no more! The church is no longer distinct from the world, for instead of the church going out into the world we have allowed the world to capture the church from the inside. We nearly all recognise the position. When will we return to Puritanism? Let us be up and clear the brushwood and the thorns that have overgrown the face of our spiritual world! Let us take unto ourselves "the whole armour of God, that we may be able to withstand in the evil day, and having done all, to stand" – yes, stand, face to face with God.'

Clearly in Baxter and the Puritans Dr Lloyd-Jones found an echo of something which he already knew in his own spirit. His own deepening sense of sin was a key to the interpretation of their 'soberness and restraint'. In a letter to a friend in 1926, after speaking of the love he received from his mother and from Vincent, he contrasted what 'they think of me' with the reality:

'They see only that which is good in me, they see me only at my best. I shudder when I realise how unworthy I am and how ignorant they are of the dark and hidden recesses of my soul where all that is

devilish and hideous reigns supreme, at times breaking through on to
the surface and causing a turmoil that God and I alone know of.'

There is reason to think that it was this sense of unworthiness
before God which was one of the ultimate obstacles to his clear
conviction that he was indeed being called to the ministry of the
gospel. And the final resolution of that difficulty was not the removal
of his sense of unworthiness, but the persuasion that God loved him,
and had saved him, in spite of all that he deserved. Salvation is
bestowed wholly apart from any human merit. He saw the gospel
more clearly as 'the power of God unto salvation to everyone that
believeth', and it was that very sight which led him to understand the
Pauline and Puritan 'passion for saving souls'. He knew the real
meaning of 2 Corinthians 5:14:

'Paul is like a man in a vice, and the vice is being screwed up and
tightened so that he is pressed. What is pressing him? The love of
Christ! "For the love of Christ constraineth us". This amazing thing
–this gospel of reconciliation! This love of God that sends his only
Son and even makes *him* to be sin for us. He has seen it, and he wants
everybody to see it, to participate in it, to rejoice and glory in it!'

No words explain better than the above what took Dr Lloyd-Jones
into the ministry. As well as knowing conviction of sin and a
profound sense of unworthiness, he drank at the fountain head of
redeeming love. Speaking of what that love meant to him in the
critical years 1925–26 he testified at the end of his life: 'I must say
that in that little study at our home in Regency Street, and in my
research room next to the post-mortem room at Bart's, I had some
remarkable experiences. It was entirely God's doing. I have known
what it is to be really filled with a joy unspeakable and full of glory.'

By June 1926 the struggle was over. He knew what the future must
be. It was almost as though the decision was made for him and he
could resist it no longer:

'Whatever authority I may have as a preacher is not the result of any
decision on my part. It was God's hand that laid hold of me, and
drew me out, and separated me to this work.'[1]

*   *   *

[1] *God's Ultimate Purpose, An Exposition of Ephesians* 1:1–23, 1978, p. 92.
The preacher's personal reference is briefer in the printed version than it was

David Martyn Lloyd-Jones

There was a second great decision reached in 1926 and one which, second only to his spiritual experience, profoundly influenced his future life and ministry. In June the girl whom he had, from the first, so admired from afar, but whose affections had proved so difficult to secure, accepted his proposal of marriage. Had the choice been solely his the matter would have been settled long before. Bethan Phillips, however, was in no hurry to commit herself to anyone, for her interests and friends were many. Besides, she did not forget that the fourteen-year-old second son of the Lloyd-Joneses who had arrived in the pew in front of the Phillips' family in the late summer of 1914 was eighteen months younger than she was, and differences between them did not stop there. Although, for example, Martyn was a moderately competent tennis player – at least at doubles – he did not share her enthusiasm for the game, and his strictures on the 'craze' for tennis left her unimpressed. Through nine years their friendship was never more than occasional, and it was an 'off' period when Martyn spoke to the Literary and Debating Society meeting in 1924. Bethan was not even present among the young ladies of the Chapel who took exception to his remarks on contemporary femininity in 'The Signs of the Times' address which he gave on that occasion. She probably had little sympathy with the indignation of her own sex – they should have known what to expect. In his March 1926 address on 'Puritanism' Dr Lloyd-Jones was to remind the Literary and Debating Society of the immediate sequel to what he now called 'his disjointed and perhaps ill-balanced remarks on "The Signs of the Times".'

Commenting on what had followed that earlier address of 1924, he recalled:

'A second meeting was arranged, largely at the instigation of certain ladies who felt that my remarks should not pass unchallenged, and I sat here patiently for about an hour and a half, listening to a torrent of eloquence, chiefly feminine in character. I was given advice freely and unstintingly . . . You may remember that one lady read out a long speech, the burden of which was that when I got to be a little older it was to be hoped I should become a little wiser. Another lady considered that my case was so serious that nothing but matrimony, as soon as possible, could hope to cure me. I am afraid that both these

---

at the time when the sermon was preached in 1954. For his convictions on the call to the ministry see his volume, *Preaching and Preachers*, 1971, pp. 103–20.

ladies will still despair of me tonight, because I am only two years older than I was on that occasion, and I have hitherto not availed myself of the infallible remedy.'

Again, the person who had 'the infallible remedy' in her hands was not present to hear the address on 'Puritanism', but, unknown to the speaker, Bethan Phillips was having second thoughts. A few months earlier the two had chanced to meet in Euston Road, she with a tennis racquet under her arm, and the amicable conversation which ensued (without a single argument!) had left Bethan wondering. It was a more significant meeting than Martyn perhaps recognised, for he failed to follow it up, as he said he would, with 'an epistle to the Philippians one of these days!' But, when the Easter week-end of 1926 came, he invited Bethan, with two other friends, to hear Dr Hutton who was supplying the pulpit that day in Westminster Chapel. The invitation being accepted, he lost no time that same Sunday in enquiring whether Bethan was free on the following day – a Bank holiday. She was! So on the Monday they went off to visit a country park and, according to Bethan Phillips, never had another argument!

With a mother's insight, Mrs Phillips was the first to recognise that something was happening and she was a ready supporter of Martyn's case. So also was Ieuan Phillips who had never allowed his sister to forget what he thought of the character and abilities of her suitor. After the sole objection that he did not approve of Bethan's absenting herself from Charing Cross for Westminster Chapel – a practice she was not to repeat – Dr Phillips was equally satisfied when he perceived the direction of events! In the week preceding their engagement, Bethan, already qualified (M.R.C.S., L.R.C.P.), obtained her Bachelor of Surgery. On the Thursday of that week Martyn wrote to Ieuan, a letter which speaks first of his trials concerning his call to the ministry and of the forthcoming marriage –evidently determined before the formal parental approval two days later!

June 16th, 1926

My dear Ieuan

At last, I am keeping my promise – the promise I made the day the General Strike ended.[1]

---

[1] The nine-day General Strike, which ended on May 12, 1926, would have paralysed the nation had it not been for the limited use of troops and the aid of many volunteers who maintained public services.

David Martyn Lloyd-Jones

I need not assure you that I have since thought of you daily and longed for your society and your encouragement. For I have indeed passed through trying, not to say crushing experiences. I have been tried to the very marrow but, thank God, I still stand where I have always stood and my faith remains unshaken and unconquerable.

You must have gathered from my last letter that great developments were about to take place. I gave you all details as I well knew that your knowledge of me and of my circumstances would enable you to fill in all the blanks. I therefore merely write to tell you how happy I was, and to let you know that I was prepared and preparing for whatever might happen, full of hope and of faith.

Ieuan *bach*, I thank God constantly for your love and for your faith. It means more to me than you can ever know.

Bethan and I were talking about you yesterday and our experiences were identical. We both felt that merely to write to you was in a sense useless, that what we desired was to talk to you for hours and hours – on into the middle of the night, even unto the breaking of the dawn. There are certain stories that improve as they go on, the hours add to them and when so many hours have gone time suddenly ceases to exist and we are in that eternity known only to souls in communion with God. You know what I mean – we have had such occasions and we have both always felt greater after them, have we not?

Well, we must wait until we next meet, then we shall commune and who knows but that we shall rise from our chairs with a new vision, a new hope, yes, even as new men, and nothing will ever be the same again.

I have been more conscious of the hand of God during the last month than I have ever been before – we count, Ieuan, and count tremendously. Nothing is trivial, nothing is unimportant, everything matters and matters vitally. There is no responsibility except within the Kingdom.

Bethan is writing to tell you about our intentions. We are going to get married. That really does not express what is going to happen but you know all that I want to say and somehow cannot.

I know that I am beyond a doubt the luckiest man on the face of the earth at the present moment. It will make no difference to you and me. Being already your brother, that I shall soon be your brother-in-law makes no difference, and yet, as you know, it makes all the difference! I want to preach more than ever and am determined to preach. The precise nature of my future activities remains to be settled, but nothing can or will prevent my going about to tell people of 'the good news'.

I spent a very happy afternoon at Harrow yesterday and I am going there to have a long talk with your father on Saturday. I am indeed overwhelmed with the love and the kindness of your father and mother.

Our partnership is about to commence, Ieuan – let the forces of Hell beware!

I shall write again soon to let you know all developments.

My mother and Vincent are well, and as I have told you, I am truly proud of them.

But I still need your prayers, Ieuan.

With all my love
I am, your brother
Martyn.

Parental approval being readily given, Martyn meant no official engagement to be announced until he could purchase a ring on the following Tuesday. But at Charing Cross on Sunday, June 18, Bethan's elation was too much to be explained solely by her University success: before the evening service the secret was out and round the whole chapel!

His long struggle over his future calling now ended, Dr Lloyd-Jones was conscious of several special indications of God's help at this point. For one thing, his mother and Vincent gave him their support. 'They have been simply wonderful,' he told Ieuan Phillips. Further, he had found that Bethan Phillips, far from being disappointed at the knowledge that she would not be marrying an Harley Street Consultant, was herself delighted to face a very different future.

In June 1926 the location and precise nature of that future remained unknown. Some things, however, were certain to Dr Lloyd-Jones. He believed that he was not meant to pursue his denomination's course of theological education, leading in a regular way to the pulpit of some well-to-do and long-established congregation. He was also preoccupied with the need for evangelistic work among poorer, working-class people. This conviction arose not simply out of interest in them as people, but equally out of a persuasion that modern Christianity, unlike the apostolic faith (which was as relevant to the 'Barbarians' and to the 'unwise' as to the 'Greeks' and to 'the wise'), seemed to appeal largely to only one social and cultural group. That was evidence to him that the

transforming power of real Christianity was largely absent. He
wanted to see the message which he believed had been given to him of
God tested in a place where social habits did not support church-
going. And one more thing was clear to him, namely, that, if it were
possible, his first endeavours should be with the spiritual concerns of
his own country. As we have already seen, love for Wales had much
to do with his two addresses on modern Wales in 1925.

This was hardly a normal mixture of motives in a candidate for the
ministry. As he talked the matter over with Peter Hughes Griffiths
(his minister at Charing Cross Chapel) the one work which appeared
to them as a possibility, if these particular hopes were to be realised,
was in the home-mission agency of the Calvinistic Methodist
Church, known as 'The Forward Movement'. The minister of
Charing Cross undertook to write to the Superintendent of The
Forward Movement, the Reverend Richard J. Rees, and Dr Lloyd-
Jones himself wrote requesting an interview. Richard J. Rees
was elected that same month to be Moderator of the General
Assembly of the Welsh Presbyterian Church. He replied from the
Movements headquarters at Cardiff on June 24, 1926:

'I was delighted to have your letter awaiting me on my return home
tonight from N. Wales and to have the links forged by our mutual
friend the Reverend Griffith Rees[1] riveted by your own welcome and
acceptable greeting. . . .
    'I feel privileged in all that the Reverend G. Rees has already
informed me and I pray that in what may ensue, whatever the result,
we shall be guided of Him to whom we owe our all.'

It happened that R. J. Rees was to be in London that next weekend
and it was arranged that they should both meet over a cup of tea in a
London café at the beginning of the following week.

The work of the Forward Movement had begun in South Wales
towards the end of the nineteenth century in an attempt to reverse the
dwindling influence of the denomination upon the unchurched.
Although it gave financial help and direction to causes which were
too weak to be regular charges, it had experienced little success in its
principal objective. The early enthusiasm to make the Forward

---

[1] Griffith Rees, who came from the Newcastle Emlyn area and had studied at
Oxford before taking a Calvinistic Methodist charge in London, was an old
friend of Lloyd-Jones who had given him advice on reading

The Call to the Ministry

Movement 'a great evangelical instrument' had 'cooled down', as the Reverend R. J. Rees discovered after he was made the General Superintendent in 1922. 'We need men,' he pleaded with the Denomination's General Assembly in 1923. This being so, it might have been expected that Rees would have given an enthusiastic welcome to this unexpected approach from Lloyd-Jones but he had been too long in the ministry to be swept off his feet. Evangelists, it is true, had normally been either men without theological training or divinity students who had failed to get pastorates. Men with University degrees were not expected to be applicants for mission work. Indeed, of the thirty students training for the regular ministry at the denomination's Aberystwyth College in 1925, only eleven were graduates; yet here was a man with four degrees, already working with some of the foremost medical authorities in the country, enquiring if he could be an evangelist! In a Forward Movement cause he might not even have the status of a regular minister for, despite attempts to change the situation, most of the causes were still 'halls' rather than chapels, and were governed by local committees rather than by presbytery-ordained elders.

Thus, when the two men met on June 28, 1926, and Lloyd-Jones spoke further of his concern to volunteer for service in Wales, it was not long before R. J. Rees gently expressed his surprise and indicated that the wisdom of the proposal scarcely commended itself to him. But that year's Moderator was pulled up short when his young enquirer exclaimed, 'Really, Mr Rees, why should you be surprised? Don't you believe what you preach?' It was a situation the Superintendent had never been in before – a doctor from Harley Street appealing for a church-extension charge! Perhaps it required a degree of effort on his part to remain non-committal in the face of such earnestness. In any case, the normal procedures necessary for a man to be recognized as a candidate for the ministry had to be followed and it was arranged that the minister of Charing Cross would raise the matter at the forthcoming meeting of the London Presbytery of the Calvinistic Methodists on July 21, 1926.

As usual, that summer, Martyn Lloyd-Jones and Bethan Phillips were both down in the Newcastle Emlyn area for holidays but with a difference. This time they spent most of the days together and the farmhouses which wanted to see the young couple for tea seemed to be endless – on one day alone there were seven or eight such calls to make! There was also time for many walks in the hills and long conversations together about the future. Of these conversations Bethan was to remember, particularly, his commitment to break through the rut of religious respectability, how on fire he was to tell people what Christianity meant, and his wish to be in some 'raw place' where people were conscious of their need. When she asked him what the answer should be for those who said, 'He can do medicine, but how does he know that he can preach?' the immediate reply was, 'I can preach to myself, I know *what* I want to preach and believe I will be able to say it.'

There being no further word from the Reverend R. J. Rees, Dr Lloyd-Jones wrote to him again on August 24 and received a reply on September 14. The Superintendent did not intend to hurry, nor indeed could he. For, as he repeated in his letter of September 13, the next step lay with the London Presbytery:

'Whatever comes of the matter in the future stages outlined by me, I shall be quite prepared, on hearing what the decision and resolution of the London Presbytery are (concerning your application to it for the status of a Preacher) to go further into the matter, if the above is favourable, and arrange an interview here with me and the Directors at the earliest possible opportunity afterwards.

'I hope you keep well and that the Divine guidance is being given you fully and clearly. Thanking you for all your confidence and assuring you of my kindest greetings and wishes in all your ways.'

Three days later, on Thursday, September 16, following a decision taken on July 21, two members of the London Presbytery visited Charing Cross Chapel to hear the mind of the people on Dr Lloyd-Jones as a candidate for the ministry. In the presence of a good congregation he gave, in the language recorded by the Presbytery, 'a clear and firm statement of his intention and decision to preach Christ's Gospel'. This course was unanimously approved by the members present. That same month he preached once more in his first pulpit, the Poplar Mission in the East End, and it was arranged that he would preach for the first time at Charing Cross on October 10.

The London Presbytery now gave their approval, and although R. J. Rees had not formally heard that news when he next wrote, he was now ready to be more definite:

> Church House,
> 2 Park Grove
> Cardiff
> October 20th, 1926
>
> My Dear Friend,
> Though I have not written to you of late, you have not been out of my mind, or absent from my prayers.
> I have been expecting to hear of the decision of the London Presbytery, and am glad to know by a letter from our mutual friend – The Rev. Peter Hughes Griffiths – that this matter has been well advanced. By intimations that I see also in the public press, I note that you are engaged in preaching from time to time.
> I trust that the vision is growing if possible, still clearer, and that signs of favour are manifest on your great act of complete surrender to the Master's Summons.
> I am surveying the field under my care, and considering where the open door for service can be found therein.
> At the present moment Beechwood Park Presbyterian Church, Newport, is about to celebrate its 21st Anniversary, and is very desirous of having your services there on Thursday November 11th. Would you please let me know per return by wire, whether it is possible for you to arrange to come to Newport for that date, so that they may proceed with their final arrangements? I hope you can, for I should also like to see you the day following, so that we may have a further conversation together on all the matters that interest us at this stage.
>
> With kindest regards and greetings
> Yours sincerely
> Richard J Rees

Dr Lloyd-Jones went to Newport and thus preached for the first time in Wales on November 11. No record survives of the congregation's response but, for his part, Dr Lloyd-Jones was not drawn to the situation. It was more respectable and affluent than the one which he envisaged. Meanwhile another invitation had arrived, this time from Mr E. T. Rees, the Secretary of Bethlehem Forward Movement

David Martyn Lloyd-Jones

Church in Aberavon, Port Talbot, asking him to preach for them on Sunday, November 28. A brief reply was to prove the beginning of a new era.

> St Bartholomew's Hospital and College
> London E.C.1.
> November 8th, 1926

Dear Mr Rees

Thank you very much for your letter, and the kind sentiments expressed therein.

I shall be very pleased to visit you on November 28th. In the meantime, I wonder whether you would be kind enough to let me have some particulars concerning the hall and the work with you at Aberavon.

Again thanking you for your kindness.

> I am
> Yours sincerely
> D. M. Lloyd-Jones

Thus far, Dr Lloyd-Jones – with no definite prospect yet in view – had said nothing to his colleagues at Bart's concerning his intention to leave medicine. But his decision was final and this was confirmed to him by an unexpected incident which occurred in this same autumn of 1926. One day as he was crossing the Square at Bart's, Geoffrey Evans, the Assistant Professor of Medicine, stopped and asked him to 'spare a moment'. Evans disclosed that his part-time post (which he combined with being a consultant physician) was becoming vacant and that it was almost certain that Lloyd-Jones would be approached and offered the job. It was a position which would have led right to the top. 'This did not shake me for a second,' Dr Lloyd-Jones was later to comment, 'I had already decided for the ministry.'

Part of the last page (page 16?) of the first sermon by Dr Lloyd-Jones which has survived. With 1 Corinthians 2:9 as the text, he preached it at the Poplar Mission, London, in September 1926, and then took it for his first sermon at Aberavon, November 28, 1926. For a printed transcription see p. 119.

6

Aberavon

The train from Cardiff across Mid Glamorgan to Swansea offers little to attract the attention of the average passenger, not, at least, until that part of the journey begins where the line reaches the coastal strip on the east-side of Swansea Bay and passes through Port Talbot. Here, with the steam and smoke rising in great columns, is one of the largest steel-works in Wales, placed between the sea and the town's narrow streets and brick-built homes. These works of men are necessarily compressed, for immediately behind the town, bracken-covered hillsides sweep steeply skywards in unspoiled beauty. Mountains, town and sea thus lie side by side in impressive contrast.

Port Talbot is very much a nineteenth-century town. A harbour and docks built in the 1830's, importing iron ore and exporting coal, established its reputation. The ore went up the valleys until Port Talbot's own steel works were opened in 1900. By 1926 the industry of Port Talbot had so overshadowed the neighbouring town of Aberavon that the two were virtually one. Houses and streets simply merged together at the western end of Port Talbot. The latter provided work while Aberavon, with its empty sand-hills and beach, gave space for recreation and for more buildings as they became necessary.

Aberavon might scarcely have been known to the rest of the United Kingdom in 1926 had it not been that it gave its name to a Parliamentary constituency. Its member of Parliament had made history in 1924 by becoming the first Socialist Prime Minister of the British Isles. South Wales in the 1920's was in the throes of a revolution of political opinion, and in that revolution the constituency of Aberavon had proved to be a pace-setter when it elected James Ramsay MacDonald, the Socialist Scot, as its representative to Parliament in 1922. A Socialist had contested the seat in the General

Election which took place at the end of the Great War. At that date Wales still held firmly to Liberalism and to Lloyd George who, as Prime Minister, had at last brought the War to a conclusion. It was therefore no surprise when a National Liberal candidate carried Aberavon with a majority of 6,000 in 1918. But in 1922 the same Liberal received the support of little more than a third of the number who voted for MacDonald, 5,328 against 14,318. The post-war boom had been short-lived, Lloyd George's prestige was in decline, and the working-classes of South Wales would never go back to Liberalism. The Conservatives of Aberavon, in an attempt to keep out a Socialist, had adopted a local employer and former mayor of Port Talbot as their candidate but he, too, was defeated.

The fact is that the slogans with which Liberalism had carried the country in 1906 – democracy, free-trade, and religious equality – provided no solution to the economic problems of the 1920's. Even during the Great War, questions were openly asked in South Wales as to the responsibility which capitalism bore for the European conflict, and pacifists – who generally belonged to the Independent Labour Party – went to prison rather than to the army in protest against the connivance of politicians in a war which, they believed, should not have occurred. While Ramsay MacDonald did not go as far as some of his colleagues in the I.L.P., it was well known that he entertained a fundamental criticism of the system which had prevailed before 1914. He held that 'a society based on the acquisitive instinct was fundamentally immoral, and that, because of its immorality, it was torn by social tensions it could not resolve.'[1]

Before the commencement of MacDonald's election campaign in 1922, a friend prophesied: 'It will be more than an election campaign, it will be a great crusade for Socialism and Internationalism, for clean politics, for high ideals'.

The swing to Socialism was not without religious significance. Among the chapel-going communities of the industrialised towns of South Wales religion was not yet being rejected. Large congregations no longer sang, prayed and heard sermons in the chapels of the Calvinistic Methodists, the Congregationalists or the Baptists, but they were still the descendants of parents for whom these activities had been a staple part of life. As yet it was too early for any general attack on Christianity, as Aberavon's Socialist candidate, a militant

---

[1] David Marquand in his *Ramsay MacDonald*, 1977, p. 278.

Marxist and atheist, had found in 1918. Crowds of children on the election day at the polling stations had booed him as 'the man who don't love Jesus'. MacDonald, far from repeating his predecessor's mistake in 1922, took care before his campaign began to lecture 'at most of the local chapels on non-political subjects, such as John Knox, or his visit to Palestine'. Nor were these efforts hypocritical. He believed in harnessing the enthusiasm of religion to the building of 'the Christian state'.[1] Nonetheless, if Christianity was not being rejected it was certainly being secularised amongst the working class electorate. The theological liberalism of former years and the broken promises of Lloyd George had opened the way for the post-war generation who came to believe that Socialism and the New Jerusalem belonged together.

*   *   *

Three men stood on the platform of the railway station at Port Talbot on Saturday, November 27, 1926, awaiting the train due at 5.27 p.m. from London. They were E. T. Rees, the Church Secretary of Bethlehem Forward Movement, Trefor Jones (another member of the congregation who had brought his Ford car to the station in honour of the occasion) and the former minister, the Reverend T. J. Lewis, now serving a pastoral charge at near-by Sketty. E. T. Rees was in many respects a personification of Welsh Socialism. Apart from a period during the World War he had lived in Aberavon since his birth, thirty-six years before. His family background was similar to that of so many others. His grandfather, David Rees, had died on his knees in a Baptist Chapel during the time of a cholera epidemic. Two days later his wife and children had been put out of their home. E. T. Rees was a grown-up fifteen by the time his father was converted in the revival of 1904 and he and his brothers were not familiar with the power of the gospel in their childhood. Politics, coupled with education, became their chief interest. He worked for

---

[1] Marquand, *op. cit.*, p. 281. Macdonald sometimes called himself a Presbyterian, but it is clear, not only that his religion had no doctrinal content, but that he was averse to doctrinal Christianity. 'Liberal theologians,' he wrote, 'have taken courage and bowed to the necessity of applying the idea of evolution to their theologies by admitting that dogma must change with thought, that it is not final, that its content is in a state of flux and flow'. *Ibid.*, p. 54.

the Co-operative Society; as a Socialist he fought a local council election (which he lost), and ultimately settled for a school-master's career. With his pacifist views it was not easy to obtain a teaching post in Glamorgan. One of his brothers went to prison for refusing military service in the Great War and E. T. Rees, having received his 'call-up' papers in 1918, would have had the same experience if the Armistice had not come in time to prevent it. Yet these views were no hindrance to the church work in which he also engaged with characteristic enthusiasm, and from the early 1920's, when he became church Secretary, much of the responsibility for the work fell on his shoulders. As a child he wanted to be a clergyman, and he enjoyed preaching a 'social gospel' in the pulpit at Bethlehem as much as he did speaking at local meetings of the Independent Labour Party.

E. T. Rees and Martyn Lloyd-Jones met for the first time when the train pulled in from London. 'We nearly missed him,' the former recalled in later years. 'I expected to see some august person in Saville Row clothes and passed by him in his over-coat and bowler hat'. A few minutes' journey took them to the Church Secretary's home on the hillside overlooking the town. The two men, ten years apart in age, presented a considerable contrast, but both could talk, and debate continued late into the evening as Rees steered through such favourite subjects as economics and politics. Rather to his surprise his visitor could both keep up with him and, at certain points, get the better of the argument. At last the different ways in which they both saw the future was wrapped up in a question to Rees from Lloyd-Jones. '"After death what?" he said to me, and the topic we finished with was everlasting life.' The candidate-preacher had already seen what Rees was later to confess, 'I put politics before the gospel and environmental change before personal change.'

Before they walked down to the church together for the first time on the Sunday morning Dr Lloyd-Jones had already received a fair amount of information about the state of the work in correspondence with Mr Rees. Bethlehem Forward Movement Mission[1] had commenced with a school hall, opened in 1897, as a result of the endeavours of two local Presbyterian churches (one Welsh and the other English) which did not see themselves able to reach the large navvy population brought into the district with the building of new

---

[1] Although still a Home Mission of the Forward Movement, its 'Mission' title was slowly giving way to 'Church' in the 1920's.

docks. The history of the Mission – by 1926 commonly known as 'The Forward' or 'Sandfields' by those who belonged, after the name of the district – had been far from even. Seven pastors and one 'evangelist' had come and gone. After an initial success the two pastorates which followed had to be recorded as failures. Again things had advanced in 1907–08, only to fall back under a fifth man until the membership in 1912 had dwindled to 31. With another pastor from 1913 to 1917, there was renewed spiritual quickening. A permanent church building had been erected in 1914 and the membership rose to 130. Once more, however, a set-back followed with a well-intentioned minister who became drawn into politics. When he left in 1921 most of the politically minded who had joined the church because of his influence also departed. Of a diaconate, established in 1907, only one man remained, and what was worse, despite the monthly help from the Forward Movement, the debt which had existed on the church accounts since the beginning was as serious as ever. In 1921 a new pastor, the Reverend T. J. Lewis, had entered enthusiastically upon the work of rebuilding. In the Church Secretary's personal notes it is recorded: 'The Reverend T. J. Lewis had built up great hopes of establishing himself in the church for many years but was greatly discouraged by the continual struggle of trying to reduce the debt which increased rather than diminished.' At length he also had left in 1926 and 'with a broken heart', as he told Dr Lloyd-Jones during the car journey from the station to E. T. Rees's home on the evening of November 27.

Without question, Sandfields was a difficult district. In a report[1] which he sent to Dr Lloyd-Jones E. T. Rees had written:

'Sandfields contains at least 5,000 men, women and children living for the most part in sordid and overcrowded conditions, and in the immediate vicinity of the Hall is a very bad patch known as the "White City" and upon which we have concentrated in our Open Air and other evangelistic work with very encouraging results. Our Pastor is loved in this very slum quarter and the "Forward Movement" to these poor unfortunate people provides a refuge when sorrow, bereavement, or trouble of any kind visits them. Indeed the Forward Movement Minister, and not the Anglican or R.C. Priest, will always be regarded as the "Local Bishop". Almost

[1] The report had been prepared earlier that year (while T. J. Lewis was still pastor) to solicit more aid from Forward Movement headquarters.

90 per cent of these people do not attend any place of worship, for there is a gross indifference amongst the respectable working class type, whilst a depravity born of sin enmeshes the great majority.

'The bookie, publican and prostitute prosper here and directly challenge us. We can confidently assert that we are the only body of Christian people in the district who have energetically taken up the challenge.'

It was the financial position which had driven an anxious E. T. Rees to Cardiff early in November 1926, to solicit an increased monthly grant from his namesake, the Superintendent of the Forward Movement. Besides the outstanding debt of £3000 there was now an overdraft of £220 at the bank. Yet other things beside Sandfields had been on his mind. The same day Wales was to play a leading overseas side in a much anticipated rugby match at Cardiff Arms Park and the interview was so timed as to allow him to do both. Things did not turn out as E. T. Rees expected. He was enthralled to hear from the Reverend R. J. Rees of a young doctor who wished to evangelise in a hard district in Wales, and responded with alacrity to the proposal that Lloyd-Jones should be invited for a Sunday. The Superintendent was far from promising that his settlement with them was likely, or even possible, but (perhaps wishing to discourage the Church Secretary from setting his sights any higher) he was sure a visit would be beneficial, 'Get him to preach at Sandfields, he will be a draw, and this will mean a good collection!' The same afternoon – without seeing any rugby match – the rejuvenated Church Secretary went straight back to Aberavon. In response to Mrs. Rees' query, 'Why are you home so early?' he poured out what he had heard, ending up with, 'Where's the writing pad, my dear?'

Such was the background to the morning of Sunday, November 28. From the moment of his arrival at the station the previous day Dr. Lloyd-Jones was drawn to the place[1] and one night was enough to cement the relationship with E. T. Rees. The latter recalls his young visitor warning him quietly on the Sunday morning, 'I hope you don't expect anything great of me'. The truth was that hitherto

[1] The attraction had really begun before he even arrived. Replying to E. T. Rees' letters he had written on November 13: 'I eagerly look forward to the 28th when I shall have the pleasure of meeting you and all the friends at Sandfields. I know from your letters that we shall get on well together in a spirit of love and comradeship to fight the forces of evil.'

he had not preached more than some dozen times in all. But Lloyd-Jones was not so quiet as they reached the church and saw a huge poster which the enthusiastic Secretary had put up, advertising their important visitor: 'I don't like that, don't do it again', he told E. T. Rees in authoritative tones that the older man was to hear more of in the memorable service of that first Sunday.

The morning congregation, normally around seventy, was unusually large to hear the unknown visitor preach on 1 Corinthians 2:9, 'Eye hath not seen, nor ear heard, neither have entered into the heart of man, the things which God hath prepared for them that love him.' His exposition of the text concluded with these words:

'The gospel tells us that our most sacred thoughts, our deepest affections, our sublimest emotions are as nothing compared with what we shall experience when we meet our Saviour face to face. . . .

'What are you out for? Believe me, you will get it whatever it is, if you are determined to do so. Are you out for the rewards of this world? They can be obtained with very little effort. They satisfy for a while, but when one begins to think seriously about them they are not even worth that little effort. But still we go on trying to get the best out of both worlds. Let us realise once and for all that the things of the Spirit can only be appreciated by the spirit. The reward for a spiritual way of life is a spiritual reward. Why do we expect to get the rewards of this world as well? Why do we so often complain that the ungodly seem to succeed while we fail? We are not out for the same thing. We must learn to judge spiritual results by spiritual standards. Whatever a man soweth that also shall he reap. If we have sown to the spirit why expect to get a worldly and bodily harvest? The man who sows for worldly results gets them, and everyone can see these and know them and appreciate them. The Christian, on the other hand, has very little that the world can appreciate. That is why the Way of Life is a difficult way – it is a life of faith. When you enter upon it, you give up everything that the world treasures most, and it is inevitable that at times we shall experience a sense of loss. You start by giving up everything. What makes it still more difficult is that as you go on the demands do not lessen but become even greater and you have no immediate reward except a loving heart and an honest soul.

'At a time like the present, as I started by saying, it is exceptionally difficult, and that is why I have dwelt on this so much with you.

'The struggle is difficult, the battle is fierce, and we are tempted on all sides to back out of it. Hold on my friends, fight on, cling to the Cross.

'The enemy is powerful, but the Son of God is on our side and His Father hath prepared a welcome for us, hath things in waiting for us such as the eye of man has never seen, the ear of man has never heard, and the heart of man has never felt.

'May God give us His blessing and His strength on the way, for Christ's sake. Amen.'

At night the congregation was larger still when the text was 1 Corinthians 2:2, 'For I determined not to know anything among you, save Jesus Christ, and him crucified.'

Contrary to all good Presbyterian procedures although it was, Dr Lloyd-Jones' future pastorate at Aberavon was virtually if unofficially settled that same day. At an 'after-meeting' (customarily held after the evening service) the people were delighted to hear him say, 'I feel this is the place I would like to work in. Will you have me?'

E. T. Rees remembers: 'We came home that night rejoicing. He said to me, "Well, would you like me to be a preacher in Sandfields?" and the impetuous Secretary said, "Like you, certainly! When will you come again?"' Before he left the next day it was agreed he would return, with his fiancée, to preach on Sunday, December 12. Meanwhile in a letter of December 3, E. T. Rees wrote:

'This week has been a never-to-be-forgotten one in my life. Your visit last weekend did it. It has passed so quickly, and has been crowded with wonderful things. On Wednesday night we had a church committee and it was unanimously decided – after many kind things had been said concerning you – to recommend you to the church for the 'call', and the following night the Joint Committee (representing the C.M. Churches of the town) adopted you as the man for Sandfields.'

Acknowledging this letter on December 6, Dr Lloyd-Jones replied:

'I feel somewhat ashamed of myself for not having written to you and Mrs Rees to thank you for your great kindness to me while I stayed with you. As I told you, I am a very poor correspondent at the best of times; moreover, I comforted myself with the thought that you must have realised how greatly I was enjoying myself. Whatever else may happen after my arrival at Aberavon, one thing is certain, and that is that you and I will be great friends, and as I have assured you time and again, I am looking forward to our work together with great eagerness.

'Your letter of this morning has naturally filled me with joy and hope. Of course, I realise fully the seriousness of the commission which I am taking up, but it is a high adventure and a crusade of hope.

'Whatever may happen, our cause must triumph, and if we fail (which God forbid!) what we stand for will go on and will in the end prove supreme. That is the spirit in which I am taking up the task, realising that human endeavour at its highest is only feeble and that our only hope is that we shall be given of the Holy Spirit freely. Of course, I am looking forward to all the various details which you will have to give to me when we meet.'

The second visit to Sandfields – where Bethan now heard Martyn preach for the first time – proved as encouraging as the first and plans commenced for the preparation of the manse to be ready after the wedding which was now fixed for January 8. There was only one difficulty, occasioned by a local newspaper reporter by the name of Lewis. After Dr Lloyd-Jones, who was not staying with E. T. Rees on this occasion, refused to give Lewis an interview on Saturday morning, the man proceeded to the Church Secretary for help, believing that he had a story likely to catch the interest of many in Wales and beyond. As a result, when the couple reached London again on the Monday they were astonished to find themselves in the midst of a blaze of publicity. Several papers for Tuesday, December 14, carried such headings as 'Leading Doctor Turns Pastor: Large Income Given Up for £300 a Year'; 'Harley-Street Doctor to become a Minister'; and 'Specialist to take Aberavon Pastorate'. For the first time Dr Lloyd-Jones had to use the area door of 12 Vincent Square, Westminster (where the Lloyd-Joneses now lived) as press reporters for two days kept watch at the front, undeterred by his consistent refusal to give any interview or even to 'stand' for a photograph. While his hearers the previous Sunday might not have taken him for a shy man, the truth is that he was. He also hated with every fibre of his being the carnal way in which the newspapers handled spiritual things. Forty years were to pass before he was reluctantly to accept photographers other than those in the family circle!

As is usual in such instances, the newspapers imagined what they did not know, and for extra copy introduced anything remotely connected with their subject. Thus one paper announced, 'For some time Dr Lloyd-Jones has been known as a local preacher in Wales'; another, 'Notwithstanding his great record, he is still under 30'. In fact he was still only twenty-six! Yet another offered the news that 'He is a brother of Mr Vincent Lloyd-Jones, a former president of the Oxford Union and a prospective Liberal candidate, who travelled in America with Mr Malcolm MacDonald recently'.

From Vincent Square Dr Lloyd-Jones wrote to E. T. Rees:

December 15, 1926

My dear Mr Rees,

I would have written to you yesterday but for the fact that I spent all the day refusing interviews with press representatives. I need not tell you how I feel about this terrible blaze of publicity, it fills me with disgust. I should have been annoyed in any case, but what has pained me especially is that the names of others should have been introduced. That man Lewis may be a good fellow, but he has done me a real disservice and has made my position difficult in a personal sense. However, I must assume that he was not out deliberately to harm me and what damage he has done must have been done unwittingly.

I simply cannot understand why all this fuss has been made. My wish was to take up the work at Aberavon in a quiet and unobtrusive manner – hence my reason for refusing to grant that man Lewis an interview on Saturday morning. The Press, of course, is always out for a story and seems to take it for granted that every man has the instincts of a politician and therefore welcomes publicity.

I have felt the whole thing very keenly and have not felt as down-hearted and as dispirited as I did last night for many a long day. However, I was given strength to pray, 'Forgive them, O Father, for they know not what they are doing.'

Bad as it has been, it failed to destroy the effect of last weekend upon Bethan and myself. To call it an enjoyable weekend is not enough, – it was inspiring and uplifting in every good sense.

There are moments, my dear E. T. (Mr Rees is becoming too official for me to use it) when I see mountains moving before the Spirit of the Lord.

There is great work ahead of us and I feel that what we have to do in the meantime is to consecrate ourselves more and more in preparation for that work.

Aberavon

What I feel about you must have been obvious to you throughout the weekend – you are one of those rare but priceless men, the practical visionary! I thank God for you.

Bethan will let you know about her brother as soon as she hears from him.

She joins me in sending greetings and all good wishes to Mrs Rees, Lynda and yourself.

Yours very truly
D. M. Lloyd-Jones

One principal reason why Dr Lloyd-Jones was so disturbed at the press reports was that he had not yet mentioned his impending change of career to some of the chiefs at Bart's. Spilsbury and Horder both heard of it first from the newspapers. The former, who was also about to terminate his work at the Hospital, wrote:

'I am exceedingly sorry to see in the Press that you have decided to leave Bart's and to enter the Ministry.

'I can appreciate the deep conviction which has led you to take this step, but I regret the loss to Medicine and in particular to the hospital.

'It lessens my regret at leaving that several whom I have come to regard as friends should have gone already.'

Horder was not so placid: understandably he felt entitled to know what was happening before seeing a newspaper announcement, and he suspected that his junior colleague's disinclination to have any discussion with him prior to making the decision was a reflection upon his capacity to judge such matters. 'Your brother is a fool,' he was to exclaim to Vincent Lloyd-Jones, 'he thinks I am only interested in bellies.' That was Martyn's view, but he was mortified at hurting the man to whom he owed so much. In a letter, Dr Lloyd-Jones sought to explain how unintentional, on his part, the press notices had been. Sir Thomas' reply was not lacking in kindness. He wrote:

'It has all been very unfortunate and, as you say, damaging. As to the main issue, disappointed as I am, I have faith in you and what you do –that you follow your best light, and will continue to do so. I think you know my creed – that it is the *man* that matters: his calling is almost an accident.'

Despite the temporary strain, the friendship with Horder was to remain intact.

Two more of the Bart's chiefs also sent letters. 'I was indeed surprised,' wrote Sir Thomas P. Dunhill, 'but I regard every man as having a perfect right to keep his own affairs private. It is no one else's business; also I admire very much a man who plans his own life and goes ahead with it regardless of the multitude who would like to arrange his life for him.' M. H. Gordon, after sending his best wishes, continued: 'There are matters that are too near the "mental endocardium" to be decided on by any but ourselves. Of course I greatly regret your giving up Medicine: you will have to come back. . . . I am looking forward to hearing your account of the endocarditis experiments. . . .'

Not without difficulty, for so many things were happening at once, Dr Lloyd-Jones continued to work at Bart's until the end of December. Meanwhile, at Aberavon, E. T. Rees, as well as being heartily involved in preparing the manse, was seeking to regularise the procedures for calling the new minister. The arrangements were little more than a formality, but in his next letter the Church Secretary of Bethlehem Forward Movement Church fulfilled the Presbytery's requirements in the following words.

> 9 Glen View Terrace
> Aberavon
> Port Talbot
> 20 December 1926

My dear Friend

On behalf of the above church I have great pleasure in extending to you a very hearty invitation to become its pastor. The decision was taken by the Glamorgan West Presbytery representatives at a well-attended meeting of members last night. We sincerely pray that God will abundantly bless you and us in the very important step taken.

I beg to submit the following terms for your consideration:

(1) Salary £225 per annum plus manse and rates.
(2) 13 Sundays per annum free.

With the heartiest greetings and best wishes of the church.

> Yours sincerely
> E. T. Rees
> (Secretary)

Along with a personal letter to E. T. Rees, Dr Lloyd-Jones sent an 'official' acceptance of the call on December 22 in which he wrote: 'It is unnecessary for me to say that I readily and gladly accept the invitation, and deeply appreciate what a great privilege it will be to be allowed to work for the coming of the Kingdom among my good friends at Sandfields. . . .' There was no comment on the proposed terms, only an exhortation to pray 'that we be given of His strength'.

The expectation was that after their wedding on January 8, 1927, the future minister and his wife should spend a fortnight's honeymoon at Torquay before travelling to Aberavon where he would preach on Sunday, January 30. In the event it proved impossible to crowd all the arrangements necessary for this schedule into the time allowed. There was his research work at Bart's which finally ended only after the Christmas holidays, furniture to buy, packing and removal to arrange, and innumerable letters requiring attention, not to speak of all the preparations for the wedding itself. Amidst it all, what was uppermost in his mind comes out clearly in another letter to E. T. Rees on December 29, 1926:

'Many thanks for all your excellent letters, particularly the one I received on Monday morning. . . .

'I preached twice on Sunday, in Welsh on a Christmas theme – my text being "*A phawb a'r a'i clywsant, a ryfeddasant am y pethau a ddywedasid gan y bugeiliaid wrthynt*" (Luke 2:18).

'My theme was the wonder and the amazement that are inherent in the gospel message and our tragic failure to appreciate this. If we could but see the real wonder in the Incarnation, the Crucifixion and the Resurrection, what powers we should be! The Son of God Himself dying for *us* – how can we remain so silent and so passive? Do we spend enough time in prayer and silent meditation? Are we not concentrating too much on what we can do in public and depending too much on our own abilities?

'Those are the thoughts that have been moving through my mind during the past few days, and above all I have applied them to my personal case.

'Oh yes! I know that the sensational side of my coming to Aberavon will soon pass – that is why I objected so much to the press reports of a fortnight ago. But, in a way, that increases my responsibility. If I could only do or say something during these first few weeks that would grip those casual people and retain them on

---

David Martyn Lloyd-Jones

our side, what a blessing it would be! Let us pray that we may be given His strength during these weeks and that the Word may be sown in fresh soil.

'I was very interested in all the news that you gave me of Sandfields and of our various friends there – I look forward to the days when I shall know them all really well – so well that we shall indeed enrich each others' lives. The Kingdom of God which is within us, is nevertheless a Kingdom that is meant to embrace all. This paradox always grips me. Our gospel, which is primarily for the individual, is nevertheless the only universal gospel. Well, I am preaching away, but it is the very bread of our lives, isn't it!'

There were three more letters to the enthusiastic Secretary of Sandfields before January 8 and they included such items as the plans for the 'Welcome Meeting', Bethan's decision on the colour for fireplace tiles, the non-existent electricity supply at the manse (to be rectified later in 1927) which did not bother them, and the lorry belonging to Trefor Jones which was to come to London to collect their belongings. He reports humorously: 'I am by now an absolute authority on furniture, as well as wallpaper'! On the eve of his wedding, and still needing 'to rush off to make a few final purchases', Martyn confesses: 'This has been a terrible week – I scarcely know what I am doing. Oh! for Aberavon!'

The wedding, at 2.15 p.m. on the second Saturday in January, 1927, was conducted at the Charing Cross Chapel by Peter Hughes Griffiths and John Thickens (Calvinistic Methodist minister at Willesden Green, London), with the members of Dr Lloyd-Jones' Sunday School class acting as ushers. Under a heading, 'Doctor Weds Doctor' a lengthy column in the *South Wales News* included the following:

'It will be remembered that Dr Martyn Lloyd-Jones recently created a sensation by announcing his intention to relinquish his practice in Harley Street for the pulpit, and he has now accepted an invitation to become lay-pastor of Bethlehem Forward Movement Mission Hall, Sandfields, Aberavon. His bride, Dr Bethan Phillips, is also giving up her medical work at the University College Hospital to help her husband in his religious duties at Aberavon.

'The bride who was given away by her father, was attired in a gown of white charmeuse and lace. Her bridal veil was of tulle

[126]

surmounted with a wreath of orange blossom; and she carried a bouquet of white roses.'

Long before Martyn and Bethan were at last able to relax at Torquay, on the South Devon coast, it was apparent that there was too much left unfinished in London for them to proceed to Aberavon as early as they had hoped. Wednesday, January 26, thus became their revised date of arrival, but that, also, was not to be. Back in London after the honeymoon, Martyn went down with 'flu and was running a high temperature and 'living in a continual bath of perspiration' on the day they had expected to reach their new home. Clearly he could not possibly preach at Sandfields, as arranged, on the following Sunday. In the event it was only three days before the 'Welcome Meeting' arranged for Friday February 4, that they arrived in Aberavon.

Their first night might have been their last. As their future home at 57 Victoria Road was not entirely ready for them, they were to be guests for a few days with one of the church families, the Robsons. Before retiring for the night Martyn and Bethan were standing talking in front of the fireplace in their bedroom when suddenly the light went out. Thinking nothing of it, they went to bed and slept soundly until early next morning when Mrs Lloyd-Jones awoke conscious of a rushing noise in the room and of a strange sensation in her head. She was attempting to alert her husband – who only responded by going further under the blankets – when she suddenly realised that the room was full of gas and, jumping out of bed, threw open a window! Their light of the night before had been a gas-light and when Mr Robson, thinking them to be in bed, had turned off the main supply, they, being used to electricity, had not turned off the gas in their own room! Because of the children in the house, it was Mr Robson's practice to do this last thing every night and then to turn the gas on again early in the morning when he rose to go out to work.

The Welcome Meetings, or Induction Services, were made up of a preaching service in the afternoon when Peter Hughes Griffiths, taking his text from Esther 4:12-14, spoke on Mordecai's 'philosophy of life', and an evening meeting addressed by several speakers. It was an event which gained much more attention in newspapers, both Welsh and English, than was usual in such cases. Nor was it merely the reporters who felt it to be an unusual occasion. Some of the ordained members of the Presbytery of West Glamorgan had mixed feelings at the prospect of receiving a new colleague who had spent not a single week in a theological college, and they did not intend to give way to the euphoria which possessed others. Dr Collins Lewis of Swansea, welcoming Dr Lloyd-Jones on behalf of the Presbytery, caused a smile by reminding the congregation 'that Dr Lloyd-Jones was after all only human', the proof being that 'he has just had a dose of influenza!' There was a veiled caution in the remark which, at least for the ministers present, would not be lost.

For Sandfields' former minister, the Reverend T. J. Lewis, who presided at the evening meeting, the occasion was also unusual. It was a new sight for him to see crowded pews in every part of the building. In his four-and-a-half years as pastor, he told his audience, 'he had often wondered how he would feel if he saw it as full as it was that evening'. Notwithstanding his affection for Sandfields, he had to confess to the people that he found it 'a hard place' to labour in, and 'he might tell Dr Jones that he would not always have such large congregations as he saw before him that evening'. T. J. Lewis concluded his address – largely a series of reminiscences – by referring to the small congregations at the Sunday morning services and appealing to the members to 'make a change'.

The Superintendent of the Forward Movement, the Reverend R. J. Rees, who was one of those who spoke in the evening meeting, had particular reasons for thinking that this was no normal induction service. His own reputation was virtually bound up with the success or failure of the pastorate about to commence. While affirming his belief that Sandfields, though a 'hard place', was one for which Dr Lloyd-Jones was suited, he candidly acknowledged that the question how 'he could get Dr Jones, with such a splendid record in his own profession, into the ranks of the ministry' had posed a considerable difficulty. 'The difficulty was that if he succeeded in getting the doctor received as a minister, and that ministry did not prove efficient, he (the speaker) was figuratively placed at the bottom of the trench, and everyone else would walk over him in exultation'.

Remarks of this kind scarcely eased the way for the new, twenty-seven-year-old pastor to bring the evening to a close with an address. The chairman had clearly hinted at the beginning that a gospel message would be appropriate for such a great gathering;

instead, Dr Lloyd-Jones left his hearers with a few stated convictions which he obviously believed the circumstances required. In the words of one of the newspaper reports:

'Dr Lloyd-Jones said he was truly astonished at the warmth of the welcome which he had received. When he took his step he had not counted on either welcome or support. He looked upon it as the only step he could have taken. Seeing the truth as he saw it, there was only one thing to do, and that was to follow it. If in the future he stood alone in the pulpit, and there was one in the church to listen to him, he would still go on. He had no use for the type of man who was always trying to produce a revival; there were men in the churches today who seemed to regard a revival as a hobby, they were always waiting for it and trying to produce it. No man had ever produced a revival, and he was not foolish enough to think or hope for a moment that anything he did or said would produce such an effect, but he hoped to live in such a way that if, and when, a revival came through the grace of God from heaven, they would be worthy of it. That was the spirit in which he took up the ministry.'

Before the benediction was pronounced the testimony of the past joined with the present as the congregation took up Charles Wesley's 'Jesu, Lover of my soul'. And no words could have been a better foretaste of the future, for there were many not in the church that night in Aberavon who would yet come to sing

> Thou, O Christ, art all I want,
> More than all in Thee I find;
> Raise the fallen, cheer the faint,
> Heal the sick, and lead the blind:
> Just and holy is Thy Name,
> I am all unrighteousness;
> False and full of sin I am,
> Thou art full of truth and grace.

'The business of preaching is not to entertain but to lead people to salvation, to teach them how to find God.'

M. L.-J.
on Psa. 34:8 (June 28, 1931)

'Taking his stand-point on the undeniable fact that during the last five and twenty years the denomination has lost ground rather than gained it, Dr J. D. Jones addressed himself to the question, What do the churches need, to become again centres of life and power? To this question he readily found the reply in the fact that the principal need of the denomination as a whole was a revival of real preaching – "preaching with a grip and passion in it".'

J. HUGH EDWARDS, M.P.
on the Chairman's Address at the Spring Assembly of The Congregational Union of England and Wales. *The British Weekly*, May 14, 1925.

7

A Different Preaching

In February 1927 the most frequently discussed subject among those in South Wales who reflected on Dr Lloyd-Jones' settlement at Aberavon was the question, 'What does he propose to do?' Not all were even agreed that his arrival had primarily a religious significance. There were ardent Socialists who, hearing rumours of his family's connections with the Liberal Party, seriously believed that he was preparing to recover Aberavon for the Liberals by standing for Parliament at the next election. After all, such a procedure was not unknown among Nonconformist ministers. Others of the medical fraternity in South Wales, incredulous of his alleged motives for leaving London, expressed the view that, once he had become known in South Wales, he would set up in general practice or as a consultant.[1]

But, assuming that the new pastor at Sandfields had come to engage in work for church extension, it was still unclear to many how he would proceed. Where did he stand, men wondered, on the much debated issue of how the decline in Christian influence was to be arrested? With good reason, no subject was more frequently discussed in the contemporary religious press. Before 1914, not far away from Aberavon, in the Rhondda Urban District, 151 Nonconformist churches had often held congregations whose aggregate number equalled three-quarters of the entire population. Such days were past. The Forward Mission church building at Sandfields, opened in the year that the First World War broke out, with seating

---

[1] Not long after his settlement, he was returning home in a bus from a meeting at which he had spoken on the other side of Port Talbot, sitting unrecognised behind two ladies who had been to hear him. He was highly amused to hear one saying to the other: 'Oh, yes, I have heard that the doctors are doing very badly in Harley Street just now, so no doubt he was glad to get away and take up this work'!

for 400, only had some 70 seats occupied on Sunday mornings, with rather more at night. In Calvinistic Methodism as a whole, with 1,497 churches, an increase of only 353 people was reported in 1926, with Sunday School attendance falling in the same period by 1,169.[1] Throughout much of Britain conditions were similar. In 1925 the Wesleyan Methodists and the Congregationalists both reported losses in Sunday School attendance of well over 100,000 since 1905, the Wesleyans losing 14,000 in 1924–25 alone. It was no wonder, then, that such subjects as 'The Lost Confidence of Nonconformity' often occupied the correspondence columns of *The British Weekly.*

Reactions to this situation were manifold. A number in Nonconformity sought to arrest the drift by a change in church services. There were those, for instance, who, critical of the plainness of congregational worship, looked for some kind of liturgy, with choir, anthem, and organ given a major role. Others, believing that people would not come to church 'to be preached at', wished to turn the sermon into an address 'relevant' to the time, or into an essay replete with many allusions to authors, poets and novelists. The religious press never lacked samples of that kind of preaching, most notably taken from the leading pulpits of London. 'Preaching at Whitefield's Chapel', *The British Weekly* tells us, 'Dr Garvie made a strong appeal for the cultivation of public opinion on behalf of the Protocol of the League of Nations.'[2] The Secretary of the Free Church Council, the Reverend Thomas Nightingale, visiting Westminster Chapel, took a text from Job and, says an admiring reporter, 'Mr Nightingale's quotations from Browning, Tennyson, Stevenson and Arnold showed us the poets of modern Christendom holding up, like Aaron and Hur, the hands of an ancient Moses.'[3]

There was agreement among the denominational leaders that modern preaching demanded a better-educated ministry and, to that end, theological degrees were increasingly required. Even colleges traditionally averse to that type of academic training were now moving with the times and thus Spurgeon's Pastors' College, London, appointed a Principal in 1925 (The Reverend Percy W. Evans) who was a warm advocate of a policy requiring students to

[1] Counting preaching stations, the buildings of the denomination could seat nearly 560,000. The membership in 1926 was 189,323.
[2] January 1, 1925, p. 343.
[3] April 23, 1925, p. 73.

A Different Preaching

take the B.D. examination of London University. In 1926 it was
reported concerning all training for the ministry in Wales: 'Notwithstanding the denominational differences which mark off the Welsh
theological colleges from one another, it is not without significance
that they have a common denominator in an identical curriculum.
Their courses are controlled by the requirements of the Welsh B.D.
degree.'[1]

This agreement was not, however, universal, as correspondence in
The British Weekly on 'Training for the Ministry' revealed in
September 1926. 'An Older Minister' writing in those columns
believed that the existing mode of training 'has very little bearing on
either pulpit or pastoral work' and asked, 'Do we exercise enough
care in admitting students, as to their spiritual character, love of
Christian work and zeal for the kingdom of Christ?' Another
complained, 'I have long felt that our colleges turn out B.A., B.D.
men with a depressing monotony.' Voices of that kind carried little
weight.

There was yet another school of opinion which was not looking to
regular church work for a renewal of influence. Church attendance,
they believed, should not be viewed as the test of success, for by many
other means, ranging from social work to religious journalism,
Christian values can be advanced irrespective of Sunday services. A
decline in the pulpit and a decline in Christianity, in their judgment,
were not synonymous. The Reverend Hubert Simpson, soon to be
appointed minister at Westminster Chapel, referred to this in
addressing the London Free Church Federation in 1926. 'According
to Mr Simpson,' *The British Weekly* reported, 'the religious outlook
is very hopeful. Literary men and journalists are preaching and
people are reading "sermons" (providing they do not recognise them
as such) with eagerness. He had been informed on good authority
that a London daily paper went up three hundred thousand in
circulation while publishing a series of religious articles.'[2]

In South Wales there was added weight to the argument that
traditional methods would not bring the people back to the chapels.
No part of Britain had suffered more from the General Strike of
1926, for while others had gone back to work on May 12 the coal
miners – a considerable percentage of the working population of

[1] *The British Weekly*, January 21, 1926, p. 397.
[2] January 28, 1926, p. 423.

South Wales – had 'remained out' for another six months. Only the threat of starvation finally took them back. During those months the only action taken by the government was to provide two meals per day for children (breakfast and at noon) and for this purpose the church hall at Sandfields was one of the many taken over for use as a communal 'soup kitchen'. A letter by an Aberavon minister under the title, 'Is the Miner's Family Starving?', published in September 1926, gives a graphic description of the seriousness of the situation. 'In our homes,' he writes, 'we do not think of keeping a child from mid-day to the next morning without food', yet this was being expected in many homes in the Aberavon area. The same writer reported that one soup kitchen in a nearby village had to be closed for lack of coal.

These events were still very much in the public consciousness in February 1927. Unemployment and dole queues were to remain a feature of the Port Talbot area in the 'Great Depression' which was only then beginning. An extract from a letter which E. T. Rees was to write to Mrs Magdalene Lloyd-Jones the following year gives an idea of conditions in some families at this date:

'Oh! how the little ones are suffering in South Wales these days. Not far from where I am writing this I have deposited a heap of shirts, trousers, jerseys, etc., which I am collecting from friends in order to clothe the poor children in my school who are half naked. Only on Wednesday I had a little fellow almost "trouserless", toes protruding from his broken boots, and cold and hungry in my room, and his brother unable to come because he had *nothing to put on*. There are hundreds and hundreds of miners' children in this sorry plight in the neighbourhood of Aberavon in J. Ramsay MacDonald's constituency. I am determined to do what I can to help. Only this morning I was with Mr MacDonald's agent at the station where he was directing many parcels sent from various parts of the country.'

Amid such conditions the case was clearly strong for the many who argued that political and economic measures were the first priority. Even those disposed to give a higher place to religion were tempted to suppose that a population with so many material needs would hardly give attention to anything being preached in chapels.

To bridge the gap with those outside, Sandfields for some years had maintained various activities, including football, musical evenings, a dramatic society, and a 'Brotherhood' on Saturday nights, although with small success, as we have seen. At Dr Lloyd-Jones' induction, the former pastor, T. J. Lewis, after referring to the fact that he had been unable to reverse the non-church going habit, advised the newcomer that 'he used to go into the streets round about their church and found he could always minister to about six times as many people as he had in his church'. There were others in Sandfields who seemed to think that the best hope lay in the area of children's work: 'Our work amongst the children is capable of great expansion,' E. T. Rees reported to Forward Movement headquarters in 1926: 'If we had the teachers, a Sunday School of 500 juniors would be obtained within a month.'

In the event, Dr Lloyd-Jones had nothing to say about any new programme. To the surprise of the church secretary he seemed to be exclusively interested in the purely 'traditional' part of church life, which consisted of the regular Sunday Services (at 11 a.m. and 6 p.m.), a prayer meeting on Mondays and a mid-week meeting on Wednesdays. Everything else could go, and thus those activities particularly designed to attract the outsiders soon came to an end. The demise of the dramatic society posed a practical problem, namely, what to do with the wooden stage which occupied a part of the church hall? 'You can heat the church with it,' the new minister told the Committee.[1] They demurred and gave it to the local Y.M.C.A.! After some hesitation on Dr Lloyd-Jones' part, the 'Brotherhood', which met on Saturday nights, was allowed to continue.

The Sunday sermons were, indirectly, to indicate the meaning of these and other changes. The church was to advance, not by approximating to the world, but rather by representing in the world the true life and privilege of the children of God. The fundamental need was for the church to recover an understanding of what she truly is.

Such was the note which was foremost on Martyn Lloyd-Jones' first Sunday as pastor in the Sandfields pulpit, February 6, 1927. The text of the sermon which he most fully prepared for that day was 2 Timothy 1:7; 'For God hath not given us the spirit of fear; but of power, and of love, and of a sound mind.' In the course of his introduction he said:

'Young men and women, my one great attempt here at Aberavon, as

---

[1] The Committee was an elected body, and was to the church at Sandfields what the diaconate is to the regular non-conformist churches.

long as God gives me strength to do so, will be to try to prove to you not merely that Christianity is reasonable, but that ultimately, faced as we all are at some time or other with the stupendous fact of life and death, nothing else is reasonable. That is, as I see it, the challenge of the gospel of Christ to the modern world. My thesis will ever be, that, face to face with the deeper questions of life and death, all our knowledge and our culture will fail us, and that our only hope of peace is to be found in the crucified Christ. May I make an appeal to you here and now at the very outset of my work among you? And in appealing to you, I pledge myself to you that I also will reciprocate in kind if you respond to what I ask of you. My request is this: that we all be honest with one another in our conversation and discussions. What I mean is this. There is a very real temptation for young people brought up in Christian homes and in a Christian atmosphere to repeat phrases which they have heard their teachers use but which mean nothing to the young people themselves. What happens is this. A young man hears his father say that he believes certain things and because he respects his father he believes that he ought to believe the same things. When he has said this to himself for a sufficient number of times the next step soon follows, and that is, that he says in public that he himself believes in these things . . .

'Now this is what I want to ask you. Do let us be honest with one another and never profess to believe more than is actually true to our experience. Let us always, with the help of the Holy Spirit, testify to our belief, *in full*, but never a word more. . . .

'Our chapels and churches are crowded with people nearly all of whom take the Lord's Supper without a moment's hesitation, and yet, without judging harshly or unjustly, do you imagine for a moment that all those people believe that Christ died for them? Well then, you ask, why are they church members, why do they pretend to believe? The answer is, that they are afraid to be honest with themselves, afraid of what their parents and friends would say of them if they got up and said that they couldn't honestly say that Christ meant anything to them. I do not know what your experience is, my friends, but as for myself, I shall feel much more ashamed to all eternity for the occasions on which I said that I believed in Christ when in fact I did not, than for the occasions when I said honestly that I could not truthfully say that I did believe. If the church of Christ on earth could but get rid of the parasites who only believe that they ought to believe in Christ, she would, I am certain, count

A Different Preaching

once more in the world as she did in her early days, and as she has always done during times of spiritual awakening. I ask you therefore tonight, and shall go on asking you and myself, the same question. Do you know what you know about the gospel? Do you question yourself about your belief and make sure of yourself?'

From this starting-point, the preacher went on to deal with the Pauline description of real religion, not 'the spirit of fear; but of power, and of love, and of a sound mind'. 'If you haven't this,' he concluded – speaking of 'a sound mind' – 'then your religion is probably nothing more than emotionalism, love of tradition, force of habit, or a sense of fear and awe.'

This sermon of February 6 was a clear indication of the direction Dr Lloyd-Jones intended to take. As he understood the times, the first need was to begin with the church herself. Once real Christian experience was recovered she would find no problem in gaining a hearing from the world. Two weeks later, on Sunday, February 20, he continued the same theme with a sermon on 'Called to be Saints'. The introductory argument was that Paul regards everyone who believes in Christ as a saint:

'The people to whom St Paul wrote were not exceptional people in any sense in which we are not exceptional. To me, every Christian is an exceptional man; at least, if a man is not an exceptional man, then he cannot possibly be a true Christian. For, remember, a Christian is one who believes in the death of Christ and the Resurrection, one who has been born again, is a new creation, has become a son of God and is therefore a brother of Christ. Yes, every Christian is an exceptional person, and those who lived in the time of St Paul were no more exceptional than we are, who are followers of Christ at the present time. Christians throughout the years have always been the same and have been called from all classes, Jews and Gentiles, bondmen and free. Their antecedents do not count, everything that has gone before does not matter, in Christ they are all one and are all exceptional. If you do not stand out in your street and in your neighbourhood as an exceptional person then I tell you seriously that you cannot possibly be a Christian. I do not mean by that that you should adopt attitudes and pose before your fellow men, because that would be hypocrisy. What I do mean is this, that the power of the Holy Spirit working in you and through you, makes such a difference to you that you become so completely changed from your former self that all those around you cannot help noticing the difference.'

There was much to be said in the coming months on the nature of the life of the Christian and the uselessness of merely nominal religion. Often Dr Lloyd-Jones' approach was staggeringly different from that to which congregations were accustomed. Preaching in July 1927, after a Sunday away from his own pulpit, he said:

'People complain about the dwindling congregations and how the churches are going down. Why are people ceasing to attend places of worship? Why is it, that last Sunday night I noticed that, while the places of worship in Cardiff were only sparsely attended, the trains coming from Porthcawl and other sea-side places were packed out. Why did these people spend their day at the seaside and in other places rather than in the House of God worshipping? Well, the answer is perfectly plain. They obviously prefer to be at the sea-side and feel that they get more benefit there than they do in their chapels and churches. Now it is no use our arguing with people like that, it is no use our telling them that they really do not get greater benefit there, because they honestly believe that they do. . . . What I feel like saying to these trippers is this: If you honestly believe (and remember it is your responsibility) that you derive greater benefit by spending your day in the country than you do by attending a place of worship, well then, go to the country. Don't come here if you honestly feel that you could do better elsewhere. Unless you feel that something is being offered and given to you here which no other institution can offer or equal, well then, in the name of Heaven, go out into the country or to the sea-side. The church of Christ is a church of believers, an association of people banded together by a common belief and a common love. You don't believe? Well, above all, do not pretend that you do, go to the country and the sea-side. All I ask of you is, be consistent. When someone dies in your family, do not come to ask the church in which you do not believe to come to bury him. Go to the sea-side for consolation. . . .'

Taken alone, such a statement might have been misunderstood, but it came in the midst of many sermons which showed the church as incomparably different in her privileges, and demonstrated that when she truly enjoys these privileges she conquers the world. There are things for which the church should weep, but confronted with 'the self-righteous, the important, the mighty of the world' she is able to laugh. The unvarnished gospel, possessed by 'a little group of men and women having apparently no influence or power', challenged the great Roman Empire so that it began 'to totter and to shake until it eventually fell, while this small body of people continued to grow and increase and spread throughout the world!'

'Surely the Christian has a right to laugh. It is to our lasting shame as Christians that we allow the world in these days to laugh at us, and we do so merely because we do not rely as we should upon the power of God. We look at the people of the world with their motor cars, their luxury, and their various pleasures, and we even seem to envy them. We, who have all the riches and all the resources of the Godhead in our grasp; we for whom God spared not his only-begotten Son; we for whom God has prepared such things as the eye of mortal man has not seen, nor ear heard, nor heart ever felt; we who, to use the words of Jesus Christ on this occasion to the woman of Samaria, have "the well of water springing up into everlasting life" within us, how can *we* be envious of those who depend upon the polluted wells of the world for their pleasure and happiness! What if we here in Sandfields but realised how great our treasures are, and realised it to such an extent that we made all the people in this neighbourhood and town feel that we were laughing at them and sorry for them in their dependence upon the fleeting things of time – why, the life of this town would be completely changed in a very short time.'[1]

Generally speaking, it was Dr Lloyd-Jones' habit from the outset of his ministry to devote one sermon each Sunday to teaching and the other to more direct evangelism, although there was often a considerable overlap and, as we shall note, both types of sermon were used to bring people to conversion. The evangelistic sermons, from his first Sundays in February, often dealt with the errors and the misrepresentations of the gospel which men confused with Christianity. Christianity is not a scheme of morality, nor a plan for social and political change, and organisations which propose improvements along such lines are only 'tinkering with the problems'. 'We may be made better men, but before we can face God we must be new men.' All by nature are dead in sin and to all men equally salvation can only come as 'the gift of God'. In no sense at all does salvation

[1] Sermon on the Woman of Samaria (John 4:16), November 20, 1927.

depend upon man. So on his third Sunday at Sandfields, preaching from Romans 6:23, he can say:

'It is a gift that is as open to the very worst man in Aberavon tonight as it is to the very best, for no one can ever get it because he deserves it. I have met men sometimes who have said to me that they know that they are beyond hope, that they have sunk so far into sin and iniquity that nothing can save them. My reply to them is just this, that the gifts of God are infinite gifts and that, were you ten times worse than you are already, God could still save you, and do so without realising that his resources had been called upon at all. The most respectable sinner in Aberavon tonight has no more claim on it than the worst and when you both avail yourselves of it you will be doing so on an equal footing. Hold on, my friends, all is not lost, no one is too bad – all are invited.'

His evangelistic sermon for the first Sunday in March – with the five foolish virgins in the Parable of the Ten Virgins as his text (Matt. 25:1–3) – brought another emphasis to the fore, the folly of being unprepared for eternity. On the previous Tuesday an explosion had occurred in a South Wales coal mine at Ebbw Vale, killing many men. From the moment that he heard the terrible news, he confessed, in beginning his sermon, that his thoughts had come back repeatedly to these words of Christ and his purpose was to ask his hearers how they had reacted:

'Reading the account in the newspapers, a hundred thoughts came rushing into one's mind – the dreadful nature of the calamity with its terrible loss of life, the extreme danger associated with the work of a coal-miner. Whatever one may have thought during the coal-strike, one must have felt this week that no work can possibly be much more dangerous and that all men doing such work should be adequately paid. The thoughts of the fatherless homes, and women suddenly becoming widows, wives who were planning things for the future for their husbands and their children suddenly being told their husbands were dead! Dreams and hope of future happiness suddenly dashed to the ground! Aged mothers mourning after their sons and wondering why young lives should have been taken before theirs, and little children in the same cases left orphans! . . .

'Well, each of you knows his own thoughts, but, for myself, I cannot remember any event which has brought home to me so forcibly the uncertainty of life. No sooner do we think that all is well, than something dreadful happens; no sooner do we feel that certain dangers have been removed once and for all, than they reappear in all their horror. Only just a fortnight ago one of the inspectors of mines had said in a lecture that "we had seen the last of pit explosions, in all probability". We boast of our advance of knowledge and of the way we have been able to harness the forces of nature to our own uses, but every now and again we are summarily reminded of their strength and our own impotence. Of everything that is uncertain in life, the most uncertain of all is life itself. No one can predict what will happen next, no one knows at what moment that final blow will come and we shall cease to be.'

To this same note the preacher returned after expounding his text:

'Life is real, life is earnest, and he who would be happy must play a man's part in it. You may be comfortable and happy now, and as far as you are concerned at the moment it may be perpetual sunshine. But I would warn you that the cloud which cast its dark shadow over Ebbw Vale last week will inevitably work its way to Aberavon. It may not appear in the same form but it is bound to come – no one can escape it. There are some laws which are inexorable and sooner or later we all become faced with the great crisis.

'My dear friends, are you ready for it? Have you catered for it in your philosophy? Are you prepared for anything and everything that may possibly meet you? Is your faith of the type "that sees through death"? For no other is of any value at all.'

A fortnight later, on March 20, the brevity and uncertainty of life was again his emphasis as he preached from Hebrews 13:14, 'For here have we no continuing city, but we seek one to come.' The introduction this time dealt with the compromise into which the church had fallen as she sought to attract the world:

'Our Christianity has the appearance of being an adjunct or an appendix to the rest of our lives instead of being the main theme and the moving force in our existence. . . . We seem to have a real horror of being different. Hence all our attempts and endeavours to popularise the church and make it appeal to people. We seem to be trying to tell people that their joining a church will not make them so very different after all. "We are no longer Puritans," we say, "we believe that they over-did things and made Christianity too difficult for people. They frightened people with their strictness and their unnecessarily high standards. We are not so foolish as to do that", we say, and indeed we do not do so. Instead, however, we provide so called "sporting parsons", men of whom the world can say that they are "good sports" – whatever that may mean. And what it does so often mean is that they are men who believe that you can get men to come to chapel and church by playing football and other games with them. "I'll fraternise with these men," says such a minister. "I'll get them to like me and to see that I'm not so different from them after all, and then they'll come to listen to my sermons." And he tries it, but thank God, he almost invariably fails, as he richly deserves. The man who only comes to church or chapel because he likes the minister as a man is of no value at all, and the minister who attempts to get men there by means of that subterfuge is for the time being guilty of lowering the standard of the truth which he claims to believe. For this gospel is the gospel of salvation propounded by the Son of God himself. We must not hawk it about the world, or offer special inducements and attractions, as if we were shopkeepers announcing an exceptional bargain sale. . . .

'The world expects the Christian to be different and looks to him for something different, and therein it often shows an insight into life that regular church-goers often lack. The churches organise whist-drives, fêtes, dramas, bazaars and things of that sort, so as to attract people. We are becoming almost as wily as the devil himself, but we are really very bad at it; all our attempts are hopeless failures and the world laughs at us. Now, when the world persecutes the church, she is performing her real mission, but when the world laughs at her she has lost her soul. And the world today is laughing at the church, laughing at her attempts to be nice and to make people feel at home. My friends, if you feel at home in any church without believing in Christ as your personal Saviour, then that church is no church at all, but a place of entertainment or a social club. For the truth of Christianity and the preaching of the gospel should make a church intolerable and uncomfortable to all except those who believe, and even they should go away feeling chastened and humble.'

From his text he proceeded to show how

'We have lost that idea and view of life which was so forcefully stressed and emphasised by the Puritans and the founders of the churches to which we belong, the idea that life is a pilgrimage and that while here on earth we are nothing more than travellers. The fathers wrote about life in that way, talked and preached about it like that, and sang of it in their hymns in that way. They were but "pilgrims in this barren land". . . . Now this idea has almost vanished out of our vocabulary and sounds strange to us. . . .

'If you have faith in Christ you will not resent the fact that life is a pilgrimage, but will rather rejoice that it is so, because you will know that the pilgrimage is but a part of your exodus – an exodus from Egypt into Canaan, from bondage into freedom, and that, an everlasting freedom. Your only regret will be that it takes such a long time, but even while you are here you will know a peace of mind and a comfort that no one else can possibly feel.'

It was preaching like this which explained the changed course of the church life at Sandfields and the quiet dismantling of much that hitherto had been taken for granted. Writing to the Forward Movement headquarters in the time of their former pastor, E. T. Rees had said, 'Our Sunday services are warm, hearty and helpful, and many find their way to the Master. The Penitent Form and the Total Abstinence Pledge are the ways of approach.' But now both 'the penitent form' and 'the pledge' were also gone! No one was summoned to 'come forward' in the brief meeting which took place after the Sunday evening service. Rather, the message was, 'Ye must be born again.' Preaching on June 12, 1927, the minister declared: 'Many churches these days make a new member sign a pledge of total abstinence from alcoholic liquors. Now I do not believe in pledges of any sort. If a man tells me he believes in Christ and desires to be a member of the church, I feel I have no right to question him. I take him at his word and leave it to his honour, but there are times when I almost feel like advocating that all members should sign another pledge, and that is, "a pledge of total abstinence from politics", for I believe that it is causing greater harm in our churches in these days than almost anything else.' E. T. Rees – still an enthusiastic supporter of the Labour party – was astonished! Despite his enthusiasm for the new minister, he had been absent from the station when the Lloyd-Joneses had arrived at Port Talbot station on February 1, as it coincided with a meeting being held by Ramsay MacDonald. 'If we must send resolutions to Parliament,' the preacher continued in the same sermon, 'I propose that we send this one, drafted by the gentle mind of St John, "He that believeth in him is not condemned; but he that believeth not is condemned already, because he hath not believed in the name of the only begotten Son of God.'

The first newspaper account of this different preaching in Aberavon came from the pen of a Mr Sam Jones who was present on Sunday July 3, 1927, and reported his impressions for his paper. After recounting the change in the career of the young man for whom fame had been confidently predicted in the medical field, he admitted that the 'romance' of Dr Lloyd-Jones' action in becoming 'pastor of a little church in a South Wales town' had been the main factor behind his going to hear him:

'Mine was a human failing of curiosity on visiting the Bethlehem Forward Movement Church, Aberavon, last Sunday. Curiosity soon vanished, however. The presence of the young doctor in the pulpit, the tremendous zeal revealed in his preaching, the air of great faith and certainty that he carried, all combined to sweep it away. I remained to wonder and to respect.

'I do not crave the reader's pardon for abandoning my usual manner of writing my impressions and for giving to the best of my ability, as much of the sermons as possible. I do this simply because the sermons in themselves were stirring, because Dr Lloyd-Jones has something to say, and because they are the words of one who has felt himself forced to speak by a greater than human power. My versions of the sermons are but a weak picture of the originals, but I dare to hope that the reader will get a faint conception of the tremendous impetus behind the preacher.'

The morning sermon, Sam Jones went on to report, was on the words of Nahum 2:1, 'He that dasheth in pieces is come up before thy face [against thee]' – words threatening Nineveh with the wrath of God and with destruction. Nineveh had sinned before but, having been reformed under the preaching of Jonah, had been spared. Now they had forgotten Jonah and turned from the God who can both create and destroy. Slow to anger and ready to forgive, there was nevertheless a limit to God's patience. He is a just God who will assert his will and his standards. Then, from an exposition of the text, the preacher turned to the contemporary world and to the church in particular. For too long the only conception of God had been in terms of 'Gentle Jesus, meek and mild'. There had been too

1. *Donald Street, Cardiff, where the Lloyd-Jones family lived until* 1905

2. *Martyn as an infant*

3. *Martyn, aged six, on a pony*

4. *The dancing class at Connaught Road School, Cardiff (see page 1).*
Martyn second from left, Harold second from right

5. *The Calvinistic Methodist Chapel, Llangeitho, with the statue of*
Daniel Rowland in the foreground

6. Henry Lloyd-Jones with Martyn outside the home and shop (as rebuilt in 1910) in Llangeitho

TREGARON COUNTY SCHOOL.

Surname	Christian Name	Name of Parent or Guardian	Address of Parent or Guardian	Father's Trade or Prof.	Pupil's Date of Birth	Pupil's Last School

7. A page from the register of Tregaron County School

8. *Llwyncadfor, the favourite of all holiday venues*

9 *Harold, Martyn, Vincent* [left to right], *taken at Aberystwyth, 1913,
after Vincent had become the third member of the family to gain a
scholarship to Tregaron County School*

10. *Henry Lloyd-Jones at the door of his dairy business,*
7 Regency Street, Westminster

11. *Dairy roundsmen*

12. *The family at Regency Street: Henry and Magdalen Lloyd-Jones,
with Harold [front] and Martyn [left] and Vincent*

13. *Martyn in a characteristic
position in his teenage years*

15. *Bethan Phillips aged about eighteen, in Welsh costume*

14. *The Square at St Bartholomew's Hospital*

16. *A firm at Bart's. M.L.-J. second from left, middle row*

17. *Sunnyside* [left], *Newcastle Emlyn*

18. Dr and Mrs Tom Phillips, with Bethan, at their home in Harrow

19. *Martyn and Bethan on their wedding day, January 8, 1927,*
Charing Cross Chapel, London

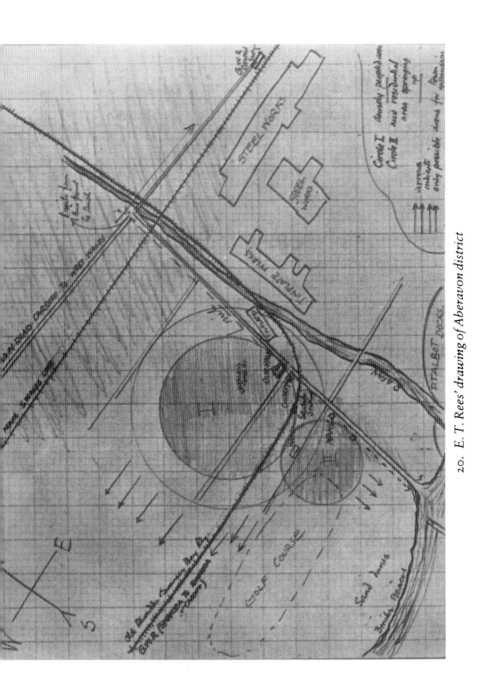

20. E. T. Rees' drawing of Aberavon district

much preaching of the Prodigal Son and of forgiveness and kindness. Nahum, with irony, advised the people to prepare to defend themselves against divine *wrath* – 'keep the fortress, watch the way, make thy loins strong, fortify thy power' – and so, in the name of God, the church ought to warn the people, 'If you will not worship God, be ready to fight and attempt to defend yourselves against the One who has power to "dash in pieces"!'

The reporter's synopsis of the close of the sermon, and of how he personally felt about what he heard, reads:

'We were the people of Nineveh – we had lost the reverence. The Sabbath meant nothing – the Bible was the Good Book no longer. We had turned our backs on God. But there was a limit to His forgiveness. God was not going to stand by and allow all the sins of this age. Let us show that God was still God, and as God's men let us stand as men with a vision and power that could not be waived.

'The cause of Christ was at a low ebb in this country. The trials of the men and women of faith were many. It was difficult for the men of God to stand before the world and still believe. But God's day would come. The world might do its worst, and all the powers of hell be let loose in the country. The people of God would not suffer! We must hold on to our faith. The day was coming when the world would be levelled.

'Dr Lloyd-Jones is a man of great courage and faith. I left the church on Sunday morning wondering.'

The writer of these words went back to Sandfields on the evening of the same day and heard a sermon on, 'The wind bloweth where it listeth' (John 3:8). The theme was God's sovereign control of all things – mysterious to us, yet absolutely sure. Man in the arrogance of unbelief supposes he is certain in his opinions. Yet the truth is that he is not even able to control his own mind: 'We think a man owns his brain. But you cannot command and order your own brain – the more you do so, the more it refuses to work'. The person who has experienced the life-giving power of the Holy Spirit, and seen God in Christ, the preacher declared, has lost his confidence in himself. He depends upon God and owns the mystery of God's ways. The great difference between the Christian and the non-Christian is that the former speaks with humility and meekness. As with the wind, the evidence of which we see in the results – the rustle of leaves and the sway of branches – so the way in which the Holy Spirit moves men. Though certain and sure, it is beyond analysis. It is the glory of the wind of the Spirit that it is beyond human control. 'It was God's saving grace and we had to go down on our knees and pray that we might share in it. . . . At present it seemed that the gale was blowing away from our country – it seemed to have vanished. . . . Let us pray,' added the preacher, 'that the wind comes again, that we experience it. But it all rests with Him.'

Sam Jones seems to have been one of the first to recognise in print that what was most unusual about the young preacher was not his change of career but his message itself and the manner in which it was delivered. Thus he closed his column with the question: 'Has the future marked him down as a great leader of the nation? Of this I am certain, if ever a man was called to the ministry it is Dr Martyn Lloyd-Jones.'

*   *   *

One thing that was clearly recognisable about this preaching was that it was based upon no contemporary models. Most of the preaching which Dr Lloyd-Jones had heard throughout his life had only convinced him what he must not do. He did not stand in the traditional Welsh succession which for some years past had confused emotionalism and sentiment with the genuinely prophetic. He shunned 'the hwyl' which J. Hugh Edwards, in *The British Weekly*, described as 'that combination of ecstatic emotion and of musical intonation which has held vast congregations absolutely spellbound with its mesmeric effect'. According to Edwards the *hwyl* was 'the distinctive and exclusive characteristic of Welsh preaching'. Dr Lloyd-Jones viewed it as an artificial contrivance to secure effect, just as he did the multitude of illustrations and anecdotes which the preachers had taught the people to expect. In contrast to this, his sermons were closely reasoned, with the main theme carefully analysed. He was certain that true preaching makes its impact, in the first instance, upon the mind. Yet he did not belong to that more intellectual type of Welsh preaching which announced a text and proceeded at once to exposition. Perhaps the most unusual feature about the form of his sermons was the importance which he gave to the introductions. He once observed:

'I am not and have never been a typical Welsh preacher. I felt that in

A Different Preaching

preaching the first thing that you had to do was to demonstrate to the
people that what you were going to do was very relevant and
urgently important. The Welsh style of preaching started with a verse
and the preacher then told you the connection and analysed the
words, but the man of the world did not know what he was talking
about and was not interested. I started with the man whom I wanted
to listen, the patient. It was a medical approach really – here is a
patient, a person in trouble, an ignorant man who has been to
quacks, and so I deal with all that in the introduction. I wanted to get
the listener and *then* come to my exposition. They started with their
exposition and ended with a bit of application.'

But beyond the form and structure of Dr Lloyd-Jones' sermons
the chief difference lay in the content of the message. Certainly there
were aspects of that message which he had heard others preach, John
Hutton on the power of God to intervene in life, for example. Yet the
combination was his own and among the elements which distinguished it from much of the best-known preaching of that period was
its absolute dependence upon the authority of the Scriptures. The
Bible was not merely the starting-point, from which he might proceed
to Browning, Tennyson or the latest novel, it was the sole source of
infallible truth and the final judge of all religious experience. To
preach from such a standpoint in the 1920's was to do what the
pulpit in general professed to be impossible without extreme
obscurantism. Church leaders almost universally conceded that
higher criticism had discredited the verbal inspiration of the Bible
and brought a change in faith which could never be reversed.
Speaking of the rejection of the 'dogmas of revealed religion' which
had become commonplace in the 1920's, one historian has written:
'This was as great a happening as any in English history since the
conversion of the Anglo-Saxons to Christianity.'[1] And yet, as
discussion on 'The Lost Confidence of Nonconformity' in *The
British Weekly* in 1925 showed, a majority of ministers were willing
to treat rank unbelief as a sign of progress rather than as a setback.
One exception was the Reverend James F. Taviner of Aylesbury,
Bucks, who wrote in the Correspondence Columns of that paper:

'For a generation we have been warned against "the worship of a
book"; we have been nervously apprehensive of what "the man in

[1] *English History 1914–1945*, A. J. P. Taylor, 1965, p. 168.

the street" might think of a simple and virile Puritan faith; we have cringed in sycophantic adulation of the sceptic and the blundering Higher Critic . . . These have been our gods, and now we are told we have lost confidence in ourselves.

'Your correspondent appears to think that unless Nonconformity gives itself up to social crusades it will perish of popular neglect. Let him ponder the words: "He that loseth his life *for My sake* shall find it". When "for His sake" and not "for the opinions and approval of others" is our motive, we shall not lack for leadership, we shall have the best of all. But with a Bible under suspicion, a Christ shorn of the miraculous, and a Gospel which has to be preached (as donkeys eat thistles) "very carefully", the wonder is, not that we lack leadership, but that Nonconformity should have anybody to lead.'[1]

These words on the displacement of Scripture were unquestionably correct. Principal W. M. Clow, writing a leading article in *The British Weekly* at this same period, after referring to 'past controversies regarding the inspiration of Scripture', which he regretted were unknown to some 'unthoughtful evangelists', declared: 'These controversies have delivered most men from that obscurantism, and its needless fears of what is called modernism.'[2] In the columns of the same paper, wonder was expressed that Dr Campbell Morgan preaching on a visit to Westminster Chapel in 1926 should uphold the biblical account of creation and say that, 'If you believe that man is the result of evolutionary process you cannot believe the Bible also.'[3] One listener who heard the visitor from America paid him a patronising 'compliment' in these terms, 'Even if Campbell Morgan held pre-Copernican theories, and rejected the testimony of the rocks, and looked on Darwin as an imposter, still I could listen to him for a month of Sundays.'[4]

Although it meant standing against the whole tide of respectable modern opinion Dr Lloyd-Jones had recognised that there could be

---

[1] *The British Weekly*, September 24, 1925.

[2] *The British Weekly*, July 8, 1926, p. 295. The sixty-five-year-old Methodist, Samuel Chadwick, was undoubtedly putting it too mildly when, preaching at Wesley's Chapel, London in January 1926, he said: 'We have no longer got an infallible Christ, some people are saying, or an infallible Bible either.'

[3] *Ibid.*, July 15, 1926, p. 307. 'How of Henry Drummond', objected the reporter in response to Morgan's assertion, 'and multitudes of orthodox theologians in all the churches?'

[4] *Ibid.*, August 5, 1926, p. 368.

no true recovery of preaching without a prior return to biblical certainties. Without this, 'the revival of preaching' for which Dr J. D. Jones of Bournemouth as Chairman of the Congregational Union had pleaded in 1925, would never occur. The whole tendency of contemporary ministerial training, as Dr Lloyd-Jones had been reminded when he went to Aberystwyth as a prospective student in that same year, involved not submission to Scripture but rather judgment upon it. Even motivation for studying the Bible (as distinct from what scholars said *about* the Bible) was disappearing. Deploring the ignorance of Scripture among candidates for the ministry in Calvinistic Methodism, Dr T. Charles Williams, a member of the Board for the oversight of candidates, declared: 'I dare say that they all keep the Ten Commandments, but there were many of them who could not write them.'[1] Perhaps the discerning Christians who sat in the pews of the churches were the best judges. When they were given opportunity to express their opinions on ministerial training, as, for instance, in the Correspondence Columns of *The British Weekly*, views such as the following were expressed:

'The number of young ministers who cannot preach is appalling. In a large number of cases there is such a painful lack of "conviction" that we sorrowfully retire from the services wondering if they really *believe* what they have been saying.'

'I am a deacon and come into close contact with a number of ministers. I have no knowledge of the method or conduct of the training of ministers. I only see and hear them in the pursuit of their high calling and for a long time past the conviction has come to me that there is something wrong somewhere . . . Ministers as a whole deliver discourses, undoubtedly clever, well thought out, and fascinating; but that is all. We get practically no Bible teaching. Why are our churches emptying? The minister will tell you it is because of other attractions. I do not agree.'[2]

Such quotations as the above are necessary to bring out the extent of the difference between the preaching of the twenty-seven-year-old missioner of Sandfields, Aberavon, and that heard from the generality of pulpits.

[1] *Ibid.*, September 17, 1925, p. 525.
[2] *Ibid.*, September 16, 1926, p. 490.

David Martyn Lloyd-Jones

There is one further feature of Dr Lloyd-Jones' preaching which needs to be added. It was customary among evangelical Christians at this date to encourage the practice of giving 'testimonies' as a form of evangelistic witness, and equally common for ministers to include personal references of various kinds in their sermons. Given Dr Lloyd-Jones' unusual career and its interest for the general public; given also, the spiritual experience which had so changed his life; it might well be supposed that references to his own story would have appeared frequently in his preaching. The case was exactly the opposite. References to himself in his sermons were brief and rare. Anything in the way of a testimony to his conversion experience was almost wholly absent. The omission was not an oversight on his part but the result of deep convictions.

For one thing, he noticed that the giving of testimonies tended to reduce all conversions to a similar pattern, to standardise experience in a way which went beyond Scripture. And yet, at the same time, testimony-givers were prone to emphasise what made their story noteworthy. No doubt the motives were often well-intentioned, but the effect could easily be carnal and man-centred. Hearers readily became impressed with the dramatic and unique features of a story, instead of with the grace of God which is identical in every conversion. In his own case – as the newspapers reporting his change of career had found – it was easy to emphasise the unusual and to speak of 'the great sacrifice' he had made in leaving Medicine, but he disliked such language intensely. To speak of any 'loss' in the context of being a Christian amounted, in his eyes, to a denial of the gospel. He never forgot the shock of once hearing a man say, 'I have been a Christian for twenty years and have not regretted it'! Further, his view of preaching was such that to talk of 'sacrifice' in relation to that work was virtually absurd.

There could be no higher privilege than that of being a messenger of the God who has pledged his help and presence to those whom he sends. When, as happened at times, people referred in admiring terms to his self-denial in entering the ministry, he repudiated the intended compliment completely. 'I gave up nothing,' he said on one such occasion, 'I received everything. I count it the highest honour that God can confer on any man to call him to be a herald of the gospel.'[1]

[1] Quoted in *The Monthly Record of the Free Church of Scotland*, 1941, p. 88.

A *Different Preaching*

Certainly his concern lest attention should be diverted to what is least important was one major reason for his lifelong unwillingness to employ his own testimony in preaching.

There was, however, a still more fundamental reason behind his divergence from normal evangelical practice. It was that he knew that the argument from experience could be matched by the claims and apparent results of other 'gospels'. Do Christians claim to have obtained happiness and deliverance from fears? So do the converts to Christian Science and to other cults. 'Our case,' he was never to tire of saying, 'is not based upon experience, it is based upon great external facts.' The business of preaching is the proclamation of the revealed truths of gospel history – truths indeed confirmed by experience, but independent of experience in their objective reality. Compared with those truths concerning Christ, as he said on the first Sunday he visited Sandfields, all else is as worthless 'as paper is to gold'. His text that first November evening of 1926 remained his pole-star: 'I determined not to know anything among you, save Jesus Christ, and him crucified.'

'Whenever lamps burn low in the Church, and love waxes cold, and watchers slumber while the Bridegroom tarries, the Restorer and Sustainer of His people is always standing at the door. He can create fresh witnesses to Himself in the most unlikely quarters, even as He raised up Paul from among the Pharisees, and Luther from among the Mendicants. The Gospel of the grace of God has been disproved a great number of times – it has been assailed and wounded and beaten down and left for dead – but it survives by the power of an endless life. Amid fightings within and fears without the modern Church can still say, I know that my Redeemer liveth. Who can guess what swift, incalculable revival Christ has in store for His desponding people?'

JOHN HUTTON
in *The British Weekly*, January 7, 1926

8

Early Days at Sandfields

The first home of Martyn and Bethan Lloyd-Jones, situated a few hundred yards from the church, was scarcely the 'dockside cottage' which one newspaper reported, yet it was nothing more than the housing typical of many of the industrial parts of South Wales. 57 Victoria Road was a single-fronted terrace house, larger in its depth than in its breadth. There was a parlour or best-room at the front, a 'middle room' behind it (with a French window opening on to a small yard), and a living room and scullery-kitchen occupying the narrow oblong extremity of the house which lay furthest back from the front door. Up a staircase near the front-door there were three bedrooms and, in the eyes of some visitors, an amazingly small bathroom. The front of the house was almost immediately on the street and behind there was a small garden.

With one exception, the accommodation suited the young couple admirably. Dr Lloyd-Jones' conviction that a pastor should live among his people and be dependent upon the means which they provide was so strong that he had given all his savings to his mother before leaving London. It meant that for some years Bethan was to count every penny of her house-keeping money, an exercise which she did not regret. The one exception, which was to trouble Mrs Lloyd-Jones, related to the location. She had scarcely arrived in the district when a well-wisher, ignorant of the fact that she was terrified of the sea, told her, 'This is the third Aberavon, the other two are beneath the sands'! The manse was on the sea-ward side of Aberavon, and although the beach was more than a mile away there was little between them and the water except a few roads, flat ground and sand-hills. When south-west gales blew up the Bristol Channel and the sea could be heard pounding on the shore, she was filled with dread and foreboding – quite unsuspected by her busy and studious husband.

David Martyn Lloyd-Jones

The 'middle room' at 57 Victoria Road, ten feet by twelve, at once became the study, where the 300 to 400 books which Dr Lloyd-Jones had brought with him from London soon lined the walls. In a real sense that room was to become the centre of the work, not only as the place where young converts were to visit him in the years ahead, but more as his place of retreat where prayer, study and preparation for the pulpit occupied the best part of the hours of each day. Mornings, and often afternoons as well, were spent in the study, and though he did not work there after supper (about 8 p.m.) there would always be a book in his hands as he sat with Mrs Lloyd-Jones in the living room later in the evening.

In his judgment, this degree of time given to the preparation of his own mind and spirit was not a matter of mere preference but an absolute necessity for an effective ministry. Many years later he was to assert: 'You will always find that the men whom God has used signally have been those who have studied most, known their Scriptures best, and given time to preparation.'[1] Again, 'I am convinced a pastor must nourish his mind, it cannot be too well stocked.' His settled principle was that nothing must interfere with preparation for the pulpit. From the outset that was a practical necessity, for the four sermons preached in Sandfields, before his Induction as pastor, had exhausted his supply. Even on their honeymoon some time was given to the preparation of the sermons which would soon be required of him so regularly.[2]

Initially at Aberavon he attempted to write both sermons for Sunday in full – an average of nine, ten or more pages, closely written on both sides. The reason for the full manuscript was not a concern for a literary form, still less for something to read in the pulpit, it was rather to be sure that he was clear in the substance of his message. He believed that a preacher should know what he was going to say from the beginning to the end. Within weeks, however, he found it impossible to write two sermons in full and thus his settled habit for many years became to write one sermon fully, and the other – though he thought it out in detail – only to record in outline. At first the full sermon manuscript went with him into the pulpit, but he soon found

[1] *The Christian Soldier*, Ephesians 6:10–20, 1977, p. 135.
[2] Mrs Lloyd-Jones has never forgotten sitting, literally, at his feet in their hotel room, while he, almost thinking aloud, went over the main points of his sermon on 2 Timothy 1:7, 'For God hath not given us the spirit of fear; but of power, and of love, and of a sound mind'.

[154]

that practice inhibiting, and his custom became to read the fully-written sermon through some three times, and then to have no more than an outline of it with him when he was preaching. In his judgment, the evening sermons (which were more specifically intended for non-Christians) were the hardest to prepare; it was therefore generally these which were written in full. Once or twice when, relying on his 'feeling' for a text, he preached with an inadequately thought-out plan, and failed miserably. Generally his experience concurred with that of Henry Rees, one of the Methodist fathers who, when asked which of his sermons had been most honoured of God, replied, 'The ones I prepared most carefully'.[1]

By no means all his hours in the study were directly concerned with the pulpit. Chief place went to reading the Bible itself, and in the first instance, for his own spiritual help, not to 'find texts'. He aimed to go through the Scriptures every year, omitting nothing – 'That should be the very minimum of the preacher's Bible reading' – and his ability to quote Scripture from memory in the course of preaching was one consequence of the time given to this practice. It could be said of him, as John Foster said of Robert Hall, one of the greatest English preachers of the nineteenth century, 'He maintained through life so assiduous a practice of studying the Bible, that he had acquired a remarkable facility for citing from every part of it, in the course of his preaching, the passages most pertinent for evidence or enforcement of whatever he was advancing.' To aid the seriousness and frequency of his study of Scripture he resolutely avoided referring to a Bible Concordance during his early years at Sandfields.

In his reading of theology the Puritans already had a major place. His 'discovery' of Richard Baxter in 1925 had been followed by other seventeenth-century acquisitions purchased in second-hand bookshops in London, and notably in R. D. Dickinson's. Wedding presents from friends had included second-hand sets of the *Works* of

---

[1] 'The Spirit generally uses a man's best preparation. It is not the Spirit *or* preparation; it is preparation *plus* the unction and the anointing and that which the Holy Spirit alone can supply', *The Christian Soldier*, p. 135. Exceptions to this will be noted subsequently. With respect to his habit of writing sermons see *Preaching and Preachers*, pp. 215–16, where he says: 'I believe that one should be unusually careful in evangelistic sermons. That is why the idea that a fellow who is merely gifted with a certain amount of glibness of speech and self-confidence, and not to say cheek, can make an evangelist is all wrong. The greatest men should always be the evangelists. . . .'

John Owen and of Richard Baxter. In the course of time, Owen was to be preferred; but he always valued Baxter's *Christian Directory* . Criticism of the Puritans which he read in *The British Weekly* left him entirely undeterred. In those columns in 1926 Professor W. M. Macgregor depicted J. Gresham Machen (whose book *What is Faith?* had newly been published) as an exponent of seventeenth-century theology concerning which he wrote: 'The glow and wonder and evangelical freedom of the Reformation were then declining and a rather hard intellectualism, in which the notion of orthodoxy was paramount, was invading.'[1] After hearing many similar remarks in the course of his subsequent life, Dr Lloyd-Jones was still ready to confess in 1971 that love for Puritan authors 'governed' his whole ministry.[2] He urged upon ministerial students the reading of the Puritans to 'help you in general to understand and enjoy the Scriptures, and to prepare you for the pulpit. . . . Those men were preachers, they were practical, experimental preachers . . . as you read them you will find that they not only give you knowledge and information, they at the same time do something to you.'[3] He was speaking from experience.

Biography and church history were also constantly pursued from the time of his settlement at Sandfields. For sheer stimulus and enjoyment there were no volumes which he prized more highly than *Y Tadau Methodistaidd* which relate (in Welsh) the lives of the fathers of Welsh Calvinistic Methodism. They were constantly in his hands in the early years. In 1926 his interest in the eighteenth century had also been increased with the dis-covery that English Methodism revealed the same spiritual lessons as were evident in Wales. This interest was awakened through Southey's very inadequate biography of John Wesley, but this book led him on to Wesley's *Journals* which he was

[1] May 27, 1926, p. 149. Machen subsequently replied tersely: 'With regard to the deadness of the seventeenth century I do not know that *Pilgrim's Progress* is exactly dead. It seems to me to be very much alive. And it draws its life essentially from that "hard intellectualism" to which Professor Macgregor is so much opposed. Even the Shorter Catechism, I think, has more life in it than all the books expressive of a "vital", as distinguished from a doctrinal Christianity, that ever were written.' *Ibid.*, p. 517.
[2] In his opening remarks on 'Puritanism and Its Origins', a Westminster Conference address in 1971.
[3] *Preaching and Preachers*, pp. 174–75.

always to acknowledge helped him much at the outset of his ministry. Before his settlement at Sandfields he wrote to E. T. Rees on December 29, 1926:

'I have been reading, recently, Southey's Life of John Wesley and have been greatly impressed with it. I see more clearly than ever that every true spiritual revival is not the result of man's witness, but is determined by God. Again I say that what we have to do is to prepare ourselves, and live in such a way that we shall not be found wanting when that time arrives.'

In the course of his reading it was Dr Lloyd-Jones' habit to make very few notes. He relied largely upon his memory. Because he had already made up his mind that he was not going to be a writer, he made no attempt to build up a stock of references for subsequent literary use. 'I have always believed,' he once said, 'that the business of reading is to make one *think*, to stimulate; the idea of obtaining quotations was almost repulsive to me.'

The one thing which he never failed to write down was any suggestion for a future sermon which came to him in the course of reading. He would record the idea at once in skeleton form and in this way was constantly accumulating 'a little pile of skeletons'. No preacher, he believed, should 'be frantic on a Saturday with no texts or sermons for the Sunday, and trying desperately to get hold of something'.

Naturally, the new pastor at Sandfields had no experience or instruction in the running of a church. He recalled that when Peter Hughes Griffiths had appointed him Superintendent of the Sunday School at Charing Cross Chapel he had told him that the secret of success in all affairs connected with church life was that the minister should not be immersed in petty details and routine and should be concerned only with the larger strategy. That was all very well; but there were many practical matters, ranging from the conduct of weddings to presbytery responsibilities, upon which he needed help. At his first wedding service he was still waiting for a bride in white to enter and walk down the aisle, with her bridesmaids, when he became aware that the lady was already standing before him, quietly dressed in a navy-blue suit! Happily, the truth had dawned upon him before the pause caused panic! It was in this practical area that the friendship of David Williams, minister of the Welsh-speaking Carmel Calvinistic Methodist Church in Aberavon, contributed much. Williams introduced his young neighbour to many details of church order and procedure with which he was unfamiliar. He also provided him with a service book in Welsh and English and guided him through such technicalities as would normally have been learned at college.

In addition to the Sunday services Dr Lloyd-Jones took a Bible Class during Sunday School on Sunday afternoons. One man who joined the class in 1928 recalled that it met in the small kitchen down some steps from the church-hall, and although there were only about a dozen present at that time, the space was so confined that he had to sit on a board placed across the sink!

While there was no mid-week preaching at Sandfields there were three evening meetings during the course of the week. These were, a prayer-meeting at 7.15 p.m. on Monday, a Fellowship meeting on Wednesday and 'the Brotherhood' for men on Saturday.

From the outset the Prayer Meeting was an accurate gauge of the spiritual life of the church. At one point before the First World War, Robert Lody, one of the older members, remembered how only five of them had gathered round the stove in the hall for prayer on Monday evenings. In February 1927 the number was perhaps around 40 and included about half-a-dozen who had been converted in the Salvation Army and were the brightest Christians in the church. 'They had very little understanding,' Dr Lloyd-Jones recalled of this half-dozen, 'but they were warm-hearted and a great help to me.' This was for him an important qualification, to be added to remarks we have already noted on the discouragement which the former pastor had experienced. Amidst the difficulties there were redeeming features and from the beginning Dr Lloyd-Jones knew that he had 'something to build on'.

The Wednesday evening meeting and the Saturday Brotherhood both took on an entirely new form. The Fellowship was an adaptation of the old Methodist *Seiat* when Christians met together to speak of their spiritual experiences and of experimental religion,[1] yet it was more than that, for one primary intention in Dr Lloyd-

---

[1] The purpose and form of the *Seiat* is well described in William Williams' book *The Experience Meeting* (translated by Mrs D. M. Lloyd-Jones and published in 1973). In an introduction to this English edition Dr Lloyd-Jones pressed upon ministers 'the importance of introducing such meetings into the life of their churches'.

Jones' mind was to convey instruction by open discussion on a question which anyone could propose at the beginning of the meeting. The only stipulation was that the question should concern a practical area of Christian living, such as 'What is growth in grace?' 'How do we deal with temptation and sin?' 'How should we read the Bible?' Once Dr Lloyd-Jones, as chairman, had accepted the question, instead of proceeding to propose answers he would encourage either the questioner himself or others in the meeting to speak. If any in attendance attempted to short-circuit the discussion by a simplistic answer which ignored difficulties, he would quickly bring the speaker to see that the question had aspects of which he was not yet aware. Only one question was taken each evening. Unused though the people were to such a meeting, it soon aroused much interest and began to teach people how to think about the Scriptures with much greater care and intelligence.

The Fellowship Meeting was not a catechising exercise and yet it provided the minister with most valuable insight into the various spiritual needs which existed among the people. One early practical result was that he devised a daily Bible-reading plan for members of the church. This was only to last until he discovered what he considered to be the superior plan of Robert Murray M'Cheyne, which he adopted and urged upon the people.

Although Dr Lloyd-Jones had at first been hesitant about continuing 'the Brotherhood', it was to become one of the most important of all the meetings. It had originated in the desire to provide an alternative to men who might otherwise go to a public house, or who, no longer wishing to go to such a place, had time on their hands on a Saturday night. They might sing, talk or pray together in an informal manner. From the outset Dr Lloyd-Jones determined that it should be a teaching meeting, and initially it appears that, with this in view, he sometimes gave an address. One evening his subject was 'Purity'. Instead of dealing with the form of moral behaviour normally associated with that subject he went to the foundations with an exposition of the meaning of original sin. Despite the slender education of some of his hearers it was teaching they could all follow:

'The problem of life, my friends, is not individual sins but Sin itself, the whole background – the thing itself, the desire process which is the cause of all these local and minor manifestations and eruptions. And that is our problem. We are not here to teach and lecture men and women about individual sins you may control and conquer. You are still a sinner, your nature is still evil and will remain so, until by the death of Christ and the resurrection you are born again and receive a new nature. Our trouble is that our nature is evil; it really does not matter how it may manifest itself.

'What is our duty then? Well, it is this. Before we talk to anyone we must find out first whether he believes in Christ or not. Is he a new man? If he is not, then he is still struggling with flesh and blood. Are we to lecture him on his sins and to preach morality to him? No, we are to preach Christ to him and do all we can to convert him, for what he needs is a new nature, a new outlook, a new mind. It is no use our expecting to find figs on a thorn bush, however much we may treat and tend and care for it. The trouble is the root. We are wasting our time and neglecting our duty by preaching morality to a lost world. For what the world needs is life, new life, and it can be found in Christ alone.

'For purity, as I say, is something for Christians only, it is impossible to anyone else. Sanctification is impossible without conversion, and first things must come first everywhere.'

Addresses like this, however, were not continued at the Brotherhood as Dr Lloyd-Jones decided to follow the same discussion practice as on Wednesdays, with one difference: amongst the men on Saturday nights he would encourage a wider range of questions, particularly problems more directly theological. So while practical Christian living was foremost on Wednesdays, the Saturday meeting centred on matters of doctrine and biblical understanding. It was intellectually demanding – in the words of one attender, 'a kind of spiritual University' – and yet the opposite, it should be added, of anything purely scholastic. Unimportant questions of mere theological interest were given no hearing by the chairmen. 'Under the Doctor's leadership,' one of the members recalled, 'the Saturday meeting truly became *the* Brotherhood.' A deeper bond developed among the men which began to be reflected in the whole life of the church. When the summer of 1927 came, the day-outing of the Brotherhood was anticipated with new enthusiasm, and with Llangeitho as the destination it turned out to be the first outing with a serious purpose: their leader had devised a way to give the men an insight into the church history of which they knew so very little![1]

So there was a guided tour of Daniel Rowland's village with on-the-spot-descriptions of what had happened there two centuries before. From that time onwards, for many of the men, the name 'Calvinistic Methodist' ceased to be a mere denominational label.

Among the things dropped by Dr Lloyd-Jones during his first year at Sandfields was a candidates' class for church membership. This institution existed throughout the denomination and almost automatically numbers of young people passed through it into the communicant membership of the church. Sometimes they joined the class at the suggestion of the minister, sometimes at their own suggestion, but seldom did their approach arise out of any spiritual concern, or out of any evidence of a saving knowledge of Christ. Moreover, Dr Lloyd-Jones came to see the candidates' class as not only spiritually unprofitable but – by its identification of entrance upon church membership with teenage years – positively erroneous. He spoke lucidly of this matter in what was probably the first book review he ever wrote. The book was A. T. Schofield's *Christian Sanity*. Much of it he was ready to commend. His strongest criticism was reserved for the lesson drawn from Dr Starbuck's figures as to the average age-incidence of conversion, which showed that 'nearly 75 per cent out of 1,000 Christians questioned were converted before the age of 20':

'From this, Schofield tends, as many others definitely do, to conclude that conversion is somehow related to puberty and its concomitant changes. One wonders whether there is not a grave danger here of confusing "confirmation or acceptance into full membership" with "conversion". To me, there is nothing which is quite so pernicious and detrimental to the true interests of Christianity as this association of "conversion" with a certain age period. There is no question but that this teaching is responsible for all the concentration upon "the young people" which characterises our church work in these days, and makes many a minister and deacon say woefully: "The young people and children are our only hope – we must concentrate upon them." Such statements and such a belief show a lack of faith

---

[1] The ignorance of the average church member on this subject is hardly surprising when it is remembered that the ignorance of ministerial candidates concerning their denominational history had been openly deplored in 1925 by one of the leaders of Welsh Presbyterianism.

and set a limit upon the power of God. The Gospel recognises no such limits – there is hope to the end, to the eleventh hour. There is as much hope today for the middle-aged and the aged as there is for the young people. It may be more difficult to teach morality and ethics to the older people or to teach one's own special fads and fancies with respect to the Christian life, but to "The Help of the helpless" and "Hope of the hopeless" there are no such distinctions. Yea, indeed, the besetting sin of most who are concerned in Christian work is to concentrate on one particular age or one particular truth instead of delivering "the whole counsel of God" to all and sundry whoever or whatever they may be. Concentration upon the young is a large part of the genius and success of Roman Catholicism, but surely it is the very antithesis of the genius of Protestantism. It is one thing to produce a religious man – men can do that – but it takes the power of God in Jesus Christ to produce a Christian man, and there is no limit to that power.'[1]

The truth is that there was no means employed at Sandfields to *bring* people to confess Christ. The new pastor believed that, if that work was to be done truly, then only God could do it. At the same time, however, he thought it well to continue the 'after meeting' on Sunday evenings. At this meeting, which lasted for only a few minutes at the conclusion of the service, he indicated that if any who were present wished to become members of the church they should raise their hand. There was no singing and no pressure of any kind. If any did so indicate, Dr Lloyd-Jones would subsequently speak to them alone.

A number of months were to pass after Dr Lloyd-Jones' settlement at Sandfields before there was any apparent response to his preaching. From the outset the congregations had quietly increased, but eighteen months were to pass before the gallery came into use. In July 1927 there was the first instance of an individual expressing his concern to join the church, but there was nothing particularly noteworthy about his case.

The real break-through, in fact, was to come from among those who were already within the membership of the church and this was led by E. T. Rees, the Church Secretary, himself. Mr Rees's unbounded enthusiasm at the coming of their new pastor to

[1] *Yr Efengylydd*, January 1929, pp. 7–8.

Early Days at Sandfields

Sandfields had continued unabated despite the degree of puzzlement he was beginning to feel. When Dr and Mrs Lloyd-Jones left for their annual holiday in August 1927 – first at Newcastle Emlyn and then at London – the correspondence which continued between them was indicative of the bond which had grown up.

Dr Lloyd-Jones wrote on August 9, 1927, from London:

'You must forgive me for not writing from Newcastle Emlyn. The country was so good and some friends were kind enough to take us about so much, that I just did nothing at all. You know that feeling that we get occasionally, particularly on holiday, in which we take a kind of brutal delight in saying to ourselves, "Well now, I'm on holiday and there is nothing that I *must* do. . . ."

'I have thought a lot about you during the past week and of all the things that have happened to us during the past six to eight months.

'I feel we ought to thank God for having brought us together and for having given us the privilege of working together in the Great Cause. I have a curious feeling these days which I have never experienced on any previous holiday – I somehow cannot relax and forget my work as I used to. The present seems an enforced pause prior to still greater effort. When I think of our little church in Sandfields, of the love and the fellowship, and of those men who are standing on the doorstep, I feel that it is indeed a community which cannot be matched anywhere.

'My weekend in Llangeitho was extremely pleasant – in many ways never to be forgotten. The shoe-maker, who was away when the Brotherhood was there, has returned and was in his best form. Many complimentary remarks were passed concerning "the nice men from Aberavon". The main impression left was that an exceptionally fine spirit was manifest between the men themselves. What better impression could have been left!'

In a reply to this letter, E. T. Rees expressed his doubts about the two venues which the Lloyd-Joneses had chosen for holidays – places where they were surrounded by relatives. To this his minister replied in the course of another August letter:

'I think that you are probably right in what you say about the respective merits of Newcastle Emlyn and London for holiday purposes. The last night we were at Newcastle Emlyn, I got to bed at 5 a.m.! Your words therefore were most appropriate.

'There is absolutely nothing of interest to tell you. My days are spent in a capricious manner. I am ashamed to say that I have only succeeded in being down-stairs before lunch, twice, since we left Aberavon! The rest of the day, I lounge about, doing nothing – my brain at the moment is probably of the consistency of a turnip.'

A further letter from 'E.T.' brought news of the Brotherhood to which Dr Lloyd-Jones responded in a final holiday letter of August 23:

'Naturally, I was very interested in all you had to say about the Brotherhood etc; very glad you had a good meeting on Saturday night. What is the matter with "M", I wonder? there seems to be a certain bitterness in his character which is holding him back. Nevertheless, I feel sure it will go, if we will only be patient with him.

'The young man with the collar is a real surprise – I felt sure we had seen the last of him.

'I don't know whether I told you that old Tucker had been down to see me the morning we left Aberavon. He said that he had seriously considered joining our church as a member, but had decided that his so doing might prove to be more of a hindrance than a help! Would that certain others were equally scrupulous in this respect.'

Perhaps Dr Lloyd-Jones did not altogether appreciate at this point the struggle which E. T. Rees was having in his own mind. Certainly the Church Secretary believed in a type of evangelical religion, but he was later to feel that he had been as ignorant of the doctrine of regeneration as Nicodemus and his long studies in Socialism had led him to suppose that the coming of the kingdom of God could scarcely succeed simply by the rebirth of individuals. But under the new preaching he was now hearing, there came increasing doubts about the rightness of his position.

The crisis came on Sunday October 2, 1927, when the sermon was on the doubt of John the Baptist which had led him to send the message to Jesus, 'Art thou he that should come, or do we look for another?' (Matt. 11:2–5). Dr Lloyd-Jones argued that the meaning of Christ's reply to John's question – 'The blind receive their sight, and the lame walk, the lepers are cleansed, and the deaf hear, the dead are raised up and the poor have the gospel preached to them' – was proof that the Baptist's problem arose out of his wrong views of what Christ had come to do. John did not appreciate the true significance of what Christ was actually doing and he supposed that the Messiah would have made political deliverance from Rome one of his priorities. 'So great was the tyranny of his pre-conceived ideas,' said the preacher, 'that he even began to doubt what he had actually seen with his own eyes and what he had actually heard with his own ears.' As the sermon proceeded, E. T. Rees' whole system of thought finally collapsed and even from the pulpit the preacher could see from the look on his face what was happening. 'I shall always remember how you rushed to speak to me before I was down from the pulpit,' Dr Lloyd-Jones was to comment twenty years later.

From that October Sunday in 1927, E. T. Rees' commitment to Christ made it impossible for him to speak for Socialism again and he left the Labour Party. Suddenly he had wider and more glorious horizons of thought and for the first time he could enter wholly into the changes which the last eight months had brought to the life of the church. Recalling the beginnings of this new era he was to say many years later:

'At the time of Dr Lloyd-Jones' coming to Sandfields there was an awful economic depression in the country and certainly in the Port Talbot area. It would be true to say that the majority of men were out of work. They were on the dole. I remember boys and girls in school who were affected by it all, in spite of the fact that their mothers sacrificed their breakfasts for them. I remember the efforts we made in soup kitchens, and the big dole queues when that iniquitous question was asked men, "Have you been genuinely seeking work?" There was no work to be obtained! That was the atmosphere, that was the setting, that was the environment. Yet this man dared to preach what would be called a simple gospel. God honoured his preaching and not only honoured his preaching but honoured his courage in reorganising the church activities. We believed in Sandfields, at that time, that to get a few pounds to meet the pressing debt, and to offset the poor collections, we should have in the church a dramatic society, a football team, and such like. Why, we even believed it was necessary to have temperance teaching in order that boys and girls might grow up to be sober. But this man believed that the preaching of the gospel was enough; "these little side lines", as he would call them, were unnecessary. How well I remember him telling me one night, "Look here, you can finish with that Band of Hope, don't waste your time with it!"'

Speaking of the slow change in the life of the congregation, Dr Lloyd-Jones recorded:

'It took some time. I was there from February to July without a single conversion. The first conversion was in July and that was not a striking one. Then we went away on holiday. After we had come back E. T. Rees was converted on the first Sunday in October and that did seem to start something. It went on from there.'

But Dr Lloyd-Jones knew that more was happening even in 1927 than was apparent, for his own wife had come into a state of concern and conviction. Having attended church and prayer-meetings from childhood, Bethan Lloyd-Jones had always believed that she was a Christian. Not until she heard Martyn preach for the first time (on his second visit to Sandfields in December 1926) was she confronted, in his sermon on Zacchaeus, with an insistence that all men are equally in need of salvation from sin. The message shook her, even frightened her, and she almost resented the teaching which appeared to place her in the same condition as those who had no religion at all. In a sense she had always feared God; her life was upright, and yet she knew that she had no personal consciousness of the forgiveness of sins, no sense of inward joyful communion with Christ. In Mrs Lloyd-Jones' own words:

'I was for two years under Martyn's ministry before I really understood what the gospel was. I used to listen to him on Sunday morning and I used to feel, Well, if this is Christianity I don't really know anything about it. On Sunday night I used to pray that somebody would be converted; I thought you had to be a drunkard or a prostitute to be converted. I remember how I used to rejoice to see drunkards become Christians and envy them with all my heart, because there they were, full of joy, and free, and here I was in such a different condition.

'I recall sitting in the study at 57 Victoria Road and I was unhappy. I suppose it was conviction. I felt a burden of sin, and I shall always remember Martyn saying, as he looked through his books, "Read this!" He gave me John Angell James' *The Anxious Enquirer Directed*. I have never forgotten what I read in that book. It showed me how wrong was the idea that my sin could be greater than the merit of the blood of Christ – His death was well able to clear all my sins away. There, at last, I found release and I was so happy.'

*   *   *

For the first eight months of Dr Lloyd-Jones' ministry at Sandfields he continued in the status of lay-pastor. His position was indeed unusual. According to the prevalent view in his denomination, anyone lacking regular ministerial training was liable to be singularly deficient in qualities necessary for a sustained pulpit ministry. Two or three years of theological training were judged to be necessities. The fact that Dr Lloyd-Jones was to be settled in what was virtually a mission-hall situation had helped the authorities to waive their usual rule. But it was almost immediately apparent to a number that Dr Lloyd-Jones' services would be required beyond Aberavon, that even at Sandfields he would be hindered if he were not ordained, and that, accordingly, his lay status should be altered without delay. The case aroused no little interest. The anonymous writer of Church Notes in the *Western Mail*, at the beginning of February 1927, drew attention to what he considered as 'the haste evidenced by some leaders to secure the ordination of Dr Martin Lloyd-Jones to the ministry of the Presbyterian Church'. In the correspondence columns of the same paper on February 5 the matter was followed up at some length by D. Winter Lewis who, while professing a neutral standpoint on the issue, underlined the difficulties:

'Dr Jones claims no training in Divinity, and has fulfilled none of the requirements necessary for recognition as minister of any English Christian Church. Yet it is desired to hasten his ordination. What will the Association do? It is this that concerns us. The Association has its rules and regulations. Will it circumvent them or discard them altogether?'

The same writer pointed out that only the previous summer the ordination of an applicant who was a graduate of Cardiff and Cambridge had been opposed by Principal Owen Prys 'because he had read Divinity at Cambridge and not at Bala'. 'What,' he asked, 'will Principal Owen Prys, the president of the Forward Movement, do in the case of one who has had no Divinity training, and who has

[167]

not spent time at Bala or Aberystwyth? We appreciate that Dr Jones finds common ground with the Divinity students in his willingness to make sacrifices. But is this sufficient ground to qualify for ordination as an efficient Christian minister? The question must be, not what a man can do, but what has he done. It will be interesting to see what line the Association will take in this case, and whether it will allow ordination next April.'

When the next Association (*Sasiwn*) of South Wales met at Gilfach, Bargoed, on April 19, requests were received from the Forward Movement, the English Presbytery of West Glamorgan, and the London Presbytery, that Dr Lloyd-Jones should be ordained at once in view of the need at Sandfields.[1] Procedure was complicated by the fact that the denomination had recently set up a Board for the examination of ministerial candidates as the feeling among the 'experts' in theological training was that the judgment of presbyteries on the gifts of a preacher might not be enough. No sooner was Lloyd-Jones' name raised in the Association than one member, who was no supporter of the new arrangement, enquired sarcastically whether the candidate had been before the Board! He had not, although the chairman of the Board was actually R. J. Rees, the Superintendent of the Forward Movement. The Moderator of the Association, Philip Jones of Porthcawl, an able preacher in his seventies, famous for his wit, and also no great patron of the Board, did not intend to be held up by such a detail. He declared (in Welsh) 'The Sasiwn is bigger than the Board in the same way that a house is bigger than a table!'

The Association proceeded to carry a proposal that Dr Lloyd-Jones should be ordained at the next Ordination Association and all rose to their feet as Philip Jones called Dr Lloyd-Jones forward to be welcomed as a ministerial candidate.

There was disquiet, however, in some quarters at this enthusiasm and waiving of proper procedures. At the next Association at Ystradgynlais at the end of August the half-ordained candidate for the ministry had to appear for questioning along with other regular applicants, with the peculiarity of the situation underlined by the fact that he was given the honour (usually accorded to mature ministers) both of preaching in one of the English chapels during the

---

[1] The decisions of the Glamorgan and London Presbyteries had been taken on January 13 and March 30, 1927, respectively.

Association period and also of addressing the Young People's Meeting along with Professor T. A. Levi of Aberystwyth. The examination proved to be almost as perfunctory as the one in Llangeitho Chapel when he had become a communicant with his brothers in 1914. There were nine 'applicants for ordination' present and the questions on matters of doctrine and experience were customarily one of the dullest parts of such proceedings. But when one of the examiners asked Dr Lloyd-Jones to 'give a word about his experience', he responded with such earnestness concerning his call to the ministry, and spoke of his assurance of salvation 'without a doubt' in such terms that the decorum of the occasion was broken as 'a brother shouted out until the building reverberated, "Praise Him," "Praise Him"!' The correspondent who reported this in Y *Goleuad* confessed: 'I have seen several meetings of this type, but this was the strangest yet. Who has been in a meeting to enquire of the religious experience of the applicants, where the congregation is in tears, and others breaking out in praise? The same writer considered that the occasion might have been called 'the meeting of the Phillipses' as, of the nine applicants, one (John Phillips) was a son of Evan Phillips, the late eminent minister of Newcastle Emlyn, another a grandson (Ieuan Phillips) and a third was married to his grand-daughter!

The conclusion of the matter came in London in the last week of October 1927 when the Association met in the English capital for the first time. With four to five hundred representatives, plus members of the Calvinistic Methodist churches in London wishing to attend, there was no Welsh Chapel large enough to accommodate the Association, of which the proceedings were to run from Monday the 24th to Thursday the 27th. As a result, Whitefield's historic Chapel on Tottenham Court Road was borrowed for the occasion. As at Ystradgynlais, Dr Lloyd-Jones was asked to address the Youth Meeting, along with two other speakers, on the Monday night. The three speakers were given the same subject, 'Life without Christ is Incomplete', but by the time that the visitor from 'Aberavon Mission Hall' (as newspapers described him) had finished, it was clear they did not all have the same message. The Reverend T. Nefyn Williams, who spoke first, believed that 'every man in life had an ideal and it was the striving towards this highest ideal that made true life and made life beautiful'. The next speaker, Dr R. R. Davies of Neath, believed that 'Christ gave man the measure of his manhood' and concluded by asking all young persons 'to stand up to show their obedience to their true religion' – which done, the whole congregation spontaneously burst into the singing of an old Welsh hymn! The final speaker's theme must have been very new to a number of hearers. If a moral life was a complete life, Dr Lloyd-Jones argued, then there was no need of Christ. To think that Christianity meant carrying out the ten commandments was a direct challenge to the doctrines of the Cross and of the Resurrection. Morality was not godliness; Saul of Tarsus was the highest example of a moral man and yet he was lost and miserable. Nor was Christianity mere belief in Christ. 'Is belief in Christ sufficient to make a man's life complete? I say emphatically it is not. Belief in Christ as a person outside yourself will not make your life complete. Christ himself must enter within.'[1] Whitefield's message of regeneration was again being heard in his old pulpit!

The ordination service was held on the night of Wednesday, October 26. *Y Goleuad* noted that Dr Lloyd-Jones' ordination in 'Whitefield's Tabernacle – his great hero' – was a pleasing coincidence and that in view of his 'great longing for revival' the subject chosen for the address by T. E. Davies of Treorchy, 'The Church Longing for its Spring' was very fitting. Dr Lloyd-Jones, however, was not there to hear it, having left immediately after the formalities of the ordination.

*   *   *

There was good reason why, on that evening of October 26, Dr Lloyd-Jones did not wait for the sermon in Whitefield's Tabernacle. Family-wise the autumn of 1927 was perhaps the most difficult they ever had to face. Many weeks before the birth of their first infant it was apparent that the birth could not be a normal one. On the advice of a Swansea specialist, Bethan Lloyd-Jones had moved to her parents in London in late September in order to have the very best attention when the Caesarian-section delivery was necessary. The day coincided with her husband's ordination and although baby Elizabeth arrived safely in the morning he had still reason to be concerned about his wife's condition as he hurried from Tottenham Court Road to the hospital.[2]

[1] My quotations are taken from the column entitled 'Sasiwn in London' in the *Western Mail*, October 25, 1927. It seems that the reporter was somewhat confused over Dr Lloyd-Jones' denominational status; he reported that Dr Lloyd-Jones 'will be fully ordained this week'!

[2] The little girl born that day, and named after her father's and mother's grandmothers, made headlines when the Welsh papers, on the following day, gave the news of the arrival of 'the Ordination Baby' – a term which stuck for some time.

For another month Bethan had to remain convalescent in London, with Martyn paying frequent visits in between the work at Sandfields, as well as preaching engagements in other places. The anxiety and burden of those weeks was shared by many within the church and not least by E. T. Rees, who was now rejoicing in his new-found spiritual liberty. The parlour light often burned late at Rees' home in Glen View Terrace as the two men talked together, and on each visit to London Dr Lloyd-Jones did not fail to send the church Secretary the latest news.

Writing from Vincent Square, Westminster, early in November 1927, he reported Bethan's progress, and went on: 'London is as usual – rush, bustle, excitement, etc., all of which depresses me. It seems so superficial and hopeless. What a difference Sandfields makes with its thoroughly *fresh* air!' Even so, he confessed, 'The thought of having to leave here on Saturday almost dismays me, but I shall have to pull myself together and face it.' There was, of course, also news of the new arrival: 'Elizabeth is in great form. I am beginning to feel that more attention should be paid to the Juniors in Sandfield, E.T.!'

The most memorable of these letters came later in the month:

> Bro Dawel
> Harrow
> Middlesex
> Nov. 22nd, 1927

My dear E.T.,

There are times when I wonder as to whether or not I am a commercial traveller – so varied are the places from which I write to my friends!

But there are excellent signs now which indicate that this constant rushing backwards and forwards is to come to an end, for Bethan is really very much better. She gets up each day for five or six hours after tea and today I got her to get up in the morning also. She looks and feels well, although, as is but natural, she feels somewhat weak and giddy at times.

As for Elizabeth, she is doing really well – has gained six ounces during the past week and looks as chubby and as happy as old Prytherch of Swansea looks when he is feeling particularly well. I feel a sense of profound thankfulness to God for his Mercy and Love towards us – which I, at least, in no way have merited.

Now, with this new responsibility and with thoughts that inevitably arise in connection with it, I find myself, at times, reviewing the whole of my faith and belief, delving at times into matters which I profoundly believe it is the very essence of faith not to examine, finding myself in many ways unworthy of my calling – indeed at times, finding nothing whatsoever to recommend myself as a preacher of the gospel, and going on and on until I again reach bedrock in the grace of God, which amazes me more and more. My experience at Bridgend last Wednesday added to all this.[1] Never, do I think, have I been so conscious of the Power of the Word and the Gale of the Spirit. It is exceedingly difficult to go on living after such an experience, especially difficult to go on preaching. But there it is, I had to preach twice the next day and the commendation of the various people at Tonyrefail who came to speak to me almost amazed me.

Of course, I know that one should not judge and I try my best not to. Blessings are controlled by God and not by man. Well, that has been my state, and if you have felt that I have been unduly sensitive and have displayed a certain amount of acrimony in my spirit, I beg of you to bear with me. Yes, E.T., we receive these things, as Paul says, "in earthen vessels, that the excellency of the power may be of God, and not of us". It is not surprising that the vessel should crack occasionally, is it? It is no wonder that "we must be born again", the "old man" could never stand it. But I must stop this. You have a great heart and there is never a day but that I thank God for you.

Bethan joins me in sending her best love to Mrs Rees, Linda and yourself.

Yours very sincerely
Martyn

Early in December Mrs Lloyd-Jones and Elizabeth arrived home and by Christmas were both out to church. That same month brought one of the most unusual occasions in Dr Lloyd-Jones' ministry as he went to speak at his old school at Tregaron on their Annual Prize Day. Perhaps it was S. M. Powell, his former history master, who was initially responsible for renewing the contact, for when Powell had heard of the settlement of his old pupil at Port Talbot he had written to one of Martyn's uncles at Llwyncadfor. The letter of the man who first introduced Martyn Lloyd-Jones to the Life of Howell Harris is worthy of preservation:

[1] The text was probably Mark 9:29 '. . . This kind can come forth by nothing, but by prayer and fasting', as his sermon notes record he preached on this at Bridgend in November 1927.

Gernos
Tregaron
Cards
Jan. 27, 1927.

Dear Mr Evans

Could you send me the address of Dr Martin Lloyd-Jones at Port Talbot, as I want it for a particular purpose?

If you do not know it and perhaps he has no permanent address yet – could you kindly give me the address of Mrs Lloyd-Jones, his mother?

I used to know it and have been under that hospitable roof, but I am not sure of it now. So I shall be much obliged if you will kindly jot one of the addresses down and send it me. You will probably guess that I am the son of Blaenywern and that your three nephews were some of my favourite pupils.

I am so glad to find that Martin and Vincent are thoroughbreds: there is a strong strain of the Llwyncadfor stock in them! Harold was as true to type as either of the two and would have been a strong character and he *was* a strong character as a matter of fact.

I often wonder how this turn in Martin's life appears to his family. You would be surprised at the amount of discussion there is in this district with regard to the step he has taken. Personally, when my opinion is asked I make no bones about it. I am very proud to have been his teacher and to find him a man of such high ideals. It is such a rare thing among us that it takes away our breath.

I hope you will not mind my writing at such length to you but when I get on this subject, I get rather eloquent in spite of myself.

I am not quite sure which of you is at Llwyncadfor, but you are all related in the same way.

With kind regards.

Yours sincerely
S. M. Powell.

Back at Tregaron for the Prize Giving on December 21, Dr Lloyd-Jones was welcomed, not only by Mr Powell but also by G. T. Lewis, then in his thirty-first year as headmaster of the County School. Mr Lewis' address on the occasion contained the usual headmaster's comments. He noted a certain decline in numbers due to the setting up of a Central school at Lampeter and went on to speak of a new arrangement whereby pupils from a distance coming to Tregaron could be brought by bus every morning. Among distinctions recorded by former pupils, Mr Lewis told the gathering, there was now something new to report: 'For the first time two of their old pupils had entered the mission field, the Reverend Martyn Lloyd-Jones, M.D., late of Llangeitho, being in charge of a home Centre, under the Presbyterian Forward Movement at Aberavon, and Nurse Winifred Mary Jones, Neuaddlas, accepted by the Presbyterian mission field of India.' The Chairman, Mrs Morgan of Llanddewi Brefi, gave her welcome to Dr Lloyd-Jones who, she said, having reached 'a high position in the medical world had obeyed the injunction, "Follow me", and had given up his profession to enter the Christian ministry'. Mrs Morgan also 'asked parents not to expect every child to be a Dr Martin Lloyd-Jones'!

Without referring to his work at Aberavon, Dr Lloyd-Jones proceeded to speak on the theme of true education. The preparation for life given at Tregaron County School, he declared, was a necessary safeguard against 'the tyranny of knowledge':

'The mere fact that a man was a B.Sc. did not mean that he was a scientist. There was great danger in thinking that people who read a lot were great thinkers. The more they read the less they thought, and the more ready they were to accept the views of other people. Speaking broadly, he feared that people today were less cultured than those of twenty years ago. The most truly cultured people he had met were not those to be found in universities, but the people he had met in Llangeitho and Tregaron, who had not received any special education. There was no real value in education unless it helped to build character. . . . It was not what one knew of geometry, history, mathematics, and chemistry that mattered, but what one knew of life and men. A cultured man was one who thought. He wished to pay a tribute to the school for the training he had received there, and to the Headmaster for the way he used to ignore the syllabus, and instead of teaching geometry deliver a sermon, and to Mr S. M. Powell for jumping from the Reformation to the Methodist Revival. While at school these things appeared as madness to him, but he had since discovered there was a method in this madness. He had received far more guidance from these side-paths along which he was led than from the orthodox teaching. He was convinced that the school gave its pupils a wider basis of culture than any other school in Wales, and he hoped that this tradition would be maintained.'[1]

*   *   *

[1] Report in the *Welsh Gazette*, December 29, 1927.

Among the things which had disappeared in the new era at Sandfields were special services for anniversaries, but when the first Sunday of February 1928, was past, Dr Lloyd-Jones dropped E. T. Rees a note on February 7 which underlined that the occasion had not been forgotten:

'I thought as I sat in the pulpit on Sunday night, during the collection, of all the things that have happened during this first year. I thanked God for all, but believe me when I say that, above all, I thanked Him for you. I often try to picture what it would have been were you not the secretary here. Of one thing I shall always remain quite sure, that what made me "fall in love" with Sandfields when I came that first Saturday was the personality and the character of him who I had anticipated was at least a middle-aged man.

'I am quite sure of that. That first surprise, filling my heart with joy as it did, and removing all sorts of obstacles and questionings, paved the way to all the things that followed.

'All I can say is that you have become to me, a brother. . . . Is it not really wonderful? Especially when we realise that it is because we both love Him and found ourselves together at His feet.'

What E. T. Rees thought, and the congregation thought, of their minister appears in a letter written in March 1928 to Mrs Lloyd-Jones, Senior, in London. Mrs Lloyd-Jones had already visited Sandfields more than once and such was her regard for the church Secretary that he had almost become another son. Early in March Dr Lloyd-Jones had been forced to take a short break from Aberavon, and no sooner was he back than E. T. Rees hastened to send his mother the news:

'Martyn returned from Gower yesterday looking really well, full of colour and energy. I am quite sure you would be pleased with your boy. I am really delighted to see him looking so well. It has been such an anxious time. How we have missed him! How the men and women have talked about his absence and prayed unceasingly for him! Tonight at the Brotherhood and tomorrow all day at the Services he will have a welcome far warmer and certainly more real than you London folk gave that Afghan King this week.'

David Martyn Lloyd-Jones

It seems that the congregation had just completed a period of special prayer, concerning which the same correspondent continues:

'It has been a wonderful week, truly stirring in the very extreme. How I wished Martyn had been here to have seen the fruits of his labours of the past twelve months! I know what you must feel concerning him, my dear Mrs Lloyd-Jones, and his leaving you and a great career: but when we face the ultimate reality of it all, what is it compared with the wonderful work he is doing in leading human souls to what is best, and making what is best out of them? You should be the proudest mother in Britain today, for Martyn is being blessed by God in the *greatest* of *all* work – a fisher of men.'

To the Editor of Y *Goleuad*

'Sir, – I read the Rev Eliseus Howells' article on Dr Martyn Lloyd-Jones with interest. He refers to 1927 as the year in which Professor David Williams and Dr T. C. Williams left us. The Association in the South was held in my old church at Crickhowell in June 1927; Thomas Charles Williams preached twice in English on I Corinthians 1:2, and Romans 6:21, and this was his last appearance at the Association in the South. Dr Martyn Lloyd-Jones spoke in the young people's meeting as well as in the open air. Thomas Charles stayed with me, and Dr Martyn Lloyd-Jones came in and they both had a most interesting conversation. Thomas Charles felt that the physician-preacher could form a new league amongst us. However, here we had a meeting in Crickhowell – in the manse – of Elijah and Elisha.

'But that which struck us was the great difference between David Williams and T. C. Williams on the one hand, and Dr Martyn Lloyd-Jones on the other hand. On the whole, David Williams was a Modernist, and Thomas Charles was a Liberal theologically (although more conservative than David Williams), but Dr Lloyd-Jones is a fundamentalist. The two Williamses were preachers of the high-festival of the Connexion, but it is highly unlikely that Dr Lloyd-Jones can be looked upon as a Festival preacher. He is a type on his own – he is not in the class of Evan Roberts the Revivalist, nor either in the class of the preachers of the great festivals.'

THE REVEREND H. P. ROBERTS, Llanfairfechan,
in the correspondence columns of Y *Goleuad*,
February 22, 1933

9

A Leader without a Party

There was a sense in which the growth of the work at Sandfields did not take Dr Lloyd-Jones by surprise: from the outset he had been given an anticipation of what could take place under the preaching of the gospel. But there were to be other events in the early years of his ministry which were wholly unexpected. The one thing to which he conceived himself to be called in 1927 was the work of an evangelist within a local community where he knew God had placed him. He desired nothing more. As a correspondent in the *Western Mail* correctly wrote of him during the week he began at Sandfields, 'He would naturally prefer to settle down to his work in peace and quiet.' This was to prove impossible, for he had scarcely settled in Aberavon before he was being asked to preach in other places. In one sense such a development was not unusual. The thirteen so-called 'free Sundays', stipulated in the terms of his call, was an arrangement common throughout the denomination. The purpose was to encourage ministers to preach away from their own pulpits for a number of Sundays every year with four Sundays remaining for holidays. But not only were there invitations to fill these vacant Sundays soon to hand for Dr Lloyd-Jones, there were also calls for him to preach at special mid-week services – often anniversaries – which were then so much a part of chapel life in Wales. Thus within twelve months of his Induction he was often away from Aberavon preaching on two mid-week evenings (Tuesdays and Thursdays), frequently with afternoon services as well and before long this had become the pattern for most weeks, apart from his holiday period.

This is not to say that Martyn Lloyd-Jones was uniformly welcomed in all sections of Welsh Nonconformity. On this point he has recorded:

'When I went to South Wales it was to a varied reception: the vast bulk of Welsh Calvinistic Methodists were delighted – not because of

David Martyn Lloyd-Jones

my beliefs but because I was, as they thought, boosting the ministry. Many in the English section of the Calvinistic Methodists, however, considered themselves intellectuals and they did not like me because they could recognise my views and my teaching. They were quite pleasant and polite but I felt they were antagonistic. The Baptists, as a whole, were most enthusiastic in my favour and received me with open arms. They were emotionalists. They all thought they were evangelical – actually they were not, they were often "praising the gospel" without any theology or understanding – yet they were really very warm in their welcome of me. Now the Congregationalists were different again: they were doubtful of me. They also regarded themselves as intellectuals and philosophers and were suspicious and critical.

'People used to tell me what their ministers would be saying to one another on their way out from services. At special services ministers all sat in "the big seat" and I was often conscious of a strong wave of antagonism. I had to preach beyond them to the people. In those days, when I went to preach on a week-day in any district, all the ministers turned up; this is no longer the case, but at that time, before the Second World War, it was customary that ministers from the several Nonconformist denominations would support special services in any local chapel. They were afraid not to be there, as their members would be watching for them and saying, "Where is our man?"'

The differences between the Welsh and English-speaking sections of the denomination, noted above, require further comment. Of the 1,497 churches in the Calvinistic Methodist Connexion, 361 were 'English' – that is to say, congregations which did not employ Welsh as their first language, and these causes constituted separate presbyteries. Thus English-speaking Sandfields belonged to the Presbytery of West Glamorgan, while 'Carmel' (Aberavon) a Welsh chapel (where David Williams was minister) belonged to a different, Welsh-speaking presbytery. The English-speaking side was less traditional and reflected a good deal more of modern religious thought. So the record of the West Glamorgan Presbytery at their monthly meeting at Terrace Road Chapel, Swansea, on March 17, 1927, that 'a cordial welcome was extended to Dr Martyn Lloyd-Jones, Sandfields', did not tell the full story. Although he was serving a cause in the English-section of the denomination, the majority of

[180]

A Leader without a Party

the invitations to preach were to come from the Welsh side. 'The Welsh and the English sections,' he later commented, 'were really entirely different. I did much more with the Welsh than with the English – much more! At mid-week services in the Welsh churches I would preach in Welsh in the afternoon and in English at night.'

Among the exceptions to this pattern was the English-speaking congregation of the Reverend Eliseus Howells, in a small mining community above Bridgend, which also belonged to the West Glamorgan Presbytery and where Dr Lloyd-Jones was early invited to preach after Howells had been to hear him. Speaking of that experience a few years later, Howells wrote:

'It was probably curiosity that made us listen to him for the first time, and that, on account of the things we had heard about him, but there was also some measure of surprise, the surprise that comes to a man awakened from his sleep with a mighty shout.

'If there was a measure of fear and a degree of doubt mixed with this curiosity and surprise, the fact that I did not stop to consider the time of my awakening would account for that, for we soon realized that it was the third hour of the day, and it was long since known in the church that the eternal Spirit himself is responsible for the events that happen at that hour.

'Indeed, who but Himself would call on this dear physician to change his plans for his whole life, shattering all his friends' expectations of him and hearing it suggested that he was going mad. . . .

'It is not strange that he won our unbounded admiration, but with him accepting a pulpit without the usual course of preparation, we felt that we should extend to him our utmost sympathy. Poor us! If we went to that first service expecting to sympathize with him, we came out pitying ourselves. He did not covet our admiration, nor was he in need of our pity. Rather, we thought not of what he had done but of what we were not.'¹

Howells and Dr Lloyd-Jones soon became close friends. Brought up in the Rhondda and about eight years older than Lloyd-Jones, it was perhaps as well that Howells was not a close neighbour, for there was nothing he loved better than to talk away the hours with a

¹ 'Doctor Martin Lloyd-Jones', an article in Y Goleuad, February 1, 1933. All my quotes from Howells are from this all-too-brief source.

fund of stories from earlier times. In a rather undisciplined kind of way, he had acquired both from books and from the older generation a considerable understanding of Calvinistic Methodist history. While he was still a youth, a cashier by the name of David Davies in one of the Rhondda collieries had befriended him. Davies' grandfather had been a deacon at Llangeitho in the time of Rowland's ministry and many incidents from those days had been passed down in the family. The result was that, with such an eager learner as the pastor of Sandfields, Eliseus Howells was ever willing either to re-tell what he had heard, or to point to Methodist books which the pastor of Sandfields had not yet seen.

Another minister who was notable in the warmth of his welcome to Dr Lloyd-Jones was W. E. Prytherch, whom Martyn had first heard at Llangeitho in 1913. Although he had retired from Trinity Chapel, Swansea, in 1919, Prytherch was still preaching after he turned eighty in 1926. In his earlier ministry Prytherch had spoken much of the judgment of God, but in middle life it was noticed how the emphasis changed, as he came to dwell much on the tenderness of divine love. Dr Lloyd-Jones rarely heard him without being moved to tears, and it was his high esteem for Prytherch which brought him into difficulties when the two had to preach together for two days in September 1927. On the first night, Dr Lloyd-Jones, speaking first, was so anxious to give full time to the old veteran that his own sermon was hastened through in twenty minutes. But he did not enjoy it and neither did Prytherch who, after himself failing to rise to the occasion, complained vigorously to his young companion afterwards: 'You have ruined the service tonight for both of us! I know what it was. You didn't want to take my time. Let us show them tomorrow night what preaching is!'

It was Prytherch who, in the early days of Dr Lloyd-Jones' ministry, encouraged him by exclaiming after one sermon, 'You are preaching the old truths but putting brand new suits on them!' But not all comments on his preaching, even from sympathetic hearers, were wholly favourable. One of the advantages of being asked to preach in a variety of places was the constructive criticism which he sometimes received. Sharing the work of preaching one week-day afternoon and evening with the Reverend Dr Cynddylan Jones at Llantrisant, he was given valuable advice by the older man who had listened to his afternoon sermon. Probably the date was Thursday, May 19, 1927, for his notes of a sermon on Romans 3:20 ('Therefore by the deeds of the law there shall no flesh be justified in his sight: for by the law is the knowledge of sin') record that he preached from that text at Llantrisant on that day. As the two men sat at tea, between the services, Cynddylan Jones opened the conversation with, 'I have only one criticism to offer of your preaching,' and when Lloyd-Jones assured him that he would appreciate knowing what it was, his adviser proceeded: 'You demand too much of the people. You watch how I do it tonight. I have only one point, but I will make it in three different ways!'

This was wise advice which it took the younger man time to learn. Not long afterwards, his old friend Ianto Crydd, the shoemaker of Llangeitho, emphasised the same lesson after he had preached in the chapel of his childhood. Martyn, he declared, was expecting too much of his hearers. With one of his characteristic similes drawn from the way in which horses and cattle have to be fed in farmyard stables, he went on, 'You are putting the rack too high – it is wonderful hay but they cannot all reach it.'

'I remember lying awake in the chapel house that night and thinking I had probably failed,' the preacher later recalled. 'I had preached a sermon not suited to a village chapel.' The greater the preaching, he came to believe, the easier it will be to understand it.

It is clear from Dr Lloyd-Jones's sermon notes that the places where he preached during his first twelve months in Wales included: Ammanford, Aberdare, Aberkenfig, Aberystwyth, Abergavenny, Briton Ferry, Blackwood, Barry, Bridgend, Bethany, Brynamman, Brecon, Blaenavon, Carmel (Aberavon), Cardiff (Cathedral Road), Cardiff (Memorial Hall), Cardiff (University C.U.), Cwmavon, Cross Hands, Crickhowell, Caerphilly, Cwmbwrla, Kenfig Hill, Ferndale, Glyn Neath, Gilfachgoch, Haverfordwest, Llantrisant, Laleston, Llangeitho, Llanharan, Morriston (F.M.), Maesteg, Neath (F.M.), Newcastle Emlyn, Pyle, Pontrhydyfen, Porthcawl, Penclawdd, Pwllheli, Porth, Pencoed, Resolven, Swansea (Argyle), Swansea (Rhyddings), Swansea (Baptist), Skewen, Tonypandy, Taibach (Wes.), Treorchy, Treharris, Tonyrefail, Tonpentre, Ystradgynlais.

Such was the additional work of his first year in the ministry, and thereafter, for half-a-century, no year was to be so quiet!

No doubt a number who invited the Sandfields' missioner initially did so out of a sense of curiosity. E. T. Rees remembers accompanying his pastor to a mid-week evening service at the church of the Reverend T. H. Morgan in Swansea. A wagon-repairer in Port

Talbot had reported to Rees that he heard Morgan say of the newcomer at Aberavon, 'He may be a doctor of medicine, but he is not a doctor of divinity! What does he know about theology?' Rees is sure that when they met Morgan in the darkness outside his chapel the Swansea pastor did not know which of the two men was his visiting preacher. Both Rees and Lloyd-Jones went into the pulpit; only after Rees had read the lesson (the parable of the Prodigal Son), and a final hymn had been sung before the sermon, did the preacher come forward! In the comparatively large congregations of Swansea and Cardiff he was still unknown – a fact which was reflected in the half-empty buildings for his mid-week preaching visits at this early date. Whether T. H. Morgan revised his opinions of the young preacher at once, we do not know, but he was certainly to come within the circle of his subsequent friends.

By 1928 it was becoming evident that Dr Lloyd-Jones' ministry was going to polarise opinion both among ministers and churches. Memorable in this connection were services which he was asked to share with the Reverend Tom Nefyn Williams at Shiloh Chapel, Aberystwyth, on February 14 and 15, 1928. 'Tom Nefyn', as he was affectionately known, was a man who professed conversion during military service in France in the First World War and came back to Wales as a flaming evangelist. His eloquent voice was often to be heard preaching the gospel in the open-air at fairs and similar gatherings. Then, however, he was persuaded to undergo theological training from which he at length emerged as an extreme liberal. In the pulpit his oratory was as persuasive as ever, but he was nothing more than a dramatic reciter, who seemed to see less authority in the Bible than he did in the latest book of modern psychology.

As recorded above, the two men had already met at the London Association meetings of October 1927 and it was probably interest arising out of the difference between them on that occasion which had led to them being asked to repeat in Aberystwyth their addresses on the theme that 'Life is incomplete without Jesus Christ'. Once more the disagreement was patent. Over fifty years later, D. J. Odwyn-Jones, who was then a ministerial student at Aberystwyth, could remember the theme of Lloyd-Jones's argument: 'The teaching of Christ is the most hopeless thing in the world apart from his Spirit. It is only when we have received the Holy Spirit that we can really see the divine glory of the gospel. A Christian is not a

Christian till he is surprised to find himself doing the things that he had always thought were impossible. Christ living in us is the complete life.'

The two sermons Dr Lloyd-Jones preached on the following day drove home the difference still further. Preaching in the morning from Luke 3:16 – John baptising with water, but Jesus 'with the Holy Ghost and with fire' – Lloyd-Jones directed the congregation to the question, By whom had they been baptised as members of the church? The church, he said, no longer provoked persecution because it no longer possessed the authority which it used to have. The church's worst enemy is the man of little faith within its membership, not the faithless man of the world. In the evening his text was Acts 3:6: 'Then Peter said, Silver and gold have I none; but such as I have give I thee: in the name of Jesus Christ of Nazareth rise up and walk.' The crippled beggar's attendance at the gate of the Temple was no help to him, the preacher declared, nor would 'silver and gold' have met his real need:

'If the apostles had had silver and gold in their pockets the probability is that they would have dropped a coin or two into the man's hand and would have gone on. But finding themselves with nothing in their pockets they could not do that, and yet they felt that they could and must do something for him. Now, my friends, the church of Christ on earth has always done her greatest things when she has been in that condition. Think of the early Christian church as shown here. Think of the young Protestant church. Think of the Methodist Revival in Wales and in England! When the church has silver and gold in her pockets she generally gives these to her people and nothing more, but when she is young she has nothing of these things to give and is thus forced back upon her real treasure.'

The church of herself can do nothing for the world, he continued, but when she falls back upon the resources of God, she will say to men as Peter did:

'I cannot give you what the world is giving and has given you. You must not expect comfort and luxury from me. It is no part of my business to find work for you and to put you in a decent house – I can do none of the things for you which silver and gold can do. I cannot improve your conditions and surroundings, but I can do one thing for you and that I do gladly: I can cure you! "In the name of Jesus

Christ of Nazareth rise up and walk!" "Let me take hold of your right hand and lift you up!" "I can make you happy in His strength. Come, let us rejoice!" And it always works, the miracle is always performed – everything is possible with Christ! Are you oppressed by a sense of your own failure in life and a feeling of hopelessness? "In the name of Jesus Christ rise up and walk!" Are you weighed down by, and heavy because of, some secret sorrow, and do you feel that you can never be happy again? "In the name of Jesus Christ of Nazareth rise up and walk!" Have you lost faith in your own will and your own capacity? Are you feeling that you are a hopeless sinner beyond recovery? "In the name of Jesus Christ of Nazareth rise up and walk!" "But it has been going on for years," you say, "surely I cannot be *cured* now? I have tried everything long ago." Remember this man who had been a cripple for over forty years, remember the converted sinners throughout the ages and those round about you at the present time and "In the name of Jesus Christ of Nazareth rise up and walk!" And you will be given strength.'

Such was part of Dr Lloyd-Jones's message on his first preaching visit to Aberystwyth in February 1928. The contrast between it and the message of 'Tom Nefyn' was almost complete. In the words of one observer, the Reverend M. H. Jones, 'These are two remarkable men. One [Lloyd-Jones] is looking to the past and the other is looking to the future.' This was certainly not a description with which Dr Lloyd-Jones would have concurred. He knew that if Tom Nefyn Williams' unbelief was allowed to spread there would be *no* future for the church.

Later in 1928, on an August Sunday, the two preachers met again in Llandrindod Wells. It was the Sunday after the Llandrindod Convention, an annual 'Keswick in Wales' week, and numbers had remained in that popular holiday town for the week-end. Lloyd-Jones, who arrived on the Saturday, was expected to preach in one of the local churches and Williams in the large Albert Hall. Among the many who had been at the Convention, and who had remained to hear the visiting preachers, discussion buzzed at Sunday breakfast time over the question which of the two men would draw the larger congregation. When Dr Lloyd-Jones, unconscious of the reason for the unusual atmosphere among the other guests in the hotel, asked what was going on, he was astonished to be told, 'If we believed in betting, the people would be betting!'

Before the respective morning services began the two preachers met in the vestry of the church in which Lloyd-Jones was preaching, which was also next door to the Albert Hall, and Nefyn could not have been kinder in his remarks to the younger man. Nonetheless he was to deliver one of his most extreme sermons in the Albert Hall in which he scorned both the deity and the resurrection of Christ. As both services had been well attended the question now was, 'What would happen in the evening?' The answer was to be that the people had exercised their own decisive judgment. The Albert Hall was half-empty while the other service was so packed that even the stairs up to the pulpit had to be employed as extra seats. The burden of one of Dr Lloyd-Jones' sermons that day was to show the falsity of any belief in man's ability to accomplish his own salvation, using as his text the words of Mark 10:26, 27: 'And they were astonished out of measure, saying among themselves, Who then can be saved? And Jesus looking upon them saith, With men it is impossible, but not with God: for with God all things are possible.'

At the meeting of the South Wales Association which was held in Nantgaredig in West Carmarthen, a few weeks later, the ministers (all Welsh-speaking), though not naturally prone to such radical action, were left with no choice but to excommunicate the preacher whose heterodox utterances had become so well known. It was an unusual event in a religious situation where discipline over matters of belief had become virtually extinct. In view of the degree of commotion which they knew the excommunication would cause, the Presbytery to which Tom Nefyn belonged decided that special services should be held on the last Thursday afternoon and evening in September in Water Street Church, Carmarthen, when a preacher able to quieten the churches and settle the people should be invited. Their choice was Martyn Lloyd-Jones. Thereafter, for fifty-one years, Water Street Church, Carmarthen, continued to hold these special services on the last Thursday in every September and always with the same preacher!

Dr Lloyd-Jones believed that the real opposition to evangelical and supernatural religion came from the pride which resents what is implied in Christ's teaching that men must be 'born again':

'By telling people that "ye must be born again" you are simply telling them that as they are, they are "*all* wrong" and that nothing but a divine, super-natural intervention from above can possibly save them and put them right. Come, let us be quite honest with ourselves and each other. Why is it that we do not like all this talk about "conversion" and "rebirth", why indeed is it scarcely ever mentioned in our chapels and churches these days? Why was it that a highly educated, cultured gentleman, whom I know well, should the other day have said to a lady, who had undergone that great change of heart, that "the word *conversion* was not a nice word and that he was surprised that a man like Dr Lloyd-Jones, who ought to know better, should allow himself to be carried away by fanaticism"?'[1]

A year later, in 1929, Dr Lloyd-Jones was asserting this still more strongly and widely. In one sermon, after tracing the spiritual decline of nineteenth-century Calvinistic Methodism, he continued:

'It is our own Nonconformist forefathers who are responsible for the churches becoming worldly institutions. Conversion and rebirth are never mentioned, they are embarrassing subjects which are dismissed when they are brought up; indeed one can almost say that the average church member is ashamed to speak about his relationship with God, but is proud of being made a Justice of the Peace! At these Presbyteries and District Meetings, votes of thanks and votes of congratulations are continually being passed on so-and-so for having been clever in some way or other – some examination passed, or office received, or other worldly honour, but I have never yet heard a vote of thanks being passed for a sinner converted, no acclamation when someone has gone from sin to saintliness. They never speak about that thing that makes a church a church – the power of God unto salvation!'[2]

It is scarcely surprising that as he preached in many parts of South Wales he was often conscious of that strong wave of antagonism from 'the big seat'! Eliseus Howells saw him as 'the man who slits the south' and, speaking of the frequent effects of his ministry, wrote: 'As the storm makes its way through the forest, hurling down all that is in its way, be that the solid pines or the stout oak, so he.'

Yet it would misrepresent the position to imply that Dr Lloyd-Jones was unfeeling in the face of opposition. He did feel it. On one occasion, when a clerical attack on him took a particularly vicious form, he was much comforted by the assurance given by Paul to Timothy

[1] Sermon on John 3:7.
[2] Sermon on Matthew 22:20, 21, April 28, 1929.

concerning faithful discipleship, 'All that will live godly in Christ Jesus shall suffer persecution' (2 Tim. 3:12).

Undoubtedly he was sometimes asked to preach simply because his name was expected to draw extra numbers. Once, preaching at a Presbyterian cause mid-week at Llantwit Major, he was shocked to be virtually told before the service by one of the church officers that he should 'do his stuff' – because the Baptists and Congregationalists had enjoyed good special services in the previous fortnight! At other times he was probably asked to speak at denominational occasions as a representative of evangelical opinion. Thus in 1929 and 1931 he was invited to give addresses at the Annual Conference of the Presbyterian Church of Wales. The published Reports of these Conferences reveal at once that the prevailing religious thought was very different from that of the preacher from Aberavon. Whereas in his addresses he quoted nothing but Scripture, apart from one reference to John Calvin, such names as A. M. Fairbairn (English Congregationalist and inspirer of the Welsh B.D. Course), Albert Schweitzer and Stanley Jones (both liberal missionaries), and C. H. Dodd were commended by the other speakers. At the 1929 Conference, Professor Edwards of Bala quoted with approval the statement of H. Wheeler Robinson, 'The doctrine of verbal inspiration is not simply untenable; it is irrelevant.'[1] Another speaker, criticising those who spoke of the failures of the modern Church, quoted another liberal, Canon C. E. Raven, who had recently declared, 'I verily believe the Church has shown during the last twenty years a power of adaptation to a new environment which can only be described as astonishing.'[2]

The subject given to Dr Lloyd-Jones at the 1929 Conference was 'The Meaning of the Sacrament of the Lord's Supper'. Another speaker, a Professor of philosophy of religion at the Calvinistic Methodist Theological College in Aberystwyth, was also given the same subject. This man was a well-known preacher in the denomination whose ministry had undergone a considerable change. When he first left Oxford, where he had taken a double first, he had employed his brilliant gifts to advance liberal theology. In the course of time, however, he had come to observe the effect of the preaching of such

---

[1] *Report of the Thirty-Fourth Annual Conference*, p. 30. The same speaker also spoke of the liberal A. S. Peake as 'one of the most enlightened and reverent students of the Bible'!

[2] *Ibid.*, p. 20.

men as Peter Hughes Griffiths. Griffiths' preaching did something to the people – sometimes they even wept – whereas his own preaching accomplished nothing. So, abandoning his attempts to give his hearers intellectual instruction in liberalism, he had adopted a new style of preaching in which he aimed at producing *feeling*. As a result he was gathering a considerable following. In Dr Lloyd-Jones' view he was a convert to sentimentality, not to evangelical Christianity, and to those with any discernment the two men's very different addresses on the same subject at this 1929 Conference confirmed that fact. Dismissing the idea that 'meaning' could properly be attached to the Lord's Supper, the Aberystwyth Professor preferred to think of it as a wonderful 'experience'. The communicant, he thought, could be likened to an old lady who, holding in her hand a 'love-letter, yellow maybe and indecipherable with age', is able to retain 'the love-experiences of long ago'. Whether the history recorded in Scripture is reliable, and whether Christ actually instituted the Lord's Supper did not matter. 'Experience' was everything and the bread and wine helped, like the old love-letter, to 'link up' with 'memories of love'.

Dr Lloyd-Jones' address which followed belonged to a different world of thought. Salvation, he declared, is not something we work for, rather we *receive* it, and it is that receiving of Christ which is symbolised in bread and wine. 'In the upper room Jesus was calling upon them to receive a gift. We are to do likewise. It is not a pathetic farewell meeting with a request that they should remember Him, so much as that they should remember always what His death has done for them. . . . According to Calvin the Sacrament gives believers the right to call everything which is His their own.'

It was about this time in the late 1920's that something happened after a Monday-night service at Bridgend which was to prove of considerable importance in the development of Dr Lloyd-Jones' ministry. The minister of the Calvinistic Methodist church in which this service was held was not at that date a supporter of the 'new' preaching at Aberavon, but its unusual emphases intrigued him. When the service was over the Bridgend minister greeted the visiting preacher with the remark, 'I cannot make up my mind what you are! I cannot decide whether you are a hyper-Calvinist or a Quaker.' When Dr Lloyd-Jones assured him that he was no hyper-Calvinist and enquired why he should make such a statement, he replied: 'Because you talk of God's action and God's sovereignty like a hyper-Calvinist, and of spiritual experience like a Quaker, but the cross and the work of Christ have little place in your preaching.'

There was a shrewd element of truth in this observation. The keynotes of Dr Lloyd-Jones' evangelistic preaching were the helplessness of man in sin, and the necessity of re-birth through the intervention of God. He preached so strongly that spiritual change is sovereignly given, not dependent upon man's own efforts, that while his message gave hope to the convicted, it did not direct them with sufficient clarity to faith in Christ as the God-appointed means of relief. The result was that the note of appeal which closed many of his sermons was not full-orbed. It included such commands as, 'Pray for the re-birth, pray for it without ceasing, pray until you experience it', but in stressing human inability he did not give equal emphasis to man's responsibility to believe on Christ for justification, nor show with sufficient clarity how that justification flows from the acceptance of Christ's atoning death.

The criticism which he heard at Bridgend was thus a fruitful incentive to further thinking. In his own words, spoken at a later date: 'I was like Whitefield in my early preaching. First I preached *regeneration*, that all man's own efforts in morality and education are useless, and that we need power from outside ourselves. I assumed the atonement but did not distinctly preach it or justification by faith. This man set me thinking and I began to read more fully in theology.'

In particular, he concentrated upon the doctrines specified by his critic. At this point he was to receive help from the Congregational minister at Brynamman, the Reverend Vernon Lewis, who was later to become Principal of the Welsh Congregational College at Brecon. Vernon Lewis had first heard Lloyd-Jones in 1928 and been struck with the apparent similarity between his preaching and that of Karl Barth. Modern theology of an evangelical complexion was Lewis's special interest and he was quick to respond to the Lloyd-Jones' request for advice on reading, frequently calling at the Sandfields manse with further suggestions and books from his own library. High among his recommendations of authors on the atonement were the two English Congregationalists, P. T. Forsyth and R. W. Dale, and the Scots Presbyterian, James Denney, author of *The Death of Christ*[1] (1903). It was Forsyth's *The Cruciality of the Cross* (1909)

---

[1] M. L.-J.'s copy of Denney's book bears the date, July 5, 1929.

which proved of especial help at this stage in Lloyd-Jones' thinking. The weakness of these authors on the *full* inspiration of Scripture did not escape his notice, but that was not his subject of study, nor did he ever have difficulties in his commitment to all Scripture as the inerrant Word of God.

*   *   *

Dr Lloyd-Jones' wider ministry soon confronted him with a problem. With invitations to preach coming from many and varied quarters it became clear that there were various groups hoping that they might attach him to their cause. The evangelicals with whom he did have a ready affinity were those who looked back to the Welsh Revival of 1904–05 as a time of true spiritual power and blessing. Yet, as in all revivals, the effects of that period of awakening had been mixed and in many places its fruits had not been consolidated within the traditional churches. Calvinistic Methodism – too often critical of spiritual babes and unsympathetic towards revival phenomena – suffered an exodus from its ranks and, in some parts of Wales, the Baptists and 'Plymouth' Brethren gained in number. Pentecostal groups, proclaiming what they considered to be the distinctive message of the Revival, also sprang into existence. They drew off men and women who were weary of the cold worship of many of the chapels.

Post-1904 Evangelicalism was thus fragmented in Wales and some of its leaders were men whose chief interests lay outside the more regular church and denominational life. One such man was the Reverend R. B. Jones of Porth who had been one of the most effective preachers at the time of the revival of 1904. A Baptist, R. B. Jones had withdrawn from the regular life of that denomination on account of its toleration of Modernism, and he now presided over four independent churches, besides running his own 'Bible Institute' at Porth. He was also active in evangelistic projects (in which he failed to discern between the old gospel preaching of the Methodist Fathers and the new which had entered Wales through the Arminian influence of Charles G. Finney) and was an enthusiastic supporter of the holiness conventions held at Llandrindod Wells and elsewhere. The 'holiness message' of 'sanctification', received by an act of 'full surrender' to Christ, he preached as the great solution to the current religious malaise.

A Leader without a Party

In the first year of Dr Lloyd-Jones' ministry R. B. Jones befriended him and urged him to unite his efforts with their own. 'You know you are like the Apostle Paul,' the Porth preacher told him, 'you are as one "born out of due time"; you belong with us, you are really one of the children of the revival, but you have come in over twenty years later. . . .' It was through R. B. Jones' son and nephew, then students at Cardiff, that Dr Lloyd-Jones was first asked to speak to the Christian Union of that University College in October 1927. R. B. Jones' magazine *Yr Efengylydd (The Evangelist)* was to give regular commendation of Dr Lloyd-Jones' ministry and, as already mentioned, even to carry a review from his pen in 1929. The minister of Sandfields, however, would never accept an invitation to speak at the Llandrindod Convention, and although he did speak, on occasions, for R. B. Jones at Porth, he knew that there was never any possibility that he could find a spiritual home in that ethos.

Along with much that was commendable in R. B. Jones there was also an erroneous conviction that his comparative isolation amidst Welsh religion was due solely to his stand for the Word of God and for experimental Christianity. There was certainly no questioning his commitment to Scripture but, like so many others of his generation, who lacked real theological understanding, R. B. Jones was prone to be swept from one idea to another. At one time he might preach that a great awakening was about to occur, and at another that the second advent of Christ was at hand. His teaching was an amalgam, a fact reflected in the absence of any clearly recognisable theological position in the teachings of his Bible Institute at Porth. Preaching tours in the United States, and the visits of American fundamentalist leaders to his Rhondda Monthly Bible Conferences, increased the mixture. Too uncritical of anything which went by the name of fundamentalism, R. B. Jones was severe in his constant opposition to the Baptist Union and to the ministry in general. Frequently his preaching was denunciatory and Porth, instead of being a centre for a growing number of Christians, became a *cul de sac* for adherents to a declining cause – a cause which, to some extent, merited the negative and anti-intellectual image which it came to possess in South Wales.

As popular as 'holiness' meetings among Welsh evangelicals at this period, were the movements which existed to propagate the pre-millennial and dispensational views of unfulfilled prophecy. In many quarters, and almost universally among the Brethren, the notes on prophecy in the Scofield Bible were unquestioningly accepted and proclaimed. Dr. Lloyd-Jones' introduction to the Brethren occurred as a result of an unusual incident in Llanelly in December 1929. A comfortably-placed business man and his wife among the Calvinistic Methodists had invited the Lloyd-Joneses for Christmas. They were not Christians but were grateful to the Doctor for his effective discouragement given to their son who had wished to become a missionary. The fact was, that for the latter the pull of the foreign field had been romantic rather than spiritual. Before accepting the advice he had received, he had dreamed largely of jungles and of big game! After mid-day dinner in this home on Christmas Day, Dr Lloyd-Jones had gone upstairs and was settling down in an armchair to rest, when he was given a most distinct impression that at nine o'clock that evening, when the family and visitors were to be assembled for party games, he must address the question to them, 'Why did Christ come into the world?' This impression he at once resisted, thinking how it would be resented at a gathering of this nature which they were attending as guests for the first time. But the conviction that he was called to do this was inescapable and his inward conflict was not resolved until he had gone down on his knees and promised God that he would do it.

The evening arrived, and it was agreed that they would all listen to an appeal on behalf of the blind which was to be broadcast on the radio before the nine o'clock News. As soon as this broadcast was over, and before anything else could begin, the Doctor addressed his question. None could answer it correctly, so he began to explain and much discussion ensued. Soon all else was forgotten save the subject in hand. Time passed, guests rose and departed, yet still the debate went on. At length the host fell down on his knees and began to pray for pardon. Later, his wife did the same and also the older daughter. But still the son, who had contributed the most heated words in the argument that had gone on, was unmoved. Eventually he was to sink to the floor on the carpet before the fireplace with an audible groan. When Dr Lloyd-Jones, who had been able to remain cool, asked 'What's the matter ——?' the now silent youth pulled two tickets for a dance the next evening out of his pocket. All along, his resistance had been stiffened by the awareness that, if he believed the truths they were hearing, his way of life would have to change radically. It

did, and also that of his parents, who thereafter became identified with the evangelical faith, while he, the son, entered the
ministry.[1]

The members of this family were prominent tradespeople in
Llanelly and what had happened in their home on the evening of
Christmas day 1929 was soon common knowledge in the area. The
Brethren, in particular, were alerted to this rather unusual Calvinistic Methodist preacher and, hoping to emulate Aquila and Priscilla
who 'expounded' unto Apollos 'the way of God more perfectly', they
eagerly proffered help. He was presented with a Scofield Bible and
encouraged to note the importance of prophetic beliefs. Perhaps they
were surprised that the young preacher was unenthusiastic. He had
never encountered this view of unfulfilled prophecy before. The
literature he was given was wholly new to him, and he might well
have taken it up as so many other pastors had done.

Commenting in later years on what had kept him detached from
associations with which it was often assumed that he would be
identified, Dr Lloyd-Jones spoke of the two principles by means of
which he had sought to determine his decisions: 'First, my understanding of the Scripture and, second, my reading of the Calvinistic
Methodist revival of the eighteenth-century. These things governed
me and when anything presented itself to me, if it did not fit into that
framework, I had no difficulty over my duty. When I saw something
which was so different from the high spirituality and the deep
godliness of the Methodist Fathers I did not have a struggle over
whether to follow it or not.' These convictions, both in his early
ministry and throughout his life, were to keep him from many things
commonly accepted in evangelical circles, and when people attributed his independence to individualism it made him the more eager
that the lessons of church history might be more widely known.
From 1927 onwards, the guidance of the past was absolutely basic to
his understanding of the purpose of preaching. Indeed, one of his
favourite quotations, adapted for another purpose, was the words
of the French novelist Anatole France who, when tired and discouraged, used to say, 'I never go into the country for a change of air

---

[1] The memory of that night never faded for those who were present. Mrs
Lloyd-Jones recalling it, said: 'As we knelt in prayer I seemed to be full of a
warm, golden glory, an indescribable joy and a hope that the consciousness
we then enjoyed of the presence of God might never pass away.'

and a holiday. I always go instead into the eighteenth century.'¹

As Lloyd-Jones surveyed the Welsh scene in the late 1920's he saw nothing to suggest that, whatever the difficulties, his work would not lie within Calvinistic Methodism. He preferred its church-centred structure, and its emphasis upon the regular and normal means of grace, to the individualism of the break-away groups with their delight in missions and conventions. His hope was that Welsh Presbyterianism could be brought back to its original position. He also thought highly of some of the older generation of ministers under whose ministry he had often profited, although, by this date, they were passing from the scene. Joseph Jenkins, the man under whom the revival of 1904 began in his area and who had invited Lloyd-Jones to join him in an evangelistic preaching tour in 1925, died in 1929. The final meeting of the two men was memorable. In the summer of 1929, when Jenkins was dying from a growth in the spine, Eliseus Howells called at Aberavon to report the seriousness of the old preacher's condition and to urge Martyn to travel to see him at Llandovery, which was some distance away. Lloyd-Jones went and as he finally reached his destination he could hear groaning through an open window. Entering the house, Mrs Jenkins informed him that her husband was not really conscious but, as the visitor sat at his bedside, holding his hand, she asked her husband in the conversation which followed, 'Do you know who he is?' 'Of course I know!' replied the dying man, attempting to turn in his bed. 'Can you pull me back out of this river?' he asked Lloyd-Jones. 'I don't know that I can do that, Mr Jenkins.' 'I didn't know that this dear old river was so wide,' said Jenkins, 'but it's all right: I am going to Jesus Christ' – then, laying his hand upon his heart, 'I wish I felt it more here.' Like the old Methodists whom he resembled, Joseph Jenkins died well.

With men such as Jenkins and Prytherch (who died in 1931 in his eighty-sixth year²) Dr Lloyd-Jones was truly at home and their

¹ 'Go to the eighteenth century!' he was later to exhort preachers. 'In other words read the stories of the great tides and movements of the Spirit experienced in that century. For a preacher it is absolutely invaluable. . . . There is nothing more important for preaching than the reading of Church history and biographies', *Preaching and Preachers*, pp. 118, 317.
² 'The Welsh pulpit has lost one of its greatest preachers through the death of the Reverend W. E. Prytherch', announced *The British Weekly*, and the Welsh Calvinistic Methodist Church Year Book for 1932 spoke of his spirit as 'simple, plain, humble – he was in spirit the least of all his brethren'.

passing only strengthened his resolve to work for the cause in which they had so long served. Yet, given his convictions, there was little possibility that he could become a 'denominational' man, or even a leader in those more evangelical circles of the Welsh section of the denomination where his wife's grandfather, Evan Phillips, had been so well known. Speaking of this, he commented: 'When I went to Aberavon, the Welsh Calvinistic Methodists thought I would drop into their mould and preach like they did. At first they were a little bit disappointed, they thought that I was going to become one of them, but I could not do it.'

The issue of temperance, as already noticed, was one of the areas in which Dr Lloyd-Jones did not fit into the 'mould'. In those days much importance was given in church courts to the cause of total abstinence, and inevitably his dissension, which was so singular, was conspicuous – even disturbing! Speaking of the temperance question, the Reverend Gomer M. Roberts recalls from his early years in the Calvinistic Methodist ministry:

'In those days much importance was given to the cause of temperance and total abstinence in our church courts. One of our ministers, the Reverend John Green of Twr-gwyn, Cardiganshire was the doughty champion of this cause. I remember, at an Association held at Borth near Aberystwyth in 1929, Mr Green had given a long and lively report of the Temperance Committee. Martyn Lloyd-Jones got up, and queried why should we worry about such matters. Our job, he maintained, was to convert the people. Converted men and women could be trusted to live soberly and justly. "Let us not be bothered any longer with such matters. Let us get on with the gospel task of converting people. . . ." His view created quite a stir at the time, and poor Mr Green was much exasperated!'

Perhaps it was because Dr Lloyd-Jones' conviction subsequently gained ground that the Editor of the Forward Movement magazine, *The Treasury*, included a moderately phrased article in defence of the temperance cause, entitled 'The Gospel and Sin, a Conversation with Dr Martin Lloyd-Jones'. The writer, 'G.H.E.', explained how, after differing with Dr Lloyd-Jones at an Association meeting, they had continued their discussion on a train journey afterwards:

'On the way home we had this matter out together, neither quite succeeding in convincing the other. Nevertheless, we both parted the best of friends. Dr Martin Lloyd-Jones contended that the way to tackle the problem of evil was not by tackling sins but sin. And the only way for us to tackle sin is to convert the sinner. And the only power that can do that is the Gospel. Therefore the sole business of Christian people in reference to the evils about them is to convert sinners and the sole way to do that is by preaching the Gospel.

'Once we understand that point of view we will understand why Dr Martin Lloyd-Jones concentrates on preaching the Gospel and condemns all other methods of evangelism as spurious and ineffective.

'In our conversation he made the voluntary admission that, even to a point of being a failing with him, once having seen what he was convinced was the true objective, he would make for it regardless of all else by the way.

'I ventured to say that, while one heartily agreed that social and individual salvation, could only be achieved by ridding the heart of its sin through the grace of the Gospel, it did not follow also that there was to be no dealing with sins as sins. After all, I maintained, dealing with sins was only a particular way of dealing with sin. . . .

'The Doctor seems to have experienced a severe reaction against the methods of the institutional Church. I am not surprised, for often these methods become ends in themselves. He will give them no quarter, not even, I believe, when limited to a Literary Society and a Women's Sewing Guild. This unqualified attitude, though obviously extreme, ought to serve to make us at least re-examine the methods of our Church work; scrap those that are unworthy and see that those that are worthy are used as means to the right end.'[1]

These words contain a perceptive observation on a prominent feature in Dr Lloyd-Jones' thought: he was much more concerned with the general principle than with a particular detail, and once he was convinced of a matter of principle it became so primary to his thought that any secondary matters hindering people from seeing the *main* thing he could sweep aside as unworthy of attention. While, at times, he might be faulted for this procedure, it was undoubtedly his ability to seize upon the overriding importance of fundamental and primary truths which made him the leader which he was soon to become. He had analysed the religious conditions with a thorough-

[1] *The Treasury*, August 1933.

ness which no one had publicly attempted for a very long time and the degree to which he stood on one side amid the long-established and varied religious circles of Wales was a consequence of that fact.

It was certainly not a feature of his temperament to want to act alone and one of the great encouragements of his early ministry was the quiet formation of a small band of like-minded brethren for mutual support and fellowship. A document still survives from the first of their meetings and is worthy of being recorded in full:

'Feeling the need of definite action and co-operation on the part of those who believe and preach the Evangelical truths of the Gospel, the following Brethren met together at Sandfields, Aberavon, on Tuesday, December 30, 1930, to consider means for promoting a Revival of Religion.

Rev. Dr D. Martyn Lloyd-Jones	(Convener)
Rev. F. W. Cole	Penarth
Rev. A. Wynne Thomas	Cardiff
Rev. D. W. Howell	Pencoed
Rev. Eliseus Howells	Hereford
Rev. W. R. James,, B.A.	Pontardulais
Rev. Ieuan Phillips, B.A.	Neath
Mr Abel Ffowc Williams	Llansannan
Mr T. King Davies	Bridgend
Mr A. E. Dalton	Swansea
Mr W. M. Jones	Penygroes

The following matters were agreed upon:

1. That we pledge ourselves that in all our meetings together for fellowship, we shall frankly exchange with one another our thoughts and experiences, paying special attention to the confession of our faults and failures.

2. That we pledge ourselves to abstention from any practice which is not of faith, "for whatsoever is not of faith is sin".

3. That we pledge ourselves to wait upon God for one half-hour daily, in particular prayer for,

    (i) A revival of religion
    (ii) For one another.

4. That we accept and subscribe to the Brief Declaration of the Presbyterian Church of Wales, but feel that in addition the

following matters be especially stressed and emphasised in our ministry.

   (a) That the call for decision, conversion and re-birth be pressed upon our congregations.

   (b) That all believers should have a full assurance of forgiveness and salvation.

   (c) That all believers be taught and instructed that it is the will of God that they be sanctified, that they receive the Holy Spirit, and that the fruit of the Spirit may be manifest in their lives. Gal. 5:22.

5. That the churches be cleansed from all worldly and doubtful means of maintaining the cause, such as Bazaars, Concerts, etc.

6. That we meet at Pencoed, Friday, April 10th, 1931.'

This group of men – and mainly young men – which in some ways resembled the Methodist 'Holy Club' of the 1730's, never gained public attention in the life of the denomination, but it was a centre of spiritual influence, and strengthened the resolve of those who came to share a common vision.

Eliseus Howells marvelled at the maturity and force with which their chairman led these meetings: 'We quickly realised that there was no theological book or any commentary of value that he did not know its contents and standpoint, and we marvelled at the extent and the exactness of his knowledge; we sometimes saw a culture that reminded us of John Wesley, as the lightning flashed way before we heard the sound of his fearful thunder.'

Another man who was helped by the fellowship of this group was wavering on the edge of the denomination when he first met Dr Lloyd-Jones. Emlyn Jones was brought up in Penuel C.M. Church at Blaenavon. Tiring of the deadness of that congregation (which was without a minister), he had begun to attend a local independent mission hall when Dr Lloyd-Jones came to preach at mid-week services at Penuel on May 26, 1931. That afternoon Emlyn Jones was to be found in the congregation along with many others who had gathered for the service. At the hour announced there was no sign of the preacher, who was delayed in travelling, and the anxious deacons could think of no alternative but that of asking Emlyn Jones (whose spiritual earnestness they knew) to begin the service himself. By the time Dr Lloyd-Jones arrived in the vestry, close to the pulpit, his

A *Leader without a Party*

substitute had begun the 'long prayer' and he was stirred to hear the fervent, pleading intercession. Emlyn Jones revelled in the sermon to which he was shortly listening and followed the preacher to the larger building booked for the evening (Horeb Baptist Church) when the text was, 'Ye shall know the truth and the truth shall make you free'. From that day the two men became friends and Emlyn Jones never missed an opportunity to hear Dr Lloyd-Jones: 'I had the privilege of receiving much blessing through his later ministry in crowded churches in the Eastern Valleys such as Garndiffaith, Pontypool and others. I remember especially a sermon he preached from Psalm 107, in which he likened it to a choir with the refrain, "O that men would praise the Lord for his goodness and for his wonderful works to the children of men".' Emlyn Jones himself not only remained a Calvinistic Methodist but became a much-loved preacher through many years.[1]

Another who benefited from the Ministers' Fellowship (in the later thirties when he was still a student for the ministry) was I. B. Davies. Having gone into the pits at the age of thirteen, I. B. Davies had little secondary education and yet under the preaching at Sandfields he believed that God had called him to the gospel ministry. Broaching this conviction at length to Dr Lloyd-Jones, he was told to 'go home and study Greek', this being his pastor's way of testing the strength of his call. A year later as 'I.B.' was leaving a meeting at Sandfields, Dr Lloyd-Jones asked him what the book was which he saw sticking from his pocket. It was a Greek grammar which the young man had been assiduously studying for twelve months. After arranging to see him for a further conversation, Dr Lloyd-Jones thereafter gave him every possible encouragement in following his call to the ministry. In turn, the Reverend I. B. Davies was subsequently to gather numbers of young men around him, including not a few who are faithful preachers at the present time.[2]

[1] He was, in fact, to be one of Dr Lloyd-Jones' successors at Sandfields. His last charge was at Neath where he retired in 1968 and died in 1981.
[2] They include his two sons, Wynford and Andrew, and a number of other preachers now serving churches in Wales and England. A fiery evangelist, Mr Davies' most fruitful years were spent at the Forward Movement Hall in Neath (1949-62). He remained close to Dr Lloyd-Jones all his days and preceded him to heaven by a few years.

'Before we deal with the position of those who are outside, let us first examine ourselves and make our confession. For every true revival in the world starts as a revival in the church, and revivals come to churches which realise their need and impotence and turn to God in prayer for forgiveness and for new strength.'

M. L.-J.

on John 10:10 (July 22, 1928)

'Thank God, the age of miracles has not ended; the Holy Spirit is still abroad and one never knows when He shall descend upon us here at Aberavon. Let us be prepared!'

'Present-day religion far too often soothes the conscience instead of awakening it; and produces a sense of self-satisfaction and eternal safety rather than a sense of our unworthiness and the likelihood of eternal damnation'.

M. L.-J.

on Jeremiah 17:9, 10, 14 (1930)

10

Revival

Revival was a subject which did not occupy a separate place in Dr Lloyd-Jones' thinking and preaching, rather it was closely related to his whole understanding of the work of God in bringing men to salvation and to assurance. He saw revival as the extension to many, at the same time, of that same divine power which is present in the conversion of every individual. It is the same life, present wherever there is true Christianity, which in days of revival abounds and overflows. The same Holy Spirit as may be known by a single Christian is then 'outpoured' upon a multitude. So a time of revival does not witness results different in nature from those attending God's more normal work, but the multiplied instances of divine grace present at such a period reveal the glory of Christ to a degree, and upon a scale, which is extraordinary, exceptional and unparalleled. True zeal for revival is therefore nothing other than zeal for the glory of God in the conversion of many.

Dr Lloyd-Jones did not regard the view that a revival can be produced or 'worked-up' by human effort as a minor mistake. He traced that error to a false view of the meaning of conversion itself. No matter how great the effort and energy expended, man cannot induce one single true conversion. This emphasis was prominent from the outset of his ministry. In an early sermon he refers to those who came to him with sad reports of the prevailing conditions and tells how he answered them: 'They draw their doleful pictures of life in the slums, and of all the sins and all the excesses, and then turn to me and ask, "Now what can you do for such people?" To which I reply, "Nothing, absolutely Nothing!" . . . I go about telling men and women that in the affairs of the soul and the spirit no man can do anything for them, no matter how dear and how near he may be to them, whether it be husband or wife, father, mother or child – no human being can do anything, but God can do everything!'¹ 'St Paul did not convert a single person, he was but God's agent. John Wesley, Daniel Rowland, General Booth, Seth Joshua, and all these glorious men, they did not save a single soul or defeat a single enemy.'²

To understand what conversion means is necessarily to deny that revivals can be produced by the activity of the church. The same sovereign and supernatural power which is essential to the saving of one individual is equally indispensable in the case of a multitude. Those who would 'rush' men into conversion and those who try to 'hasten' a revival have fallen into the same error:

'Pray for revival? Yes, go on, but do not try to create it, do not attempt to produce it, it is only given by Christ himself. The last church to be visited by a revival is the church trying to make it.'³

Revivals are 'special times' in the history of the church, 'made "special" not by the schemes and devices of men, but by the intervention of God'. The church, Dr Lloyd-Jones preached, has her 'great days' and her 'ordinary days': 'There are not only the great experiences but also the ordinary, everyday experiences, and a church that is *always* praying for a continual revival is a church that has not understood her mission. The church is not meant always to be in a state of revival but is also to do ordinary, every-day work. But some remember this fact so well that they forget that the church is meant to have special occasions!'⁴

Dr Lloyd-Jones' early emphasis on the necessity of God's action, far from encouraging passivity, pointed men to the one source of true hope. And if conversion is God's work, then it is as possible for a hundred or a thousand simultaneously as it is for one. Yet Dr Lloyd-Jones would not have been in the ministry had he not also believed that God uses means to fulfil his purposes. Men singly or in multitudes are not brought to faith without hearing the Word of God. The Holy Spirit employs the truth in order to bring about conversion and he does so supremely by the agency of preaching. Thus Paul, speaking of his ministry, could assert, 'Our gospel came not unto you in word only, but also in power, and in the Holy Ghost

¹ Acts 11:9, July 5, 1927.   ² 1 Samuel 17, May 3, 1927.
³ Mark 4:26–29, March 16, 1930.   ⁴ Acts 19:11, February 10, 1929.

Revival

and in much assurance' (1 Thess. 1:5). Upon which statement Dr Lloyd-Jones commented to his people at Sandfields:

'Paul knew while he was preaching to them that something was happening. He knew he was being used of God, he knew the Holy Ghost was driving his words deep into their hearts and souls, he was conscious of that power which changes men and women and which had changed him. So he says, that he had preached with "much assurance". Of course he did! He knew he was but the mouth-piece and the channel. God grant in His infinite mercy that it may be the same here tonight and that we all may experience that power and the blessed, gracious influence of the Holy Ghost! There is no greater joy which any minister may ever have than that, to know for certain that it is not he himself, but Christ in him, who is doing the work.'

Further, Dr Lloyd-Jones believed that the Scripture reveals the kind of preaching which is owned of God, and it was his persuasion upon this matter which was to render his own ministry so significantly different from that of many of his contemporaries. Much preaching, in his judgment, was controlled, not by Scripture, but by prevailing fashions of opinion and especially by the wishes of those in the pew. So-called 'intellectual preaching' was patently at variance with the Bible: 'As I read the Gospels,' he told his congregation as he began his second year in Aberavon, 'any man who gives the impression that "the mind of Christ" is open only to scholarship and learning is false to the very fundamentals of Christ's teaching. The words "absolute", "reality", "values", "cosmos", "Christology" and "Logos" are not the every-day words of our vocabulary, and yet, in reading contemporary literature and in listening to religious addresses in these days, these things seem to be vital and essential.'[1] Yet despite its uselessness, this 'learned style' was sometimes treated with respect, and in another sermon he gave an illustration of this from his own experience in Llangeitho:

'I remember a man who used to come to preach in the country and who preached in such a way that no one could follow him or had the slightest idea as to what he was talking about. The general verdict about this man, especially by the deacons who considered themselves

[1] Acts 27:22, February 5, 1928.

intelligent men, was this: "No, he is not much of a preacher," they said, "but no doubt he is a great thinker"! Great thinker indeed! The great thinkers are those whose thinking is so great and so clear that they can express in a simple and lucid manner the greatest things of all, namely, the Mystery of God and His love. Great thinkers? Was there ever anyone who thought as Jesus of Nazareth did – was there ever such great thinking as that? Was there ever so much of the mind of God revealed as in His sermons and addresses? And yet it was delivered to ignorant, uneducated people and – wonder of wonders! – they actually understood Him and grasped His message. The same applies to the great disciples who have followed Him, with this qualification – that none of them have been as simple as He was. Here they are, St Paul, St Augustine, Luther, Calvin, Pascal, Wesley and so on. Giant intellects every one, and yet any man who wishes to do so can follow their reasoning and their argument.'[1]

Modern preaching, Dr Lloyd-Jones believed, had gone fundamentally wrong. He saw the main proof of that fact in the failure of the pulpit to recognise that the first work of the Holy Spirit is to *convict* of sin and to humble men in the presence of God. He knew that any preaching which soothes, comforts and pleases those who have never been brought to fear God, nor to seek his mercy, is not preaching which the Spirit of God will own. The truth is that he was going back to a principle once regarded as imperative for powerful evangelistic preaching, namely, that before men can be converted they must be convinced of sin. In 1883 C. H. Spurgeon declared: 'In the beginning, the preacher's business is not to convert men, but the very reverse. It is idle to attempt to heal those who are not wounded, to attempt to clothe those who have never been stripped, and to make those rich who have never realized their poverty. As long as the world stands, we shall need the Holy Ghost, not only as the Comforter, but also as the Convincer, who will "reprove the world of sin, and of righteousness, and of judgment".'[2] It was this same principle, so largely forgotten even before Spurgeon's death in 1892, which reappeared at Sandfields, Aberavon, in the late 1920's.

Among the varied features of Dr Lloyd-Jones' preaching nothing was to be more prominent than his insistence that, before the gospel

[1] 1 Corinthians 4:20, October 23, 1927.
[2] *The Metropolitan Tabernacle Pulpit*, vol. 44, p. 421.

Revival

can do good, men must be brought to understand the radical nature of sin. 'It is made perfectly clear in the pages of the New Testament that no man can be saved until, at some time or other, he has felt desperate about himself.'[1] Accordingly, a large number of his sermons were preached with the specific intention of awakening spiritual concern. 'The way to obtain salvation is to seek it, and what makes one seek for it is that one realises one's need of it. That is, in reality, the great theme of the New Testament.' In an introduction to a sermon on John 8:32 he comments on the complaint that 'Present-day preaching does not save men, the churches are not getting converts':

'There is something even worse than that about the situation as I see it, and that is that present-day preaching does not even annoy men, but leaves them precisely where they were, without a ruffle and without the slightest disturbance. . . . The church is regarded as a sort of dispensary where drugs and soothing mixtures are distributed and in which everyone should be eased and comforted. And the one theme of the church must be "the love of God". Anyone who happens to break these rules and who produces a disturbing effect upon members of his congregation is regarded as an objectionable person. . . .'

Judged in those terms, he went on, Christ himself must be found blameworthy:

'If ever anyone knew the love of God, if ever "the love of God" was preached and understood by anyone, that one was Jesus Christ. Yet what was the effect He produced upon His congregations? Did all go home from the service smiling and happy, and feeling very self-satisfied and complacent? Was His perfect ministry one in which no one was offended and at which no one took umbrage? Do His services suggest the type so popular today – the building with "the dim religious light" where nice hymns are sung, nice prayers are offered, and a fine and cultured "short" address is delivered? Look to the pages of the New Testament and see the answer.'

The Jews, he went on to preach in this same sermon, failed to receive Christ because they were unconvinced of sin, and all his unconverted hearers were in the same condition:

'Have you ever seen yourself as one so hopelessly involved in sin and so

[1] Acts 16:30, c. 1928–30.

David Martyn Lloyd-Jones

helpless face to face with life and the power of evil that nothing but Christ's death could save you? If not, then you are in the precise position of these Jews.'

In another sermon from John's Gospel he reminded his hearers that the method of preaching which dealt first with sin was also followed by the apostle Paul:

'The great apostle finds it necessary not only to point out the glorious salvation in Christ Jesus, but also, before that, to bring to men conviction of sin, to point out to them the fallacy and the folly of their ways and their outlook. Many object to this and say that there is no purpose in it; indeed they go further and say that such preaching, which they call "negative", is wrong and is contrary to the love displayed in the life of Christ. . . . I say, with due reverence and consideration, unless we realise our deep and desperate need of it, the love of God is of no value to us and will make no difference to our lives. It thus behoves all of us, as we preach, not only to give our testimony as to the love of God towards us, but also to emphasise the equally great truth that all who have not felt a need of it are outside it.'[1]

Preaching on the Prodigal Son, and on how the prodigal was brought to know 'that he was a sinner, that his very nature was vile and filthy', he told his hearers:

'Now, my friends, until you experience that, you know nothing; that is the first thing a man or woman can ever really *know*. What is more, unless you have experienced that, unless you have known that, you are not a Christian, you do not believe in Christ as your personal Saviour. Until you realise that, you cannot possibly have felt the need of Christ; you may have felt the need of help and advice and comfort, but until you awake to the fact that your nature itself is evil, until you realise that your trouble is not that you do this and that which is wrong, but that you yourself are wrong, and that your whole nature is wrong, until you realise that, you will never have felt the need of a Saviour. Christ cannot help or advise or comfort you until He has first of all saved you, until He has changed your nature. Oh, my friends, have you yet felt this? God have mercy upon you if you haven't. You need not be a rotter or a scamp to be a sinner. It makes

[1] John 9:25, January 15, 1928.

[208]

no difference who you are or what you are, it makes no difference how good you may appear to be or how much good work you may do. You may have been inside the church all your life and actively engaged in its work, but still I say (and I am merely repeating what is said repeatedly in the Bible) that unless you have at some time or other felt that your very nature itself is sinful, that you are, in the words of St Paul, "dead in sins", then you have never known Jesus Christ as a Saviour, and if you do not know Him as a Saviour you do not know Him at all. "They that be whole need not a physician, but they that are sick."'[1]

This same teaching he applied with equal strength to what must be the church's vision of her work. Preaching near the end of 1928 from Nehemiah's words of distress at the state of Jerusalem, he urged that true prayer and spiritual work arise out of deep *feeling* for others: 'This is the beginning of all Christian work. Our time should be taken up in bringing conviction of sin to the sinner. The sinner must *feel* his own sin and the Christian must *feel* for the sin of others. We are called upon to *feel* the burden of sin around us, so to feel it that we drop on our knees and weep and pray.'[2] A right understanding of sin and of the gospel will, he declared, certainly lead to prayer for the Holy Spirit:

'We say we are concerned for the sin of the town! How much prayer do we offer for the sin of the town? When we pass a drunkard it is not our business to say, "What an awful man, what a beast!" No! judge not, but pray without ceasing. Christ came not to destroy – sin does that – but to save and release men from their sin. Will you as a church pray for the sinners of Aberavon and pray for God to save them through His Spirit? That is the meaning of a church. . . . May God give us this power to pray for a visitation of His Spirit! God give power to all doing this in all places!'[3]

By 1929 conversions had become a regular feature of the life of the church at Aberavon. Church membership had steadily increased, from 146 (as the official figures stood in 1926) to 165 at the end of 1927, and then to 196 at the end of 1928. These figures, of course, included some Christians who had moved into the district and

[1] Luke 15, June 19, 1927.   [2] Nehemiah 2:17, December 2, 1928.
[3] Luke 9:55, 56, February 24, 1929.

transferred their membership to Sandfields, but they do not show the considerable number who were already church members and yet were not converted until this period. The Robson family was one household which was profoundly influenced. Mrs Violet Robson, in whose home the Lloyd-Joneses had had the alarming experience of their first night together in Aberavon, was a leading figure in the church and a member of its Committee. Following one of the early Committee meetings soon after Dr Lloyd-Jones' arrival – the meeting at which he announced that there would be no more stage dramas in the hall! – Mrs Robson said grimly to herself: 'You'll learn, young man, you'll learn!' 'But,' she said, telling the story years later, 'it was *I* who learnt.' Although already a Christian in 1927, her spiritual life was greatly changed in the years which followed. Her elder daughter, Peggy, who was already a church member (having entered *via* the candidates' class), after a great inward tussle, was to come to the realisation that she was not a Christian at all. By 1930 she knew that she had passed from death to life, and with a friend, Dorothy Lewis, who was another church member with an identical experience, she went to Dr Lloyd-Jones to ask what she should do. His reply was that they could bear testimony to their change of heart in an 'after-meeting' one Sunday evening and when this was done, their words encouraged a number of others to make the same confession. The result was that Dorothy Lewis, Peggy Robson, with her young sister, Marjorie, and forty others, were baptised by sprinkling on November 2, 1930.

By that date the number of those who were coming to a saving knowledge of Christ from outside the church was markedly increasing, some of them being among the forty-three whose baptism we have just noted. Church membership in 1930 was to increase by 88 of which number 70 were recorded as 'from the world'. With deductions made on account of 'deaths, transfers and expulsions', the nett increase in membership that year was 63 (from 248 to 311).

One of the forty-three of November 2 was a certain Harry Wood. In his youth Wood had played soccer for Cwmbran and Monmouthshire but by the late 1920's, when he was one of the many out of work, the sporting enjoyments of those carefree earlier years had gone. When, at length, he became a Christian, the old sportsman, who loved a picturesque turn of phrase, would relate his testimony in such words as these: 'I sought satisfaction in many ways. I had my problem, I was all wrong. I would go into the cricket match and there I would see the white splashes on the greensward. I would go in through the north gate with my problem, I sought satisfaction watching as they wielded the willow and there my problem would be forgotten, but as I went out through the south I picked it up again. Then I came into this church one Sunday evening, sat in the gallery, and heard the doctor preach. He preached to me and showed me the way whereby I could enter by the north gate, and go out through the south, with all my problems solved!'

Perhaps few who saw Harry Wood as he tramped the streets looking for work would have supposed that *all* his problems were solved. He had once been well employed as a colliery sawyer, but neither that work nor any other could now be found. Yet the one thing which now concerned him was his service to Christ, and when he was asked by the officials in the local Labour Exchange, 'Have you been genuinely seeking work?', he was so sensitive to the implications of that question that he walked all the way up to a colliery which was working part-time at Bryn, a village in the hills some miles above Port Talbot. There his enquiry to the under-manager was answered by the exclamation, 'Work? We haven't got work here!' Concerned at only having a verbal reply to report at the Labour Exchange, Harry Wood proceeded to the school where E. T. Rees was teaching, with a plea that the Church Secretary should obtain the under-manager's refusal in writing – a request which the Church Secretary gladly fulfilled later in the day.[1]

The pastor of Sandfields had few more joyful conversations than those with Harry Wood and he was often surprised at the spiritual perception of one who, though well on in years, was such a young Christian. No one was more fully involved in the life of the church, and especially at the prayer meeting. After one especially memorable prayer meeting on the morning of a Good Friday, Dr Lloyd-Jones was surprised when Wood expressed his disappointment as he left. In response to his pastor's enquiry why he should feel like that on such an occasion, the older man replied that it had been his

---

[1] At the mine, the under-manager proposed that Mr Rees should write a statement, which he would sign. Mr Rees wrote, 'This is to certify that Mr Harry Wood of Sandfields, Aberavon, applied at this colliery today for work and I was unable to offer him any work.' On reading it, the under-manager declared, 'That's not good enough. Write, "I deeply regret that I cannot offer such a man any work"!'

prayer that he should be allowed to go 'straight Home' from just such a prayer meeting.

At the Monday night prayer meetings it was Dr Lloyd-Jones' practice to take no active part himself, save to give out an occasional hymn if it seemed appropriate in the course of the meeting. Otherwise the time was given wholly to prayer. Each week a different male member was asked – without prior notice – to commence the meeting with a reading from Scripture and with prayer. At a prayer-meeting early in 1931 Harry Wood was called upon to open the meeting. He did so by reading Christ's High-Priestly prayer recorded in John 17, and then he prayed with such 'glorious unction' that Dr Lloyd-Jones felt that he had heard nothing like it. The man seemed to be more in heaven than upon earth. When he stopped, and went to take a seat in the front row, Dr Lloyd-Jones heard heavy breathing and, opening his eyes, had only just time to catch the beloved Harry Wood as he fell to the floor, dead. Although there was no more prayer in the church that night, for the pastor pronounced the benediction and asked the people to leave quietly, the departure of Harry Wood was one of the events which marked the beginning of an extraordinary spiritual stirring. In the winter of 1930–31 the whole church seemed moved as by a consciousness of the presence of God and Dr Lloyd-Jones traced a quickening of his own spirit to this same period.

The year 1931 saw an addition of 135 to the membership of the church, of which 128 were 'from the world'! A number of the Sunday evening sermons of that year were to be remembered by those who were present as long as they lived. The text for the evening sermon on the first Sunday in March 1931, was Isaiah 55:8–9, 'For my thoughts are not your thoughts, neither are your ways my ways, saith the Lord.' At the close, fifteen people asked to be received into the membership of the church. On a similar evening, another twelve expressed their desire to be publicly identified with Christ and his people. One hot summer's evening, July 19, 1931, when the text was, 'For thus saith the Lord to the men of Judah and Jerusalem, Break up your fallow ground . . .', the message was to be particularly spoken of for years to come. The life of the natural man, the preacher declared, is like a farm in which the most important field is left waste, uncultivated, 'fallow'. Man neglects his soul and gives no thought to God and to eternity. He then proceeded to deal with the reasons for this neglect: first, ignorance of the fact that we have such a field; too many suppose that 'religion' is only for certain types of people. Second, laziness and thoughtlessness – objecting to the effort involved and desiring just to 'enjoy' life and pleasure. Third, 'Too busy in the other fields.' The next head of the sermon was the command of God, 'Break it up!' After emphasising that *man* has to do this, for 'he that cometh to God must believe that he is, and that he is a rewarder of them that diligently seek him' (Heb. 11:6), Dr Lloyd-Jones showed how the fallow ground was to be broken. His brief sermon notes listed: 'Realise you have it; Chapel going; Prayer; Bible-reading; Meditation; Giving up sins; Turning to God.' The sermon then concluded with reasons why this command of God must be obeyed: because the 'fallow ground' is the best part of the farm, the only part truly worth farming: 'Nothing else yields a real crop. What does sin give us at the end? What have we to show for it?' But the fallow ground is capable of yielding a crop of love, joy, peace, longsuffering, gentleness, goodness, faith, meekness and temperance. And, finally, the crowded chapel heard on that July Sunday evening, that the farm is only held on lease-hold, a rent-day is soon coming. Our actions will be judged, and all who do not break up the fallow-ground and bear fruit unto righteousness will be without excuse. In the silence of that crowded building every person was called to immediate obedience to the divine command.[1]

Such is an outline of one of many such sermons preached at this period for conviction and conversion. Without question it was deeply disturbing to many who came to listen. Morgan Beddow, for example, first came to Sandfields twice in 1928 and then decided that he would listen no more to the man who 'put the breeze up him'. He

[1] It needs to be noted that the command was always to faith and to repentance and not to an immediate public profession of conversion. Far from encouraging anyone to stay to the after-meeting and 'join the church', Dr Lloyd-Jones frequently gave warning against the danger of a premature profession of Christ: 'There is a sense in which it is true to say that the church is a very much more dangerous place than the world for the unbeliever. . . . The church has been far too anxious to put people into church-membership . . . church-membership, unless it is based upon a true and definite belief in and experience of Jesus Christ, the Son of God, can be exceedingly dangerous and can even be the cause of damning a soul' (sermon on John 6:66, April 23, 1933). When a new convert made his wish to join the church known at the after-meeting he would be given a very warm welcome and the church would all join in singing, 'Praise God from whom all blessings flow . . .' often with tears of joy.

had never been distressed over spiritual things in all his life and he did not intend to start. But, scarcely knowing why, Beddow was soon back in Sandfields and the sermon he heard so awed him and led him to the fear of God that he was never to be the same man again. With assurance of salvation, he became a member in 1930 and men marvelled at the change in his life.

The guiding principle in Dr Lloyd-Jones' evangelistic preaching was that pride and ignorance are the chief reasons why men trust in themselves and will not turn to Christ. Men suppose that they know God and therefore confidently argue that in 'a moral universe of love it is not possible that only a few Christian people are to be saved', but the truth is, that they are at enmity against the God of whom they profess to speak:

'What accounts for the fact that so few ever speak of the judgment in these days is that they do not believe in God. They think that they do, but when you come to analyse their belief you find that it is but a projection of certain ideas which happen to please them. Their god is something which they created themselves, a being who is always prepared to oblige and excuse them. They do not worship him with awe and respect, indeed they do not worship him at all. They reveal that their so-called god is no god at all in their talk. For they are for ever saying that "they simply cannot believe that God will punish the unrepentant sinner to all eternity, and this and that". *They* cannot believe that God will do so, therefore they draw the conclusion that God does not and will not. In other words, God does what they believe he ought to do or not do. What a false and blasphemous conception of God! How utterly untrue and unworthy! Such is the new paganism of today.'[1]

'The man who is concerned most of all about his public appearance before men is never much concerned about his private attitude before God . . . The world thinks highly of you. Men honour you and praise you. And so you are proud of what they say, you accept their honour and revel in it and live for it. You allow them to think, and to go on thinking, that you are exactly what you appear to be! Ah! the fraud and the dishonesty! What if they saw your heart? What if they knew the recesses of your mind and your imagination? What if they discovered all the details of your past record? What if they knew you

[1] Acts 17:30, 31, February 23, 1930.

as your family knows you? Above all, what if they knew you as you know yourself, really, in your heart of hearts? You have a great and a good name, bouquets are thrown to you during your life and wreaths innumerable will be placed upon your grave. You are proud of yourself and satisfied with yourself. Men and women think highly of you, you are praised as a "good sort" and as a "good fellow", for your good nature is proverbial. What a farce! What deceit! What if you were found out? What would they think of you if every act and every thought of yours were suddenly placed before them? What if they could but enter your heart and mind for just one day and find out what is taking place there? What if they knew your secret life as well as your public life? . . . As long as you are content to go on fooling others about yourself, you will never face yourself, and until you face yourself honestly you will never feel the need of Jesus Christ our Lord as your personal Saviour.'[1]

The evangelistic sermons of this period were taken from a wide variety of Scripture. From Old Testament examples and teaching, from Christ's parables and miracles, from the narratives of Calvary and the resurrection, from the records of the Book of Acts and the words of the Epistles, the gospel was constantly proclaimed. Instead of being deterred by the claim of some that his emphasis upon sin was 'too negative', he employed those very objections to drive home the difference between the world's solution for man's need and the remedy announced in the Bible:

'The world's medicine is always nice, always a "soothing syrup". "Come on, old chap, don't be so depressed," says the world. "Don't go to that chapel, don't go and hear that man preach if it makes you feel down in the mouth! Why should you be turned inside out Sunday after Sunday? Why should you read the Bible and think about death? My dear chap, cheer up!", says the world with a slap on the back. The world is crying "Peace" when there is no peace. . . .'

Instead of healing man, all the world can do is to offer stimulants with short-lived effects:

'When we are facing the worst, what has the world to offer? You cannot get up from your deathbed to go to a dance or to the races.

[1] John 5:44, September 14, 1930.

The world cannot help us to face God and eternity . . . But God be praised! There is a way whereby man in the last stages of the disease can find peace and healing. "*I*", says God, "will heal him and will cure him." God will not pamper us or give us some temporary measure to tide us over. He will not put a soothing plaster on the open sore of our soul. The remedy of God is radical. It tackles diseases beneath the surface – it reaches to the very centre of our being and scrapes out the core of matter which is poisoning us. The gospel does not pat you on the back, and tell you that all is right. No, the gospel says all is *not* right; not "all is well", no, but, "In the name of God, all is *wrong*". And you can never put it right. The remedy of God is different from the remedy of the world.'[1]

Again, towards the close of another sermon, he says:

'I am not afraid of being charged, as I frequently am, of trying to frighten you, for I am definitely trying to do so. If the wondrous love of God in Christ Jesus and the hope of glory is not sufficient to attract you, then, such is the value I attach to the worth of your soul, I will do my utmost to alarm you with a sight of the terrors of Hell.'[2]

It should be said at this point Dr Lloyd-Jones believed that, while the truth ought to result in profound emotion, the cultivation of 'emotionalism' was thoroughly alien to true Christianity. Feeling *alone* he saw as not merely valueless, it was positively dangerous. 'Emotionalism is ever the most real, because the most subtle, enemy of evangelicalism.' True feeling must be the result of truth believed and understood, and he frequently gave warning against that type of service where attempts are made to induce emotion by 'working up' the meeting with music and choruses, or by the telling of moving stories. 'Tears are a poor criterion for faith, being carried away in a meeting by eloquence or singing or excitement is not the same as committing oneself to Christ.'[3] To aim at emotion is the surest way to produce counterfeit Christians.

Thus his belief was that in a service where feeling could be restrained it ought to be restrained. The power of God was more likely to be known in a solemn stillness than amid noise and

---

[1] Isaiah 57:21, June 16, 1929.   [2] Mark 6:20, March 5, 1933.
[3] John 2:23–25, September 9, 1931.

excitement. Silence and an expectant seriousness, born of a realisation of the nearness of God, were striking characteristics of the
services at Sandfields. Audible interruptions, traditional in some
branches of Welsh evangelicalism, were noticeable by their absence. This fact was not always appreciated by occasional visitors,
and on one Sunday evening, after E. T. Rees had given the notices
at the middle of a service, he recalls how Dr Lloyd-Jones directed
him to go to speak to a man in the gallery. Before the first hymn
had been concluded this stranger had made his presence known by
a loud 'Amen!', and his interruptions were to continue until the
Church Secretary finally reached him with the message he had
been commissioned to deliver. 'Brother, I am sure you would like
to see souls saved?' Mr Rees began. 'I would, Hallelujah!' was the
exuberant response. 'Well,' said Mr Rees, 'shut up!' The silence
which followed confirmed Dr Lloyd-Jones' opinion that the
man's shouts had not been the irrepressible exclamations which
may spontaneously occur when God stirs men's souls to their
depths.

In the midst of the rising tide of blessing in 1931, one older
Christian member, who could remember the beginning of the century, exclaimed, 'Why, this is revival! The power of the Spirit is
greater here than in 1904.' What was occurring at Sandfields was
certainly a repetition of what has been seen whenever there is a
real spiritual awakening. In true revival, conviction of sin, sometimes amounting to agony of guilt, is widespread, and in the case
of those who are finally brought to salvation no human endeavours can unloose them from their sense of bondage. A God-
given persuasion of being lost and condemned can only be removed by 'the Spirit of adoption' who follows his first work of
conviction with the assurance that sin is forgiven. The man who
has truly felt his sin will not be prepared to stop short of a conscious persuasion of his salvation, and when he has that assurance
the height of his jubilation may correspond to the depth from
which he sees himself to have been delivered. Thus Dr Lloyd-Jones
believed that, as in the days of the Acts of the Apostles, when a
truly serious view of sin takes hold upon men, the ultimate result
will be a glorious conception of the gospel. Believing this, he was
not surprised that the vague, contemporary religion which professed to be Christian and yet said nothing to convict men of sin,
should be equally silent upon the joy of true assurance. On this

subject he says in a sermon on 2 Corinthians 1:19–20, preached on May 15, 1928:

'You remember that the first question which George Whitefield put to Howell Harris on the occasion of their first meeting was this, "Do you *know* that your sins are forgiven?"[1] That, to me, is the question which every minister and every man who claims that he is a Christian should be made to answer. For if you are not certain about that, your so-called belief in Christ is valueless, for if He taught one thing more than anything else, it was that God forgave all the sins of those who believe in His Son. In my agony when I am worried about my sins and sinfulness and wondering whether God can ever possibly forgive me, it is of no value to me to hear men's opinions, it is of little value for me to listen to a man who talks in general about life and expresses his opinion on this and that. The man who can help me is the man who can tell me that once he was in my position, knowing the agony of it, thinking at times that there was no hope for him, but, one day, realising in his heart that what Christ had said applied to him also, found relief and had never since been tormented by that agony. The man who is doubtful about it is of no help to me, however learned he may be and however much he may know, for all his knowledge and learning are of no value to me as long as he is doubtful about the one thing which really does concern me. I ask him bread, but he gives me a stone.'

Similarly, in a sermon on the words, 'Many of the Samaritans of that city believed on him for the saying of the woman, which testified, He told me all that ever I did' (John 4:39), he showed what happens when a person delivered from conviction of sin becomes a witness to others:

'This sinful, forlorn, notorious character, who had fallen so low that she had even ceased to be a topic of conversation, was so desperate in her sin that no one was any longer shocked by what they might hear about it! Such was the one who called upon the townspeople to come out of the city to see Christ! Why! there is enough gospel in that fact alone to save the whole world if we could but see it. . . . But if the messenger was strange, the message or the way in which she put it was even more remarkable. "Come", she said, "see a man, which

[1] The two men met for the first time on March 8, 1739.

told me all things that ever I did". What an extraordinary message! "Come see a man, not which told me all my good points, not one who praised me and told me what a good woman I was, but one who told me my faults, told me about my sins, revealed to me my own past life with all its horror." Ah! that is the very secret of the gospel of Christ. Christ exposes our sins and weaknesses, but God be praised, He does not stop at that. Why was this woman shouting about the streets? Simply because Christ had not merely exposed them but had removed them. Why are Christian converts less ashamed than others to refer to their past, why are they so free to speak about it? Simply because they know it is gone and no longer counts.

'Well, here were these men, listening to this woman. Seeing the change in the woman and hearing her story, they determine to try it for themselves. There is a danger of their sins also being exposed, but what does it matter as long as they get the happiness which she had! What does it matter though the whole world may know your past, and all the town laugh at you because of your penitential tears? What does it matter when you know that God has forgiven that past and you are filled with the joy of salvation and are thrilled with a new life? And off they go with the woman to see Christ. . . . You remember the sequel. What had happened to the woman happened to them. Their lives were changed, they knew their sins were forgiven, they also became filled with this joy and they turned to the woman and said, "Now we believe, not because of thy saying, but we have heard him ourselves and know that this is indeed the Christ, the Saviour of the world." In other words they said, "You made us believe that there was *something* in it, but what you said was a very poor picture of it. Why! This is life and life eternal! This is joy unspeakable. This is release from Hell to Heaven. This is darkness turned into light. This is misery turned into joy." It seems a little unkind for them to turn to her and say that, and yet it is not. No one would agree quite so readily with them as the woman herself. How can one describe the glory of the knowledge of the forgiveness of sins? Who can paint an adequate picture of what salvation means? How can one tell fully to others the difference that conversion makes?'

There were many listeners in Sandfields who, in their new-found freedom, could assent entirely to these words. In the Monday prayer-meetings earnest intercession had increasingly mingled with fervent praise. Assembled for prayer, the church came to know such a sense of liberty in the presence of God that there were nights when all sense of time seemed lost. Certainly the prayer-meeting, once so poorly attended, could not now be contained within two hours on account of the numbers who were ready to pray and to engage in thanksgiving. One Monday night, about May 1931, the prayer-meeting began as usual at 7.15 p.m. and was stopped by Dr Lloyd-Jones at 10 p.m. after forty-four had taken part in prayer![1] There were other occasions when the Wednesday Fellowship spontaneously turned into a time of praise. On one such evening, a man, new to spiritual things, rose to ask Dr Lloyd-Jones the question, 'What is a Christian?' The reply, as E. T. Rees remembers it, was this, 'To define a Christian would take all through the night, and all through tomorrow and all through the next night.' But, to the surprise of the whole gathering, a woman who was never known to speak at the Fellowship, and who was later to die of cancer at Bridgend, rose to declare: 'A Christian, Doctor, is the heir of salvation, the purchase of God, the born of his Spirit, the washed in his blood'. 'Thank you, Mrs B.,' her pastor replied, and addressing the people continued, 'Those who can say – "I am the heir of salvation" – get up and thank God in just a few words!' A prayer-meeting resulted in which more than forty were again to take part before the close.

One of the clearest memories of E. T. Rees from those days is of the eagerness with which the congregations gathered. On a Sunday evening the building would start to fill as much as an hour before the 6.30 hour of service, with sometimes not a seat remaining empty by 6 p.m. The Monday and Wednesday meetings had both to be removed to the church itself on account of the numbers attending. Shopkeepers would arrive straight from their business without an evening meal. Night-shift workers, due to report for work at 8.30 p.m., would come in their working clothes, preferring to miss part of the meeting rather than the whole.

This new life witnessed at Sandfields required neither publicity nor organisation to carry news of it to others. The word spread in all manner of ways. Women spoke over their shopping of how their husbands now preferred prayer-meetings to the cinema. At school, one afternoon, a teacher was told by a boy in her class, 'We *had* a

[1] It is almost certainly this evening to which Dr Lloyd-Jones referred in preaching on 'Praying in the Spirit', *The Christian Soldier*, Ephesians 6:10–20, 1977, p. 348.

dinner, today, Miss! We had gravy, potatoes, meat, and cabbage, and rice pudding' – they had rarely had such a meal at home before, and the reason followed: 'My father has been converted!' So the money this man had formerly spent on drink, when he got his pay on Fridays, now came home for his wife and children.[1] Others saw a neighbour, who had been a well-known spirit-medium in Aberavon, abandon the only livelihood which she knew, for the gospel. Every Sunday evening she had been paid three guineas – quite a large sum in those days – for leading a spiritist meeting. Then one Sunday when she was ill, and unable to go out, her attention was attracted to the numbers who were passing her house on the way to Sandfields. The very sight of these people, and their evident anticipation, awakened a desire in her to attend a service herself. This she did, to be herself transformed and thereafter to live a consistent Christian life until her death. Included in the testimony which she subsequently gave to the messenger who had led her to Christ were these remarkable words: 'The moment I entered your chapel and sat down on a seat amongst the people, I was conscious of a supernatural power. I was conscious of the same sort of supernatural power as I was accustomed to in our spiritist meetings, but there was one big difference; I had a feeling that the power in your chapel was a *clean* power.'

Some of the most unlikely characters were brought to Sandfields by friends. One such was Mark McCann, whom Mrs Lloyd-Jones still remembers from the night when he entered the chapel for the first time – 'A thin, tallish, raw-boned man, his grey hair well plastered down, a slightly embarrassed expression on his face and an incredible moustache!'[2] As his Christian companion passed her pew

---

[1] The school-teacher who heard these words was Mrs E. T. Rees. In Mrs Lloyd-Jones' opinion drink was a greater problem in the town than actual poverty. Dock workers were often given liquor in addition to wages. When a man was converted he often handed in a bottle on the manse doorstep with such words as these: 'I asked the Doctor to keep this for me . . . it's good stuff, the Captain gave it to me when I finished the job . . .' Converts were unwilling to trust themselves with it in their own homes. When the Lloyd-Jones' finally left Aberavon a large wall cupboard in the Doctor's study was full of bottles – a fact which posed a considerable problem for them. The solution was for a medical friend from Cardiff, able to put the cupboard's contents to wise use, to call one night with a van!

[2] Mrs Lloyd-Jones' memories of some of the Christian converts at Sandfields, upon which I am dependent both here and in following pages, will be found in *Memories of Sandfields, 1927-38*, due to be published in 1983.

he whispered, 'I've got one of the Devil's generals here tonight, Mrs Jones, pray for him to be converted.' McCann, of Scots and Irish parentage, was then probably in his early sixties. Once a miner, his living and his enjoyment had centred largely upon the fights in which he engaged at fairs. With his vicious temper, and considerable strength, it was only the providence of God which had restrained him from actually killing anyone. Once, when his dog had eaten the dinner intended for him to consume, he had cut off its head with a bread knife! McCann was one of those whose conversion was swift. On his first visit to the Chapel he was arrested by the Spirit of God. The next Sunday evening he was there again and, to the surprise of his companion, when the service ended he indicated his intention to stay to the after-meeting. When the usual question was put at that meeting, amidst the solemn joy of many witnesses, Mark McCann stood to profess the name of Christ, 'And from that moment,' writes Mrs Lloyd-Jones, 'he showed himself to be a changed man, unfailingly faithful, truly born again – another, somewhat elderly, "babe" for the Church to love and nurture.'

There were others who came, not as the result of Christian testimony, but simply because they heard about what was being preached in Sandfields. William Thomas, or 'Staffordshire Bill' as he was commonly known, was drinking in the Working Men's Club in Aberavon one Sunday afternoon. As usual, he was by himself, for even men who had few moral standards had long since learned to avoid his 'filthy language and general unpleasantness' whenever they could. In the words of Mrs Lloyd-Jones:

'There he was, drinking himself into his usual sodden condition, and as he afterwards confessed, feeling low, hopeless and depressed, trusting to the drink to drown those inward pangs and fears which sometimes disturbed him. There were several men in little groups of twos and threes in the Club room, drinking and talking, and suddenly he found himself listening, at first involuntarily but then anxiously, to a conversation between two men at the table next to his. He caught the words "the Forward" and then something about the "preacher", and then a complete sentence that was to change the whole of his life. "Yes," said the one man to the other, "I was there last Sunday night and that preacher said nobody was hopeless – he said there was hope for everybody." Of the rest of the conversation he heard nothing, but, arrested and now completely sobered, he said to himself, "If there's hope for everybody, there's hope for me – I'll go to that chapel myself and see what that man says."'

But William Thomas' intention was not easily fulfilled. That first Sunday he walked to the open gate of the railings that fenced the church, stood for some minutes, then, his nerve failing him, he turned and went home. Although throughout the wretched week that followed he waited for the next Sunday evening to arrive, somehow he reached the chapel only to hear singing. Faced with the realisation that he was late, 'with his heart in his boots and full of some nameless fear, he once more turned away and went home'. Now, though his misery was increased, he had no thought of attempting to drown his terrors of conviction in drink. The Spirit of God had already begun a work in his heart which would prevent him from going back to his old ways. The third Sunday evening he was again at the gate, 'wondering nervously what he should do next', when one of the congregation welcomed him with the words, 'Are you coming in, Bill? Come and sit with me.'

That same night 'Staffordshire Bill' passed from condemnation to life. 'He found,' Mrs Lloyd-Jones tells us, 'that he could understand the things that were being said, he believed the gospel and his heart was flooded with a great peace. Old things had passed away, all things had become new. The transformation in his face was remarkable, it had the radiance of a saint. As he walked out that night, lovingly shepherded by J. M., they passed me, and J. M. said, "Mrs Jones, this is Staffordshire Bill." I shall never forget the agonised look on his face, for he flinched as though he had been struck a sudden blow. "Oh no, oh no," he said, "that's a bad old name for a bad old man; I am William Thomas now."'

The change in the man was apparent for all to see. He lived some three or four miles up the valley from Aberavon and in the years when he had employment he had carried on a door-to-door fish business. It was no uncommon sight in those days for people to see Staffordshire Bill's pony taking the fish-cart home, while the man himself, having fallen backward off the driver's seat as the cart went up the steep hill, lay drunk among the unsold fish! He was nearly seventy at the time of his conversion, the pony and cart gone, but, in the words of Mrs Lloyd-Jones, 'He thought nothing of those three or four steep uphill miles when once "the light of the knowledge of the glory of God in the face of Jesus Christ" had shined in his heart. He was at every meeting – twice on Sunday, Monday night prayer-meeting, Wednesday night Church Fellowship and Saturday night Brotherhood – that old battered face transformed and radiant with an inner joy.'

*   *   *

The unusual nature of what was happening in Aberavon was common knowledge in South Wales in the early 1930's, though very little information appeared in print. Such secular papers as did report it scarcely saw more than what was externally observable, and yet that was amazing enough. The words of J. C. Griffith-Jones, South Wales Correspondent of the *News Chronicle*, who supplied an article entitled 'A Physician of Souls', are worth quoting:

'Seven years ago Martin Lloyd-Jones, M.D., M.R.C.P., was on the threshold of a brilliantly promising career in Harley Street. He renounced it to labour in one of the most difficult fields of Forward Movement evangelism in Wales. The Sandfields district of Aberavon is a dead end. Even when the sun shines, sandy wastes and dreary, crowded houses convey a sense of desolation, almost of hopelessness. What could a man denied work, disillusioned by social callousness, do here but live for a day, deteriorate, drift and die?

'Into this desperate little world came the young physician-minister, preaching, living the gospel of old-new hope. He shocked the locality out of its despair. This world had failed them; there was another world.

'Men listened amazed. Here was one who practised the gospel that he preached with such tremendous conviction. He had given up a great career – fame, money, leisure – to live and work among the poor and the hopeless.

'Christianity was not a mere fable, then, but a living modern fact!

'The little church filled. Under the previous pastor it had not been a dead letter by any means, but now it awakened to a galvanic new life.

'Not only in Port Talbot, but all around the district, the word went forth that surprising things were happening at the "mission hall" on the sand dunes. Curious, sceptical, doubting, hoping, believing, people flocked to the church.

'It was no passing wonder. Today, years after the first revelation of new power, the congregations still overflow the church. Every meeting is a "big meeting".

'More than 500 members, the faithful augmented by "hard cases", sinners whom others considered, and who regarded themselves, as beyond redemption, irretrievably lost . . . No whist drives, bazaars or worldly side-shows, no dramas except the great drama of salvation.

'A working-class (and unemployed) membership raising £1,000 a year for church work. Crowded prayer meetings, a crowded "seiat" (church meeting) in mid-week, a crowded brotherhood meeting on Saturday, of all nights, when men discuss the problems of spiritual salvation and the pastor sums up the discussion.

'Sandfields now shares the glad tidings with all Wales. The "physician of souls," who shuns publicity, draws thousands to hear his message in all parts of the Principality. He will not stand for a Press photographer. But his name is a household word in Wales.

'He will not preach in the "Sasiwn" [Presbyterian quarterly meeting], but his every engagement becomes a Sasiwn. Public emotionalism leaves him cold, yet his passion for human salvation sets his people on fire.

'The doctor's sermons penetrate the innermost secrets of the heart.

'Spellbound, but sorrowful, men sometimes go back into the world after hearing the message, saying: "It is terrific. We ought to take that road, but it is too hard, too completely revolutionary".

'This note of certainty permeated the only sermon I have ever heard Dr Martin Lloyd-Jones preach.

'I doubt whether there is any other preacher in Wales today who could extract such dramatic power out of a text of two short words, "But God", as this dynamic evangelist. There was man, and there was God, with this tremendous "but" always between them.

'As preaching it was mesmeric in its appeal: as a message of hope to a world that has tried everything but Christianity, it was electrical.

'An awe-inspiring new force has arisen in the life of Wales.'

Interesting though such words may be to us, it was, in fact, this kind of reporting which confirmed Dr Lloyd-Jones in his silence over the blessing they experienced in the church at the beginning of the fourth decade of this century. He never referred to what they had seen in their midst as a 'revival'. Compared with the rain which the land needed, it was only a shower. Yet they had experienced a glimpse of the glory, and it left him more persuaded than ever that the supreme need of the church was to 'cease from man'. He had seen things of which he felt it was almost too sacred to speak. He preferred to suppress all information rather than to risk anything which gave glory to man. So no one in Sandfields ever put pen to paper, and the figures recording the remarkable increase in church membership were never released. E. T. Rees himself could have written a book upon the years which we have touched upon in this chapter, but deference to his pastor restrained him. Had such a book been written we do not doubt that Mr Rees would have concluded it as he once did a conversation which he had many years later with a few friends about the converts of 1929–31: 'I say these things not because of the personal influence of Dr Martyn Lloyd-Jones, for he was ever reminding us, even to his last night, his farewell night, "Don't talk about me, talk about my Saviour". It was not his personal influence or his personal attraction that led to the salvation of those men, but a realization that they were lost souls and that Jesus Christ came to seek and to save that which was lost.'

For Dr Lloyd-Jones himself, probably the clearest lesson he gained from this period was the lifelong assurance that, in days when the church's influence is limited and restrained to certain types of people, the power of the Holy Spirit is able to reach and convince *all* classes. No single section of the community was left unrepresented in Sandfields, and the reason is best explained in words he preached in the midst of those days of blessing. Speaking of the reaction of the Christian Jews to the conversion of the first Gentiles, with Acts 10:25, 26, as his text, he said:

'We tend to regard certain people as being "beyond hope", and assume that they must of necessity continue in their grooves as they are and die unrepentant and unredeemed. We just shake our heads over them and express our sorrow. We have talked to them and tried to persuade them. We have appealed to them and preached to them. Everything that human agency can possibly do has been tried and has failed. We cannot get them to come our way, so we feel that their case is hopeless and desperate. Ah! what lack of faith all that reveals! How different from what we find here in the New Testament and always in the church during days of revival and true faith! If you and I are to save men and women, then indeed the case is hopeless. All our efforts will most certainly fail. But that is not our gospel. It is Jesus Christ who saves! There is no limit to what He can do! His methods are not confined as ours are. There are no prescribed and definite ways where He is concerned. Ah! what a shock those Jews had when they found these Gentiles suddenly converted! And what glorious shocks do we also get here from time to time! Straight from paganism to Christ! Yes, quite easily, for there is no limit at all. He creates anew. His power is endless. Do not give up hope for any sinner. Pray to God to save them. Let not any conversion astonish you; be astonished rather, that anyone should possibly remain unconverted.'

'I want to get back the discipline of the church – discipline for the minister as for the members – and to recapture the glorious conception of the Christian life, that men may feel that there is no honour which can be conferred upon them so great as their church membership, and that ministers may feel that there is nothing in life to be compared with the preaching of this glorious and incomparable gospel.'

M. L.-J.
on Matthew 16:24, c. 1929

11

The Church Family

With so many newly-arrived members in Sandfields, differing so widely in age and, often, in background, it might be supposed that a certain degree of disunity was inevitable. Many had no previous experience of what was expected within a church; instead, they had to learn from the beginning. The members of the church Committee themselves were faced with a novel situation, for they had never seen such an enlargement of numbers before.

But the truth is that one of the chief features of Sandfields, noted by many outside visitors in the early 1930's, was the extraordinary degree of closeness and inter-dependence among the people. Although so many were new-born babes in the Christian life, far from feeling strange in their new position, they were instantly conscious of belonging to a family. The unity which they now knew was instinctive. And, for their part, the older Christians needed no directions on how to receive and help those for whom the gospel was so new. They had no greater interest than in the signs of grace and of growth which week by week were to be observed in the church.

The eagerness to be together which marked the young converts was indeed prominent throughout the entire membership. The Reverend R. J. Rees of the Forward Movement describes a visit he made to Sandfields one Sunday about the summer of 1931. Dr Lloyd-Jones was away, but that made no difference to the size of the morning congregation which filled the building to its utmost capacity. Mr Rees writes:

'The service was for me a breaking forth of God's glory, but I believe I rejoiced just as much on the Sunday afternoon to find myself seated in the midst of a Bible Class of some 80 in number. And what, think you, we discussed? Where did I find them? Nowhere else but in the midst of the Eighth Chapter of the Epistle to the Romans and there

for the long but interesting, bright afternoon, I had to sit it out, the
target of questions asked by young and older men arising from the
dialectic of the Apostle concerning "the mind of the flesh", the carnal
mind, the new man, and the leading of the Spirit. It was a beautiful
afternoon. The sands were near, but there they were – 80 strong –with
me, not Dr Martin Lloyd-Jones.'[1]

Not long after this, Eliseus Howells was to make similar observa-
tions. Writing in *Y Goleuad* of the prayer and fellowship meetings at
Sandfields, he says:

'These meetings are noted for their length because hardly one of them
ends in under two hours, and we have seen between 160 and 200
present in them on cold, stormy, winter evenings. The rejoicing that
we commonly link with the feelings is hardly present, although a great
measure of deep joy is present. Sometimes between fifteen and twenty
take part, and it is easy to perceive that the atmosphere is too laden
with the law for the wicked to live in it, and too abounding in grace for
the legalist so much as to breathe in hypocrisy.'[2]

At least one ministerial reader of the above words found their
implications extraordinary and wrote to the correspondence columns
of the denomination's paper to say so:

'I tend to think that Dr Jones' people do not have a taste for anything
outside religious meetings – "it is exceptional to finish any of them in
under two hours". Is there another church in Wales ready to be in a
religious meeting for two hours? If so, then they are few and far
between! Usually people complain if the meeting runs over the hour.
Should every church be like Sandfields, or is there a place for
variety?'

The same writer goes on to express the opinion that, if Sandfields
were to be regarded as the pattern, then it would require a 'great
revolution' to bring the rest of the churches into line! He did not seem
to realise that the attendance at the Sandfields mid-week meetings,
and the duration of the meetings, was the result of something much
deeper than 'taste' and akin to the experience of the multitude who

[1] *The Treasury*, March 1932.   [2] *Y Goleuad*, February 1, 1933, p. 38.

after Pentecost continued daily in a unity of doctrine and fellowship.

Perhaps no meeting brought out more clearly what was happening in the church than the Brotherhood on Saturday nights to which we have already referred. E. T. Rees remembers how dozens of men 'came, whose evident concern was to grow in grace and in spiritual knowledge'. On Sundays they heard from the preacher, 'I hope that none of you is dependent upon what I say from this pulpit'. They were to think, read and pray for themselves, and the questions ready for discussion at the Brotherhood showed how the exhortation was being obeyed. Each Saturday night the meeting began in the same way, first prayer, then the familiar words from the minister, 'Well, what is the question?' If the question put was not entirely clear, or if it did not get close enough to the questioner's mind, the suggestion came from the chair, 'What you mean is this . . .', a procedure which almost invariably brought the response, 'Yes, that is right, Doctor!' The one thing that the chairman would never allow was a 'Yes' or 'No' answer. If a man rose to say, 'Doctor, I am still being tempted. Is that a sign I am growing in grace?', he would refer the question to the gathering with such a non-committal expression as, 'Well, there it is, what do you make of that?' Only at the end would he summarise the full answer and press it home with an exhortation. On some occasions if a visiting minister happened to be present, he might be presented with the duty of the summing up – an undertaking which was often found to be none too easy! E. T. Rees recalls the stirring discussion at one of the gatherings when the question was, 'Should a Christian live with his eye on the future reward?' At the end a startled visitor was asked to summarise; he did so in the abrupt sentence, 'What I feel is this, that if Moses "had respect unto the recompence of the reward" (Heb. 11:26) I do not see why E— B— should not do the same!'

The Bible was ever central in the Brotherhood meetings, but after their first outing to Llangeitho in 1927, church history became an increasing interest among the men. In the succeeding years practically all the major places of spiritual interest in South, West and Mid-Wales were to be visited, including Trevecca, Llandovery and parts of Pembrokeshire (scenes associated with the eighteenth-century leaders, Howell Harris, William Williams and Howell Davies respectively). These trips were always concluded with an address related to what they had seen and with advice on books which would supply more information. On one occasion when Dr Lloyd-Jones was unable to go to a spot associated with William Williams, E. T. Rees had to be the spokesman. The answers given to Dr Lloyd-Jones' questions at the next meeting of the Brotherhood proved that he had been a worthy deputy. When asked for their impressions of what they had seen and heard, Richard Lody, a Port Talbot Corporation road sweeper, replied: 'As I stood at the graveside of Williams, Pantycelyn, I thought what a wonderful man he was and how he was made wonderful in the same way that I was made a new creature – by the grace of God! And I said to myself, "William Williams was the greatest William Williams that ever lived, and you know the secret; well, Dick, you are the only Dick Lody, and just as William Williams was the greatest William Williams, so – God help me! – by the grace of God you can be the greatest Dick Lody that ever lived!' Such impromptu reflections did much to make the Brotherhood what it was.

It was noteworthy that the composition of the Brotherhood was far from being as homogeneous as that of the other church meetings, for curiosity often brought visitors from other churches and from backgrounds alien to any kind of Christianity. Some who were not yet ready to venture into the chapel on Sundays might well put in their first appearance on a Saturday night to see what 'this little fellow'[1] had got to say. 'All sorts of men they were,' E. T. Rees has recalled, 'with all sorts of opinions. Roman Catholics were there as well as Protestants; sceptics as well as Christians; there were people who belonged to such bodies as the Apostolics and the Pentecostals sitting alongside one or two deep-dyed Calvinists. We were an odd mixture and sometimes things would get pretty hot! A man would say, "It's all right for you, Doctor, to talk about being a Christian, how can a man be a Christian on an empty belly?" Then you would have a clash between the man in the chair and the man on his feet.'

Not infrequently objections of that kind would be voiced by visitors who were convinced Socialists, persuaded that chapels stood for the interests of capitalism. One Saturday night in the midst of the Depression a stranger rose to ask why Christians were doing nothing about the prevailing conditions: 'The church should *do* something,' he protested. That same day, he went on, he had been at Abergwynfi

---

[1] *Y dyn bach*, literally 'the little man', in Welsh, has an aura of affection not obvious in the English term.

where he found not a man working. The only help anyone had offered him came from a woman who, with baby in arms, had dragged herself across the soup kitchen to give him three pence! 'What is your profession?' Dr Lloyd-Jones asked him. 'Insurance agent,' was the answer, to which Dr Lloyd-Jones responded, 'If you were a *Christian* insurance agent you would have given the money back to her!'

Generally speaking, all political questions were refused. Had he allowed political debates he would have lost the ears of many of the community at once. Instead, to men who regarded Ramsay MacDonald as a saviour, he was content to urge the general principle, 'Put not your trust in princes, nor in the son of man, in whom there is no help' (Psa. 146:3). When, at length, MacDonald astonished his former constituents by heading a National Coalition and abandoning his distinctive Socialism, there were not a few in Aberavon who began to consider that, with the thousands in the country unemployed, their trust had indeed been misplaced. More than once, a man who came to the Brotherhood believing in political solutions was ultimately brought to confess that there was only one solution to life's problems, and that was to be found in the New Testament.

The Saturday night discussions were commonly hard-hitting and intensely serious. Next to the spiritual impact, the thing which so often struck E. T. Rees was the demands made upon the minds of those who came: 'I used to be amazed at the high educational standard attained in those debates which went on between 7.15 and about 9 p.m. It was comparable with University extension classes, which some of us had attended and some of us had conducted.' Anything of the nature of entertainment was entirely absent; on the contrary there was an element of severity about the leader which is not generally associated with church activities. On one occasion an individual was literally put out! The man rose to complain, 'I cannot believe in the deity of Christ.' After a moment's careful scrutiny of the speaker, with an instant and, as it proved, accurate assessment, Dr Lloyd-Jones, replied, 'You have said that more than once. Very well, you will say it no more here, you must go!'The man left, only to return subsequently in a different spirit and to take his place among believers.

Dr Lloyd-Jones' penetrating analysis of those who spoke on Saturday or Wednesday nights was a regular feature of the meetings. While the shy were encouraged, any 'Mr Talkative' was soon put down. Commenting on this, Eliseus Howells wrote:

'He does the interviewing, counselling or rebuking as the need arises, and what Williams says of Daniel Rowland is also true of Dr Lloyd-Jones, "If anyone strays from the paths of divine grace he reveals their error, so that others see the offender in a hateful light". Williams (Pantycelyn) commended the act of rebuking sinners, believing that if this was overlooked it gave nourishment to tares, and that a gospel without law prospered wickedness.

'It is here in his *seiat* that we saw the strangest combination of a keen questioning as to the state of mind and conscience, coupled with the unmistakeable tenderness of the gospel in its application to every instance. If Calvin ruled with an iron rod in Geneva, and if Howel Harris was severe in his large building, the Doctor is just as strict in this respect. But if there is in him an unusual degree of severity, there is also a matchless tenderness, and the fathers were not more beloved by their converts than he is by his.'

If love for the children of God is the mark of all who have 'passed from death unto life', as emphasised in the First Epistle of John, it is not surprising that there was an abounding love evident in Sand-fields. We have already mentioned some of the converts, but the truth is that they were representative of many others, and in them all there shone a devotion to the messenger from whom they learned the truth. It was in profound affection that they all called him 'the Doctor'. Not E. T. Rees only, but a whole host of them counted it their privilege to serve alongside their pastor and to be with him whenever possible. Frequently after evening meetings or services Dr Lloyd-Jones would stay behind to talk with individuals, yet, no matter how late the hour, when he finished there would always be one or more of 'the men' waiting to accompany him back to his house. Often one of the inner band, of which E. T. Rees was the head, would offer to go with him on pastoral visitation. Mr Rees remembers one night when a case of peculiar difficulty kept them both out late at the home of one of the members after a mid-week meeting. Finally they left, hungry and tired, and not before Dr Lloyd-Jones had spoken sternly to the member of the household who was responsible for the trouble. Despite the late hour, E.T. set off as usual to the manse gate, before going to his own home. Deep in conversation as they walked, Martyn suddenly stopped on the bridge between Sandfields and his home and, looking back on the church silhouetted in the moonlight, he exclaimed, 'That's our church – a truly Corinthian church! Now for ham and eggs!'

The love of the men for their pastor took various forms. On one occasion in the early years at Sandfields, the foreman of the tin-plate factory, then on night-shift, enthusiastically agreed to wake the Doctor daily at 7 a.m. so that the two could have a six-mile walk on the moors before Lloyd-Jones' day began. But he was soon alarmed to find that these early-morning outings, far from benefitting his minister, brought him to confess that if he did not give them up he would have to abandon preaching! Another admirer of the outdoor life and would-be helper was a local army drill sergeant whose work gave him the use of some fine horses. Hearing of Dr Lloyd-Jones' love of horses, the sergeant arrived unexpected at the manse on horseback one day before breakfast, leading another fine stallion, with empty saddle, on a rein beside him. In this instance the Doctor was not to be enticed!

More normal occasions for one or more of the men to accompany Dr Lloyd-Jones were his twice weekly preaching visits to various parts of South Wales. Even before the 1930's, the afternoons of Tuesdays and Thursdays each week were regularly employed for this purpose. He had no car and generally went by train, but sometimes when trains were not available he accepted the ready offers of transport from willing assistants who were ready to borrow a car from anywhere rather than leave the Doctor in difficulties. Morgan Beddow – whose first hearing of Dr Lloyd-Jones had put him to flight – was to become one of his travelling companions. In later years he was to recall how once he borrowed a car from Briton Ferry for this purpose. On another occasion, when the Doctor had missed the train to Llandilo, it was a Fiat which a friend had recently purchased for £5, which was pressed into service. Despite the Doctor's misgivings at the appearance of the Fiat, it somehow held together as they sped over the Black Mountains at 'over forty miles per hour'. 'We looked', said Beddow, 'like a couple of race goers, I in my slouch cap and he in his old bowler (from his student days) which had become flattened in our rush.' Their destination was reached by 2.45 p.m. in time for the afternoon service!

Driving did not end Beddow's welcome duties. By the close of such afternoon services the preacher had perspired so freely that a change of shirt would be needed, and before the fresh shirt (brought with him) was put on, his companion would 'rub him down with a towel as though he were a pugilist'. With the burden of preaching over, there might well be some good-humoured banter on the drive home. All the men enjoyed trying to score at the Doctor's expense, an experiment in which they rarely succeeded. Then, as later, Dr Lloyd-Jones, even without owning a car,[1] was an expert on routes and roads, both major and minor. Though he rarely advised his chauffeur as to driving he was always ready to assert the best route. Returning from a preaching service with Beddow late one night, his expertise failed him as they became hopelessly lost in mist somewhere in the area of Pontypridd. But Dr Lloyd-Jones did not intend to allow Beddow the pleasure of enjoying the temporary eclipse of his sense of direction. When at last they stopped beside a signpost on some high ground, Beddow, matches in hand, had to climb the post before he could read the direction in which it pointed. 'It says to Pontypridd,' Beddow called from his perch, only to hear from the muffled figure still inside the car, 'Well, why didn't you go there instead of driving up here!' Home was not reached that night until 2 a.m.

Much as the Doctor enjoyed Beddow's company, perhaps he was not entirely at his best at a car wheel; in any case borrowed cars became unnecessary as another man, Jack Williams, who was converted later, offered the use of the car which he had for his business as a commercial traveller with a shoe company. Although they may not have realised it at the time, the truth was that Lloyd-Jones often took these men with him, especially on journeys by road for their own help and encouragement. On a train journey he generally preferred to be alone so that he could devote the time to reading. There is no doubt that Beddow and many others were strengthened by the personal fellowship which these opportunities provided. One unusual incident during an outing which Beddow recalled concerned a clash between the Doctor and the Church Secretary of a chapel building which a smaller church had borrowed for the special occasion. When Dr Lloyd-Jones heard this Secretary telling his counterpart from the small church that they required £5 for the use of their building, he did not hide his anger, convinced that £1 would have been quite sufficient and that the smaller church which he had come to help was in need of funds. 'I will never come to

[1] He had experience of driving but did not own his own car until 1952.

your church again,' he exclaimed. The Secretary, mortified and alarmed, stuttered, 'Oh, Doctor, don't say that. I was only having a bit of fun'. But his rebuker was in no mood for 'fun' and spoke his mind very plainly.

Much could be written on this bond between the pastor and his men for it showed itself in so many ways. From George Jenkins, whose conversion had occurred on the same day as his own birthday, Dr Lloyd-Jones was to receive a birthday card on December 20 as long as this grateful Christian was alive. Another man, despite his good position as a docks pilot, had been a hopeless drunkard. After his conversion three photographs adorned his mantelpiece; one, taken during his pre-Christian days by a former friend, showed him leaning helplessly against a lamp-post; a second showed him sitting beside Lloyd-Jones on the sea-shore, where he had joined the Sunday-school outing one Whit Monday and been drawn into spiritual conversation for the first time; while a third showed him as a smart and clean-shaven figure whose life now centred in the church and the gospel. Each picture had its own one-word caption written beneath, 'Lost', 'Found', 'Saved'.

Sometimes a few words from these men would reveal the depth of their feelings. When, some years later, George Jenkins whose life was so radically changed lay dying in London, a former friend from Sandfields visited him. One of the old man's first enquiries was to ask for 'his beloved father in Christ' and, he added, 'I would rather see him, than Paul himself!'

The fellowship of the church was, however, a great deal more than the relationship between pastor and individuals. It was pre-eminently a family unity and, no matter what the background of the once broken elements of mankind which now filled the pews, all that was needed in order truly to 'belong' was a common attachment to Christ. While Acts 4:32 was not literally followed at every point, the resemblance between Sandfields and Jerusalem was indeed real: 'And the multitude of them that believed were of one heart and of one soul: neither said any of them that ought of the things which he possessed was his own; but they had all things common.'

Many works of brotherly love lay hidden from public view. The case of J.J. was typical of scores of others. Before he became a Christian the greater part of J's money was constantly squandered on drink. His house was literally a shambles, with hand-rails torn off the staircase to light fires and the bath used for the storage of coal. This

David Martyn Lloyd-Jones

was the man already mentioned whose sons so enthusiastically told
their teacher of the new dinners they were enjoying because of the
change in their father. J.J. was now troubled at the broken-down
state of his house, especially as it stood not far from the church in
what was known as the 'White City' district. One day as he walked in
Port Talbot with one of his new Christian friends, E. T. Rees, the two
men happened to meet Mr Thomas, the Town Clerk. Looking at J.J.,
and addressing Mr Rees, Thomas began, 'Oh, this is one of the
converts in Sandfields, is it?' 'Yes, Mr Thomas,' replied E.T., 'this is
one of the new men'. And seizing the opportunity to put in a word
respecting his companion's housing problem, he went on, 'Now he is
a new man, Mr Town Clerk, he needs a new house – that's the order,
isn't it? New man, new house! Not new house for "the old man"!'
Scarcely disguising his surprise at this mixing of theology with
housing problems, the Senior Corporation official went away
promising to see what he could do. At this date there was an
arrangement whereby houses could occasionally be bought on a
corporation mortgage system, provided that a sufficient down-
payment was available and that a bank guaranteed that the promise
of further weekly payments was realistic. During the week that
followed the street meeting the Town Clerk informed Mr Rees that a
house was available for J.J. provided the necessary requirements
could be met. There was, however, no prospect that the would-be
purchaser could meet them, but the Church Secretary and Dr Lloyd-
Jones themselves offered the deposit and guaranteed that weekly
payments would be met. J.J. himself had no experience of banks, he
did not even know how to sign his name on a cheque, and when the
Manager, behind his desk, in one of the local banks, heard the
proposal from E. T. Rees and Lloyd-Jones that they would stand
guarantees 'for one of these *converts*, as you say', his amazement was
complete. Soon the new home was acquired, help being gladly given
with decorations and curtaining. Its most valued piece of furniture
was the harmonium upon which J.J. played hymns every Sunday
evening and thereafter this 'new' man's payments never failed until
the house was his own.

There were a multitude of other ways in which the gospel had a
practical out-working in the church family and in some of these Mrs
Lloyd-Jones was involved. By this date, with her early spiritual
difficulties past, she was almost as closely involved in the care of
others as her husband. Although she did not then speak of it to

[238]

others, there was one particular experience which, in strengthening her faith, prepared her for future service. Despite her assurance of divine forgiveness, the south-west gales blowing in from the sea still terrified her as her imagination continued to picture how the first two Aberavons had come to their end! In her own words:

'I had even bought a time-table of the tides, so that I would know the times of the high tides, especially when the moon was at the full!

'One night when Martyn was away, and I was alone with the baby, there was an exceptionally severe gale blowing in from the sea, and I lay, beside myself with fear, tossing feverishly in my bed, full of terror and panic – if the tide came up Victoria Road, could I escape with the baby? get out of the window? on to the roof? etc. At last, in sheer helpless despair, I got out of my bed and on to my knees, and I prayed: "Lord, if it is all true, if you are really there and will answer my prayer, *please* give me peace and take all my fear away". As I spoke, it all went away, my heart was flooded with perfect peace, and I never had any more fear of gales and tides. I was completely delivered and asleep in two minutes. As the hymn says: "The Lord is rich and merciful, the Lord is very kind".'

Small though the problem might have been to others, it was great to her, and when the prayer *was* answered her thanksgiving was profound. It was an end of the terror which even Martyn did not know was troubling her so much.

A Thursday afternoon 'Sisterhood' already existed at Sandfields in 1927, but when feminine converts were added to the church Mrs Lloyd-Jones began a small Bible class in the parlour at 57 Victoria Road. As the numbers of those wanting spiritual help grew, it had to be moved to the church. The class included such women as the converted spiritualist medium who, when asked by Mrs Lloyd-Jones in the course of Bible study in 1 Samuel, what she thought of the action of the witch of Endor in relation to Saul and Samuel (1 Samuel 28), hung her head and confessed that she preferred never to think of such evil any more.

In Mrs Lloyd-Jones' case, however, the practical aid to young converts went well beyond the imparting of instruction. Not long after the conversion of Mark McCann, noted in the last chapter, the following incident occurred which we give in words which Mrs Lloyd-Jones recorded for another purpose:

David Martyn Lloyd-Jones

'One evening as we were leaving the hall at the end of a weeknight meeting, I passed a small group of three or four people talking to McCann. As I said "Goodnight", and went by, one of the group said: "Isn't it a shame, Mrs Jones, Mr McCann can't read?" "Can't read?" – I was quite surprised, "No, there's the pity, he never learnt, see; he'd love to be able to read; he can't read his Bible." A veritable chorus of murmurs and comments broke out, McCann meanwhile shuffling his feet and hanging his head. "Can't you read at all, Mr McCann?" "No, I never learnt, I never went to school regular, see, I was always running away, so I can't read." Despair and hopelessness all round! Well, I knew it was easy enough to teach a child to read, and even as the thought came to my mind that it might be more difficult with a man in his middle or late fifties, it was immediately snuffed out by a mental picture of my mother teaching old Mr Matthews – well on in his seventies – to read, and she never seemed to have any difficulty. I am sure that the memory of that convert of the 1904 revival helped to dispel, in a split-second, the doubt concerning the possibility of teaching an elderly man to read. Be that as it may, I said, with the complete confidence of comparative youth and inexperience, "I'm sure I can teach you to read, Mr McCann, if you would like to try." Pity help me! I little knew what I was taking on! Mr McCann was delighted and jumped at the offer and we arranged the times for the sessions.

'The first few minutes of the first session told me all! I had picked out one of Elizabeth's reading books. It was a small book with a picture on one page and a few simple words on the facing page, and it was called "The Little Red Hen"! We got nowhere. Phonetics? we might as well have tried Chinese characters. Inwardly I was in despair and grieving for what I knew would be a bitter blow for him. We ploughed on, with no hope at all on my part, for two or three sessions. Then – it must have been the third or fourth time he came – as I got out the book and put it before him on the table, he pushed it away. Half apologetically and half rebelliously he said: "I don't want to read that, I want to read the Bible." I confess I felt rebuked! "Right," I said, "let's do that", and I fetched a clear print Bible and opened it at the Gospel of St John, chapter 10, "I am the good shepherd . . .". With his finger pushing along under each word, he started, spelling each word aloud, getting an occasional little word by himself, looking for prompting over the big ones: "I . . . a, m, [very hesitantly] am, t, h, e, ???" Seeing him floundering, I said, "It doesn't sound like anything, does it? You must remember that t, h, e, always spells *the*." Complete satisfaction! He never forgot. And now the door was wide open and the light began to dawn. The method with Mark McCann was memory and the sound of the words, perhaps some familiarity with some of the sentences, but above and beyond all a sense of the preciousness of the words and an overpowering desire to read them. The Gospel of John became his chief love – he would sometimes say, in his half-apologetic, half-hesitating way, "Can't read Mark, see, though it's my own name. I'd rather read John." '

Mark McCann and J.J. were only two of a whole crowd of men and women who in many different ways required the loving care of the whole church. And the response with which the church rose to the challenge was not confined to their own membership. For the first time there was an evident concern for the church across the world and, despite the Depression, funds began to flow to aid the work of Foreign Missions. In 1930 it was evident to Dr Lloyd-Jones that much money was now being saved because so many of the people were living different lives. He therefore suggested that, instead of spending that additional money upon themselves, a large box be placed in the porch of the church for the service of the gospel overseas. This proposal was zealously taken up by the people and indeed, in some cases, quite beyond what Dr Lloyd-Jones was asking or suggesting. Violet Robson, convicted of the amount of money she had long spent on her dress and appearance, sold all her jewellery apart from her wedding ring! A piece of paper, found by her family after her death, revealed that she did not do this without first giving her own self to the Lord, as Christians before her in Corinth (1 Cor. 8:5). In part her solemn covenant read:

'Having had this morning, April 12 1932, a fresh revelation of my hopeless inability to keep the Law, and that Jesus Christ the Son of the most High God was the fulfilment of the Law, and gave himself to save me from its terror, I desire with all my mind, heart and strength to consecrate myself and everything I hold dear and that I possess. . . . I consecrate myself, mind, soul, strength, to the will and purpose of my Heavenly Father and his Son Jesus Christ. . . . I give my home and everything I possess or shall possess, I desire to adorn the doctrine of our Lord and Saviour Jesus Christ, by being humble, consistent, faithful, long-suffering, truthful, careful in small things, patient, tolerant, and no "respecter of persons." Honest in the sight of all men, prayerful, to make myself of no reputation, that Jesus Christ might be glorified and that I may be accounted worthy of the fellowship of his sufferings. Amen.'

While the spirit of the apostolic age was indeed present at Sandfields, it is also true that the faults which marked the early churches were not absent. Many of the converts had behind them the greater part of a lifetime spent in bad habits, many had minimal knowledge, and not a few upon their conversion found themselves wholly without any support or sympathy in their own families. One young Christian, returning joyfully from a Monday night prayer-meeting, was greeted by his wife with the words, 'I would rather have you coming in drunk than coming in from a prayer meeting!' It is scarcely surprising if there were problems. Many had to struggle with difficulties and not always with success. As in the fast-growing churches of the New Testament, the situation required the corporate care of the whole membership one for another. Preaching on that theme from Galatians 6:1–5, 'Brethren, if a man be overtaken in a fault, ye which are spiritual, restore such an one in the spirit of meekness . . .', Dr Lloyd-Jones told his people:

'That is the rule of Paul. We are a family – one in Christ Jesus. If a brother falls the whole family suffers from the same and is dragged down by his fall. If a member of the church falls into the gutter the whole church falls with him. When a member goes down, this church goes down – we must all go down into the gutter after him and pick him up. You never know, one day you may be the one who falls into the gutter, and you will be glad that day if the church comes and pulls you out. It is no good turning your back on this fallen member, the world will only laugh at you, you may brazen it out, but the world will know. "Restore such an one in the spirit of meekness; considering thyself, lest thou also be tempted," says Paul, "for if a man think himself to be something, when he is nothing, he deceiveth himself." That verse ought to be hanging on our walls, always before our eyes; not the usual nice little verses about the love of God, no, get a card printed with these words: "For if a man think himself to be something, when he is nothing, he deceives himself!" If we read that every morning, what a difference it would make to us and to the people working with us. It brings us back to the realisation that we are broken earthenware, saved by the grace of God.'

These words were spoken on February 3, 1929, and the evidence of the years which followed showed how they were received. Burdens were borne together, and no small care was needed for those faced with all the temptations of the devil. Some came to assurance of salvation, only to be plunged again into temporary darkness. Old 'Staffordshire Bill', for example, or William Thomas as he now wished to be called, did not have the rapturous joy of his new life for ever unbroken. No sooner had he come to the Lord's Table for the first time than, reflecting on his privilege as he sat at home that same Sunday night, he was thrown down by a thought which came as a bolt from the blue. Many years before, as a young man in a public-house argument, he had called the Lord Jesus Christ a bastard. As this far-off memory came back to him, it seemed to him as though the gates of heaven were suddenly shut against him. His grief and misery were almost complete; perhaps it was the barest gleam of hope which took him prematurely from his bed the following morning to seek help where he knew it would be given. Speaking of that same Monday, Mrs Lloyd-Jones writes:

'Very early that morning there was a knock at the manse door. The unusual hour drove the Doctor and me to the door together. We are not likely to forget the sight that met our eyes as we opened the door. Poor William Thomas looked as wretched, hopeless and woebegone as he felt. He came in, and I left them together while he told the Doctor his pitiful story. It was no easy task to persuade him that he could be forgiven. The enormity of his sin was all he could see at first, but lovingly and patiently he was shown from the Word of God that he could indeed be forgiven and that this heinous sin, like all the others, had been washed away by the precious blood of Christ. So he was healed and restored and the dark night of his soul passed away.'

Prior to this, William Thomas had already been delivered from another trial in a way that brought great joy to the church, although, in that case, he had left the problem behind before his fellow church members knew of its existence. After his conversion his humble demeanour at Sandfields, where he listened much and spoke little, had not revealed that he was still struggling with his lifelong use of bad language. It was not that he meant to use it, but a sentence

David Martyn Lloyd-Jones

without oaths and blasphemies was as foreign to him as cravats and starched-collars. 'He could not help it,' writes Mrs Lloyd-Jones, 'and he could not stop it. The truth is that he did not know that he was doing it until the words were out, and then the realisation that these horrible terms and words came from his own lips, sickened and shamed him, and he was driven to a frenzy of despair and an abject misery. It may seem strange that he never sought the help of a fellow Christian in this matter, but he was too ashamed, and he suffered for some weeks, little dreaming that deliverance was at hand. It came about in this way – he was getting up one morning and gathering his clothes together to get dressed. But there were no socks among his clothes. He went to the bedroom door and shouted to his wife "I can't find my —— socks! where are the —— things?' As he heard himself speak and realised what he had just said, a great horror possessed him and he fell back on the bed in a paroxysm of despair, and cried aloud, "O Lord, cleanse my tongue. O Lord, I can't ask for a pair of socks without swearing, please have mercy on me and give me a clean tongue." And as he lay there, and as he got up from that bed, he knew that God had done for him what he could not do for himself. His prayer, his cry of agony was heard and answered, and it was his testimony that from that moment to the end of his days no swear word, or foul or blasphemous word, ever again passed his lips. Hearing his account of this amazing deliverance on a subsequent Wednesday (Fellowship meeting) night is something that we who were there will never forget. His face, wet with tears and alight with an inner joy and wonder, his faltering voice broken with emotion, brought a warm wave of response from every heart. He was not a speaker and I do not think that I ever heard him speak in the Fellowship meeting either before or after that, but he would always learn some words of Scripture and repeat them as his own testimony when called upon. He was particularly drawn to the Psalms and read much in the Old Testament as well as the Gospels.'

In connection with the theme of this chapter it should be said that, through Dr Lloyd-Jones' weekly ministry in places other than Sandfields, something of the fellowship that was known in his own congregation spread to other Christians further afield. One consequence of this was the increasing number of letters arriving at the manse. Believers unable to obtain counsel from their own pastors looked to Sandfields and joined earnestly in prayer for the spread of the power of true religion across the land. Morgan Beddow is sure that one week in the thirties, when Dr and Mrs Lloyd-Jones were away from home and it was his duty to forward mail, he forwarded no fewer than ninety letters. Whether Dr Lloyd-Jones, without a secretary, answered them all, we cannot say, but it is clear from correspondence which survives that he often gladly responded to this further demand upon his time. The following reply to one regular correspondent near Swansea, whose only connection with Dr Lloyd-Jones was their common Christian experience, is characteristic:

Dear Mr Thomas,

I rejoiced to receive your kind letter this morning and to read all the good news you have to give. It is glorious to think that the life which we have received in Christ Jesus is Eternal Life, is it not? Though we have not heard from or of one another for sometime, still the life goes on, and I rejoiced to find it in all its freshness in your words. Whatever may happen, whatever difficulties and obstacles may be in the way, still we know with St Paul that 'neither death, nor life, nor angels, nor principalities, nor powers, nor things present, nor things to come, nor height, nor depth, nor any other creature, shall be able to separate us from the love of God, which is in Christ Jesus our Lord'. That is the Christian confidence. Nay, also, we know that to the extent that we are faithful and loyal to that Lord, we shall never be separated from one another, but as fellow-believers, as joint-heirs, as brethren and sisters in the Lord, we shall go on together to all eternity. I thank God for you and for all who acknowledge Jesus Christ as their Saviour and their Lord. I thank you for the interest you take in me, and above all, I thank you for your prayers.

The question you ask me is difficult and yet I believe the answer is quite clear. It is difficult and galling for you to have to sit and listen to such doctrines from the pulpit and you naturally feel you should make some sort of a protest. My own view on the matter is that it would be inadvisable for you to make any public protest. It would lead to argument and disputation. But what I think you might do is to have a chat with such people 'in private'. And when you talk to them, do so in the spirit of meekness and prayer, and pray much before doing so. I would just tell them simply your experience of God in Christ and the difference He has made to you. Talk of the New Life, the New Nature, and the New Power that you have received, etc., etc. And having done all this, pray for him when you get home again, and go on doing so. Remember that such people are in darkness, and have not seen the Light and that I

Corinthians 2:14 applies to them. Nothing but the Power of the Holy Spirit can ever bring them to a different state. Arguments never will.

Such is the way I deal with people of that type and I feel that it is the way indicated in the New Testament. I am always glad to hear from you and to be of any help that I can.

You will hear fairly soon of my being not very far from you, preaching.

May the Lord continue to bless you and yours.

Yours in His service
D. M. Lloyd-Jones

From the experience of these years Dr Lloyd-Jones was immovably confirmed in a truth which he had first seen in the New Testament. It was that evangelism is pre-eminently dependent upon the quality of the Christian life which is known and enjoyed in the church. The community around Sandfields was reached not by advertising or organised visitation, but by the manner of life of men and women whose very faces seemed to be new. No one in the congregation was offered courses on 'personal evangelism', nor told how to 'witness'. It was done in a whole variety of spontaneous and natural ways, differing according to the circumstances and temperaments of individuals. Some were not gifted at making public speeches. The soft-spoken, William Nobes, for example, who somehow on his meagre pension managed to keep his little bachelor room, would often be found sitting on a window-sill, outside the entrance to the market, 'chatting happily in his gentle, kindly manner to any and all who had time to stop and talk to him'. Despite his poverty in this world's goods, says Mrs Lloyd-Jones in her portrait of him, no one ever heard him grumble or complain. 'There's just four of us now,' was his contented answer to someone who asked him about family and relatives, 'my bed and my table, my Book and me!'

The converts witnessed, too, by death as well as by life. Even the most thoughtless in the community were sometimes arrested by what they heard or saw of the home-going of those who had confessed themselves pilgrims in this present world. Certainly the market was subdued and onlookers stood silent, the day when the body of William Nobes was carried from his few earthly possessions, through the town, and up to the cemetery on the mountain side. Few who saw the large crowd of church members, led by their minister, following the coffin, and not grudging one step of those long three miles, could have doubted that Nobes did indeed have a family!

'Staffordshire Bill' had just three years at Sandfields before people spoke of how the old man whom the church family had nursed as a spiritual babe departed this life. When Dr Lloyd-Jones and E. T. Rees arrived at his bedside it was clear from the high fever and the stertorous breathing that the end was not far off. William Thomas was dying from double pneumonia. As Mrs Lloyd-Jones heard the scene described later that day by her husband, from the moment of their arrival in the room:

'William Thomas was far away somewhere, but responded to a greeting and a prayer. He was obviously at perfect peace and all the evidences of the old sinful, violent life were smoothed out of a now child-like face. The minutes passed and became an hour, and more. Then suddenly the painful sound of the difficult breathing seemed to stop. The old man's face was transformed, alight, radiant. He sat up eagerly with upstretched arms and a beautiful smile on his face, as though welcoming his best of friends, and with that he was gone to that "land of pure delight where saints immortal reign".'

The whole tragedy today is that the Christian Church is moving ponderously, slowly, heavily, while the world is in the grip of the devil. She is setting up committees to investigate the problems, and commissions to examine various situations, and calling for reports, interim and final, to be produced in a year, or perhaps several years, which will then be considered. And she is doing this while the world is on fire, and people are going to hell, and the devil is rampant everywhere!

M. L.-J.

12

Enlarged Work

In the early 1930's preaching visits to North Wales became a regular part of Dr Lloyd-Jones' ministry. In October 1931, *Yr Efengylydd* subsequently reported that his 'lively and substantial ministry caused a great stir' in parts of Anglesey. Four months later, in February 1932, he preached for the first time in another area of North Wales, at Rhos (Rhosllanerchrugog), near Wrexham, where he was often to be in subsequent years. Although little more than a village, Rhos was a place of vast Nonconformist chapels – buildings which had been none too large for the memorable events which had accompanied the 1904 revival in that district. But times had changed, as one of his first hearers at Rhos has recorded. John Powell-Parry was a miner, converted as a young man of nineteen in 1904. In the years which followed, Powell-Parry found little spiritual help in the local chapels and it was this which made the coming of Dr Lloyd-Jones into his neighbourhood all the more striking:

'It was something which I had not heard for a very long time when I heard the Doctor preaching. My impression was of a very humble man who spoke with conviction and holy boldness. The text of his first sermon in Rhos was Matthew 16:3, "O ye hypocrites, ye can discern the face of the sky; but can ye not discern the signs of the times?". The people came from far and near to listen to him but the ministers were not sympathetic, Oh dear, no! There was a great change in Rhos compared with what it had been at the end of the nineteenth and the beginning of the twentieth century. It was different entirely. There was a turning from the Word of God and Modernism came in like a flood, especially after the first World War.

'Dr Lloyd-Jones preached the Word and believed what he preached. I remember two ministers sitting right in the very back row of the chapel on the occasion of that first visit. The place was packed and they were there, looking to me like two critics or spies. Of course, the Doctor would not know them, but I knew them. They were rank Modernists. Today they have passed away and left nothing. Both their chapels are empty.'[1]

The same reporter spoke of how, subsequently, still larger crowds would gather whenever it was known that Martyn Lloyd-Jones was going to preach in that vicinity. 'One winter's day in February, in the midst of a heavy shower of melting snow, I remember people – many young men, young people – queuing five or six abreast for some distance to get into the chapel before the doors were opened.' He noted one particular emphasis in the visitor's preaching which had become a rarity by that date, namely the stress upon the exceeding sinfulness of sin:

'I remember his preaching at Wrexham on "The deep things of God" from the second chapter of 1 Corinthians. He disturbed a number of people, including many of the Modernist ministers whom I knew. I recall overhearing them outside the chapel discussing the man, discussing his message, and quite a number disagreeing with him. He was preaching something they did not know, and did not believe, but they had to recognise the authority with which he spoke.'

This lack of ministerial sympathy was common throughout North Wales and yet it was not universal. One Calvinistic Methodist minister, J. J. Morgan of Mold, sent the itinerating preacher the following note of encouragement, which Mrs Lloyd-Jones managed to preserve:

'I have been weighing your preaching in the balance of "The Treasury". Of course, you will remember that these are not the balances of Heaven so that you must not rejoice on the one hand nor grieve on the other whatever weight the scales record. 1. Freedom from the aim of entertaining: 95%. Some of the dramatic situations elaborated. 2. Freedom from the aim of soothing: 100%. 3. Freedom from the exhibition of one's own cleverness: 99%. 4. Freedom from detracting mannerisms: 95%. A tendency to pick the cheek (unconsciously) with the right-hand finger and thumb sometimes. A slight

---

[1] These words were given to the author on a visit to Rhos in the early 1970's. John Powell-Parry died in June 1978.

screwing of the face in making palpable hits. The screw mustn't grow. 5. Audibility: 100%. 6. Length: 100% Monday. 99% Wednesday. 7. Freedom from uncouth expressions: 99%. 8. Simplicity:99%, "Re-action" and "negatived" would try the simple souls of the audience. 9. Pointedness: 100%. 10. Fervour: 100%. 11. Spirituality. I will not presume to put that in the balances. This will help you to keep in mind that there is such a place as Mold.'

The extent of the spiritual need in North Wales led Dr Lloyd-Jones to be in the North, often as frequently as once a month, normally taking engagements in the week when he was not due to be in his own pulpit the following Sunday. One typical letter sent to him from Ruthin, North Wales, spoke of daily prayer for his ministry and of 'a number of people here willing to go anywhere within a radius of 50 miles' to hear him preach again.

A good description of the character of Lloyd-Jones' preaching at this date is given in an issue of *The Cymric Times*, April 1932, following a visit which he made to Water Street Chapel, Carmarthen. The writer of this lengthy account, who was not a Calvinistic Methodist, and signs himself 'An old Reader', began by asserting the inappropriateness of the word 'enjoyment' in connection with such preaching:

'Frankly, Mr Editor, I did not enjoy, but I did appreciate. He held us up before a mirror, where we were face to face with the Almighty God and His Son, on the one hand, and ourselves, poor miserable sinners, on the other hand, facing our "eternal destiny" – implying that today is an integral part of eternity. Honestly, could you, after gazing in that mirror, say you enjoyed your experience? I doubt it. The afternoon session was in Welsh, and the congregation a most inspiring gathering. His subject was Peter and the raising from the dead of Tabitha (alias Dorcas), Acts 9:36-43. The dead body symbolised the modern problem facing the Church of Christ today –the women, the weeping, the fuss over garments, the weak, quite inadequate shallow faith utterly unable to accomplish the solution of the problem, the intensely wished-for revival. Hence Peter shuts them out, for not only were they useless, but real hindrances. Peter looks not at the dead body, typifying the magnitude of the problem, but turns to Heaven, goes down on his knees and appeals to the source of infinite power for strength and guidance, then intuitively feeling it will be granted faces the dead body – the problem – and calls out, "Tabitha, Arise." She rises and he leads her out by the hand to the assembled disciples – the outwardly impossible problem was solved. Peter had healed before, but in those cases there was life, and where life is, where hope also is, but here was death, stark remorseless death. He was not discouraged, why should Christ's church today be dismayed with the enormity of its problem? The post-war world, the Huxleys, the Keiths,[1] the schools and colleges with their often agnostic professors, the cinema, the dance, the football craze, the motor urge, the hypocrites and their doubts – these were the 'dead body', the modern problem, but why should we forget the infinite power of God?

'The evening session was in English and drew a bigger congregation still. His text was Genesis 26:17-18. The subject was Isaac driven from one region to another, coming to Gerar. Here he was faced with the water problem, simple everyday water, but an absolute necessity of life. He knew the wells his father Abraham, an expert at well digging, had dug here, but the Philistines had filled them up with rubbish. In spite of this and the protests of his servants, he insisted upon opening up the old wells of his father. His appeal was that the church today, instead of seeking new wells, should go back to the wells of the Christian fathers who drew from them the living water which followed them through the wilderness of life; leaving modern theology with its doubts, back to the one book as the inspired Word of God, back to Peter and Pentecost, to Stephen the first Christian martyr, back to Calvary and the empty tomb, back to Christ the only-begotten Son of God; back to the Spirit of Christ, the Holy Spirit and his power, fully conscious of our sinful nature, but believing in the power of Calvary to recreate man and the world. Today the demand is for learned men with titles and degrees, but the reverend doctor would sooner accept the simple ordinary man who had found the fount of living water and could lead others also. Then in the ring of the true coin in word and gesture came a powerful appeal, possibly to a modern multitude profoundly respectable, educated, perhaps stoical, not to say cynical, his appeal fell on deaf ears. But I went away convinced that this man had power, had known Christ and Life Eternal personally, had personality, was

---

[1] A reference to Sir Arthur Keith (d. 1955), surgeon, a foremost exponent of evolution.

deeply sincerely anxious to win souls for the kingdom. The call of the pulpit today, in all churches, whatever their denomination, is for such men as this evangelist.'

Also in 1932, *The Montgomeryshire Express and Radnor Times* gave a long account of 'that renowned preacher, Dr Martin Lloyd-Jones, Aberavon'. Under the sub-heading, 'A Warning to Ministers', the paper alluded to remarks which would not have endeared the preacher to some of his clerical hearers. He had referred to the description of true religion given in the Epistle of James – 'To visit the fatherless and widows in their affliction, and to keep himself unspotted from the world' (James 1:27) – and went on to point out that visitation was not the sum total of the duty required: 'that was not enough; unitarians and atheists could do that much. The whole art of helping is to do good and not lose our souls in doing so. He felt that the words, 'to keep himself unspotted from the world', were a warning to ministers. How many had lost their fire and zeal by being "nice" and by giving themselves to beneficent work? He knew of a minister who felt, when the Miners' Welfare began, that he ought to take it up. After about six months he had lost all the pleasure he used to take in preaching on Sundays. He felt he had nothing to say; he worked so hard that he was too tired to study anything. He was doing excellent work, feeding and clothing the body, but in doing that he was neglecting still greater work.'

The necessity of constant study for the work of the ministry remained one of Dr Lloyd-Jones' deepest convictions and was one of the main features of his own daily living. Next to his Bible it was probably Jonathan Edwards' Works which provided the greatest stimulus to him at this date. While still in London he had asked a Welsh Presbyterian Minister for the name of books which would help him prepare for the ministry. One recommendation he received was *Protestant Thought Before Kant*, written by A. C. McGiffert. Although the book did not live up to his expectation, while reading it he came across the name of Jonathan Edwards for the first time. His interest aroused, Dr Lloyd-Jones relates: 'I then questioned my ministerial adviser on Edwards, but he knew nothing about him. After much searching I at length called at John Evans' bookshop in Cardiff in 1929, having time available as I waited for a train. There, down on my knees in my overcoat in a corner of the shop, I found the two volume 1834 edition of Edwards which I bought for five shillings. I devoured these volumes and literally just read and read them. It is certainly true that they helped me more than anything else.'

While authors such as Edwards were regular reading, certain large works, less directly related to preaching, he reserved for holiday reading. By the late 1920's he had come to organise his annual holidays so that the mornings were almost invariably spent with a major theological volume. One of Elizabeth's childhood memories is of herself in a bathing costume playing in and out of the pools on the beach, while her father sat, fully clothed in a dark grey suit, complete with shoes, socks and hat, leaning against a rock and reading Brunner's *The Divine Imperative*!

Another major work which he read about this period was *The Vision of God* by Kenneth E. Kirk, being the Bampton Lectures for 1928,[1] delivered at Oxford where Kirk, nine years later, became Bishop. 'These lectures,' he commented later, 'had a great effect on me. Kirk dealt with the pursuit of God and the different methods by which men have sought God, but he did it historically and went right through – the medieval mystics, the later mystics and so on. I found that book absolutely seminal. It gave me a lot of background. It made me think. It helped me to understand the Scriptures and also see the dangers in such movements as monasticism and the anchorites. I regard *The Vision of God* as one of the greatest books which I ever read.' Thereafter he frequently took Bampton or Gifford lectures for his holiday reading. A year or so after Kirk it was Norman Powell Williams (Lady Margaret Professor of Divinity at Oxford) on *The Ideas of the Fall and of Original Sin*.[2] 'From the standpoint of style that was the most brilliant book I ever read.' Lloyd-Jones liked the detached standpoint from which these Lectures were generally given. What he valued was the information which they gave and he could make the application himself either in terms of warnings on what should be avoided, or guidance respecting what was worthy of further pursuit.

The summer holidays for 1929 were to be remembered for the sheer enjoyment which he had in reading Luke Tyerman's two-volume *Life and Times of George Whitefield*. Part of that holiday was spent at an ancient farm-house, St Mary Hill Court, in the Vale

---

[1] Published 1931.   [2] Bampton Lectures for 1924, published 1927.

of Glamorgan and not far from Llangan. This beautiful old building possessed historical interest in its history as a pre-Reformation abbey, while the district in general had a special appeal on account of the ministry of one of the Calvinistic Methodist Fathers, David Jones of Llangan (1735–1810). One of the oldest features of St Mary Hill Court was a dovecote no longer inhabited by pigeons. When Dr Lloyd-Jones enquired of the farmer concerning its present use he was told that it had been full of 'old books' and that in order to make space for storage they had very recently put a match to all of them! In Mrs Lloyd-Jones' opinion, her husband's look on receiving that information (and in a district once full of revival Christianity) was indescribable! According to one paper, *Yr Efengylydd*, which reported the Lloyd-Jones' holiday, 'this untiring worker managed to hit upon a spot far from "the noise of the world and its pain"'. The writer went on, however, to say that on the first Sunday of the holiday Dr Lloyd-Jones had preached at Penllyn Chapel, as the expected preacher was unable to be there, and in the evening of the second the Anglican incumbent of Llangan parish church had asked him to take his pulpit.[1]

It was after this second Sunday at St Mary Hill Court that the peacefulness of the 1929 holiday was rudely interrupted. A bull in a field close to the farm had already disturbed Mrs Lloyd-Jones who enjoyed walking Elizabeth in her pushchair while her husband was absorbed with Tyerman's account of George Whitefield. A crisis came after lunch one day, early in the second week, when as they looked on to the farmhouse yard from the kitchen window, they were amazed to see the bull lift the yard gate off its hinges and make triumphantly towards the house! Mrs Lloyd-Jones refused to stay one day longer and so it was agreed that she and Elizabeth should go on to London where Martyn would join them some days later. But St Mary Hill Court had other problems to raise and this time nocturnal ones. Scarcely was Dr Lloyd-Jones in bed with the light out, on the day of Bethan's departure, before he was arrested by a strange pattering on the linoleum around the bedroom. With a light on, the noise departed, only to return as soon as it went out. There was

---

[1] It was rare for Dr Lloyd-Jones to preach in Anglican churches in Wales and the incumbent's wife scarcely seems to have appreciated this visit. Having responsibility for the music in the evening service she picked a hymn before the sermon 'suitable for lay preachers', and was heard to say afterwards how appropriate that particular hymn had been!

nothing for it but to pull the sheets tight about his head and to find an excuse to leave promptly the next morning. Bulls and farm-yard livestock were one thing, facing mice quite another! It was the last stay at St Mary Hill Court! But the kindness of the farmer and his wife was never forgotten.

Two years later, in 1931, Dr Lloyd-Jones spent a summer holiday with his brother Vincent, doing some 'mild climbing' in the hills of Carmarthenshire. Pembrokeshire was another favourite place for holidays.

Besides summer holidays there were occasional 'days off' and a particularly memorable one, taken spontaneously, occurred during this period. Lloyd-Jones had been preaching in Monmouthshire where he heard that the next day the famous Scottish evangelist, John McNeill, then seventy-eight years of age, was to preach for R. B. Jones at Porth. This was probably McNeill's last visit to Wales, for the veteran preacher, who had packed his first churches in Edinburgh and London in the 1880's and 1890's before he became a world-wide itinerant, died some twelve months later. Not a few regarded John McNeill as the greatest preacher of his generation, an opinion with which Lloyd-Jones might have concurred had it not been that the Scot had a great ability to entertain and too often was ready to indulge his hearers with a wit which drove all else from their minds. McNeill went further than a restrained use of humour, such as might legitimately drive home a truth, as he literally convulsed congregations with mirth.

After the afternoon service in Porth, Dr Lloyd-Jones was invited to have tea with McNeill at the local Bible College, when the most surprising feature of their personal meeting turned out to be the enormous appetite of this jovial Boanerges! After consuming a generous meal, rounded off with two or three platefuls of fruit and cream, McNeill faced a hesitant enquiry from his hostess, 'Would you like biscuits and cheese?' Indeed he would! and he proceeded to empty a round box of cheeses together with a packet of digestive biscuits![1] Yet despite such a repast the preacher's alertness was in no

<hr/>

[1] 'Arriving one night in the Highlands of Scotland, after a long and weary journey, tired, cold, and hungry, the lady of the house met him with the enquiry, "Will you take an egg to your tea, Mr McNeill?" To which he quickly replied, "I will that, my good woman, and the hen that laid it, too!"' *John McNeill*, His Life and Work, Alexander Gammie, p. 256. It is interesting to note that about 1890 McNeill was pressed to consider a proposal – which he declined – to become minister of Westminster Chapel, London. He died on April 19, 1933.

way impaired when he began the evening service. Knowing that R. B. Jones did not approve of jocularity in the pulpit, and probably suspecting Lloyd-Jones of the same dullness, McNeill gave the first part of his evening sermon to 'the place of humour in preaching'. He told the congregation that he not only believed in the Fall but he could say something further; he knew *where* Adam fell. Adam fell on his head and it had been cracked ever since! After some twenty minutes of this kind of thing, he concluded, 'So much by way of introduction to the blind man in John chapter 9.' 'Then', as Dr Lloyd-Jones remembered, 'he began to preach on that theme and he was rollickingly funny, so that even R. B. Jones was laughing uncontrollably. But it was tragic, because he was a very powerful preacher: he could produce a tremendous effect, then foolishly throw it away with some quip. Far from establishing his case for the use of humour he showed me that this was ruinous.' It was not that Dr Lloyd-Jones failed to enjoy his jokes, for he was well endowed with a sense of humour himself, but it was his lifelong conviction that entertainment and jocularity in preaching 'are not compatible with a realisation of the seriousness of the condition of the souls of all men by nature, the fact that they are lost and in danger of eternal perdition, and their consequent need of salvation'.[1]

*   *   *

In addition to itinerant preaching, Dr Lloyd-Jones' work had also expanded by this date in a different and unanticipated direction. We have already noted how, when a number of his friends first heard of his conviction that he was called to preach, they had urged him to continue in medicine and to be a lay-preacher. Speaking once at Sandfields on the peril of compromise, he had referred to this advice as an instance in his own experience: 'Before I came here, the Devil said to me, Why don't you go on practising medicine and preach on Sundays? I listened to him and I tried it; but I did not go far before I found what a hopeless failure it was. When God calls a man to preach, he calls him to preach and nothing else.'[2] He was convinced that he had to say farewell to medicine. Had he needed

[1] See *Preaching and Preachers*, pp. 140-41. A fine imaginative anecdote of McNeill's which Dr Lloyd-Jones heard on this occasion he re-tells in *Christian Unity*, Ephesians 4:1-16, 1980, pp. 87-88.
[2] On Genesis 19:16, November 17, 1929.

David Martyn Lloyd-Jones

any help in carrying out this decision it was provided by members of the Welsh medical fraternity. At the time of his arrival at Sandfields the local branch of the British Medical Association at Swansea held a special meeting to decide what to do about him, the common opinion being that he only intended to preach until he was well enough known to set up either in a general or consultant practice. Speaking of this meeting (of which he heard from one who was present and who later became a good friend), Dr Lloyd-Jones recalled, 'They solemnly decided to have nothing whatever to do with me, and they carried it out!' His contacts, medical or social, with fellow doctors in the Port Talbot area were to be non-existent.

At a later date, however, the situation underwent a change which was so radical that Dr Lloyd-Jones regarded it as one of the most remarkable episodes in his life. There was one doctor in the town, David Rees, whose father was a deacon at Carmel Welsh Methodist Chapel, and whose brother Illtyd Rees was a local chemist. This brother became very seriously ill and nobody could do anything for him. In Dr Lloyd-Jones own words:

'One day Bethan had been up in the town and when she came back off the bus and into my room she said, "You know, I've suddenly had a strange feeling. They are going to call you in to see Illtyd Rees, the chemist." I said, "You are talking rubbish, that's the one thing that cannot happen!" "Well," Bethan responded, "I know. I'm telling you. It suddenly came very forcibly to me in the bus."

'Two days later Bethan and I were at tea when there was a knock and we found that Dr David Rees, with a consultant from Swansea, were at the door. When we invited them in and asked what they wanted their question was, Would I go and see Illtyd Rees? I had to go and preach up in the valleys that night, but there was just time for me to make the visit first, so I finished my tea and got into the back of their car. I remember well saying to them, "Would you mind telling me the history as we are going along?" They did, and before we arrived at the patient's house I knew exactly what was the matter with him. The explanation was that I held a research scholarship for 18 months – the Baillie research scholarship – to investigate Hodgkin's disease (Lymphadenoma) and a particular type of it called the Pell-Epstein type. I had done nothing else, more or less, for eighteen months. The disease was characterised by tremendous bouts of temperature, up and down, with periods of remission, then the same thing again. So as the car drew up outside Illtyd Rees's house, I didn't move when they opened the car door. The consultant from Swansea, looking daggers at me, enquired, "Aren't you coming out?" "Well," I said, "there is actually no need for me to come out. I know what is the matter with this man, and do not need to see him." "What are you talking about!" the senior man exploded. "The patient," I explained, "is suffering from the Pell-Epstein type of Lymphadenoma." "Good God!" he retorted, "what is that? I have never heard of it." "However, I will come in and examine him," I said.'

The examination fully confirmed Dr Lloyd-Jones' diagnosis and afterwards the two medicals were ready to listen to advice on possible treatment. Horder, Dr Lloyd-Jones told them, could treat these cases and obtain some temporary relief, but such was the pattern of the disease that ultimately it was bound to lead to death. Illtyd Rees was sent to London and his subsequent history was exactly as the minister of Sandfields had predicted.

Dr Lloyd-Jones saw in this incident a clear indication of the providential hand of God. It became the talk of the town and it gave him a new relationship to men from whom he had formerly been alienated. A few days later the leading doctor of Port Talbot – a man with an Oxford M.D. who had previously passed Dr Lloyd-Jones in the street without so much as looking at him – arrived at the manse door and announced himself by saying, 'My name is Phillips'. 'I recognise you, Dr Phillips,' replied Lloyd-Jones who had answered the door himself. 'Will you come in?' 'If I were half a man,' the visitor at once responded, 'I would drop on my knees in front of you and beg your pardon for the way we have treated you!'

Understandably, this revolution in medical attitude, good though it was, led to unforeseen consequences, for it encouraged others to appeal for Dr Lloyd-Jones' medical advice. Previously he had on occasions given advice, without fee, if a patient's doctor had consented to his being consulted, but now, with almost all the local doctors only too glad to consent, calls for his help multiplied.[1] Dr

---

[1] One local doctor was to remain hostile. When a patient (from Sandfields) who had this man as his general practitioner was failing to recover from an illness and required a certificate to that effect, the doctor, instead of supplying it, wrote the following sarcastic note to the patient's minister: 'As you had no confidence in my diagnosis or treatment it is quite possible that the Under Sheriff would take the same view. Perhaps Dr Martin Lloyd-Jones will issue the certificate required.'

Phillips himself became a considerable culprit in this respect, for he let it be known that the only opinion outside London which he recognised was that of Dr Lloyd-Jones!

To a limited extent Dr Lloyd-Jones was thus compelled to re-enter medicine when cases were referred to him for help which he felt responsible to accept. When these cases were outside the church he might take a fee, which invariably went to the Sandfields funds, and these amounts became an important factor in finally paying off the debt on the building. On one occasion a prosperous individual, who had benefited from medical consultation at the Sandfields manse, pulled out his wallet to settle his account as he was leaving; but when he heard that any fee offered went 'to the church' he promptly replaced his wallet and searched his trouser pockets for any loose coins to be found there!

When Lloyd-Jones was preaching away from home it was quite common for individuals to seek his help. The Reverend D. J. D. Jones remembers how when Dr Lloyd-Jones came to preach at Rhiw-bwys, Llanrhystud, Cardiganshire, 'before the service our front room at the Manse was used for the Doctor to examine several people who had heart trouble or other illnesses and he gave his advice free'. An unusual case occurred on one occasion at Gilfachgoch, where the local doctor was mystified by the illness of a young woman and sought his assistance. Dr Lloyd-Jones was told that the patient in question had been doing her nursing training at Bart's when illness had compelled her to return home to Wales; also that the Matron sympathisingly had permitted another girl to return with her in order to provide nursing care. This illness had some strange aspects; for example, her temperature, taken regularly by her nursing companion, night and day, rose steeply at night, sometimes to 103 or 104, yet the doctors and consultants called in confirmed with their own instruments that there was no rise of temperature during the day. The general medical opinion seemed to be that she was suffering from the last stages of T.B. of the bowel (Tubercular Peritonitis).

When Dr Lloyd-Jones examined this young woman he soon arrived at a very different diagnosis and one which he could easily put to the test. The other doctor and the nurse present were asked to leave the room, and then, addressing the patient, Dr Lloyd-Jones told her that while he did not want to alarm her, he wanted to know why she had been turned out of Bart's! The patient's general condition, the disparity between the nightly high temperatures (taken by her companion) and those which others had taken in the day time, and his knowledge of the Matron at Bart's (not renowned for sympathy!) all led him to believe that the illness was a fiction invented for some purpose not yet clear. There was also an additional piece of evidence, in fact the first thing that led him to suspect malingering. He had never known a dying girl to have any interest in 'make-up', but this young woman's face was very expertly and carefully 'made up'. His direct question was no sooner put than the patient's reaction at once confirmed his suspicions. Instead of lying languid in the bed as formerly, she immediately sat upright and vigorously denied that she had been 'turned out'. But when Dr Lloyd-Jones promised to help her and cover her if she co-operated, the story came out. The girl confessed that she and her companion had been expelled for having boy-friends in their room at the hospital – a serious offence in those days! Not knowing how to face their parents in such a situation, the two nurses had devised the scheme which they had successfully operated until that afternoon.

Dr Lloyd-Jones fulfilled his promise not to expose her. He told her not to do anything sudden or dramatic, and returning to the local doctor who waited below he informed him that she would slowly get better and make a complete recovery!

It is scarcely surprising that one minister, writing to the press, gave his opinion that 'Dr Lloyd-Jones is a perfect diagnostician –and is one of the best and safest judges of character I know. He sees through men.' Dr Lloyd-Jones himself only regarded the Gilfachgoch case (which he told to his family some fifty years later) as a proof of the necessity of working from first principles, a practice which he regarded as essential both in theology and in medicine. In the case of the dismissed nurse, others had been misled because, assuming that certain things were facts (including the false readings on the temperature chart), they had failed to credit what ought to have been their initial conclusions following an examination of the patient. They had failed in first principles, especially in the first step in diagnosing – observation.

Of course, Dr Lloyd-Jones' diagnoses were not always 'perfect', and he once gave a medical gathering an amusing illustration of a failure which he spoke of as 'one of the greatest blunders of my life in a medical sense!' It happened when he was preaching for the first time in a chapel in the Vale of Glamorgan in 1928 on a Tuesday night and on the Wednesday afternoon and evening:

'I was having supper before leaving for home, when the old lady with whom I had been put to stay – and she was a real old lady worthy of the name, quite a tyrant in her local community – suddenly leaned across the table halfway through the meal and said, "Will you do an old woman a favour?" I said, "Yes, if I can, I will be glad to do so." "Then," she said, "will you come and preach again next year at these meetings?" "All right," I said, "I will." We went on eating. After a while she leaned forward again and she said, "Look here, will you do an old woman another favour?" I said, "Well, it depends on what it is." "Oh, it's all right." she said, "you can do it." I said, "What is it?" "Will you promise to come and preach at these meetings each year as long as we both live?" She had already told me she was aged seventy-nine – her skin was more like parchment than skin – and I in my cleverness came to the conclusion that there was no risk at all in acceding to her request, so I entered into the contract.'

About 1936, when he had fulfilled the promise faithfully for eight years, the old lady took ill, with severe bronchitis and broncho-pneumonia. With no antibiotics in those days she lay desperately ill, with constant nursing supervision, day and night. 'All the relatives had been sent for, and they were all convinced, the medical men included, that she was dying. Early one morning, about 3 o'clock, she suddenly sat up in bed and said, "Give me that calendar, that almanac on the wall." They all thought, of course, that this was part of her delirium. However, she insisted upon having it, and they gave it to her. She looked at it and turned over the pages back and fore for some time. This was typical delirium of course! Suddenly she said to the nurse and the relatives, "He will be here in six weeks." She had worked out the date of my annual visit. From that moment she began to get well!'

Dr Lloyd-Jones told this story only to illustrate how there are often factors entering into the 'delicate mechanism of health and disease' other than those which can be explained in purely scientific terms.[1] But the story also shows well the profound attachment and esteem which so many had towards both his ministry and his person. Her health recovered, he was to continue to preach there until 1939, and had it not been for the Second World War, when the presence of a near-by areodrome resulted in the lady's evacuation to mid-Wales, he would have had to go on until 1942, when she died!

[1] *The Supernatural in Medicine*, Christian Medical Fellowship, 1971, pp. 17-18.

Enlarged Work

Naturally, it was in Aberavon itself, with its comparatively poor working-class population, that the demands upon his medical skill were most frequent. Although it remained his profound conviction that it was far more important to prepare men for eternity than to see them restored to health, his natural sense of sympathy, trained by his years of medicine and heightened by his Christian experience, had made care for the body a primary instinct. Nor were soul and body necessarily distinct, for there were cases where both were healed together. One memorable example occurred in the home of three sisters whose lives had been rendered sad by the early loss of both their parents.

Two of these sisters began to attend services at Sandfields, the eldest with some religious interest, the second only as a very reluctant companion. A third sister, the youngest, remained at home where she had been a bed-ridden invalid for many years with a condition which never seemed to improve. At length Dr Lloyd-Jones was asked if he would see the youngest of these three women. When he made the visit, far from being welcomed by the patient it seemed 'as though the devil was looking out of her eyes'. After an examination he was convinced that there was really nothing physically wrong and he told her to begin getting up gradually. Before long this youngest of the three sisters was being half-dragged by the eldest to the chapel and within three months she was both converted and perfectly well! Her recovery was used, in turn, to influence the indifferent middle sister. All three were to become bright Christians.

Next door to these three women lived the docks' pilot mentioned in the last chapter whose addiction to drink not infrequently both disturbed and alarmed his neighbours. The three sisters now viewed him in a different light and when he became ill it was at their instigation that Dr Lloyd-Jones visited the home. This interest in his physical need proved to be one of the first steps leading to his conversion.

Perhaps it is in connection with medicine that a personal episode in Dr Lloyd-Jones' own life can be best told. In his early years at Sandfields he was to smoke, as he had done at Bart's, some ten cigarettes per day, often with a pipe as well. When reflecting on particular medical problems it had become virtually instinctive to reach for a cigarette. Returning to the manse one evening after seeing a lady whose illness was a real enigma, he threw himself down in a chair to think through the case in conversation with Bethan.

Opening his cigarette case, as he began to talk, he was pulled up short at unexpectedly finding it empty. There could be no proceeding until tobacco was found, but a thorough search of the house for the next three-quarters of an hour revealed nothing save part of a mangled cigarette in an old pouch. With her husband now on edge, Bethan sent their maid down the road to the Robsons for the loan of cigarettes from their lodger, who generally had a plentiful supply. That night, however, it so happened that the lodger had entirely exhausted his own stocks! There was nothing for it, as Martyn attempted to turn his thoughts back to the medical case, save to make the best of the mangled remnant he had found in the pouch. The first whiff of that tobacco did not have its accustomed effect: on the contrary, he felt thoroughly ashamed of himself – a feeling which did not wholly leave him even when the discussion with Bethan had resolved the problem of the lady's illness.

Soon afterwards he found himself preparing a Sunday night evangelistic sermon, a sermon which both at Sandfields and elsewhere he was subsequently to preach with much power. The text was John 8:32, 'And ye shall know the truth, and the truth shall make you free.' In the midst of his work on the sermon the conviction suddenly came to him like a dart, 'You are not free!' He was convinced that his dependence upon smoking was unworthy of a Christian. For two to three weeks he had an 'awful struggle' over the matter, Bethan would say that it was the only time she ever saw him depressed. Then, to prove that as a Christian he was not in bondage, he resolved to smoke only once a day. This he did for about a year, until April 1, 1930, when he gave up smoking entirely.

Dr Lloyd-Jones never preached against smoking and he had no sympathy with those who regarded the practice as necessarily sinful. But he felt more at liberty without it, and at the same time it also enabled him to enter more fully into the spirit of self-denial which had come to characterise the giving of the members at Sandfields to the work of Christ. The financial record of the congregation, in the midst of severe economic depression, bears its own testimony. For the four years 1930, 1931, 1932, 1933, the annual receipts from the freewill offerings of the members were £1,074, £1,069, £955, and £1,102 respectively. Within those years the debt on the property was cut from £1,750 to £615 (shortly to be cleared entirely) and the church indicated to the Forward Movement headquarters in 1932 that the Movement's annual grant of £90 was no longer required.

The value of money at this date is indicated by the fact that, with the church's annual expenditure around £500-£600, the surplus was enough to build a new manse, install electric lighting and additional seating for more than 60 in the church, provide new heating apparatus in Church Hall and Vestry, and to enlarge the church still further by the building of a large classroom adjacent to the main building and separated only by a sliding partition. The new classroom both served the Sunday school and enabled an overflow of people to be accommodated at Sunday night services.[1]

*   *   *

It was during this same period that the question of mental illness forced itself upon Dr Lloyd-Jones' attention in a new way. In medical thought it was already by this date almost universally accepted that any powerful and distressing 'conviction of sin' was a form of neurosis requiring psychiatric treatment. The kind of 'symptoms' which appeared in a number of cases of conversion recorded in *The Acts of the Apostles*, or indeed in such men as 'Staffordshire Bill' in Sandfields, would commonly have been regarded as types of mental illness. Indeed, there were those at Bart's who had not disguised their belief that Dr Lloyd-Jones himself was suffering from a 'mental complaint' when he gave up his medical career.

From the medical standpoint Dr Lloyd-Jones was, of course, familiar with true mental disease and its distressing symptoms. Nor, as there will be occasion to notice more fully in his later ministry, did he dismiss the value and need for psychiatric help in many instances. But at this date he began to meet with individuals who were being treated as 'mental' cases, and yet, he had reason to believe, were only in spiritual trouble. Nothing except spiritual remedies could help them. One instance of this particularly impressed him.

'I was told one day that there was a man at the door in a state of great agitation, and a younger man with him. I went to the door and there, indeed, was a man in a state of very great agitation – a tall fellow,

[1] The only additional source of income which contributed to the cost of these additions and improvements was 'a quiet appeal' in 1931 which brought in £238. In recognition of the many improvements in the property the Forward Movement Directors also gave a grant of £120, which sum was deducted from the debt due to them.

with hair all ruffled, who could scarcely contain himself. Well, when I brought them into my study and began to talk, I found that this man had just discharged himself from a nursing home where he had been treated for six weeks for religious mania. He really was desperate, virtually tearing his hair, and when he took hold of me in his desperation I had the terrible feeling that he could crush me if he wanted to – he was such a powerful man and was beside himself. The story was this. This man had been converted in the Welsh Revival of 1904–05; he was delivered from drunkenness and became a fine Christian. Partly as the result of that change he began to prosper in business. But after a number of years he began to grow a little careless. A spiritual decline commenced which first showed itself in worldliness and proceeded with his returning to drink, so that he became a thoroughgoing backslider. In this state he had gone on for several years, outwardly doing very well indeed, so that he became a wealthy man. Then suddenly and without any warning, he knew not why, the reality of his position came home to him, and he began to worry about it deeply. His self-accusation took this form. He would reason, "Of course, when I was unconverted and did these things, I did not know any better, and I was forgiven; that was all right, but now I have sinned against the light. While living as I have been doing I knew the truth, I knew better, and now there is no forgiveness." So his concern increased. His doctor diagnosed his case as one of religious mania, and he was put in this nursing home. There, despite various kinds of treatment, he became worse rather than better.'

As the above description reveals, Dr Lloyd-Jones had come to the conclusion that the man needed purely spiritual help, and as he began to speak to him in terms of Scripture, and of the true basis for an assurance of salvation, the apparently deranged man slowly became as calm as a child. He was not completely delivered at once. A week or so later, although he lived at Bridgend – some distance from Aberavon – he was back at the manse door seemingly as distressed as before. Once more the truths of Scripture were urged upon him and with less difficulty than before he came to rest on them afresh. Other similar visits followed until the man was clearly re-established in the assurance of the love of Christ and he needed no further help.[1]

[1] A fuller account of this story will be found in *The Sons of God*, Romans 8:5–17, 1974, pp. 229–30.

This experience confirmed Dr Lloyd-Jones in a principle which he regarded as crucial in counselling. He saw that just as it is disastrous to attempt to treat a case of real physical or mental illness with spiritual remedies, so it is equally wrong to treat a *spiritual* case with what may be of benefit to those who are genuinely mentally ill. Yet as symptoms in the two classes can be very similar, how can one discern to which class a distressed person, in need of help, belongs? His conclusion was that where, in a regenerate person, distress arises out of a sense of sin and an absence of assurance – in other words, where the condition has spiritual causes – then the person will respond to a correct application of the truths and promises of Scripture suited for that condition. Such response may not be immediate and total, but it will be recognisable to the careful pastor. On the other hand, where this use of Scripture is of no avail in removing the distress of persons of whom there is reason to believe that they are Christians, then the likelihood is that medical psychiatric assistance should be sought.

It would be premature at this point in Dr Lloyd-Jones' life to discuss his views on divine healing. But it is notable that some of his most powerful evangelistic sermons were based upon miracles of healing and of the resurrection of the dead as recorded in the Gospels and the Acts of the Apostles. As a physician he looked closely at the misery of disease and of death, and as a preacher of the gospel he gloried in showing that it is the same power which in those instances delivered the body from sickness and death that is supremely glorious in transforming the soul.

'It was my pleasure and privilege to preach for nine Sundays in Canada, in Toronto, in 1932.'

M. L.-J.
Preaching and Preachers, p. 147

13

In North America

At nine on a June morning, close to mid-summer's day in 1932, a small party stood on the platform of Waterloo Station in London to see Dr and Mrs Lloyd-Jones, with Elizabeth, off on their first crossing of the Atlantic. Besides members of his family, the M.P. for Cardiganshire, Mr D. O. Evans, was there, and also Eliseus Howells who by this date had become one of his closest friends. Maybe the last-named had some eighteenth-century reading matter to offer as the best employment for an Atlantic voyage, for Martyn was never known to be a lover of fresh air. In their common judgment, the highest pleasure offered by such travel was the opportunity to read undisturbed!

The destination was Toronto where Dr Lloyd-Jones was to preach for nine Sundays at the United Presbyterian church on Sherbourne Street at the invitation of Dr Richard Roberts. Roberts, who belonged to an older generation of Welsh ministers, was serving this Toronto congregation, having previously been minister of the Calvinistic Methodist church at Willesden Green in London. From the United Kingdom he had received news of the young preacher in Aberavon whose ministry was becoming so influential in Wales, and he thus hoped that an extended visit might serve to rally the Sherbourne church. At this period it was common for all the principal Toronto pulpits to be supplied by prominent preachers from Britain during the summer months.

If, before giving the invitation, Dr Roberts had concerned himself with finding out Dr Lloyd-Jones' doctrinal commitment, then the likelihood of a strong contrast appearing between their respective ministries had not troubled him. Like many other Welshmen of his generation Roberts admired 'good preaching' regardless of the content of the message, but with respect to creed his own sympathies were decidedly liberal. Although he was on vacation when Lloyd-

Jones began to preach at Sherbourne Street, he remained in town and introduced and welcomed the visitor whose name was completely unknown to his congregation. Unintentionally Dr Lloyd-Jones immediately ran into a fundamental difference between their two standpoints. As he has recorded it:

'In responding to the welcome I thought it would be wise for me to indicate to the congregation my method as a preacher. I told the congregation that my method was to assume generally on Sunday morning that I was speaking to believers, to the saints, and that I would try to edify them; but that at night I would be preaching on the assumption that I was speaking to non-Christians as undoubtedly there would be many such there. In a sense I just said that in passing.

'We went through that morning service, and at the close the minister asked if I would stand at the door with him to shake hands with people as they went out. I did so. We had shaken hands with a number of people when he suddenly whispered to me saying, "You see that old lady who is coming along slowly. She is the most important member of this church. She is a very wealthy woman and the greatest supporter of the work." He was, in other words, telling me to exercise to the maximum what little charm I might possess. I need not explain any further! Well, the old lady came along and we spoke to her, and I shall never forget what happened. It taught me a great lesson which I have never forgotten. The old lady said, "Did I understand you to say that in the evening you would preach on the assumption that the people listening are not Christians and in the morning on the assumption that they are?" "Yes," I said. "Well," she said, "having heard you this morning I have decided to come tonight." She had never been known to attend the evening service; never. She only attended in the morning. I cannot describe the embarrassment of the situation. I sensed that the minister standing by my side felt that I was ruining his ministry and bitterly regretted inviting me to occupy his pulpit! But the fact was that the old lady did come that Sunday night, and every Sunday night while I was there. I met her in her house in private conversation and found that she was most unhappy about her spiritual condition, and did not know where she stood. She was a fine and most generous character, living an exemplary life. Everybody assumed – not only the minister, but everybody else – that she was an exceptionally fine Christian; but she was not a Christian. This idea that, because people are members of the church and attend regularly, they must be Christian is one of the most fatal assumptions, and I suggest that it mainly accounts for the state of the church today.'[1]

For the first and second Sundays at Sherbourne Street church the building was only half full, but the evening service of the second Sunday was broadcast and this had the effect of filling the building for the third weekend. The broadcast also had another consequence. Before he reached Toronto, Dr Lloyd-Jones had some acquaintance with the ministry of the leading orthodox preacher of that city, Dr T. T. Shields of Jarvis Street Baptist church, having heard him once in Britain.[2] Shields' paper *The Gospel Witness* circulated among Christians known to Dr Lloyd-Jones in South Wales and the Canadian preacher was particularly admired by R. B. Jones and his circle at Porth. Like R. B. Jones, T. T. Shields was a vigorous denouncer of all denominational apostasy. In theology Shields and Lloyd-Jones stood close to one another: both were Calvinists, both amillennial in their view of unfulfilled prophecy. But there was an important aspect of Shields' ministry with which Lloyd-Jones was not in sympathy. He thought the Baptist leader was sometimes too controversial, too denunciatory and too censorious. Rather than helping young Christians by the strength of his polemics against liberal Protestants and Roman Catholics, Lloyd-Jones believed that Shields was losing the opportunity to influence those whose first need was to be given positive teaching.

The morning after the broadcast service from Sherbourne church, while the Lloyd-Joneses were at breakfast, the phone rang and the caller announced himself as T. T. Shields. His purpose, he went on to say, was to ask if Lloyd-Jones would come and preach for him. 'You know,' Shields went on to explain, 'a most remarkable thing happened. My wife died at the dinner table last Friday night. The result was that I wasn't preaching yesterday, so I thought I would listen to the radio and hear what these infidels are saying. I left your church to the last because the man you are preaching for I regard as the arch-infidel. But I switched on to it and, Man, I found myself

[1] *Preaching and Preachers*, pp. 148–49.
[2] Thomas Todhunter Shields, born in England, 1873, emigrated with his parents to Canada in 1888, where, after serving three or four congregations, he was called to the premier Baptist church of Canada, Jarvis Street church, Toronto, in 1910 when he was 37. There he was to remain as pastor until his death in 1955.

listening to the gospel! You must come and preach for me.' When Dr Lloyd-Jones responded that this would be impossible, Shields asked that the visitor would at least come and meet him and this was agreed for lunch-time the next day.

As Dr Lloyd-Jones spoke with Bethan, who was not to accompany him, of this forthcoming meeting and they prayed about it, he came to the conviction that if Shields gave him any kind of opportunity he would raise the matter which limited his admiration of the older preacher's evangelicalism. In Dr Lloyd-Jones' own words:

'Shields came to fetch me and we had lunch. We talked on general subjects and then we went to sit in the garden. There, as we drank coffee, he suddenly turned to me and said, "Are you a great reader of Joseph Parker?" I replied, "No, I am not." "Why?" he asked. "I get nothing from him." "Man!" he said, "what's the matter with you?" "Well," I said, "it's all very well to make these criticisms of the liberals but he doesn't help me spiritually." "Surely you are helped by the way he makes mincemeat of the liberals?" "No, I am not," I responded. "You can make mincemeat of the liberals and still be in trouble in your own soul." "Well," Shields said, "I read Joseph Parker every Sunday morning. He winds me up – puts me right." I felt my opening had come, so we began. We had a great debate. He was a very able man and we argued the issue about which I disagreed with him. In defence of his attitude he said, "Do you know, every time I indulge in what you call one of these 'dog-fights' the sales of the *Gospel Witness* go right up. What about that?" "Well," I replied, "I have always observed that if there is a dog-fight a crowd gathers, I'm not at all surprised. People like that sort of thing." Then he brought up another argument. He said, "Now, you are a doctor and you are confronted by a patient who has got cancer. You know that if that cancer is not removed it is going to kill the patient. You don't want to operate but you have to do so because it is going to save the patient's life. That is my position. I don't want to be doing this kind of thing, but there is this cancer and it has got to be removed. What do you say to that?" I responded, "What I say to that is this: I am a physician but there is such a thing as 'a surgical mentality', or of becoming what is described as 'knife-happy'. I agree, there are some cases where you have got to operate, but the danger of the surgeon is to operate immediately. He thinks in terms of *operating*. Never have an operation without having a second opinion from a physician."'

21. *Bethlehem Forward Movement Hall, popularly known as Sandfields*

22. *A group at the Induction Service, February 4, 1927. Behind Dr Lloyd-Jones [centre], E. T Rees [behind and to his immediate left], Richard J. Rees (Superintendent of the Forward Movement); [further to the left], T. J. Lewis (the former pastor) [Extreme right, second row], David Williams (minister of Carmel Calvinistic Methodist Chapel)*

23. *A Brotherhood annual outing*

24. *M. L.-J. talking to a school teacher from his childhood while on a*
Brotherhood outing to Llangeitho

21 *M.L. leading a 'Whit March...*

26. *Bethan Lloyd-Jones' Sunday School class*

27. *M. L.-J. and Eliseus Howells*

28. *M.L.-J. and E. T. Rees – Twm Siôn Cati's Cave*
(the Welsh Robin Hood)

29. *On the beach with Elizabeth at Cwm yr Eglwys, Pembs., c. 1934*

30. *Bethan Lloyd-Jones with Elizabeth and her mother*

31. *The day of the Cardiff broadcast service, January 1, 1935. M. L.-J. is between the Rev. J. Penry Thomas [left] and Dr Llewellyn Williams*

32. *En route to New York, with his mother [second from left] 1937*

33. *Westminster Chapel, sometimes known as 'Westminster Church'*

34. [overleaf] *Westminster Chapel congregation, with Campbell Morgan in the pulpit, 1930's*

35. *The International Inter-Varsity Conference, Cambridge, 193*

Douglas Johnson is on the extreme right [second row]

36. *Family group, summer 1938. Taken upon leaving Sandfields*

In North America

'At this point Shields got up, walked down the garden and then came back to re-open the conversation: "Well," he queried, "what about this: you remember Paul in Galatians 2? He had to withstand Peter to the face. He did not want to do it. Peter was an older apostle, a leader and so on. Paul did it very reluctantly, but he had to do it for the sake of the truth. I am in exactly that position. What do you say to that?" "I would say this," I responded, "that the effect of what Paul did was to *win* Peter round to his position and make him call him 'our beloved brother Paul'. Can you say the same about the people whom you attack?" Shields was finished. Then, after we had stopped arguing, I made a great appeal to him. I said, "Dr Shields, you used to be known as the Canadian Spurgeon, and you were. You are an outstanding man, in intellect, in preaching gift, in every other respect, but over the McMaster University business[1] in the early twenties you suddenly changed and became negatory and denunciatory. I feel it has ruined your ministry. Why don't you come back! Drop all this, preach the gospel to people positively and win them!" '[2]

Dr Lloyd-Jones continued this appeal as they drove back in the car. With tears in his eyes, Shields – then fifty-nine years old – at length confessed, 'I have never been spoken to like this in my life before and I am most grateful to you. You have moved me very deeply. I will tell you what I will do. I will call a meeting of my board tomorrow night, tell them exactly what we have discussed and put myself in their hands. If they agree with you I will do what you say. If they don't, I won't.' The meeting, as Dr Lloyd-Jones eventually heard, took place as arranged and Shields' men told him not to listen to the advice he had received.

Thus no change was to follow the memorable meeting of the two men, except that Dr Lloyd-Jones became more firmly convinced of the way in which an orthodox ministry can be spoilt by a wrong spirit and by wrong methods. T. T. Shields in his later years was even to drive away from the Jarvis Street church some of his warmest supporters and eventually to finish his ministry with a congregation much reduced in size. To Dr Lloyd-Jones the warning of this experience, confirmed by what he saw of the same danger in R. B.

[1] Shields had anticipated an appointment at McMaster University but was blocked by liberals.
[2] Another account of this conversation, with slight variations, will be found in *Preaching and Preachers*, pp. 259–61.

David Martyn Lloyd-Jones

Jones' later ministry at Porth, when he modelled himself on Shields, acted as a salutary check in subsequent years and he was often to pass on the same warning to other ministers exposed to the same temptation.

Almost all of Dr Lloyd-Jones' nine weeks' stay in North America was to be spent in Toronto, apart from a few excursions. With Mrs Lloyd-Jones and Elizabeth he was able to make a first visit to the Niagara Falls, a site which he never tired of revisiting in later years. There was also an outing into the country from Toronto for fishing with Richard Roberts, when he proudly brought back his catch of a splendid lake trout! By far the most important days away from Toronto, however, were five which he spent on a first visit to the United States where he was engaged to speak at the Chautauqua Institution. This was a large vacation conference, meeting for the fifty-ninth occasion, and running, with a large number of different speakers, from July 6 to August 28. Founded by the Methodist Bishop Vincent, the Chautauqua conference had originally aimed at helping Sunday-school teachers and was thoroughly biblical and evangelical in its vision. The passing of the years, however, had brought many changes until by 1932 the organisers were happy to claim that the Chautauqua Institution – now attended by several thousand people – taught everything, including religion – the latter being relegated to a comparatively minor place in the daily programme. The main sessions were now given to addresses on literature, history and politics, or to drama and concerts. Two of the principal speakers in 1932 were Mrs Franklin D. Roosevelt and the famous agnostic, Professor Julian Huxley of London.

Each week at Chautauqua the conference had a different chaplain and those who wished could attend his 'Devotional Hour' at 9.45 each morning, or the 'Chaplain's Hour' at 4 p.m. Attendance at this conference had not been originally intended as part of Dr Lloyd-Jones' overseas trip, but before the conference programme was published, an English chaplain booked for one week had withdrawn and it was hurriedly arranged that Dr Lloyd-Jones should come in his place. Unlike the sessions to be taken by the other chaplains in other weeks, the published programme gave no titles to the sessions for which Dr Lloyd-Jones was to be responsible. For the 'Chaplain's Hour', he was told, he could say 'anything he liked', and judging by the titles printed against the names of the other chaplains they availed themselves of this liberty. Their subjects included, 'Humour, a

Human Asset', 'Not Thrills but Joy', 'The Mystery of Life', 'The Gospel and the Poets', 'Slang, a Human Revelation', with some more specifically Christian.

After a full Sunday at Sherbourne church, Dr Lloyd-Jones travelled on a hot Monday, July 11, to Chautauqua, near Buffalo, in New York State. He was there in time for the first 'Chaplain's Hour' at 4 p.m. and the sight of the little group of some thirty people who were present to hear him (from among the thousands present at the conference) was a clear enough indication of what the majority thought of chaplains who could 'say anything'! Later that same evening – his first in the United States – he had a long and ineffective debate with a Baptist professor of theology who scorned the evangelical faith. When at last he prepared to retire to bed he was weary, lonely (for Mrs Lloyd-Jones and Elizabeth had remained in Canada), and thoroughly downcast at the prospect of the week before him. It was just at this moment that, in prayer beside his bed, he knew afresh that not only can we speak to God, but He can speak to us. There was indeed no audible voice, yet he was unmistakably conscious that God had directed him to that place, and the words of encouragement once given to Paul at Corinth came also to him with great clarity and force, 'Be not afraid. . . . for I am with thee. . . . I have much people in this city' (Acts 18:9–10). The experience transformed his whole spirit, and the next morning, thoroughly roused, he was able to preach with exceptional liberty and power. At the end of that first morning meeting, attended by about one hundred and fifty, an older Christian was waiting to ask him, 'Where do you come from?' 'From Toronto,' was the reply. 'No, I don't mean that, where have you come from?' 'From Britain – Wales,' was the preacher's second answer, only to be swept aside with, 'No, no, I will tell you, God has sent you here.' He went on to explain how he had attended the Conference for years, only to see it become more and more secularised and bereft of the gospel. But he and some other Christians had hung on and prayed that better things would yet come. He was sure that the Welshman's visit was an answer to prayer. By the time of Dr Lloyd-Jones' final service on the Friday morning the venue had to be moved to the huge concert auditorium, able to seat 6,000, which was well filled!

For Dr Lloyd-Jones there was something uniquely helpful about the week at Chautauqua. It was not the numbers nor even the sense of answered prayer. In Wales his critics often expressed the view that his influence had no particular spiritual significance: it was due, they argued, to the exceptional interest which would attach to any prominent man who thus changed his profession and became a preacher. It was his switch from being a medical doctor to a minister which explained the attention which his services attracted. Such arguments Lloyd-Jones had often heard, and though he never believed them, the Chautauqua week was, to him, a final confirmation of their falsity. He was there as someone entirely unknown, a stop-gap substitute from whose 'talks' – as the Monday meeting demonstrated – nothing particularly helpful was expected.[1] In all his subsequent visits to the United States there was to be no single experience which he valued more highly than this week at Chautauqua.

It was while Dr Lloyd-Jones was in Toronto that a Canadian reporter came out with the first interview which any newspaper reporter had succeeded in obtaining with him. A Welsh paper, unable to give its readers similar copy, later explained that Dr Lloyd-Jones had made an exception to his rule out of deference to his hosts at Sherbourne Street church who said, 'He would be expected to make some response to the "interviewing" methods of the Dominion'. What went into print, however, under the heading, 'Departure from Old Ideals, says Minister', suggests that the reporter, who was a well-known Canadian interviewer, had no great success in acquiring personal details from the visitor. After explaining how a friend had advised him to go to hear one of 'the greatest living pulpit orators', the reporter proceeded:

'This Chrysostom man, now and for five further Sundays in Sherbourne pulpit, is the Rev. Dr Martin Lloyd-Jones, one of the outstanding pulpit orators in Wales, home of melody, oratory, politics, theology – and of a mysterious language that has no alternative but a cry.

"How often have you visited Canada?" was my first enquiry of this 46-year-old keen-eyed, black-hair begirt son of Wales. "Never before," was the melancholy answer.

"Enjoy the trip across?" I pursued. "No, I didn't," was the candid reply.

[1] The elaborate Chautauqua Institution programme for 1932 does not name Dr Lloyd-Jones among its twenty leading speakers. In small type he enters the programme on July 11 as 'Dr Martyn Lloyd-Jones, Fort Talbot, Wales'!

"Stormy passage?" I presumed.

"No, fine – but I don't like the sea," was the strange confession of a man who lives near Llandudno and its incomparable glories.'

It was not the last time that Dr Lloyd-Jones was to be credited with being considerably older – fourteen years in this case – than he actually was and perhaps this was more forgivable than the placing of his ministry 'near' the *North* Wales holiday resort of Llandudno! The writer went on to relate how he had spoken to Dr Lloyd-Jones of two of Canada's 'greatest preachers' who were both Welshmen, Dr Richard Roberts and Dr Trevor Davies, and of how startled he was by the visitor's assertion that, not knowing the Welsh language, Davies 'can't be a real Welshman'. Dr Lloyd-Jones' reservations on Richard Roberts were left unexpressed, but there was this exchange on how he felt to have the senior preacher present to hear him every Sunday. 'Was he not embarrassed to have the minister of Sherbourne Street present in the church?' asked the interviewer, from whose article we continue to quote:

' "Not a bit," was the calm reply.

' "Perhaps the Welsh never embarrassize," I suggested. "Oh yes, we do – we're really a very sensitive and nervous race."

' "You have it under fine control," I informed my interesting subject; "but tell me how many Joneses are there in Wales?"

' "Why do you ask that?" "Oh, nothing – I'm only trying to keep up with the Joneses. Is it possible, in Wales, to be a Jones and still be distinguished?"

' "A bit difficult – but we all have appended names, of course."

' "Yes," I replied, "I know a man, a Jones, in Hamilton, whose parents made him all but immortal from his birth. They called him 'Seneca'. Wasn't that fine? – all Canada knew Seneca Jones. Just imagine the edge a Seneca Jones has over a William Jones!"

' "Quite a fine antidote, I'll admit," replied this witty visitor whose legitimacy reposes in the Welsh, whose fame in the English language.

' "Which kind of church are you the minister of in Wales?" I went on.

' "Really a Presbyterian church, the name of the denomination – the strongest one in Wales – is the Welsh Calvinistic Methodist Church."

' "Surely there's a mistake somewhere," I opined; "please say that over again."

'Once more the name rolled out, a civil war in language. "I'm bewildered," was my confession. "Surely the term 'Calvinistic Methodist' is about as harmonious as 'white black-bird' or 'east-west wind'. Are they not antipodal terms?"

' "Not at all – you evidently think that John Wesley was the only Methodist who ever lived. George Whitefield was a Calvinist – that's why he and Wesley quarrelled."

' "But aren't the Welsh people naturally Calvinistic – isn't that their religious genius?" I returned.

' "I don't believe nations are ever of any religious stripe, nationally and naturally."

' "Look at Scotland – isn't it nationally and naturally Presbyterian and Calvinistic?"

' "No! – due mostly to John Knox."

' "Why has Wales never had any great – I mean monumentally great – preachers?" I diverted.

' "She has had them," rolling off two or three gnarled names of which I had never heard.

' "Tell me," I asked, "how much is left today of the result of the great Evan Roberts revival?"

' "I affirm this – that the best Christian leaders we have in Wales today, a vast proportion of them are the product of that Roberts revival. The world's departure from the old foundations, in theology, is in large measure the cause, I believe, of the moral wreckage that marks our modern life." '

The conversation then turned to politics and Dr Lloyd-Jones parried questions with which he did not mean to become involved. But his lost enthusiasm for his one-time political hero was not disguised. 'Does Mr Lloyd George ever preach now?' asked the reporter. 'Far too often,' was the reply. A second question, 'Has he a future?' elicited the non-committal response, 'No mere man can say.' When the interviewer proceeded to speak with enthusiasm of the new National Government in Britain (headed by Ramsay MacDonald and supported by his old opponent, Stanley Baldwin) the preacher conceded that MacDonald has had 'a great triumph, for the moment at least', at the same time indicating that neither of the men – 'both sentimentalists, both much of the same type' – had his confidence. Dissatisfied to leave it there, the reporter tells us how the interview came to a conclusion:

' "Don't you consider the National Government a good thing for the nation?"

' "I believe it has gone far to bring about a religious revival, such as I expect soon to visit our land [Wales]," was the startling reply.

' "What on earth can the two have to do with each other?" I exclaimed.

' "Just this: The people – oh, how they did idolise Ramsay MacDonald! – the people have seen the feet of clay. The scales have fallen from their eyes. They are disillusioned. Their faith in men, in man as such, has been shattered. No longer will they put their 'trust in princes', or potentates, or politicians. Thus, the only alternative is God. They are thrown back on the divine. And this spells spiritual quickening. The religious revival that is to be," was the concluding opinion of this mystic-minded and original man.'[1]

One noticeable feature in Dr Lloyd-Jones' character was underlined in his Canadian visit, namely, his capacity to win the friendship of men with whom he could disagree strongly. Such was the case with his host, Dr Richard Roberts, and equally so with the pugnacious T. T. Shields. When, with the family, he boarded the Canadian Pacific liner *Empress of Britain* early in September 1932, for the voyage home, he found, waiting for him, a greetings cable from the Baptist who was nearly thirty years his senior.

Prior to this date Dr Lloyd-Jones' name was practically unknown in the religious press of England. The situation was to change even before he had reached home. *The British Weekly* of September 8, 1932 – in different vein from the criticism expressed by its Welsh correspondent in 1925 – reported the news that 'Dr Lloyd-Jones' preaching in Canada had made a very deep impression upon the large congregations that assembled to hear him.' The Editor of *The Christian World*, under the heading 'An Evangelistic Leader' went further, after reminding his readers that 'Dr Jones is the young medical man who gave up medicine to enter the Welsh ministry and has been

[1] Having just gone to hear Dr Lloyd-Jones in a professional capacity the interviewer's own personal interest was to bring him back to subsequent services.

making a deepening impression in Wales'.[1] His source of information was a personal letter received from Richard Roberts in Toronto from which he quotes the words:

'It is no exaggeration to say that Dr Lloyd-Jones has taken the city by storm. On the last two or three Sundays large numbers of people have failed to get into the church. He is pre-eminently an evangelistic preacher with a mighty passion for souls.'

The Editor's note continued:

'Dr Roberts, who heard him several times, says that "Dr Jones' preaching is easily the finest of its kind I have heard for many years". "Probably," he adds, "he is that evangelistic leader you seem lately to be calling for." '

The British Weekly for September 15, 1932, gave still fuller information from the pen of the Reverend William Paxton of Liverpool who had also been preaching in Toronto. Under the heading 'Summer Sundays in Toronto', Paxton described the service rendered by the various British preachers who had recently been in Toronto, but there was no doubting what he considered to be most noteworthy:

'Each summer it is customary for the pulpits of the leading churches in Toronto to be occupied by preachers from the Old Country, and the people show their appreciation by filling the pews in the "dead" months.

'The pioneers in this movement were warned that in August people like to spend Sunday motoring in the country, or "everyone" had gone to their weekend cottages, or that it was too hot for sitting in church.

'The surprise, from our point of view, has been the amazing success of Dr Lloyd-Jones at Sherbourne church, as deputy for Dr Richard Roberts. He comes from a small Welsh town and it is no reflection upon him to say that he is the least known of the British delegation.

'Dr Lloyd-Jones has attracted congregations of such dimensions

[1] By a printing error, another paper inadvertently changed the words to read 'a deepening depression in Wales' – a fact gleefully noticed by *Punch*, September 14, 1932, which quoted it under the heading 'Gathering Gloom'!

that the large church was too small to hold them, and he has done so by the quality of his preaching, without any of the meretricious aids sometimes given to professional preachers on this side of the Atlantic.'

The references made by Roberts and Paxton to the numbers who came to Sherbourne church were not exaggerated. On Dr Lloyd-Jones' last Sunday night in that pulpit the service had to begin an hour early at the request of the police.

The *Empress of Britain* docked at Cherbourg and as the family trio crossed the English Channel on Thursday September 8, bound for Southampton and London, Dr Lloyd-Jones wrote to E. T. Rees of his anticipated arrival at Aberavon the following Saturday night. He would be too late for the Brotherhood but was ready to preach on Sunday, 11 September. That first Sunday home, Sandfields had more visitors than usual, including a reporter from the *South Wales News* who the next morning offered his readers two lengthy columns of type, headed 'Dr Martin Lloyd-Jones Home, Aberavon Preacher's Canadian Tour'. Characteristically, however, the preacher had said not so much as one sentence on his trans-Atlantic experience and, despite the caption, all the paper could give was the substance of his two Sunday sermons. In the morning sermon, on 1 Corinthians 4:20; 'For the kingdom of God is not in word, but in power', he declared that power did not mean 'ecstasies, dreams or trances': true spiritual power is to be tested by scriptural truth and its presence will always result in conviction of sin and in the spirit of prayer. For the evening sermon he was once more in the Book of Acts, with chapter 20, verse 21, for his text.

For the Lloyd-Jones' family themselves the return from Canada was memorable in that it marked their entrance into a new manse, the building of which had been going on over the previous twelve months. The new home, 28 Victoria Road, was only a few hundred yards from the old – nearer to the sandhills – but, semi-detached and on a corner site, it was to provide more adequate room. As the plans for its erection were discussed, the Sandfields men discovered that their own minister, aided by a good local builder, was all they needed for an architect! It was Dr Lloyd-Jones who decided that although the house would be deep and narrow fronted in the common style, the kitchen should be in the middle of the ground floor with the parlour behind it at the rear (the normal place for a kitchen). He also designed the parlour fireplace so that its fire would also heat a back boiler in the kitchen. Only at one point did the men, as they first thought, have the pleasure of indicating an 'error' in the 'architect's' guidance. He had recommended that it would be easy to enlarge the maid's bedroom – planned for the head of the staircase and beside the main front bedroom – by taking into it part of the space designated for the landing. After duly weighing this proposal, the builder came back to tell 'the Doctor' that such a curtailment of the landing area would make it impossible for a coffin ever to be carried out of the main front-bedroom! The doorway space would not permit it. But, Dr Lloyd-Jones quickly pointed out, that was no problem: all that was needed was a connecting door between the main front-bedroom and the room behind it (Elizabeth's future room). So the proposal, with this modification, was duly carried out and the maid given her larger space. The real sufferer proved to be Elizabeth because that front-room was the guest-bedroom and when the visiting preachers came to stay once a month the connecting door provided no defence against their sonorous and stentorian slumbers. She came to dread the weekend her father was away. Sometimes it seemed as though her very bed shook in unison with their snoring.

Only at one point did the amateur house designer, after a little experience of the new home, believe that his plans had contained a weakness. The placing of the fireplace in relation to the window in the sitting room created what, above all things, he hated most, namely, a draught! The only thing to be done was to rig up a moveable partition between his fireside seat and the window. That partition was to be a curiosity and a source of amusement in the congregation for years to come!

When Dr Lloyd-Jones went to Canada in June 1932 there were those at Sandfields who, despite the preparation of the new manse, made known their fears that they were about to see the last of their beloved pastor. Had they known the full picture their fears would have been increased. The month after his return, the Official Board of Sherbourne United church wrote urging a second visit in July and August of 1933. 'I know that you will be guided by your sense of duty in this matter,' wrote James Hales for the Board, 'but I hope that you will be able to see that it is your duty to come to us. There are thousands of people who will look forward to your coming with great expectation.' T. T. Shields also wrote asking him to supply Jarvis Street for several months and promising that their difference over baptism need be no deterrent, as he could make special arrangements for its administration without the participation of Dr Lloyd-Jones. On the heels of these letters came an approach from the congregation of Trinity United Church, Toronto, currently without a minister, asking if he would be willing to negotiate with them before they looked elsewhere or made a decision. Other letters and cables from the same congregation stressed the spiritual opportunities arising out of Trinity's central position in the city – close to the University – and also the ease of accessibility from Toronto to the many parts of Canada into which his ministry could be extended.

The invitations to return to Canada in 1933 were not accepted and Dr Lloyd-Jones had no hesitation in declining to proceed with the enquiry from Trinity United Church. Encouraged though he was by his experience in North America, his mind and heart were set on the need for a spiritual awakening in his own country. He saw, later, the danger that his head might have been turned by that sudden wave of popularity and spoke of the old literature of biography and revival history as a principal means which preserved him from that danger. 'When I read of Whitefield and of other similar men,' he could say, 'I felt I had not started.' More than that, amidst those records of the mighty works of God he felt the utter insignificance of any human acclaim and endorsed the testimony of Isaac Watts:

> Had I a glance of thee, my God,
> Kingdoms and men would vanish soon,
> Vanish as though I saw them not,
> As a dim candle dies at noon.

'Observe how all the fathers in the early church revere Paul and, without the slightest hesitation, include his epistles in the New Testament canon. And then consider the way in which these very epistles and their teachings have been honoured and used by the Holy Spirit. Their very essence is in all the creeds and doctrinal statements of the church universal, they form the basis of all true dogma. And who can forget the fact that the words of Paul were the means used by the Holy Ghost in the conversion of Augustine, Luther, and Wesley, not to mention scores of others. Let us put it quite plainly. The one who rejects what he calls Pauline theology is flying in the face of everything that has been most wonderful and noble in the history of the Christian church. Yea, let us boldly go the whole way and say with St Paul, "If we, or an angel from heaven preach any other gospel than that we have preached, let him be accursed".'

M. L.-J.
in a sermon on 1 Timothy 2:3–6, July 1933

'Dr Lloyd-Jones is a man of one idea, and, judged by the false breadth all too prevalent in Christian circles today, might be regarded as "intolerant". If he is intolerant, it is precisely the same way as the Apostle Paul, who wished that anyone preaching any other gospel might be anathema. So he refuses to compromise, or to adjust the Evangel to human speculations.'

'Preacher – Physician', The Christian, November 28, 1935

14

The Pauline Note

Dr Lloyd-Jones' Toronto visit of 1932 occurred eleven years after the death of the American whom he was later to describe as 'undoubtedly the greatest theologian of the past seventy years in the English-speaking world'.[1] Benjamin B. Warfield died at Princeton, New Jersey, in 1921, at a time when the Protestant Churches across the world appeared to be in almost full retreat from the doctrinal Christianity which he so eminently represented. When Oxford University Press, New York, ventured to issue a limited edition of Warfield's works, in ten volumes, between 1927 and 1931, interest was comparatively small. Warfield, and the old Princeton Theological Seminary where he taught, were, for many, symbols of an outmoded past.

A review of one of the Warfield volumes in *The British Weekly* had first alerted Lloyd-Jones to the existence of his collected writings, but not until the Canadian visit of 1932 did he make his own discovery of the biblical stature of Princeton's late Professor of Didactic and Polemic Theology. Richard Roberts and his wife, unable to accommodate the Lloyd-Joneses in their own Toronto home, had arranged for them to stay at 74 St George's, and it was this location which placed them, for nine weeks, directly opposite Knox Seminary, a leading Presbyterian theological school. Dr Roberts saw no significance in the near proximity of the two places, unused as he was to holiday preachers who spent their mornings in study. Dr Lloyd-Jones, however, hearing that Knox possessed a fine theological library (something not to be found in Port Talbot), was scarcely

---

[1] Review of *Biblical and Theological Studies*, B. B. Warfield, *The Inter-Varsity Magazine*, Summer, 1952, pp. 27–28. For his estimate of Warfield as a theologian see also his Introduction to *Biblical Foundations*, a collection of Warfield writings published by Tyndale Press, 1958. The entire O.U.P. set of Warfield was reprinted by Baker in 1981.

settled in Toronto before he decided to ask permission to use its facilities. This the librarian readily granted and the visitor had not even begun to explore the library building when his eye fell upon the cream cartridge-paper covers and the crimson bindings of Warfield's works, standing on the shelves reserved for new acquisitions. His feelings at that moment, he was later to write, were like those of 'stout Cortez', as described by Keats, when he first saw the Pacific. In the mornings of the many days which followed, Dr Lloyd-Jones never went beyond that shelf of Warfield. He revelled in the ten volumes to a degree which he had done with no other modern writer. As in the older Reformed authors, here was theology anchored in Scripture, but with an exegetical precision more evident than in the older authors, and combined with a devotion which raised the whole above the level of scholarship alone. 'Such was Warfield's own knowledge and experience of the truth, and of God in Christ through the Holy Spirit,' Dr Lloyd-Jones was to write in the review already quoted, 'that more than most writers he gives a profound impression of the glory and wonder of the great salvation we enjoy.' Once back in Britain, he was to lose no time in becoming, in his own phrase, 'a proud possessor of the original ten volumes'.

We have already noted the usefulness of such writers as James Denney and P. T. Forsyth to Dr Lloyd-Jones, yet, partly because of the deficiency in their doctrine of Scripture and also because of weakness in other areas of doctrine, the impression which they made upon him was neither so profound nor so influential as that which he now received through Warfield. To Warfield more than to anyone else he was to attribute a development in his thought and ministry which occurred at this period. Hitherto Dr Lloyd-Jones' reputation was built very largely on his evangelistic preaching. Intellectual though he was by aptitude and training prior to this date, he showed no great interest in distinctly doctrinal teaching or in the defence of the Faith against modern error. No one would have described him as a 'theologian' or 'teacher'; there were even occasions in his early preaching when he decried the niceties of doctrinal correctness. The Gospels and the Book of Acts were his first love and, while he rejected the claim of liberals that our Faith must come from these sources rather than from the Pauline Epistles, the Pauline element in his thinking and teaching was as yet comparatively weak compared with what it was to become. Warfield gave him new insight into the necessity for doctrinal teaching. While not ceasing to be an evangelist, he was now brought to the strong conviction that more was required.

Certainly this major development was not due to Warfield's influence alone. In the providence of God there were other factors at work in Lloyd-Jones' life which were pointing in the same direction. The many young converts at Sandfields needed to be established in the Faith. Further, because of his leadership as a preacher, ministers were increasingly looking to him for counsel on a number of contemporary religious issues, and evangelical students in the Welsh University Colleges – particularly those at Cardiff and Swansea – were asking for his help in the defence of the truth from the attacks of unbelieving scholarship. It was the presence of these demands upon him which made the 'discovery' in the Library of Knox Seminary of far-reaching significance. In the years to come the words which he wrote of Warfield could well have been written of his own ministry: 'He not only asserted the Reformed faith; he at the same time demonstrated its superiority over all other systems or partial systems.'

Such was the even tenor of Dr Lloyd-Jones' work at Sandfields in the mid-thirties that it permits of no extended comment in these pages. Although the period of awakening witnessed in 1931, with large numbers of converts, was not repeated, there was no decline either in spiritual interest or in numbers. *Yr Efengylydd* reported in December 1933, that at Sandfields 'it is necessary to hold the week-night meetings in the chapel because the spacious schoolroom is too small'. Three years later, the Editor of *The Treasury*, the magazine of the Forward Movement, wrote of Sandfields in April 1936: 'Every memory of this Church brings joy. Its ministry is blessed of God in the building up of a great community rich in numbers, experience and devotion. A further added testimony of this is the announcement that the debt on all the buildings has now been extinguished.'[1]

These quotations tell their own story. Instead of attempting to expand them further we shall trace something of the growing influence of Dr Lloyd-Jones among ministers and students. He met

[1] Mrs Lloyd-Jones, recording her own memories of these years, writes: 'There were confessions of faith, conversions and requests for membership throughout the Aberavon ministry – not always in large numbers, but usually one or two in the after meeting on most Sundays. We always sang the doxology after their reception by the minister and there were not many Sundays when the doxology was not sung.'

many of them in the course of his itinerant ministry and in addition there was now an increasing number of private meetings and conferences where he was asked to address men in this category. In 1931 and 1932 he visited the Calvinistic Methodist training college at Trevecca. Of the first of these occasions, *Yr Efengylydd* reported, 'He encouraged the students there to resort to prayer together and to read the Word'. On his second visit, when *Y Goleuad* referred to him as 'the evangelist Dr Martin Lloyd-Jones', he urged more preaching upon holiness, speaking from the words, 'He must increase, but I must decrease' (John 3:30). Thereafter invitations to address ministerial students and ministers multiplied. In 1933 he gave a series of addresses at the Calvinistic Methodist College at Bala, North Wales, on themes related to the pulpit and the pastoral office. From his own few pencil notes which survive, it is evident that many of the points which he urged upon ministers at a later date were already uppermost in his mind at the age of thirty-three. 'A preacher', he began, 'is a man who has a distinct call to his work. He is not looking for something to say; he is a witness who testifies. He is not always talking about himself and his own experience, but preaching the truth.' He then proceeded to develop the significance of this principle. Preaching is not an end in itself. It must not ignore the people, yet it must not be ruled by the people. 'But it must follow Paul's method; truth and the Faith are committed to us to be applied to different people in different ways.' There must be a plan to a sermon and, in content, the sermon needs to include 'teaching, conviction and appeal'. Doctrine must precede moral duties, 'the right way is to make the ethical *inevitable*'.

In another address on 'The Minister as Pastor' he covered the organisation of church life, also dangers to avoid in accepting new members, together with such things as personal work and visitation. He warned that visiting is not to be undertaken as a duty in order to quieten one's conscience. 'The secret of all church work', he urged, 'is to realise our calling and our terrible responsibility (2 Cor. 5; 1 Cor. 3)'. Speaking further on 'The Minister as a Man', he began:

'This matter is difficult and may seem uninteresting but it is vitally important. The ruling idea ought to be that the pastor is a shepherd, *not* a pet lamb. He must be alert to the danger of trying to be nice and popular and chatty. The minister is to be always and everywhere "the man of God" and not merely when he is in chapel or taking a service. It is our duty to remember our calling. The minister should always move amongst the people as one who has been with God. His chief object should be to please God rather than to please men. What is needed is not the spirit but the Holy Spirit. What the minister thinks of himself is of vital importance. He can only win his place and have respect by a holy life.'

'Beware', he warned them, 'of becoming socialisers and tea-tasters.' Equally, they were to be on their guard against dissipating their strength on good causes, not essential to their true calling. The minister is not a public servant but God's servant. 'He is to be a specialist on the soul, not on everything. He votes, etc., as a citizen but takes no active part in political affairs.'

On 'The Minister in Private' he spoke first of 'the supreme importance of system and regularity' and then turned to the subject of Prayer, which he illustrated from 'Praying Hyde' and David Brainerd. Next he spoke of Bible reading and of general reading. Under 'special dangers' he dealt with ambition and the love of applause, jealousy, worldly-wisdom, unbusiness-like and unreliable traits, and laziness.

It is greatly to be wished that more than Dr Lloyd-Jones' skeleton notes had survived from these addresses to the students at Bala in 1933.

Two movements in particular were in vogue in Welsh, and indeed in British ministerial circles in the 1930's and in both of them Dr Lloyd-Jones became involved as an opponent of popular religious trends. The first was the so-called 'Oxford Group Movement', later better known as 'Moral Re-Armament', and inspired largely by the influence of Frank Buchman (1878–1961), a Lutheran clergyman from the United States. The Oxford Group, to use the name coined by Buchman in 1929, offered Christian renewal, not on the basis of a recovery of Christian faith in the truth, but rather in terms of the 'Christian ethic' and 'Christian experience'. Partly because it by-passed controversial matters of faith, and partly because of its surprising and widespread support among the young, church leaders of all shades flocked to Oxford Group conferences and pledged their support. Evangelicals, with no sympathy for the spiritual coldness of liberalism, were attracted by the Group's emphasis upon 'the Holy Spirit' and by not infrequent reports of remarkable and miraculous experiences – sometimes in dreams and trances – enjoyed by members of the Movement.

When Dr Lloyd-Jones first heard of the Oxford Group Movement from evangelical students at Aberystwyth, and before the Movement's character was commonly known, he was somewhat impressed. Urged by students to attend a Group Conference at Oxford he agreed. This decision, which he later viewed as a serious mistake, he failed to carry out, but only because of what he came to believe was a direct intervention of God. During the Sunday night before the morning when he was to travel from Aberavon to Oxford, he awoke feeling desperately unwell. A thermometer revealed a high temperature and accordingly all thought of travelling a few hours later was abandoned. Yet when he did rise, somewhat later than his normal time, all trace of the overnight illness had disappeared!

By 1932 when the Oxford Group influence was in the ascendancy in many quarters, Dr Lloyd-Jones was almost a lone voice in speaking against it. He was convinced that the *truth* must come first, irrespective of what experiences people claimed to have received. Any movement which gave *chief* attention to the subjective and the experiential was necessarily deviating from Scripture. So, on the first Sunday after his return from Toronto, as already mentioned, he had argued that 'the power of the Holy Spirit' must be defined and understood in terms of Scripture. 'Ecstasies, dreams and trances do not matter. We should ascertain how we stand with these essential definitions. . . . Let us turn to the holy mirror – the Bible – and continue to look into it steadfastly day by day.'

While not attacking the Oxford Group Movement by name from the pulpit, he was often to debate it and oppose it in ministerial circles during the course of the next few years. As a result some men, previously moving in that direction, were brought back. The *South Wales Evening Post* in 1936 reported a 'theological debate' at the presbytery of the West Glamorgan English Presbyterians, meeting at Clydach, when there was discussion of 'some recent manifestations of religious feeling in our valleys, and particularly with regard to the Oxford Group Movement'. The discussion, the paper reported, was led by Dr Lloyd-Jones, and it centred upon the subject of 'the working of the Holy Spirit in Christian experience'. The Presbyterian minister at Clydach was himself delivered from Buchman's influence as a result of Dr Lloyd-Jones' decisive advocacy of biblical principles.

A second controversial subject with which Dr Lloyd-Jones often became involved in the 1930's (and later) concerned the teaching of

Karl Barth (1886–1968) whose eminence as a theologian had become world-wide. Against liberalism, Barth called not only for a recognition of the supernatural, but also for a restoration of 'the Reformed Faith' itself. Once more, the names of Calvin and other reformers were heard with respect in Barthian circles, and Presbyterians, in particular, on both sides of the Atlantic came to view Barth with admiration. The Swiss theologian's belief in a universal salvation, and his wish to construct a theology which did not rest upon an infallible Bible, were scarcely noticed. In British Universities and elsewhere voices were raised acclaiming Barth as a restorer of 'orthodoxy' and – in contrast with the Westminster divines of the seventeenth century – as a 'true interpreter' of John Calvin.

Lloyd-Jones was drawn into reading Barth, and subsequently Emil Brunner, another Swiss theologian, in order to help students whose lecturers had come under the new spell. Unlike the writings of the Oxford Group, the Barthian literature was intricate and profuse. The pastor of Sandfields did not find its study to be of any personal profit, but it certainly had the effect of making him a resolute opponent of what he regarded as a serious deviation from the Reformed Faith. Accordingly, when asked to speak at ministerial gatherings, there were times when, to the surprise of his hearers not yet accustomed to think of him in a theological role, he chose to demonstrate why Barthianism was not orthodox Christianity. One such meeting occurred in Liverpool in the mid-thirties. As an evangelistic preacher he was already known in that city. He had preached in the great Chatham Street Calvinistic Methodist Chapel in Liverpool for three nights early in 1934, when his hearers included more than 1,500 young people. The same paper which reported these figures confessed, 'Many of us have not seen or heard anything similar for a long time.'[1] Not long afterwards, when asked again to Liverpool, to share in an evangelical Convention, there was consternation, and a vigorous debate ensued among some of Barth's admirers when he seized the opportunity to address a gathering of ministers on Barthianism.

While Dr Lloyd-Jones' growing influence among ministers might have been anticipated by observers of the religious scene, there was perhaps at this time little to indicate a similar development of his influence among students. Much of his ministry seemed to be carried

[1] *Yr Efengylydd*, April 1934.

on as though he was oblivious to all age distinctions. Certainly there was no 'youth work' at Sandfields, and the larger gatherings popular among evangelical students – the Keswick Convention, for instance – were places where his voice was never heard. Furthermore, unlike so many of his evangelical contemporaries he did not hold the view that the various inter-denominational youth movements represented the most hopeful field of labour: indeed his doctrine of the church left him with little sympathy for that attitude. Consequently, although, as already mentioned, he spoke occasionally for the Christian Union of evangelical students at Cardiff University College, he had no connection with the wider 'Inter-Varsity Fellowship of Evangelical Unions' which had been formed in 1928.

One of the few inter-denominational societies with which Sandfields came to be connected in the early thirties was the China Inland Mission. As spiritual concern deepened in the congregation, so did commitment to foreign missionary endeavour which was faithful to Scripture, and in 1934, for the first time, a member of Sandfields – Peggy Robson – was accepted as a candidate for the C.I.M. That same year, on May 8, Dr Lloyd-Jones spoke for the first time at the Annual Meeting of the C.I.M. held in Westminster Central Hall, London. C.I.M. had close links with the Inter-Varsity Fellowship and several of the youthful leaders of I.V.F., including the honorary secretary, Dr Douglas Johnson, were present that evening. Johnson, who had qualified at the Medical School of King's College Hospital in the late twenties, had known of Lloyd-Jones' reputation at Bart's. He also recalled having seen him, on one occasion, crossing the square at Bart's, when the thought occurred to him that Lord Horder's assistant looked 'too streamlined and severe' to be a physician! When Lloyd-Jones left London for Wales in 1927 Douglas Johnson and other evangelical Christians in the medical schools were left wondering what was the nature of the cause of the change of profession and his going to Port Talbot as a preacher. After all, Lloyd-Jones had not been known as a Christian at Bart's, he had no ties with the Evangelical Union in that hospital, and his closeness to the agnostic Horder was common knowledge. Some evangelicals in the student world were thus left to question whether the Welshman's unexpected entrance into the ministry was only motivated by the same 'Social Gospel' concerns which were then so prevalent in Nonconformity. These doubts as to his orthodoxy can be better understood when it is realised that adherence to the Evangelical Faith was extremely weak in all University and academic circles. The Student Christian Movement – from which the Evangelical Union was a breakaway – had shared in the departure from the Faith, its General Secretary affirming in the 1920's that 'the doctrine of the verbal inspiration of the Bible is as dead as Queen Anne'.[1] Professor A. Rendle Short, writing in 1933 of the state of Christianity in English Universities, believed that before 1914, 'the situation was disquieting, almost calamitous, except at Cambridge, and at a few London medical schools. . . . The real message of the gospel of forgiveness of sins in virtue of our Lord's atoning death had almost died out in the provincial universities.'[2]

Not without reason, therefore, Douglas Johnson and friends with him were not prepared to listen to the China Inland Mission's new speaker uncritically in May 1934. Perhaps even the C.I.M. was not always as discerning as the times required! Nor were Johnson's reservations immediately resolved. The building was large, and the microphone, which was left in front of the chairman when the speaker rose to address the meeting, very inadequate. When Dr Lloyd-Jones announced Romans 1:14 as his text, and proceeded to speak in the quiet tones which always marked the beginning of his sermons, he could only be heard by those seated near to the platform. As the microphone was at length moved closer to him, and more, as he rose to his subject – the fact that every Christian is 'a debtor' – the attention of the whole three thousand who filled the Central Hall was arrested. Before he had finished, the doubts of any critical evangelical hearer were entirely swept away. Afterwards, Douglas Johnson and other medical friends managed to exchange a few words with the speaker before he left, but their hurriedly mentioned enthusiastic hopes that he would accept an invitation to speak for the Inter-Varsity Fellowship received no immediate encouragement.

There the matter lay in Douglas Johnson's mind until a month or two later in the summer of 1934 when a letter arrived from his friend, Dr W. Melville Capper, then on the staff at St Bartholomew's Hospital, and subsequently to be Consultant Surgeon at the Bristol General Hospital. The letter revealed that Capper was on holiday in

[1] Quoted by Douglas Johnson in *Contending for the Faith*, a History of the Evangelical Movement in the Universities and Colleges, 1979, p. 131.
[2] 'Testimony for the Truth in the British Universities' in *The Evangelical Quarterly*, October 1933, pp. 338–41.

Wales, staying with a friend at the Mumbles, near Swansea, but he had news to tell Johnson which could not wait until his return to London:

'On Sunday, with an old friend, I drove across to Aberavon to hear a preacher in a growing church who, I understand, used to be on our hospital staff. His name is Martyn Lloyd-Jones and, as for his preaching, I have never heard anything like it! He took texts both morning and evening out of Paul's Epistles and then talked to all those people just as the Apostle Paul, I'm sure, used to do in the earliest churches. I have discovered the modern Apostle Paul! I really have!'[1]

Melville Capper went on to urge Johnson to see that everything possible was done to get Lloyd-Jones to an annual Inter-Varsity Conference.

Clearly the Pauline element had come strongly to the fore by the time these two visitors came to hear Dr Lloyd-Jones. Paul as a teacher had become his own model. In one sermon preached in 1933 he describes one feature of Paul as a preacher in these terms:

'There is nothing vague and nebulous about St Paul's writings. He tells you exactly where he is; his method is essentially dogmatic. There is no need for any prolonged search and study and enquiry in order to discover where he stood and what his attitude was, he hurls it at you, he shouts it, he proclaims it with all his might. And, in order to make doubly certain that it is quite clear – that there can be no doubt at all – he compares and contrasts it with all rival teachings and pronounces his terrible anathemas upon all opposing teachers. What he calls "my gospel" in his second letter to Timothy was as plain and as clear as daylight.'

The I.V.F. Executive Committee met shortly after the arrival of Melville Capper's letter and the question of how Dr Lloyd-Jones could be secured for the Annual Conference of 1935 was high on the agenda. The discussion was not far advanced before the Welsh Representative declared that he was not hopeful that any invitation which they might give would be accepted, and he went on to explain

---

[1] This is not a verbatim quotation from Capper's letter (which does not survive) but these sentences made such an impression upon Douglas Johnson that he was often to quote them.

that Dr Lloyd-Jones was a 'high-churchman' in the Presbyterian sense. Only with some difficulty had he been persuaded to agree to speak at the Swansea Evangelical Union which began in 1930. After further deliberation it was at length resolved that Dr Douglas Johnson himself should make a personal visit to Wales to put before Dr Lloyd-Jones the I.V.F.'s need of his help.

Johnson did not go unprepared for the discussion which he knew lay ahead. From Bart's men he sought an accurate description of Lloyd-Jones, and a Welsh graduate who had been to Sandfields a number of times was able to provide more information on his theological outlook. Next, he obtained a letter, commending the work of I.V.F., from the Reverend W. H. Aldis, the much-respected Home Director of the C.I.M., and finally, before leaving Highbury (where he was then staying at the Foreign Missions Club, close to the old C.I.M. headquarters), he received the assurance of the help of others in prayer for the success of his mission. The journey itself presented a problem, for the Lloyd-Joneses were not in Port Talbot, but on holiday at Talybont near Aberystwyth, one of the less accessible parts of Wales. Taking the over-night 'milk train', via Shrewsbury, Johnson at length alighted at Borth station – the nearest to his destination – about 8.30 a.m. From there a taxi took him to the schoolmaster's house at Talybont where Dr and Mrs Lloyd-Jones were spending their holiday.

Breakfast over, Douglas Johnson explained to his host how the I.V.F. annual residential conference had increased so greatly in size since the first at High Leigh, Hoddesdon, near London, in 1926, that it would be necessary for the next conference to be held at Swanwick, Derbyshire. It was likely that three hundred students would be there. Lloyd-Jones made no mention of his own memories of High Leigh, but they formed a part of his judgment on the general condition of English evangelicalism. On a train to London after the memorable Sunday when he and Tom Nefyn Williams had preached in Llandrindod Wells in 1928, he had met Mrs C. T. Studd who had urged him to visit a forthcoming 'Victorious Life' Conference at High Leigh. He had done so, and had returned home confirmed in his impression that the English scene was even further removed than the Welsh scene from the Christianity of brighter days. Evangelism and 'holiness' teaching were alike far too man-centred, a consequence of the prevailing Arminian theology. Some men prominent in I.V.F., whom he had also met, confirmed his misgivings by their superficiality.

[295]

David Martyn Lloyd-Jones

'So,' Dr Johnson records of this memorable meeting at Talybont, 'Lloyd-Jones imagined that I was a sentimental, empty-headed evangelical, having no church principles of consequence and only caring for an interdenominational organisation loosely attached to the churches. Accordingly when I sought to put to him our invitation to give three addresses at the forthcoming Swanwick Conference, and said that I had come so that he could satisfy himself about Inter-Varsity before he committed himself, a curl of his lip and a slightly hostile expression was his initial response. He had clearly made up his mind not to be drawn into what he thought to be a shallow, American-type evangelistic and activist society. He seemed set on analysing the I.V.F.'s nature and views either (i) to give me a bad time and to help me to mend the error of my ways, or (ii) to get a clear picture of this type of English religion for his own future information and future use. So he began by asking questions on our doctrines, aims, methods and ecclesiastical outlook, and watching me like a hawk! But we also had a tyrannical, Socratic-method teacher at King's College Hospital, so I was quite used to coming back at a forceful questioner.'

Nonetheless, Douglas Johnson was hard-pressed until he managed to divert the conversation from I.V.F. in general to his own personal beliefs in particular. Here the visitor had an element of surprise on his side, for having commenced to read Charles Hodge and B. B. Warfield he was already a moderate sympathiser with the theology to which Lloyd-Jones was committed. The I.V.F., Johnson then returned to urge, despite the broad spectrum of evangelicals from which its membership was drawn, was committed to the gospel and to the full authority of Scripture. If the leadership was strengthened there was no reason why it should not represent serious, biblical Christianity still more fully. Hence the importance of their appeal which he had come to make to Lloyd-Jones for support. But, queried Lloyd-Jones, was it not the case that Anglican evangelicals were predominant in I.V.F. and how could their commitment to the Establishment coincide with Johnson's hopes? The visitor replied by contrasting the Welsh episcopal clergy with the school of moderate Calvinists which had succeeded Charles Simeon in England, and which was represented in I.V.F. by such figures as Archdeacon T. C. Hammond. These English Anglicans, he argued, were a very different proposition from the generality of the High-Church clergy in the episcopal churches in Wales.

As the morning's discussion went on, Douglas Johnson's hopes of an acceptance of the I.V.F. invitation rose. Lunch was followed by a further exchange, during which some doubt as to the outcome returned to him. When he left to catch the train from Borth back to Shrewsbury around 4 p.m., all he took back was a promise that his host would write to him in due course and make known his decision.

A week later the letter came and Douglas Johnson was delighted to hear that his journey to Talybont had not been in vain. Dr Lloyd-Jones would come to Swanwick for the Conference scheduled for Tuesday, April 9, to Monday, April 15, 1935, though with the provisos that he would only give one address – the subject he did not specify – and that he must return to his own church on the Saturday before the Conference concluded. Disappointed with the small place the preacher from Wales would occupy on the programme, the General Secretary subsequently urged, with success, that Lloyd-Jones should also chair a 'Question Meeting', and give 'concluding remarks' at two sessions where speakers would deal with 'Effective Witness'.

From the standpoint of I.V.F. the 1935 conference was a great success. Besides well-known figures such as Bishop J. Taylor Smith, who was Conference Chaplain, there were several new I.V.F. speakers from various countries, including Dr Robert P. Wilder from the United States, and missionaries home on furlough. A report of the Conference in the *Inter-Varsity Magazine* spoke of splendid scenery, 'very happy fellowship', sports, 'a delightful lantern lecture', and commented briefly on some of the speakers, excluding Dr Lloyd-Jones. Perhaps the writer detected a different note in the visitor from Wales and had not yet made up his mind what he thought of it!

For his part, however, Dr Lloyd-Jones was far from satisfied with his first I.V.F. Conference. It confirmed his earlier impression that he was out of his element amidst English evangelicalism. In his view, the Conference, while strongly emphasising evangelism and missionary endeavour, lacked seriousness. Bishop Taylor Smith's sense of fun was as large as his physical frame, and others present were almost equally well able to show that to be a Christian there is no need to be 'solemn' – hardly a lesson which students found difficult to learn. Speakers and hearers alike, Dr Lloyd-Jones felt, had little interest in the kind of literature which meant so much to him. Their sense of church history seemed to be practically non-existent. Theology of any kind was viewed with suspicion, and the degree of concern for an intellectual understanding of the Christian Faith was almost childish in its proportions. Despite his personal liking for Douglas Johnson, which deepened with this second meeting, Lloyd-Jones went back to Aberavon persuaded that his own ministry lay elsewhere.

Uppermost in his assessment of the contemporary situation was his conviction that national religious trends could only be changed by an outpouring of the Holy Spirit in true revival. As he read his Bible, and turned afresh to such men as Jonathan Edwards and George Whitefield, he knew that there was nothing in the past which could not be repeated. The church needed to be called back to her true work of prayer and preaching and, given existing religious conditions, he saw more hope of that occurring in Wales than in England. In England the evangelicals, in their preoccupation with evangelism, were failing to see that the real problem lay within the church herself.

There were also particular reasons why, in 1935, the longing for a great awakening was much upon Dr Lloyd-Jones' spirit. Several times that year there were such marked evidences of God's presence and blessing that he could do no other than anticipate a revival. Others felt the same. On January 1, 1935, preaching on the Ten Lepers (Luke 17:11–19) at a broadcast civic service in Cardiff, held in Wood Street Congregational Church, there was a general sense that something unusual was happening. One Cardiff newspaper, commenting on the spirit of the 2,000 who packed the building, asked the question: 'Are we on the eve of another religious revival in South Wales? Not only ministers, but laymen as well, state with conviction that there is a new spiritual stir among the people.' The same paper described Dr Lloyd-Jones, whose sermon was carried by the radio to thousands of Welsh homes, as 'the new John Elias'. Unlike the usual radio sermon it was not read from a script!

In many parts of Wales during the same year Dr Lloyd-Jones was to see similar intense attention given to the Word of God. After he had preached at the Tabernacle Chapel, Haverfordwest, reported the *Western Telegraph*, 'the building – capable of holding more than a thousand people – was crowded out an hour before the service commenced'. 'The service,' continued the same reporter, 'shows that the alleged "coldness and indifference of the times" is greatly exaggerated, and that when there is a man with a message the people are ready to respond.'

The Pauline Note

The most remarkable service of 1935, however, was to occur in the South Wales Welsh Presbyterian Sasiwn held in Llangeitho because it was the bicentenary of the conversion of Daniel Rowland. As usual, a number of preaching services were to be held during this Sasiwn, which met in the third week of August, but there is no doubt that the principal reason for a public attendance unprecedented for many years lay in the anticipated sermon from Dr Lloyd-Jones on the Thursday afternoon. The *Western Mail*, August 16, under a heading 'Amazing Scenes at Llangeitho', gave their reporter's eye-witness account of what had happened the previous day. People 'from all parts of Wales poured into this little village throughout the night and during the greater part of the day. Many of them slept in the open air'. When it was learned that Dr Lloyd-Jones was to preach, not in the great marquee – erected on the ground used in the open-air services of two hundred years before – but in the chapel which could hold no more than 800, there was consternation and confusion:

'An hour and a half before the meeting opened the chapel was crammed and thousands of people surrounded the doors in a frantic effort to get inside.

'A few went round the back of the chapel where a small door from an ante-room leads on to the pulpit. The outer door of this ante-room was locked, but so eager were the people to gain admission that it was forced open and a rush was made into the building.'

A rebuke from the pastor of the church restored a measure of order and the withdrawal of the offenders, yet the respite for the harassed organisers of the Sasiwn was only temporary. The situation was, in the words of the *Western Mail*, 'fast becoming out of hand', when, an hour before the meeting was due to start, it was announced that, after all, the service would be held in the marquee. 'At this stage the people moved in a solid mass along the narrow road towards the field, and the marquee, which is capable of seating 6,000 people, was soon filled to the doors, where hundreds of people stood outside.' The reporter estimated that 7,000 heard the preacher, who spoke for nearly an hour from Acts 2:38, 'Then Peter said unto them, Repent, and be baptised every one of you in the name of Jesus Christ for the remission of sins, and ye shall receive the gift of the Holy Ghost.' The sermon, carefully and fully prepared,[1] while not dealing with

[1] His manuscript filled thirty sides of average size writing-pad paper. It was first preached at Aberavon on June 9, 1935.

the subject of revival, presented the very truths which had heralded all the great awakenings from Pentecost onwards – man in sin, face to face with God and the certainty of death and eternity, together with true repentance and faith in Christ as the only means of deliverance. The preacher spoke as though he had entirely forgotten that the multitude before him were churchgoers. Peter's hearers, he told them, had begun by thinking that all was well with them. It was only as they heard the truth that they were 'awakened, shaken, disturbed and frightened', so that they began to cry out, 'What shall we do?' Ignorance alone, he argued, kept modern men from a like concern. After nearly an hour it was a subdued multitude which sat or stood in motionless silence as the preacher began his final exhortation:

'What can you say in reply to the case I have held before you? What is there in earth, or life, or amongst men, that is worthy of consideration in comparison with this? Earth's best must inevitably pass, as well as all it contains, but at the end you will be left with your immortal soul and spirit which will have to face God. I warn you to flee from the wrath to come!

'But I would also attract you to God by asking you to consider again this amazing offer of His in Jesus Christ. If you but come and submit yourself to Him, then all your sins will be forgiven, you will be clothed with the righteousness of Christ, and He will fill you with His own Holy Spirit. . . . Here is God's greatest gift to men; here is God's last and ultimate offer. For here He offers Himself and gives His own Spirit. . . .

'On the day of Pentecost three thousand souls gladly received the word and were added to the church and began to enjoy these blessings. Since then, countless thousands of others have in a like manner gladly received the same message and have been added to the same church throughout the centuries. The numbers grow, the church expands, the work goes on towards its glorious consummation and will go on until the end, when Jesus Christ the King will come and lead all who have believed in Him into the very heaven of heavens. Oh, how glorious will the sight be!

> Ten thousand times ten thousand,
>   In sparkling raiment bright,
> The armies of the ransomed saints
>   Throng up the steeps of light:
> 'Tis finished, all is finished,

Their fight with death and sin;
Fling open wide the golden gates,
And let the victors in.

"Ten thousand times ten thousand"! O wondrous day! Will you be amongst them? Yield now, and make sure of it.'

In the opinion of the *Western Mail*, the Sasiwn was rendered outstanding by 'one of the most remarkable services that has been seen in West Wales since the revival of 1904'.

Almost despite himself, Dr Lloyd-Jones was to be back in England more than once before the end of 1935. His name was now beginning to come regularly to the attention of evangelicals outside the Principality of Wales. On March 16, 1935, *The Sunday Companion* had printed a summary of his broadcast sermon on Luke 17:11–19, introducing it with a statement that it was 'by a minister whose preaching is having a mighty influence in South Wales'. On November 28, 1935, *The Christian*, one of the best-known of evangelical weeklies, gave a page of comment on 'Preacher – Physician: Dr Martin Lloyd-Jones'. The same issue of *The Christian* carried an advertisement of a 'Great Demonstration at the Royal Albert Hall, London, under the auspices of the Bible Testimony Fellowship, when the Rev. Martin Lloyd-Jones, M.D., M.R.C.P., from Port Talbot (late of Harley Street) would be the closing speaker'. Despite a foggy winter's day, the evening of Tuesday, December 3, 1935, saw the vast spaces of the Albert Hall filled for this meeting which was intended to assert foundation truths and particularly the full inspiration of the Bible. Not only was Dr Lloyd-Jones in accord with that object, he told his hearers, but he was prepared to assert that 'the real cause of the present state of the Church of God on earth is to be found in the Church's voluntary departure from a belief in the Bible as the fully inspired Word of God, and from a stressing and emphasising of the great evangelical doctrines which had been so stressed and emphasised, especially in the eighteenth century'. He declared that the common opinion which traced the decline of religion to the First World War and to changing social conditions was an error. At the same time, he was not there to argue merely in defence of the Bible: the paramount need of the hour was rather that its truths should be announced and preached, simply and boldly.

Thus far he knew he would carry his hearers with him, but he did not intend to allow such an opportunity to pass without indicating the area in which the English evangelicals were themselves, in his opinion, less than biblical. The constituency from which he had so many representatives before him was too often looking for evangelistic 'results' without first being sure of those truths which were essential to the advance of the church:

'You will find that there are quite a number of people who are always ready to join in an evangelistic campaign in order that they may fill their church, who thoroughly disbelieve the doctrine of justification by faith only. Again, I do not want to be controversial, but must we not admit and confess that there is far too much heard at the present time of the word "decision", as if the great thing is that you and I should decide for Christ, rather than that He should do something for us. Yea, is not there a tendency on our part to emphasise results at the expense of regeneration? Let us face this question quite honestly. Can we, I wonder, from the Word of God itself, justify all the present tendency to concentrate on youth and on youth movements? Let me go still further. Can many of the evangelistic methods which were introduced some forty or fifty years ago really be justified out of the Word of God? As I read of the work of the great evangelists in the Bible I find they were not first and foremost concerned about results; they were concerned about proclaiming the word of truth. They left the increase unto Him. They were concerned above all else that the people should be brought face to face with the truth itself.

'I watch St Paul going into the town of Corinth, and I like to listen to him as he soliloquises just outside the city. I imagine he thought he might resort to many expedients in order to win the town of Corinth. He might have consulted the Mayor of the town. He might have thought of many other expedients which I am not going to mention this evening, in order that he might have results. But I hear him say: "I determined not to know anything among you save Jesus Christ and him crucified." The great Apostle was afraid of rhetoric, eloquence, oratory; I think he was terrified lest a man might join his church simply because he had been carried away by Paul's own speaking. I am very certain he would be afraid of many of the evangelistic methods that are being freely employed at this present moment. No, No, my friends, our business, our work, our first call is to declare in a certain and unequivocal manner the sovereignty, the

The Pauline Note

majesty, the holiness of God; the sinfulness and the utter depravity of man, his total inability to save and to rescue himself; and the sacrificial, expiatory, atoning death of Jesus Christ, the Son of God, on that Cross on Calvary's hill, and His glorious resurrection, as the only means and the only hope of human salvation.'[1]

One of the most thoughtful of Dr Lloyd-Jones' hearers on that December evening in 1935 was the tall, scraggy figure of Dr Campbell Morgan. Dr Lloyd-Jones had been surprised to meet the seventy-two-year-old veteran behind the platform before the meeting began and, noting his surprise, Morgan had exclaimed, 'I tell you that no one but you would have brought me out on such a night!' After visits to Britain from the United States in the 1920's, Campbell Morgan had finally returned in 1932 and, despite his age, resumed at Westminster Chapel as a helper of its minister, Dr Hubert L. Simpson, whose health was failing. After Simpson retired in 1934, Morgan had continued alone in the pulpit which he had made famous at the beginning of the century. Although Lloyd-Jones as a teen-ager had seen him from afar, it was not until January 1933, while Morgan was taking meetings in Cardiff, that the two men first met personally in the home of a Christian lady. Their paths again crossed in Liverpool in 1934, when both were speaking at the same church, though we do not know whether Morgan heard Lloyd-Jones on that occasion.

What Campbell Morgan thought of the preaching which he heard in the Albert Hall on the first Tuesday of December, 1935, was clear enough two days later when a letter from him arrived at the Aberavon manse urging the Aberavon pastor to come to fill the pulpit of Westminster Chapel for the last Sunday of that same month. Despite the shortness of the notice, Lloyd-Jones accepted, being mindful of the debt which he owed to Westminster Chapel for the ministry he had received in Dr Hutton's days and, as it happened, free to take a break from his own pulpit on that day. Thus on December 29, 1935, he stood for the first time in Westminster Chapel's large circular pulpit and gained a new view of the building which he had first entered twenty years before.

The morning sermon was on John 6:66–68, 'Will ye also go away?' In the evening he preached on 'The Narrowness of the Gospel' from

[1] *Proclaiming Eternal Verities*, 1936, pp. 25–26. This booklet contained the addresses given at the Albert Hall meeting.

Matthew 7:13–14, 'Enter ye in at the strait gate . . .'. Both sermons were heart-searching and evangelistic, though not in the usual sense of that term. Even relatively evangelical congregations were not used to being asked, 'Are you ready for the judgment? Have you a personal conviction of sin, and a personal knowledge of God?' Equally unusual were such assertions as the following:

'The narrowness of the Gospel – I speak with reverence – is the narrowness that is in God himself. Oh, that we all became narrow that we might enter in through this strait gate. "Few there be that find it," says our Lord. On the broad way there is a great crowd. "Many there be which go in thereat." It does not take an exceptionally great man to sin. Any fool can sin, and every fool does sin . . . .'[1]

This visit to Westminster Chapel was probably the first time Lloyd-Jones had preached in England on a Sunday to other than Welsh Calvinistic Methodist congregations. Inevitably, other congregations in England, noting the variation from the Welsh preacher's norm, followed Morgan's lead with more invitations. Possibly the only one which he accepted at this period came from Spurgeon's Tabernacle, now vacant after the pastorate of H. Tydeman Chilvers who had worked to restore the congregation to the spiritual condition from which it had fallen earlier in the century. *The Baptist Times* for April 23, 1936, reported:

'Dr Martin Lloyd-Jones, who gave up a brilliant career in Harley Street because he saw the proclamation of the gospel to be today a greater need than the healing of the body, drew a large congregation to Spurgeon's Tabernacle last Sunday morning. For more than nine years he has travelled up and down the country preaching the message of the Book.'

The same writer went on to speak of Lloyd-Jones' sermon on 'The Christian Hope' based on Hebrews 6:11–12. The preacher proclaimed the necessity of right doctrine as indispensable to the Christian life. The writer of the Epistle, he reminded the congrega-

---

[1] The substance of the morning sermon was printed in *The Christian World Pulpit*, January 16, 1936, and in *The Christian Herald and Signs of Our Times*, April 2, 1936; the evening, from which I quote above, in *The Westminster Record*, April 1936, being the first time that Dr Lloyd-Jones' name appeared in Westminster Chapel's monthly magazine.

tion, reproached the Hebrews for their neglect of doctrine, 'If I could only tell you the great truths of God, but you have neglected the intellectual side of your profession. So you are babes and could not understand.' The Christian life, Dr Lloyd-Jones declared, cannot be lived aright unless 'the doctrine that our salvation is mainly future' is known. In this life Christians have only the first instalment, 'the mass of salvation lies ahead'. The acid test of our real spiritual position, he asserted, is our attitude towards the Christian hope.

Many at Spurgeon's Tabernacle responded to this Pauline theology, indeed there were immediate moves made by some to ascertain whether the preacher would consider a call, notwithstanding his denominational affiliation. It was more than the question of baptism by immersion which restrained Lloyd-Jones from giving any encouragement to their enquiries. The convictions with which he had left the I.V.F. Conference at Swanwick just twelve months before were still with him. At the same time it was true that concern for the wider situation in the British Isles was being awakened and he was finding that English hearers were not all as uncomprehending of the convictions which moved him as he had feared. Perhaps the lady who wrote to him on April 6, 1936, was representative of others:

'I am a perfect stranger to you and must apologise for writing to you. My only excuse is my longing to be of some use in a small way to my church. I was at Westminster Chapel and heard you preach the last Sunday in December. I am a member of Dr. Morgan's Bible School, and rarely go up on Sundays, but I did on that occasion. I felt when I heard your earnest gospel message, Oh! if only I could get him to come to our church, Tetherdown, what good might not result! . . . . The church Secretary told me last night they were going to ask you, and if they do, will you come if you possibly can? We do want the plain gospel message so much, so I plead with you again, if they write, *do come* . . . I shall never forget your sermon that night, although I have been a Christian ever since I was a young girl and I am now 67 years old, but I feel so keenly that our churches need revival and some of us pray earnestly that it may come . . .'.

Such letters served to prepare him for the future.

'When Paul says, "I have great heaviness and continual sorrow in my heart . . . for my brethren, my kinsmen according to the flesh", it is not the Jew in him speaking, but the Christian. I do not wish to disregard Paul's natural feelings as a Jew totally; I am merely saying that they are completely subject to and take second place to his zeal and feelings as a Christian. We see clearly, therefore, that differences between nationalistic features have very little, indeed nothing, to do with the great central matter – our salvation. To place more importance on these things, than on the fact that every man, of every tribe and every language, is a lost soul before God, and consequently without any right to boast, is contrary to the teaching of this great Jew who became the apostle to the Gentiles.

'The truth is one and the same to everyone. God in Christ through the Holy Spirit is the one who saves. Nothing else counts in this context.

'But salvation or re-birth does not erase natural and national characteristics. It is the man or the soul which is re-born and not his characteristics, his abilities, or his temperament. The gospel does not produce a number of people who are exactly the same as one another like postage stamps. The innate characteristics of man's personality remain the same – the factor which changes is the master who rules and the direction which is given. We must guard against drawing the conclusion that religion has nothing to do with national characteristics at all.'

M. L.-J.

in broadcast addresses on 'Religion
and National Characteristics', 1943

15

Mainly through Welsh Eyes

With Martyn Lloyd-Jones being as distinctly Welsh as he was, there were many Welshmen who saw no possibility of his being lost to another country. They supposed that the capacity to value aright such preaching as he represented lay almost wholly within the chapels of the Principality. Thus *Yr Efengylydd*, in January 1936, while expressing the pleasure of Welsh Christians at the prominence given to Dr Lloyd-Jones at the recent Albert Hall meeting in London, also commented, 'It is slowly – yes, a slowness which is at fault – that English people give way to having Welsh preachers in their prominent places.' Another Welsh paper put it more plainly, 'I doubt if the English people are capable of appreciating his preaching as we do in Wales.'[1] *The Christian Herald*, London, publishing one of his sermons in 1937, described him as 'The Famous Welsh Preacher', and Wales, his fellow countrymen believed, was where his fame would remain.

The response to Lloyd-Jones' preaching in Wales in the 1930's certainly gave weight to this opinion. The sheer size of the attendance upon his itinerant ministry in all parts of the Principality was a matter of Welsh national news, and the Welsh press followed his preaching to an extent scarcely to be imagined elsewhere. Aneurin Bevan, and a few other Socialist leaders, could gather occasional large crowds in the mining valleys of South Wales, but no one, it seemed, could gather such numbers in all parts of the country, on any week-day, as did the preacher from Port Talbot. Speaking of the extraordinary national following with which Dr Lloyd-Jones' preaching was attended, Eliseus Howells wrote in 1933:

'Dr Lloyd-Jones' primary difficulty is entering the chapel where he is to preach for, like his Master, the crowds press on him. We know of

[1] *The Express*, April 19, 1947.

[307]

some of the poor of the valleys keeping back some "dole" money
for weeks in order that they might travel to listen to him and throw
their mite into the treasury. Yes, returning to empty, bare homes
with a song in their hearts.

'We have seen people standing in the rain outside chapels for two
hours in the hope that some word would come to them in his shouts
and we heard that one crowd asked permission to break the
window so that they could hear him, promising to pay for the
damage done.'[1]

Numerous newspaper reports substantiate the degree of eagerness with which Lloyd-Jones' preaching was attended. Throughout the 1930's what was seen at Siloh Calvinistic Methodist
Chapel, the largest chapel in Tredegar, at mid-week meetings in
1931, was to be repeated. Both afternoon and evening, records a
local paper, 'the chapel was full nearly an hour before the commencement of the service, and hundreds of people went away
disappointed'. *The South Wales Evening News* in its account of
another typical service held in Alexandra Road Chapel, Swansea,
on a stormy October day in 1934, records:

'In the evening, for a meeting timed to start at 7.30, people gathered
at the doors before six o'clock, and in less than half-an-hour every
seat in the church had been taken. . . . Dr Jones was brought from
the house of his host before the announced time, and when he
entered the pulpit, with the Rev. W. Davies, of Craig-lâs, who read
Scripture and made the offering of prayer, the church was an
inspiring sight. From the pulpit steps to the galleries there was no
unoccupied spot.'[2]

The *Herald of Wales*, October 24, 1936 reported:

'The two-and-a-half-century-old Baptist stronghold of Felinfoel
mustered a congregation of 2,000 to listen raptly to the former
medical man's discourse. Up and down the country the story is the
same.'

The location certainly seemed to make little or no difference to
the attendance. Even from such an improbable place as Cardiff

[1] Y *Goleuad*, February 1, 1933.   [2] October 26, 1934.

Mainly through Welsh Eyes

Docks a *Western Mail* reporter could describe his experience as follows:

'I went to Bethel with my leaflet in my hand. It was as I expected; the chapel was full, but I was fortunate in securing a seat in the topmost aisle. "I have been coming to this chapel for 70 years, and I have never before seen such a large congregation," said my neighbour. . . .

'The doctor was as dark as ever, and half-closed his eyes when he looked in my direction. He has a natural accent and is without conceit and affectation. I had to listen; there was no wandering when he was reading or preaching. He was very earnest; it was fortunate that his thick eyebrows diverted the perspiring streams from his prominent forehead so that they did not interfere with his vision. He had no place for humour in his sermon, which occupied our rapt attention for an hour.'

After describing the sermon and the silence which gathered over the congregation until, at length, it was broken by the organ for the final hymn, the reporter concluded:

'When I got out I did not know where I was in the streets around Cardiff Docks. "After five p.m. this is the poorest part of Cardiff," said somebody. I am not sure; gold is where you find it.'[1]

James Evans, another newspaper correspondent, describes the preacher as he appeared when he first heard him at the Tabernacle, Ystradgynlais, in 1937:

'I found he was not unlike the mental picture of him that I had been carrying about with me. His outward appearance gave no suggestion of the pulpit. He looked quite dressy, but his clothes were in every respect those of the ordinary citizen. I must confess that I fully expected to see the "collar". But no!

'A man of medium stature, his white hands were rather fat and short-fingered. As for his head and features, however, there was nothing fat about those. His pale, thoughtful face, his forehead high and wide, his black shiny hair, keen eyes, and thin lips often brought to mind the features of the late Sir John Morris Jones. His gestures, like the inflexion of his voice, were perfectly natural.

[1] *Western Mail*, March 20, 1939.

[309]

There was no attempt at that peculiar intonation known as the Welsh hwyl.'

Dr Lloyd-Jones' abiding seriousness was frequently noted and so also were his eyes, although, upon the latter, there was less unanimity of judgment. The reporter at Cardiff Docks, quoted above, evidently felt that he was being scrutinised by the preacher's gaze, while another observer thought that 'the preacher's dark mystic eyes stare straight ahead as if seeing worlds of their own'.[1] His own people at Sandfields were quoted as believing that there was often a quality in his eyes which tempered the near severity of his look: 'He is seldom seen to smile, but everyone speaks of the subtle laughter that dwells at the back of his eyes.'

Besides such accounts of his preaching, reasons for his influence were often offered by the press.

'What is the secret of the drawing power of Dr Martin Lloyd-Jones?' was the question often asked and by way of answer several points were usually agreed.

First, in the words of the *Herald of Wales*, 'It is not the oratory of Dr Lloyd-Jones which draws the crowds.' Many said the same, although for the assertion to be rightly understood it needs to be remembered that the commentators were equating 'oratory' with the dramatic and emotional techniques popularised by nineteenth-century Welsh preachers. Even the language which Dr Lloyd-Jones commonly employed frequently differed from that tradition, as one reporter noted after attending at a service in Swansea:

'One of the attractions of the Doctor's preaching is that his language is entirely his own. Not an out-worn phrase. Not a platitude. Not an age-old expression. He used the language, not of the street, but of the average cultured man. . . . It may be that his freedom from the language of the pulpit – the language inevitably fixed upon a student of theology who spends his youth and manhood immersed in its phraseology – is one secret of his drawing force.'[2]

Second, it was agreed that the drawing power of his preaching was in no sense restricted to any one group or class of hearer. Considerations of age, sex, or social background appeared to make

[1] *The People*, April 30, 1939.
[2] *The South Wales Evening News*, October 26, 1934.

no difference to the effectiveness of his ministry. Working-class men were certainly prominent in the congregation at Sandfields, yet the variations to be found in the pews were many. One curious newspaper reporter, visiting Aberavon in 1938, was surprised to find that another visitor, an expensively-dressed lady, had drawn up outside the chapel in a large car in order to inquire, 'Is Dr Jones preaching today?' Her home was in the far west of America where she had heard of the preacher through a woman whom he had once helped.

Third, it was almost universally accepted that the note of authority was the most arresting feature of Dr Lloyd-Jones' preaching. Observers of his ministry at this date wrote: 'The secret of his power is the note of certainty that pervades his preaching.' 'There is evidently no diminution in the extraordinary drawing power of Dr Jones, due largely to his intense earnestness and the definite message which he so confidently proclaims.' 'A dominant personality, intensity of conviction, clarity of thought and directness of speech, with an entire absence of striving after oratorial effect, portray this modern Puritan.'

All this, however, is not to say that those who assessed his preaching were agreed as to the nature of the influence which his ministry exercised. No one thought that the power of which they were conscious as they listened to him was contrived; no one questioned his sincerity; but some wondered whether what they felt was anything more than a fleeting impression of the preacher's own vision.

James Evans, writing for one of the Welsh newspapers in 1937, seemed to be at a loss to offer any explanation:

'Like his person, Dr Lloyd-Jones' sermon displayed no fripperies, no adjectival adornments whatsoever; though he often proved himself a master of a very pointed and illuminating phrase. . . .

'The sermon was even more characteristic of the preacher. The subject, Herod being attracted by the noble qualities in the character of John the Baptist but failing in the end to take the vital step. Herod had "heard John gladly" again and again, but failed in the end to step beyond the border line and place himself in safety within the kingdom. The phrase, "So near and yet so far" became the burden of his message.

'Very soon after he had commenced we began to feel that taking that step was the most important thing in this life. How did he work us all up to that? How did he produce his effects? He did not in the least rely on flights of oratory like the old masters; he never attempted to bewitch us through our natural senses. He relied solely on something beyond this seen world. That something became a great reality, nay, the only reality, for us all, at least for the time being. We believed in it, somehow, because we could not help ourselves. His own faith was so compelling and domineering as to be irresistible.'

More vivid but less sympathetic is the account of the novelist, Rhys Davies, which occurs unexpectedly in a chapter on 'The South Wales Workers' in his book, *My Wales*:

'That a preacher with a romantic mantle can still draw a crowd was proved to me, nevertheless, one week-day evening in the Rhondda. Dr Martin Lloyd-Jones was to give a sermon in one of the largest chapels. Still a young man and possessing first-rate pulpit gifts, Dr Lloyd-Jones first attracted celebrity by abandoning his prosperous Harley Street medical practice and going down to Wales as a full-time missionary in a poor Glamorganshire district. The romantic heart of Wales was touched: it was won when chapels all over the country invited him to prove his oratorical gifts in their pulpits. He looks like a less emaciated James Maxton: intense, vibrant, and unwavering.

'The doors of the chapel where he preached were opened two hours before the service began. I have never seen a building so unhygienically packed. The ground floor seethed in slow, awful movements of wedged humanity. The enormous gallery, which ran all round the building, steamed with bodies that were piled up to the walls in a warmth that was stifling. Not a window was open, for winter was outside. At last, with the utmost difficulty a man climbed to a sill and opened a window six inches. A minute afterwards a woman sitting under the window climbed up and shut it again. Little ventilation could come through the open doorways and passages; they were tightly wedged with people, who also dripped over the staircases and filled each aisle. A pie could have been cooked nicely in the warmth.

'Dr Lloyd-Jones picked his way up the steps of the pulpit, also crowded with late-comers. He wore an overcoat, which he astonishingly kept on until he began his sermon twenty minutes later. Outside were special coaches and buses which had brought people from up and down the valley. The hymn-singing shook the building; it rose to a deafening demand, it sank to a sweet plaint infinitely gentle.

'The over-melodramatic technique of the old-time preachers was not used by Dr Lloyd-Jones. The opening of his sermon had almost an intellectual primness; his sincerity had a cold ruthlessness, very attractive, at least to me. But the congregation seemed to be holding back; it had not the old customary glow, in spite of the heat. The deacons gathered in their Big Seat under the pulpit began to give their encouraging "Amens" and "Aye-Ayes"; some of the congregation followed suit. The preacher began to talk of Belshazzar's Feast and the writing on the wall. This was promising. For me there was writing enough on the wall-like mountains outside, even if there was no feast beneath them. But the opportunity which I imagined the preacher would take was spurned.

'He became revivalist, though not in the old furious way. The key-word of the sermon was Surrender. Surrender to God. Not a word about the evils outside the chapel, the raw bitter life concentrated in the broken valley. Why should there be! Surrender to God was the palliation: it was enough to announce it, perhaps. Dr Lloyd-Jones' fine violin-like voice was exquisite enough in its entreating. And there was one thrilling moment when, by use of that magic which all the great preachers of Wales possess, he called on the name of God with tremendous passion and, opening wide his arms, he seemed like a great black bat swooping down over the congregation.

'At the close of the sermon an invitation was issued. Would any members of the congregation who felt the need of further guidance, or who wanted to give themselves anew to God, remain behind? There was a closing hymn, magnificently sung. The difficult exit began. I was one of the last to leave. No one remained behind. The air was thick as glue. At last, as I got away from my front seat, a man approached me, smiling. For a fearful moment I thought he was a chapel official coming to try and induce me to be "saved," as others had tried to induce me in my youthful Rhondda days. Not so.

'"Well, Mr Davies," he said frivolously, "I suppose we'll find all this in your next novel?"

[313]

'I was far away from thought of novels just then. He was a studious collier who had worked in the mines, but now had his own coal-level on a hill-side. I asked him what he thought of the preaching. His reply was revealing.

'"Well, as a Welshman it held and roused me, but as another man it left me cold."

'Which explained the presence of that vast eager crowd, and its curious lack of response, so impossible in the old days. Something more is needed than the old pleasures of surrender, however seductively they are painted. These Welsh are new people now.

'Outside, groups of women chattered domestically, knots of men shared cigarettes. I did not expect blatant evidences of surrender to the bliss recently offered us. But the conversation of the big crowd lingering in the road was shockingly mundane. Perhaps the religious bliss was being more subtly absorbed than used to be the case. The coaches and buses swept off with their loads that had come from afar. Feeling dingy after the wicked air of the chapel, I went through some breathing exercises and then tottered across a square to a public refreshment house.'[1]

Such comment neither deterred nor excited Dr Lloyd-Jones. But he was well aware of the mixed character of his congregations and the blind admiration of some of his hearers concerned him more than the flippancies of a Rhys Davies. Though few seemed to realise the fact, it was his close assessment of the Welsh character and temperament which vitally influenced his preaching. Nationality, he was to argue a few years later in three broadcast addresses for the Welsh B.B.C. on 'Religion and National Characteristics', does affect a man's approach to religion.[2] Although spiritual rebirth is God's sovereign gift, it does not erase natural or national characteristics. After expounding this truth he went on to analyse the difference between the Welsh and the English. The basic point of difference, he believed, was that the English character is more simple and integrated than the Welsh. The Englishman's tendency is to function as a whole –feeling, mind and will operating together. The Welshman, on the other hand, has a character which is capable of operating on 'a number of

---

[1] *My Wales*, London, 1937, pp. 117–120.
[2] These addresses, 'Crefydd a Nodweddion Cenedlaethol', were given in 1943 and published that year, in Welsh in *y Drysorfa*, vol. cxiii. They were reprinted in *Crefydd Heddiw ac Yfory*, 1947.

different levels which are not organically connected together'. The level of feeling and imagination lies nearest to the surface in the Welshman, yet it is a complete mistake, he argued, to say that the Welshman is *basically* emotional. Merely to move the Welshman emotionally is to accomplish nothing, because much stronger in its final influence in his make-up is his mind which does not necessarily move in accordance with his feelings:

'It is easy to touch the feelings of a Welshman and to arouse his imagination. He is prepared to be moved by the eloquence of expression, or by singing and music, or by beauty. His reaction to these things is fast and expresses itself outwardly and obviously to everyone.

'Many believe that this is the whole truth concerning the Welshman. The reason for this is that they think his character is woven on the same simple pattern as that of the Englishman. In this respect the Welshman's character is truly deceptive, because the Welshman's feelings constitute merely a thin layer on the surface, and underneath is the thick, strong layer – the most important and the strongest in the Welshman's character – namely, the mind. That which characterises the mind is its love of reason and of definitions. It must have everything plainly and clearly and orderly. It follows the argument to its furthermost point and it demands consistency. . . .'

Believing that this analysis was correct, Dr Lloyd-Jones viewed the tendency of Welsh preaching to entertain the emotions as a dangerous mistake. He would have agreed entirely with a reporter of the *Western Telegraph* who, contrasting the Doctor's 'barrister's style' with the more normal type of pulpit oratory, drew this conclusion:

'Phillips of Bloomsbury once declared at the Bethesda Chapel, Haverfordwest, that, if Wales could have been saved by eloquent sermons, salvation would have been general and complete long ago. So far from that being the case, he said that in Wales the road to Hell had been paved by "the eloquent sermon". I suppose he meant that Wales had produced a race of actor preachers, and that their pulpit eloquence merely pleased the ear but had no permanent effect on the heart and conscience of men and women.'

In reply to the charge that he encouraged 'emotionalism' Dr

Lloyd-Jones used to say, 'It is very easy to make a Welshman cry, but it needs an earthquake to make him change his mind'! It was an earthquake which his country needed and at the end of his broadcast addresses he gave his own conclusions on what that would mean:

'The chief need of Wales is great theological and doctrinal preaching which will emphasise the sovereignty of God, the ugliness of sin, the uncertainty of life, the judgment and eternity, the glory of the Person of the Lord Jesus Christ, and the all-sufficiency of His saving work for us on the Cross, the Resurrection and the blessed hope we have.

'These are the only truths which will produce great preaching and which will prove a foundation to sweeping eloquence. . . . To reach the Welshman's will, nothing will suffice but the strength and might of God, as it is in Christ's Gospel. But this Gospel at the same time is large enough to answer all the questions of the mind and reason, to quench the thirst for wholeness in the realm of the mind and also to move us to the depths of our being.'

Abundant spiritual confirmation of this judgment existed in the hundreds of individual lives across Wales changed by the grace of God through Dr Lloyd-Jones' ministry. Deliberately he never attempted to keep anything in the way of a record. But glimpses of a spiritual influence, hidden from Rhys Davies, occur occasionally in the letters which he wrote to his mother at this period. After a preaching visit to North Wales, he commented in the course of a letter dated November 18, 1933:

'My visit to Holywell this year actually surpassed that of last year. It seems to be one of the most responsive places to which I go. And yet it has the reputation of being one of the deadest places in Wales.

'The sermons preached were "Aeneas", "The Truth shall make you free", and Mark 5:17, 18. The second was in Welsh. The last night was a memorable occasion. I knew during the meeting that things were happening and I was conscious of being given unusual strength and power. But I never anticipated what I saw at the close. I had said in my usual way that if any had been given to see that night that Jesus Christ had died for them, and wished to thank Him and acknowledge Him, that they should stay behind. Some 30 to 40 did so and nearly all were young people somewhere between 20 and 35 years old. There were 7 or 8 men amongst them. I saw them all separately one by one and questioned them and listened to their experiences. It was 10.15 p.m. before I left the Chapel. Yesterday morning, I was visited by the lady who owns the local cinema. She had been present at my last meeting last year and she had come again on Wednesday night. She came yesterday morning to the house and began by saying "I should have stayed behind last night but I was too much of a coward to do so." She told me her whole story. She is somewhere between 66 and 70, I should think. Her husband had died worth £300,000 but she and her children between them had lost it all in business and speculation. She is highly intelligent and cultured. She said that my sermon last year had convicted her, but that she had not seen things plainly and clearly until this time. She confessed that her life had been selfish and that she had lived for herself and her children, instead of living to please God and to serve Him. Her one desire now was to know that God had forgiven her for certain in and through Jesus Christ and to serve Him for ever. Indeed she said that in her loneliness she had felt that our Lord was near to her and that she was not alone. It was a remarkable interview.

I kept feeling that a good deal of myself was left behind in Holywell.'

Another source of information on the fruit of his ministry lies in the letters sent to him at this period. One such tells a large story in few words:

Cardiff
Monday 22/10/34

Dear Mr Jones,

Many thanks for your masterly exposition of last night. It was a sermon I shall remember for all time. May God prosper your ministry – is the fervent prayer of

Yours in Him,
Gratitude

P.S. I am unemployed and put my last few coppers in the plate last evening, and not having the heart to pass the plate tonight, I decided to put this in instead; my gratitude is none the less sincere however.

Very few of the letters sent to him survive but another exception is a batch of forty-nine letters and cards which he received following his first broadcast on January 1, 1935. The occasion was his civic sermon in Cardiff already mentioned, on the subject of 'The Ten

Lepers'. Radio was still a comparative novelty and a number of letters expressed the element of near surprise at the clarity with which they heard the preacher over the air. A Bridgend hearer, who had listened to the Doctor thirty times, reported, 'This is the first time your voice has ever reached my home and it filled the whole house.' Another from Ogmore Vale, Glamorgan, wrote:

'I heard every word as plain as if I had been by your side. In spirit I was with you and earnestly prayed throughout the service, that God would drive home every word by His Spirit, to the hearts of all who listened. I thought it was wonderful, marvellous, and so overjoyed was I at times that I could hardly sit in my chair, but felt like jumping around the room and shouting "Amen".

'Surely God's strength was made perfect in your weakness yesterday; I was afraid, at times, of the old body collapsing as you seemed to put forth every ounce of strength it contained.'

Many wrote to say what the message had meant to them and to others who listened with them. 'Many of God's people were blessed and edified, I can assure you of that,' declared one correspondent from Llanelly. 'I felt the power of God behind your words'. A group of people who listened together were so certain of the spiritual results which would follow that their spokesman wrote to say, 'We had a thanksgiving meeting at the close – thanking God for the conviction of hundreds, and ending in conversion; thankful that the angels had joy, and above all that the Lord Jesus was pleased with His servant.' Others spoke similarly: 'I am certain your message has been a blessing to thousands of people and I am thankful to God for giving the country such a privilege on the first day of the year 1935; the fruit, I am certain, is assured.'

Several who wrote were ministers. The Baptist minister of Sirhowy, Tredegar, giving his impression of the service, wrote: 'The only thing I shall say of the message, wonderful! That was *preaching*. I have heard you declare the message of salvation many times but never so effectively as this morning. I write to you out of a very full heart. May God be praised and I trust the Lord will continue to strengthen you with all might, to preach the glorious gospel as you have done this morning.' Another minister, who served a Cardiff congregation, declared, 'Your message has disturbed scores of people and I hope that the disturbance will end in surrender.'

Mainly through Welsh Eyes

A Christian in Gorseinon reported a similar effect in his place of work:

'I have heard you preaching the gospel a few times at Gorseinon, Gowerton, Penclawdd, and Llanelly. It has been a great blessing to my soul. It has sent me to my knees crying in shame. On Monday last I had the privilege of hearing you on the wireless. It was wonderful. I praise the Lord for giving you the grace to lift up His Son on such an occasion. May God bless you, Sir, in these hard days when so many so-called scholarly men are trying to deny the Word of God.

'When I went to work on Monday night, a man working on the afternoon shift (one of the most ungodly men) came to speak to two of us who were talking about your address. He asked us if we had heard you, he went on to say that he had never heard the gospel proclaimed in such a way. He was greatly moved by your message – I may say he missed his usual bus that he comes to work on. He wanted to know, "Why don't they all preach like that?" I have spoken to him on several occasions about his soul. His reply to me had been that there was nothing in it. Sir, I praise God that you succeeded by proclaiming the Word of God to move this man. I trust that it will mean his salvation.'

Several wrote in similar terms. In the summary of one, 'The saints were edified and mere chapel goers were really concerned.' Another confessed of himself, 'In the rebellion of my spirit, because of certain circumstances, the vision that God vouchsafed to me has certainly been disobeyed. To God be the glory for making that message a means of grace!'

One or two who wrote were clearly old friends of the family. For example a Grocer and Provision Merchant of Brynmawr, Breconshire, as his note paper designates him, wrote:

'I feel too full to express myself. How I wish your father was alive to listen to your inspired discourse. May God give you health and strength to carry on the good work. The London Correspondent talked of Williams (Brynsiencyn) and T. C. Williams. He was talking through his hat. If he spoke of Spurgeon I would agree.[1] I could not

[1] Evidently a newspaper had compared Lloyd-Jones favourably with these two famous Welsh preachers who, while preaching glorious sermons *about* the gospel, never seemed to touch the conscience or the will, while stirring the emotions. The writer was correct in believing that Spurgeon was the nearest real parallel to Lloyd-Jones.

help myself today when listening to you. Your dear father came to me so vividly. . . .'

Such was the good done by this one sermon of January 1, 1935.

It will be apparent already that Dr Lloyd-Jones' pro-Welsh prejudice was moderated by a considerable measure of critical objectivity. He early determined to follow no religious custom simply because it was Welsh. Scripture, not nationality, must rule in the church. Thus, though he greatly admired the Welsh language, and always used it with Bethan in the home, he would never agree to its usage in the pulpit if he had reason to believe that an opportunity to help non-Welsh speakers would be lost. Often, as indicated above, his mid-week itinerant preaching would include a Welsh afternoon service, followed by an English service in the evening, but more than once he changed to English in the afternoon for the sake of his hearers. One such occasion occurred at Trecastle in 1931. The chapel intended to hold the afternoon Welsh congregation proved to be too small and it was therefore arranged that he would preach instead from a cart in the open air. Recognising the presence of a number of non-Welsh speakers, including students from Trevecca, he preached in English, only to be confronted afterwards with a very indignant Welsh language zealot who had hitherto been a great admirer of his preaching! After listening to heated words from this man on the wrongness of dropping Welsh, Dr Lloyd-Jones rebuked him sharply for putting his language before the gospel.

For the same reason, Dr Lloyd-Jones had little interest in the discussions of linguists who wished to compare his effectiveness in the two languages. Some regarded him as equal in both as a preacher, others considered he was inferior in Welsh. Certainly as a Welsh preacher he was not a purist. During his early ministry he was occasionally inhibited to some degree in that language by its lack of certain technical terms or unusual words, unfamiliar in everyday Welsh. Once he had to stop to ask a fellow minister the Welsh word for 'suburb', a procedure he soon recognised as ridiculous, for while few in the congregation knew the correct Welsh word, they were all aware of the English. This led him to the conviction that his care to avoid any English in a Welsh sermon was chiefly due to a regard for his own reputation. Thereafter he was prepared to use an English word when at a loss for a Welsh equivalent and, with his inhibition broken, he became as free in Welsh preaching as in English.

Sometimes one of his favourite English expressions, 'Very well, then . . .' was even known to creep into a Welsh sermon!

Bethan Lloyd-Jones comments: 'In the early days I used to feel that he was rather "shackled" when preaching in Welsh – he would have ten words he could use in English to one in Welsh. His pulpit Welsh certainly got easier with every year that passed and in the end presented no problems or inhibitions!'

Few things disturbed him more than the occasional experiences when he saw fellow-countrymen, professed Christians, allowing national pride to take precedence over the need of men's souls. Once when visiting Atherstone in the Midlands of England where he was to preach at an inter-denominational service, he was met at the station by the local Congregational minister – a Welshman – who soon showed considerable concern that the forthcoming service, to be held in the Church of England, should be 'a good one'. When Dr Lloyd-Jones enquired further about the nature of this concern, his host declared, 'They haven't heard preaching yet!' The Welsh exile clearly felt that his future reputation at Atherstone lay in the hands of the visiting preacher. It was not Dr Lloyd-Jones' custom to hide his impatience when he met this kind of attitude.

*   *   *

Dr Lloyd-Jones' preaching in Wales in the 1930's was by no means confined to the large churches of the more populated areas. There was nothing he enjoyed more than to be in some remote and isolated country chapel with a congregation of shepherds and farmers who often scarcely knew if they would see a preacher in their pulpit the following Sunday. In such a category belonged the chapel at Soar y Mynydd, almost inaccessible in the wild Berwyn mountains between Tregaron and Llanwrtyd. To those who approached it by the rocky track from Fanog, and across the river Towy, there was a final steep ridge to be climbed and then, where the track finally crosses the mountain crest and begins its descent into the valley of the Camddwr, Soar chapel would finally come into view 500 feet below. Amidst a clump of pines and with nothing to lessen its loneliness except a chapel house and stables, the long grey building stood much as it had been when first built in 1822. No car ever approached its doors and no word of English was heard within, for that language was unknown to the chapel-keeper and perhaps to most of Soar's

shepherd congregation. Here from the late 1920's onwards, Dr
Lloyd-Jones loved to come. Sometimes it was for 'Big Meetings' –
Cyrddau Mawr – as in August 1937, when by horseback, bicycle, or
on foot, people would come from Tregaron, Llanddewi Brefi, and
beyond. But, more often, when holidaying quietly with his family in
the district, he would preach to the normal congregation at Soar y
Mynydd or to the same people at a more accessible location.
Recalling one particular holiday in this area Bethan Lloyd-Jones
writes:

'We would spend a long week-end at Nantstalwyn sheep farm. On
this Sunday morning we set out early for "Soar", some nine miles
away. The farmer, Mr James Edwards, would take the preacher in
the trap (a light kind of gig) while the rest of us made our way –
precariously, some of us! – on mountain ponies. Now, my pony was
the best friend of the pony in the trap, and if the latter broke into a
little trot, so did mine – panic on my part, but gleeful amusement on
the preacher's! However, even if one did fall off, it was not far to fall
off these sturdy little beauties.

'I remember this Sunday best because it was a glorious day, and the
beauty of the scenery indescribable. I shall never forget the sight,
looking down at the chapel in the valley, while still some four miles
away. Half a dozen or more paths led down to it from various
directions, and these were all alive with streams of ponies (bearing
the congregation!) converging on the little grey-stone jewel in its
lush green setting.

'On arrival, the great stable under the church was soon full to its
doors, and the rest of the ponies were turned out to the near-by field
or enclosure. Then we all trooped into the little chapel and soon
filled it. Every farmer had his devoted sheep dog sitting between his
feet, behaving perfectly and seemingly enjoying everything to the
full. We never had trouble with the dogs, though occasionally there
was the sound of a short sharp fracas from beneath, as the ponies in
the stable below had an argument. This morning we counted over
seventy ponies. As for the service, never in the whole of Wales would
one find a more attentive and appreciative congregation, and the
singing was joyous.

'It was the custom for the evening service to be held in the
neighbouring farms – each farm in its turn. On this particular
Sunday, it was to be at Nantstalwyn, as we were staying there. It was

a large farm house, close to the banks of the *very* young River Towy. It had been so built that the enormous kitchen had, as its floor, one great flat stone – it looked like one gigantic blue slate "flagstone" – worn smooth as satin by the river's ministrations. But this night it was too small to contain the congregation for the evening service, even with doors to other rooms being opened, to hearing if not seeing. So it was arranged that the service be held outside in the great farm yard, and out came benches and stools and chairs, and behold, there was a ready-made pulpit – the sheep-dip! It was already raised and railed, being the place where the shepherd stood with his special rod, to push the recalcitrant sheep under the disinfectant dip, when the great dipping day arrived. Now it had a different purpose and made a really good pulpit. It was a glorious summer evening and no one who was there will ever forget the occasion.

'A notice such as the following would often be fixed to a farmyard gate or the chapel door, for the sake of any visitors from other parts. The usual members always seemed to know.'

These words in Dr Lloyd-Jones' hand were written on an envelope:

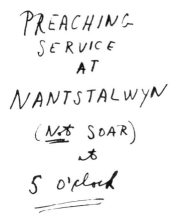

It was at the sheep-dip at Nantstalwyn that he was to preach for the last time in the open air about 1938.

The wild scenery around Soar never failed to inspire him. He could well understand how the precipitous mountain 'roads' had helped William Williams, Pantycelyn, to compose his famous line

Cul yw'r llwybr imi gerdded.[1]

[1] 'Narrow is the path I have to tread.'

And in the same area where, to survive the gradients, men had to cling to the backs of their mountain ponies, he realised and relished the fact that he had not lost the horsemanship learned nearly thirty years earlier at Llwyncadfor.

Yet despite Dr Lloyd-Jones' love of solitude and open spaces, it was in the industrialised South of Wales – amidst the coal-mines, narrow terraced houses and factories and smoky valleys – that the influence of his preaching was so far reaching. One observer of the period, with no sympathies for Calvinistic Methodism, and who became a Professor of Law at the University of Liverpool, was of the opinion that two men were foremost in keeping South Wales from Communism in the 1930's. One was Aneurin Bevan, who held back the politically-minded; the other was Martyn Lloyd-Jones who kept such large numbers of chapel-goers to the Christian Faith.

'*Dr Martyn Lloyd-Jones is the modern Moody for whom we are waiting.*'

DR JOHN SHORT
summing up the meetings of the National Free Church Council at Bournemouth.

The British Weekly, April 7, 1938

16

Leaving Aberavon

In November 1936, *Yr Efengylydd*, after reporting a service conducted by Dr Lloyd-Jones near Llanelly, added a note of concern over the preacher's future movements: 'We heard someone say that he intends going to preach again in America. If this is so, let him not remain there long, our need of him in Wales is great.' The rumour was correct. Dr William Klein of the Department of Evangelism in the Presbyterian Church in the U.S.A., had invited him to speak on behalf of the League of Faith, at a Conference on Evangelism to be held on May 25–26, 1937, immediately prior to their denomination's One Hundred and Forty-Ninth General Assembly at Columbus, Ohio. Probably the fact that this was a critical juncture for evangelicals within the Presbyterian Church in the U.S.A. helped Lloyd-Jones to agree to the invitation. For more than ten years the denomination had been torn with controversy over the liberal theology now firmly established within its ministry. The tide was so much against those who stood for the Bible that at the General Assembly of 1936, J. Gresham Machen, the foremost opponent of that liberalism, had been suspended from the ministry – seven months before his death! While some Presbyterians, in sympathy with Machen, had already left the denomination, others were still trying to rally evangelical opinion from within – a view which corresponded with Dr Lloyd-Jones' own position in Wales at this date.

Accordingly, in May 1937 Dr Lloyd-Jones crossed the Atlantic for his second visit to North America, this time alone except for his mother who was to visit friends and return on her own, at the end of the summer. The recent birth of a second daughter, Ann, completing their family circle, was one reason why Bethan Lloyd-Jones remained at home, and, influenced also by an overriding concern for work in the United Kingdom, her husband had arranged for only a short stay of three weeks. *Yr Efengylydd* had no need to be concerned.

Once arrived in New York, his first destination was Pittsburgh where Dr Clarence E. Macartney, President of the League of Faith, ministered in the down-town First Presbyterian Church. It was Macartney in 1936 who, disagreeing with Machen's separation, had attempted to rally conservatives by forming the League of Faith which had now invited Dr Lloyd-Jones to America. To make the visitor feel more at home for his first week-end in the United States, it was arranged that he would stay with an influential fellow-countryman, J. R. Jones, who was an elder in the cathedral-like East Liberty Presbyterian Church in the same city. On the Saturday night, J. R. Jones was host to his guest at a gathering of Welsh friends at the Fort Pitt Hotel – an evening which closed with Dr Lloyd-Jones telling the gathering of his aim and purpose as a preacher of the gospel. On Sunday, May 23, he preached at East Liberty, morning and evening, and for Macartney at First Presbyterian in the afternoon, when he spoke from one of his favourite texts at this period – the miracle wrought by the Apostle Peter in the healing of Aeneas (Acts 9:33–34). One Pittsburgh paper reported:

'Dr Jones' preaching made a profound impression generally and at the outset it may be said that his brief visitation to America will prove highly successful and compelling.'[1]

From Pittsburgh, Lloyd-Jones travelled with Macartney on Monday, May 24, to Columbus where the Pre-Assembly Conference on Evangelism began at 9.30 the next morning. Four sessions in all were allocated to him, two being 'Seminars' related to Evangelism which had the general title, 'The Present Situation'. At the first of these he dealt with 'Investigation and Analysis' and at the second, 'How to Deal with it'.

The Presbyterian for June 3, 1937, reported: 'Dr Martin Lloyd-Jones set a fine keynote in his pre-Assembly ministry, and its effect was felt.' The same paper, however, also indicated that there was some division in the response of his hearers: 'Dr Lloyd-Jones fulfilled the old-time test John Wesley set for effective gospel preaching. He won followers and provoked enmity, but this time the enmity was on the part of noted theological indifferentists and religious Liberals. Dr Lloyd-Jones laid down Christian truth and called to repentance on

[1] *The Druid*, June 1, 1937, 'Pittsburgh Greets Famed Welsh Divine'.

lines that were so forthright and particular, that some of his audience felt uneasy. . . .'

At the time Dr Lloyd-Jones wondered whether this unease was not shared by some of the League's leaders themselves. Strong doctrinal preaching and experimental Calvinism were by no means common even among conservative Presbyterians. A number of the other speakers at the Conference certainly belonged to a different spiritual tradition. Yet at least one of their number was outspoken in his approval. The Reverend Dr E. Cynolwyn Pugh in a newspaper article entitled 'Prophetic Preaching' wrote:

'No gift or equipment of a preacher is wanting in him. He has a well placed voice of pleasing timbre and quality, and is distinctly heard in the largest buildings. He is a complete master of vivid, direct English speech, and he has the lively Celtic imagination combined with real prophetic insight.'

Immediately after the Conference, Dr Lloyd-Jones left for Dayton, where he preached on the Thursday evening, and for the remainder of his visit he was to be similarly engaged in centres as far apart as Utica, Scranton and Philadelphia. The Philadelphia engagement was followed by others in New York where he was to spend his last weekend in the States until 1946. *The New York Sun* for Saturday, June 5, announced in a headline, 'Three City Churches to Hear Visiting Minister Tomorrow', and went on to explain that Tremont Presbyterian Church was uniting for morning worship with the congregation of West End Presbyterian Church to hear Dr Lloyd-Jones, while the Welsh Presbyterian Church would hear him in the evening. With these services behind him, he spent Monday and Tuesday in sight-seeing and shopping. His purchases included two dresses (later judged 'perfect in every way' by his wife), a brown Teddy for Ann and a doll for Elizabeth. The five-day voyage home on the *Queen Mary* began on the Wednesday and one unexpected pleasure for him was the presence of an old friend from Bart's, Geoffrey Keynes.

In later years, Dr Lloyd-Jones came to believe that of all that occurred during his 1937 trans-Atlantic visit the most significant event was one which no observer noticed at the time. It concerned his one night in Philadelphia at the beginning of June. He had been driven there by car from Scranton in a heat-wave and arrived at the house of the minister with whom he was staying in a state of almost complete exhaustion. After initial greetings his host said, 'Well, I don't know what sort of a congregation we can expect tonight. It is very hot, as you know, and people are away.' But, he proceeded to say, he did have one piece of definite information which he seemed to think might encourage his visitor: 'As I say, I don't know what sort of a congregation we are going to get, but this I do know; I can tell you who will be the most distinguished person in the congregation. Dr Campbell Morgan! He arrived last night from England with his wife. They are staying with his son Howard, and the moment he heard that you were preaching here tonight he said "I am going to be there"'.

Dr Lloyd-Jones later recalled that at that moment Morgan was the last man whom he wanted to see. It was common knowledge that the minister of Westminster Chapel was looking for an associate and there were some who already linked Lloyd-Jones' name with that London charge. Eliseus Howells had done so as early as 1934 and Mrs Lloyd-Jones, senior, hearing of it, had received the following comment from Martyn in a letter dated January 22, 1934:

'As for Westminster I feel that it is extremely unlikely that I shall ever visit there while Campbell Morgan is alive or has anything to do with the place.'[1]

He was wrong, as his visit to Westminster on December 29, 1935, had already proved, and, facing his Philadelphia congregation that summer's evening in 1937, it was hard for him not to suppose that the tall figure prominent in the front of the congregation, who took out his watch to time him as he began to preach, had other things besides the message on his mind. Before the night was over Lloyd-Jones was sure that his intuition was correct. Morgan was the first to speak to him when the service was over and when the old veteran walked away up an aisle on the side of the building Dr Lloyd-Jones, then engaged talking to others, noticed how he would stop every now and again and, deep in thought, turn back and look towards him.

Although Dr Lloyd-Jones preached for a second time at Westminster Chapel on June 27, 1937, this episode in Philadelphia had no immediate influence upon subsequent events and it certainly did not enter into the belief to which Dr Lloyd-Jones came in the latter half of

[1] This judgment was based upon the obvious differences in their theological standpoints.

1937 that his work at Sandfields was done. That conviction came to him almost as unaccountably as the awareness with which he had been led there eleven years before. Subsequently he spoke of his consciousness that his Aberavon ministry was about to be concluded as being as definite as if 'a shutter had come down'. Far from it being an experience which he welcomed, 'I was', he later said, 'really quite upset by it.' This is not to say that there were no considerations that pointed to the need for a change. Foremost among them was the weight of work which had become inseparable from his weekly routine, including as it did the full responsibility for the thriving work at Sandfields, and the strain of addressing large congregations in all parts of Wales. These things, and the insistent and constant calls for his medical counsel, had combined to make physical demands upon him which could not be long sustained by any man. Concern that Dr Lloyd-Jones was working 'at the edge of his strength' was being expressed in the Welsh press by the mid-thirties and the preacher himself shared in it. In particular, Dr Lloyd-Jones was aware for the first time of having trouble with his voice. The large chapels of those days generally had no microphones and sometimes there was the even greater demand made upon him by preaching in the open-air. For no apparent reason there were now times when his voice failed and twice at Aberavon during this period he had to sit down in the pulpit without being able to complete his sermon. The cause, as he subsequently came to see, was that his voice production was wrong. He spoke far too much 'from the throat'. As long as he had the physical and nervous energy of youth to carry him through, this mistake was neither serious nor obvious, but with the lessening of that energy the problem had become manifest and for some years, until his practice changed, it gave him real concern.

It was in these circumstances that Dr Lloyd-Jones in the autumn of 1937 received a pressing request to preach for Marylebone Presbyterian Church, London, who were without a minister. Situated in George Street, off Edgware Road, with institutional buildings 'among the finest in London', the Marylebone church was one of the most influential Presbyterian congregations in England. Besides not a few émigré Scots, including Jane Stoddart who had just retired after fifty years' editorial work with *The British Weekly*, the church had recently had the support of such prominent figures as the American Ambassador and his wife. After an early evangelical tradition, the congregation – as so often in English Presbyterianism – had become accustomed to a more nondescript message, and when the previous minister had accepted a call to Australia in 1937 there were some who saw the possibility of a change. A few years earlier the Moderator of the General Assembly of the English Presbyterians, in a discussion as to why the denomination made such small appeal to the masses, asked the question, 'Is it that we have not discovered the best method of preaching the gospel? Is the preaching of Presbyterian ministers in England for the most part too academic in character?'[1]

It was because he also felt the force of such questions that J. Chalmers Lyon, the Interim Moderator at Marylebone for the vacancy, took the unusual step of turning to Welsh Presbyterianism and, in his letter of invitation to Dr Lloyd-Jones, he confessed that he was unable to get his name out of his mind.

The result was that the first Sunday of 1938 found Dr Lloyd-Jones in the pulpit of Marylebone Presbyterian Church where he preached in the morning from the story of the widow and the cruse of oil (2 Kings 4:1–7) as illustrating the secret, supernatural nature of the Christian life. In the evening, from the miracle of the raising to life of the son of the widow of Nain (Luke 7:11–16), he preached one of his characteristic evangelistic sermons. Only the power of Christ, he told his hearers, could halt the funeral procession which made its way out of Nain, and only the same power can change the world's hopelessness as it stands in the presence of failure, sin and death.[2] The Marylebone congregation heard nothing of the prose or poetry which visiting preachers too often brought to the pulpit and they do not seem to have missed it. Even before a church meeting was called, Jane Stoddart could not resist contributing in the Table Talk of *The British Weekly* for January 27 an entry under the heading 'A Medical Minister' which read:

'Dr Martyn Lloyd-Jones, of Port Talbot, a correspondent writes, seems destined to a place in the great succession of Welsh pulpit orators. He had a brilliant career as a medical student and took the London M.D. degree.

'He is now 38, and good judges have compared his preaching to that of the young J. D. Jones. Dr Lloyd-Jones has recently preached

---

[1] *The British Weekly*, May 5, 1932, p. 88.
[2] Outlines of these sermons were taken down by a reporter of *The Christian Herald* and published, in reverse order, on March 17 and October 27, 1938, respectively, in that paper.

to very large congregations in London, and it is expected that he will shortly receive a call to an important London charge.'

In the issue of the same journal for the following week the full news was out:

'At a largely attended meeting of the Marylebone Church on Thursday evening it was decided to invite the Rev Dr Martyn Lloyd-Jones, of Port Talbot, to succeed the Rev. J. Golder Burns as minister. The call was unanimous and enthusiastic.'

At the time of the press announcement on February 3, 1938, Dr Lloyd-Jones was inclined to view the call to Marylebone as the guidance of God. Although London was not a preaching sphere which naturally appealed to him, the Marylebone pulpit offered an important opportunity. In London there would be no question of his medical counsel being needed as had been the case in Wales, neither would he have the four or five mid-week preaching engagements which had become so much part of his Welsh ministry. For the moment he said nothing, nor did he yet need to reach a decision, for the call to London had first to be approved and passed on to him by the Presbytery of London North (of which Marylebone Church was a part) and it was not due to meet until April 12, 1938.

Before that date, however, other developments had occurred. The National Free Church Council Assembly, one of the most important annual events in English Nonconformity, took place during the last week of March. With 800 delegates, the venue was Richmond Hill Church, Bournemouth, and Dr Lloyd-Jones had been invited to speak on the Wednesday evening, March 30. When Dr John Short subsequently gave a lengthy account of the Assembly in *The British Weekly* it was to the meeting of that evening that he drew particular attention under a sub-heading, 'Voice from South Wales'. He wrote:

'The Rev. Dr Martyn Lloyd-Jones, who gave up a fine career in order to become a Methodist minister, informed us that he was to preach a sermon and not deliver an address. It was an inspiring experience, fresh, arresting, challenging, moving. This man is a born preacher and is destined to become a great force in the religious life of our land. He is orthodox in his theology and thoroughly convincing in his mode of presentation of his message. . . .

'Taking as his text Acts 9:32–35, he applied the miracle as a parable to our present situation. . . . The vast congregation was gripped and held from start to finish. If the National Council is thinking of adding to the number of its evangelists, it ought to do its utmost to secure the services of Dr Martyn Lloyd-Jones. He is the modern Moody for whom we are waiting.'[1]

The week after Bournemouth, on April 6, 1938, Dr Lloyd-Jones was asked to meet with six brethren, appointed by the South Wales Association of his denomination, who were anxious to confer with him prior to his reaching any decision on the call to Marylebone Church. The President of the Association chaired the meeting which met in the vestry of the Forward Movement Hall, Neath, and, after speaking of their 'sadness and sorrow', 'beseeched him in the name of the Connexion not to leave us'. After the other members of the deputation from the Association had spoken to the same effect, Dr Lloyd-Jones explained the reasons which were compelling him to consider the call to Marylebone. As later reported back to the Association by the six deputies these reasons were:

'(a) He felt that he had completed the work he had been called to do in Sandfields.

'(b) He felt that he could not labour in another church in Wales and also do all the travelling and preaching that he had been doing lately.

'(c) He believed that by centralising his efforts in some way or another he could best attain his purpose in the ministry.

'(d) It was because he believed that the Marylebone church could be made into a centre of evangelical preaching, as it is now in the Westminster church, and as it was in the Methodist church in Central Hall, that he was considering the call that he had received from this church.

'He stated further that he had no desire to leave the Calvinistic Methodist Connexion, which was dear to him, but his present heavy

---

[1] *The British Weekly*, April 7, 1938. The sermon was the one which the preacher once described to his mother as 'my Aeneas sermon'. Like Whitefield, he had no hesitation in preaching the same message forty times, though once a sermon was printed (as this sermon was in *The Westminster Record*, April, 1940) he did not preach it again.

duties had become a physical burden and he did not see how he could fulfil his ministry satisfactorily if he continued. He therefore felt that he had no other alternative but to consider other fields which were in harmony with his thoughts on true usefulness.'[1]

In response, the deputation, while recognising the force of his argument, pressed upon him the possibility of a post of wider influence within the denomination, without the responsibilities of a pastoral charge. They foresaw 'within two years' an opportunity for him to become directly involved in the education of men for the ministry. What they had in view was that the principalship of the denomination's college at Aberystwyth was about to fall vacant with the retirement of the Reverend Harris Hughes. If, as they thought probable, Principal D. M. Phillips was transferred to that position from the denomination's other college at Bala, then Phillips' present work would be ideally suited to Dr Lloyd-Jones' gifts, for it was at the Bala College that all students for the ministry did a year's course in pastoralia.

While Dr Lloyd-Jones was faced with this unexpected development, another consideration arose which was to prove decisive to him. It precluded one of the possibilities at once. When the Presbytery of London North met on April 12, as no mutual eligibility for ministerial interchange existed between English and Welsh Presbyterianism, they would only authorise the call on condition that the candidate applied for transfer to the ministry of the English Presbyterian Church – a step which would include an examination as to his ministerial competence! Before the end of April Dr Lloyd-Jones formally declined the call. The *Sunday Dispatch* reported Marylebone's reaction in the words of J. Chalmers Lyon:

'It is a great disappointment to us that Dr Jones prefers to remain in Wales but we understand his position. The Welsh Presbyterians –his own denomination – have great need of him down there. He will carry out important work all over Wales. He is a wonderful man. If he had remained a doctor, and ignored the call of the church, he would have been earning £15,000 a year, and probably have had a title.'

[1] Printed (in Welsh) as part of the deputation's report, Appendix VI, in the published *Agenda of the Quarterly Association of the Presbyterian Church of Wales to be held at Salem, Llandeilo*, June 14–16, 1938.

Meanwhile, during this same month of April 1938, yet other possibilities arose. Dr Lloyd-Jones received a letter of enquiry from the Free Church Council concerning his availability. The Council had not needed the published remarks of Dr Short to prompt them to recognise the good which the Welshman might do by preaching at interdenominational services under their auspices in different parts of the country. Also, as we have earlier noted, there was another party deeply interested in Dr Lloyd-Jones' future. Campbell Morgan had been on the verge of approaching him when, to his consternation, Marylebone forestalled him! He had not forgotten Lloyd-Jones since his last meeting with him in Philadelphia, and confidential conversation with other leaders in Congregationalism – notably with his old friend, Dr J. D. Jones, recently retired from his famous pastorate at Richmond Hill church, Bournemouth – had confirmed his growing conviction that the Calvinistic Methodist from Aberavon was the best man both to hold the congregation of the denomination's citadel in London and also, from Westminster, to exercise future leadership within English Nonconformity.

Concerned with the outcome of the matters under discussion, Campbell Morgan had asked Lloyd-Jones to keep him informed, and accordingly, when the latter phoned on April 27 and gave the news that he had declined Marylebone, the old man was delighted. But also hearing at the same time of the other possibilities Morgan did not immediately reveal his mind. Instead he wrote the next day:

My Dear Friend,

I want to thank you very much for phoning me up yesterday. It was good of you to let me know your decision, and I greatly rejoice in it, and believe you have been guided aright.

I am tremendously interested, moreover, in what you have told me about Bala.

Now I do not know how far you have committed yourself to the Free Church Council after July, but I am wondering whether you could postpone anything definite until you hear from me again. I have an idea in my mind that I should like to talk to you about; but before doing so, need a little time. Please write me.

With abiding affection
Ever Yours
G. Campbell Morgan.

Joy at Sandfields over their pastor's decision not to proceed with the

Marylebone call was short-lived. Uncertain of the outcome of the various considerations now before him, Dr Lloyd-Jones could not escape the conviction that he was nearing a point of exhaustion and that, irrespective of his future work, a real break was urgently needed. On Sunday May 1, 1938, the church family at Sandfields was stunned to hear their pastor announce his resignation as from the end of July. Not without the usual inaccuracies the press at once gave headlines to the 'Aberavon Pastor Sensation'. His 'ill-health' was over-emphasised in some papers, in one case under the heading 'A Long Rest Necessary': 'He informed a church meeting at Aberavon of his decision to retire from the ministry.... An astonished diaconate asked Dr Lloyd-Jones to reconsider his decision.' There was, of course, no question of 'retirement' from the ministry. The statement of another paper was much closer to reality:

'He said that he was resigning because he was grossly over-worked, and he was a tired man and had the desire for a complete change and rest before he undertook the further work which his denomination had for him in the future'.[1]

Meanwhile, the same weekend as this news was announced at Aberavon, another letter was in the post from Campbell Morgan. Hearing in reply to his first letter of April 28 that Lloyd-Jones was not committed in the immediate future Morgan lost no time to seize an opportunity. In the letter which arrived the morning after his resignation, Dr Lloyd-Jones read:

'You know I am serving here under limitations. I consented to continue for a year, taking two services only a week. That year really comes to a conclusion at the end of June. I am taking July and August off, going into the country, and lying fallow. I know that it is the wish of my officers that I should continue on the same arrangement, and I believe a Church Meeting is definitely being called to make that statement an official one to me.

'This, as you will be aware, involves the finding of varied supplies for half the Sunday. Now at last to the point. Would you be at all inclined to come and share the pulpit with me for, say, six months? To me it would be a great joy if you could do so; and I believe that

---

[1] The *Glamorgan Gazette*, May 6, 1938, 'Resignation of Dr Martin Lloyd-Jones'.

you would find here a real opportunity for the work for which you are so marvellously fitted, namely, that of preaching. Any such arrangement would leave you free for half of every Sunday, and the whole of the week. Before going to my officers I want you very frankly to tell me your own reaction to the suggestion. Mr Marsh and I have talked the matter over, and he thinks with me that it would be a splendid arrangement.'

Dr Lloyd-Jones replied stating his willingness to consider such a temporary arrangement, if it met with the approval of the Westminster Chapel congregation which was due to meet on May 26. The invitation interested him, but it was no more than that, his thoughts being principally turned to Wales, as is clear from a letter which he wrote shortly after to the Secretary of the South Wales Association:

28, Victoria Road,
Aberavon, Port Talbot.
May 16th, 1938.

Dear Brother,

I write to inform you (and through you the other five representatives of the Association whom I met at Neath together with you on April 6th, and through them the South Wales Association which will meet at Llandeilo on June 14th) of the response which I have made to the appeal of the Association in the matter of 'the call', which I had received to the pastorate of the Marylebone Presbyterian Church, London.

My decision has been given publicity already in the religious press by the friends at Marylebone.

I write, therefore, not primarily to acquaint you with the fact that I have declined that invitation, but rather to express my feelings and sentiments with regard to the action of the Association in appointing the six representatives to meet me.

I say quite honestly and sincerely that the action came to me as a very great surprise, and that its main effect upon me has been to humble me and to fill me with a sense of my unworthiness. It would be affectation on my part to conceal the fact that I regard this as the highest tribute that has or ever can be paid me or any one else.

Nothing can be more precious than the thought that one has the affection and the trust of one's brethren.

As I indicated to the deputation, it was not my desire, nor indeed my intention, to leave the Connexion.

My consideration of 'the call' to Marylebone was dictated solely

by physical causes and the desire to render to the Kingdom of God
on earth the maximum amount of service of which I am capable.

The opening-out before me, therefore, by the brethren, of a field
of service within the Connexion which is of the very first
importance, immediately decided my course of action.

I informed the friends at Marylebone of my decision and of the
reasons which dictated it.

It is but right and just that I should say that I fully realise that the
six brethren whom I met had no power to commit the Association
to anything definite, and that I have acted solely and entirely on
their personal pledges and on my estimate of them as leaders
within the denomination.

I should like to place on record my deep sense of gratitude to
them for their courtesy and their kindness, and for their over-
generous estimate of my performances in the past and of my
possible services in the future.

I thus leave myself in the hands of the brethren, assuring them of
my love in Christ Jesus and of my determination to labour and to
strive 'according to his working which worketh in me mightily', so
never to betray their confidence and their trust.

With warmest greetings,
Your brother and fellow-labourer,
D. MARTYN LLOYD-JONES[1]

During the week following the writing of this letter a telegram
from Campbell Morgan, dated May 27, read: 'Large and enthusiastic church meeting last night asked me to go on again and ratified all
arrangements. This gives me great satisfaction as I look forward to
your co-operation.' The same day Dr Lloyd-Jones wrote to confirm
his acceptance of this interim arrangement and also to urge that any
announcement of his coming to Westminster should be kept in low
key and not given to the 'press hounds'. He was already too late.
Arthur E. Marsh, Westminster's church Secretary, who had first
visited the Lloyd-Joneses in 1915, had already sent out a news release
to fourteen papers! Dr Lloyd-Jones' only consolation was that Marsh
had judiciously kept his words to a minimum:

'Dr G. Campbell Morgan shall continue to work as during the past
year, taking two major services each week, one of which has been
and will continue to be his Friday evening Bible School . . . At the
same [church] meeting it was announced that arrangements had

[1] Printed in the *Agenda of the Quarterly Association*, op. cit., pp. 36–37.

been made with Dr. D. Martyn Lloyd-Jones to take the second service for a period of some months, commencing on the first Sunday in September. The Church is looking forward hopefully to a further period of useful service in the interests of the Kingdom of God.'

*   *   *

Shortly before the time came for Dr Lloyd-Jones to leave Aberavon, one English national newspaper carried the kind of lengthy article which the minister of Sandfields had always sought to avoid. The reporter had no access to Dr Lloyd-Jones himself but by means of a number of enquiries in Aberavon he was able to record some facts under the heading, 'The Harley Street Doctor who became a "Modern Saint"'. He rightly discerned that the almost unique relationship between Dr Lloyd-Jones and many of the people of the town was based primarily upon a conviction about Dr Lloyd-Jones' personal life:

'For eleven years now Dr Martin Lloyd-Jones has been a minister in Aberavon, and around him has grown a living legend of sainthood.

'I came through dull streets to learn something of this legend –the legend which you will never learn from the "beloved doctor" himself. Hundreds of humble dwellers in Aberavon, church members or not, regard Martyn Lloyd-Jones, the man to whom all men are brothers as a matter of course, with a reverent gratitude that holds a touch of awe.

'There are a thousand splendid deeds of Aberavon's doctor-saint over the past eleven years, that will never, perhaps, be told, yet, in their cumulative influence, they seem to sweeten this little town even as the strong winds from the Severn sweeten and cleanse it. He has spent, they say, a small fortune in giving practical help to people in need of money, has helped them to clear off arrears of rent and even to buy their homes. His constant question at meetings of his church committee is: "Now, who is there in *real* want?"

'Here in Aberavon they pray he will come back to them. When I asked why he had decided to leave Aberavon and the little wind-swept church, a friend told me: "I do not know. I only know that he has decided nothing in his life – not the slightest thing – except after many hours of prayer."'

We cannot close the record of Dr Lloyd-Jones' ministry in Aber-

avon without adding something more on the closeness of the bond
between him and the people whom he served. As the above quotation
rightly states, it was not only the spiritual interests of the church
community which concerned him. Mrs Lloyd-Jones writes:

'We had been in Aberavon for a few years, when I discovered that my
husband had a keen business acumen! People had often said to me,
"He'd make a marvellous barrister", or "He'd be a wonderful
politician" and I would agree with them, with an inward sigh of
thankfulness that he wasn't either. But business? One Wednesday
night, we had come home from the Fellowship Meeting rather later
than usual. By the time we had had some supper, it was getting late,
and Martyn, tired after a long day, was relaxing with a book before
going to bed. The door bell rang. There stood Mr and Mrs ——,
business people in the church, looking drawn and haggard and as
though they had not slept for a week. Could they come in? They just
wanted to know one thing from the Doctor. And in they came, and
their question was – Would they have to go out of membership of the
church if they went bankrupt? The answer, "*Why* go bankrupt?"
That was the start. They had gone over everything a hundred times,
tried this and tried that – it was a sorry story, and now they were
giving up – but *not* the minister! By about 2.30 a.m. he had gone into
every detail and had worked out a plan for them to carry out. They
left exhausted but seeing a gleam of hope. The end of the story was
that there was no bankruptcy, but a sound and satisfactory little
business and a very happy family, in a few weeks' time. I saw this
happen two more times in a big way, and many, many times in minor
business crises, and I was always amazed'.

At the end of July 1938 came the final packing at 28 Victoria
Road, Aberavon. It was far from easy and still less was the parting
which followed. Sandfields had long become much more than a place
of gathering for various activities. It was a spiritual home; a place
where, for many, the 'family' life was a true taste of coming glory.
Whatever their future ministry, Martyn and Bethan sensed that they
could scarcely experience again the closeness of the spiritual ties
forged since those first memorable visits in 1926.

Immediately before them lay a holiday at Talybont, Cardiganshire, and then removal to Vincent Square, London, where they were
to stay with Martyn's mother during the period of months which they

David Martyn Lloyd-Jones

expected to be in London. A few days after their departure from Sandfields, Martyn wrote to E. T. Rees on July 30, 1938:

'I could say much, but in a sense I told you everything when I told you that you were undoubtedly the most vital factor in my ever going to Sandfields. And throughout the years you have ever been the same.

'I find it quite impossible still to realise that we have left and that I am no longer the minister of Sandfields, Aberavon. But I know that as the months and the years, God willing, shall pass, I shall be ever more and more grateful for all the help and the friendship, indeed the love I received from you.

'What the future holds we do not know, but it cannot possibly be happier than the past years. Accept my deepest thanks then for all, and may God continue to bless you and Mrs Rees and Linda and Roger even as He has done. We all join in warmest love to you all.'

It was, in part, because of all that Sandfields meant to Dr Lloyd-Jones that fifteen years were to pass before he was to preach there again.

'M. L.-J. used to describe his understanding of guidance in this way: Think of a train standing at the departure platform. Everything is ready and waiting. Everything is checked, the engine driver has the steam up (n.b. the old days of steam trains!), the guard stands, green flag in hand, but the train does not move. Why not? Because they are waiting for the signal to drop! And now he was waiting for the signal to drop, waiting for that internal certainty.'

BETHAN LLOYD-JONES

'No worker for God need sit down and chant a dirge. David had to lay down this work [his preparation for the building of the temple] unfinished. Every one of us has to do the same thing; but God is there, and there is the next man coming on.'

G. CAMPBELL MORGAN
Preaching, 1937, p. 80.

17

Wales or Westminster?

Dr Lloyd-Jones' first service at Westminster Chapel in September 1938 was fully recorded in the *Western Mail*. The paper's London reporter estimated the congregation at 'not less than 2,000' for the evening service at 7 p.m. when he preached. 'A large crowd had assembled outside when the gates of the chapel were opened at 6.30, and strangers waited patiently in queues in the aisles until stewards showed them into the seats. When Dr Lloyd-Jones, accompanied by Dr Campbell Morgan, ascended the rostrum, there were not more than half a dozen places available. These were quickly taken up. Dr Lloyd-Jones wore a plain black robe over his ordinary dark suit, with a layman's collar and tie.'

The praise included 'Rock of Ages', Psalm 23, and 'When I survey the wondrous Cross'. Dr Campbell Morgan gave out the announcements and welcomed Dr Lloyd-Jones 'who, I say with very great gratitude, by the grace of God has come to my side to help me for a little while in the ministry here which I cannot myself fulfil as in the early days'. Without the slightest reference to his new duties the newcomer proceeded to direct the congregation to his text – the parable of the two sons and the vineyard in Matthew 21:28–32. In the words of the same reporter:

'Dr Lloyd-Jones preached for about 40 minutes a discourse on repentance, purely evangelical, which magnetised his listeners. So far as I could tell he spoke without notes, beginning in his pleasantly conversational voice, his hands holding his gown on the lapels of his coat and occasionally being used to emphasise a point.

'He urged the fundamental place of doctrine in the Christian life and gradually became more forceful and more eloquent.

'His command of language and his wonderful choice of words enriched and strengthened one of the finest and most searching sermons that has been heard at Buckingham Gate for a long time.'

At this point of time the decisions which Dr Lloyd-Jones had been called to face since the beginning of 1938 were far from over. Largely unknown to the congregation at Westminster Chapel, and owing to no fault of his own, the coming months were to find his name at the centre of a difficulty and a controversy in Wales. He was on the eve of a crisis which became the turning point in his life.

By September 1938 the deputation from the South Wales Association, which had conferred with him in April, had not made any real progress in their hopes of finding an appointment acceptable to the denomination and to the preacher himself. A vacancy at Bala remaining an uncertainty, it appears that the deputies' thought had turned to the possibility of Dr Lloyd-Jones becoming a 'general missioner' within the denomination, although for this to be feasible he would probably need to become superintendent of the Forward Movement. As early as May 1938 an anonymous major article in the *Western Mail*, entitled 'Man Who May Stop Backward Trend of Forward Movement', cast Dr Lloyd-Jones in this role. The writer asked: 'If Dr Martin Lloyd-Jones could accomplish so great a revival in one Forward Movement Hall, what could he not do if the whole line of the movement were put under his charge?'[1]

When the Association met in London in November 1938 it was clear, as the *Western Mail* announced, that this hope could not presently be fulfilled. The desirability of the proposal was not in doubt: 'It was felt that under his leadership, with his great gift of popular appeal, the various mission halls could be galvanised into a state of unprecedented vigour.' The practical difficulty was simply that the Reverend R. J. Rees was not ready to retire from the superintendentship of the Forward Movement. Thought, therefore, had returned to the possibilities at Bala, and so, while the Association was being held in London, the *Western Mail* came out with an article entitled, 'Dr Martin Lloyd-Jones and the Bala College Principalship'. Though not on the agenda for discussion, the paper reported, the matter overshadowed its proceedings, and the anonymous writer backed the proposal that Principal Phillips be translated to Aberystwyth and Dr Lloyd-Jones replace him at Bala. Given such an arrangement, the writer believed, 'Dr Lloyd-Jones would be in a strategic position for moulding the Welsh pulpit, as regards both its message and its power of appeal, in such a way as to leave the impress

[1] *Western Mail*, May 14, 1938.

of his labours on the life and thought of our churches for a whole generation.'

The same writer pointed out that the need for a denominational appointment for Dr Lloyd-Jones 'has become accentuated afresh by reason of his phenomenal success as a temporary co-minister with Dr Campbell Morgan; he is drawing congregations as crowded as those that wait on Campbell Morgan's ministry – a fact which had been regarded by the office bearers of the church as beyond possibility . . . the members at Westminster Chapel already regard him as Dr Morgan's successor in the full pastorate. They are determined that now they have him they will not let him go when the period of his temporary ministry comes to an end.'[1]

After Campbell Morgan's initial letter to Lloyd-Jones proposing a 'six-month' arrangement, he had deliberately dropped any reference to a specific period of time. Despite his knowledge of what was afoot in Wales, he clearly hoped to retain his new-found colleague. The *Western Mail* was reporting the feeling at Westminster correctly. Even as early as October 1938, at Campbell Morgan's instigation, the proposal was moved that Lloyd-Jones should join him on a permanent basis in a joint pastoral charge. When this invitation was renewed and unanimously carried at a church meeting on December 8 (the day before Morgan entered upon his seventy-sixth year), the *Western Mail* announced that the Bala position had 'failed to attract Dr Lloyd-Jones' and that 'the invitation [to Westminster] will be accepted by him.'[2]

These newspaper assertions were alike erroneous, for the position with respect to Bala was by no means settled and Dr Lloyd-Jones was still disposed to accept a call to the college if it was given him. Unknown to the general public, a controversy over his nomination to Bala was reaching its height among the Welsh Presbyterian leaders. In part this controversy was due to the differing interests of North and South Wales which from time to time surfaced in an evident rivalry between the separate Associations representing the two areas. For the sake of harmony in the denomination, Moderators for the annual General Assembly were chosen in strict alternation from North and South. A similar balance was also aimed at in the United College Board which had the oversight of the colleges at Aber-

[1] *Western Mail*, November 5, 1938.
[2] In an article entitled, 'Effect of Dr Martin Lloyd-Jones' Settlement in London'.

ystwyth and Bala. When the forthcoming vacancy at Aberystwyth came to be discussed in the North their candidate was not Phillips but the Reverend G. A. Edwards who was a professor or tutor at Bala. Seeing this, the six Southern deputies, concerned to obtain a position for Dr Lloyd-Jones and without waiting for the formal backing of their Association (on which they knew they could depend), wrote to the committee of the United College Board urging that as soon as they appointed the new Principal to Aberystwyth, they should proceed to nominate Lloyd-Jones to fill the Bala vacancy. They do not seem to have anticipated a blockage to their plan. After all, the South was willing to support Edwards – a North Walian – to the highest position at Aberystwyth and it was reasonable to expect that the North would reciprocate with respect to Lloyd-Jones going to Bala.

But when this letter from the six brethren of the Southern Association came under the consideration of the College Board Committee it encountered a storm of protest from Northern members. They claimed that the communication was irregular and that it should not even be read, for it lacked the formal backing of the South Wales Association. As was later to be revealed, 'Accusations of Hitlerism were hurled, and similar epithets used, charging South Wales with thrusting a candidate down their throats.'[1] Disturbed but undeterred, the Committee referred the matter back to the next Southern Association which met at Bridgend in March 1939. Here a resolution was unanimously passed – members rising to their feet to record approval – that the College Board be again asked to nominate Dr Lloyd-Jones for Bala and that the Association of the North, due to meet the following month at Chester, be respectfully asked to do the same.

By March 1939, after seven months at Westminster, Dr Lloyd-Jones felt the difficulty of his position acutely. He remained true to the commitment he had expressed by letter to the Southern Association nearly a year before, but doubts had now arisen in his mind as to whether, in the continuing absence of any firm appointment in his own Church, he was not – as Campbell Morgan urged upon him in private – 'fighting against God'. Thus far he had positively declined the call to settle at Westminster: now the conviction deepened in his mind that the decision of the North Wales

[1] 'Our Readers' Views', *Western Mail*, May 23, 1939.

Association would be of crucial significance in determining his future.

When the Northern Association duly met at Chester in April 1939 it was soon plain that a majority had no intention of backing the South's proposal. At the first discussion of the Bala vacancy the request from the South was ignored. In the words of one observer, 'When the South Wales message was subsequently considered, it was rejected contemptuously as being entirely out of order and against the usual rules of procedure.' The Association simply postponed any action on Bala – an example followed, with characteristic diplomacy, by the College Board at their next meeting. By a strange providence two men who had both intended to speak at Chester on behalf of Lloyd-Jones' nomination were prevented from doing so. One was taken ill and unable to be there. The other was a liberal who nevertheless favoured the South's proposal on the grounds that Lloyd-Jones would 'teach the men to think'. Arriving at Chester, as this man stood on a pavement kerb before the Association began, he was struck by a passing lorry and required hospital treatment.

In the light of this situation, the men to whom Dr Lloyd-Jones had committed himself in South Wales released him from his promise, and thus, a year after the call from Marylebone had been declined, he accepted the call to Westminster. The news was announced to the congregation by Dr Campbell Morgan on Sunday, April 23, 1939, when he briefly reminded the church of how their call had been given to Dr Lloyd-Jones:

'I felt he had a very difficult decision to make. He has now accepted our invitation, and becomes not assistant, but associate-pastor. Those of you who do not know the difference, you had better get out your dictionaries when you reach home.

'Dr Lloyd-Jones will be perfectly equal with myself in the oversight of the church, and especially in the work of preaching. To me personally it is a very great satisfaction that he has accepted. This pulpit has for many years stood for biblical preaching. It has become a national pulpit – indeed an international pulpit – with a world-wide influence'.

The same day Morgan also commented to a reporter:

'We all have waited patiently for him to come to a decision. It seemed a very long time, but I fully understood what he had to face.

Personally I feel perfectly sure he has come to the right decision. He will be a great gain to the preaching power of London, and I think I might say without being misunderstood that Westminster Chapel gives him a great pulpit.'

Despite Dr Lloyd-Jones' acceptance of the call to Westminster Chapel the controversy over him in Wales was far from closing. Indeed his settlement in London was a signal for the debate to become more public. Recognising it as a matter of public concern, various Welsh newspapers now ran articles which reviewed what had happened. The headings indicate their subject matter: 'Is South Wales Ruled by the North? Disagreement Over Vacant Chair at Bala College'; 'Differences on Bala College Appointment'; 'Why Wales Lost Dr Martin Lloyd-Jones'; and 'Secrets Behind the Loss of a Prophet to Welsh Presbyterianism'.

When the South Wales Association met in May 1939 at Conwil Elvet, near Carmarthen, feelings ran high as the trouble over Bala was uppermost in all minds. Notwithstanding the fact that Dr Lloyd-Jones' future was now decided, the South had been shocked and stung by the attitude of the North. There were even fears of the extent to which the division between the two Associations might yet go. Thus, before the South Wales Association opened, a Committee judiciously proposed a resolution to be sent to the North Wales Association, strong enough, it was hoped, to satisfy the resentment felt and yet ending on an eirenical note:

'We are much distressed by the action of the Association in North Wales meeting at Chester in reference to the message which the Association in South Wales transmitted to you relative to nominating the Rev. Dr Martin Lloyd-Jones to the selection committee of the United Colleges Board. It was our conviction that a great benefit to our Church would be derived from it, had it been carried through as we desired, and this is still our conviction. We have been seriously perturbed by the way in which our message was dealt with by your Association lest it indicated that we were becoming more alienated one from the other and that it brought in an estrangement of spirit. It is now our hope that any threatened disagreement may be averted.'

Not without debate – for some favoured stronger action – this resolution was carried, and another resolution was sent to Dr Lloyd-Jones 'to the effect that though the Association rejoiced that

Dr Jones had been given a wider field in which to labour, they sincerely prayed that his service might not be wholly lost to their church and that he be preserved for still greater service'.

Although these resolutions did not silence all further discussion it is unnecessary to pursue the subject further. What is of material importance for these pages is the reason behind the degree of opposition to Dr Lloyd-Jones' proposed appointment to Bala, affecting as it does our understanding of his whole ministry. The newspapers' emphasis on the rivalry between North and South – and the North's alleged wish to hold 'the denominational plums' – is by no means an adequate explanation. The real meaning lay deeper than mere provincial bias. One contributor of a major article in the *Western Mail* believed that the root of the difference was to be found in the fact that, like Amos, Lloyd-Jones did not come from the normal 'school of the prophets':

'After the manner of the Hebrew prophet he has sprung from the laity and consequently he lacks those traditional accoutrements as regards training, deportment, and jargon, which have come to be regarded as the hall-mark of preachers as a class. That is why so many of them are ready to regard him with disfavour. . . .

'The fact that the most popular preacher in Wales is one who has never undergone a theological training, after their example, manifestly serves to demonstrate to the point of proof that such training is not really necessary for a successful ministry. It is that consideration which has upset their professional equilibrium and made them jealous of his phenomenal success. They would rather see him leave the connexion than remain in it as a perpetual reproach to the men who have emerged from the denominational colleges with the full flavour of academic distinction, but who, notwithstanding, are utterly unable to attract the masses to their half-empty churches.'[1]

There is reason to think that the attitude depicted by this writer did enter into the controversy and contributed to the procedural blockage inspired in the North, but it would be unfair to suppose that it summarises the position of all who disapproved of Lloyd-Jones' appointment to Bala. The main hindrance to his being welcomed in the North, and in some parts of the South, was theological rather than personal. Ministers of liberal beliefs, whose

[1] *Western Mail*, May 27, 1939.

main strength lay in the North, argued that Lloyd-Jones' success should not be attributed to his message, because, after all, were there not others preaching the same doctrines as he with very meagre results? On the other hand they knew that almost all the most influential pulpits in Britain, and certainly all the leading theological schools in the United Kingdom, had adopted the liberal form of Christianity with which Lloyd-Jones was so clearly unsympathetic. They saw his theology as a dangerous anachronism in an age when, as they believed, the credibility of Christianity depended on a far more flexible approach to Scripture. To insist, literally, on all biblical testimony, to accept the Old Testament as though it were as dependable as the New, or Paul's words as though they were equal with Christ's, was, in their opinion, reverting to the times when Thomas Charles and John Elias preached on the Green at Bala. It was treating modern 'biblical scholarship' as though it were non-existent and, to that extent, condemning no small part of the very work which the theological colleges existed to promote. In other words, they pitied the superficiality of the judgment of those who wanted Lloyd-Jones at Bala simply because he was an eminent Welshman and an eloquent preacher. Anyone who was familiar with the kind of speakers who came to the annual meetings of the Bala Theological College Union ought to know that the permanent introduction of Dr Lloyd-Jones would mean an influence intolerably different. Without question, although ministers did not care to debate it in public (for the masses of the people were still little acquainted with their leaders' change in belief), the principal cause of the failure of the nomination to Bala was doctrinal.

For those who only knew Dr Lloyd-Jones in his London ministry of later years it is difficult to conceive how the quietness and isolation of the little town of Bala, beside Lake Tegid and amidst the mountains of North Wales, could ever have satisfied him. Yet there was a side to his character which did respond, not to possible controversy at Bala, but to the life which such a situation might offer. 'Though some may not think it,' he was once heard to say, 'I am by nature a pacific person. . . . In some moods there is nothing I would more like to be than a mountain shepherd – above and away from it all, upon the silent slopes of the hills I love.'[1] It needs to be added that in all the controversy in Wales Dr Lloyd-Jones took no part at all.

[1] *Maintaining the Evangelical Faith Today*, 1952, p. 3.

Recalling her husband's state of mind as he faced his decision in 1939, Bethan Lloyd-Jones writes:

'It might seem to the looker-on, as though ML-J was waiting and biting his nails with anxiety, to see whether the North Wales Association would have him. Nothing could be further from the truth. His one desire at this time, as it was when leaving medicine, was that he should be in the will of God in this matter, and he was happy to wait until he had that certainty. I doubt if his feelings pulled one way or the other; the opportunities seemed quite limitless in either direction – to influence a great congregation or to influence the future leaders of many congregations. And so he could wait with a quiet mind.'

The successive decisions which he had to face in 1938–39 he faced alone in private. Amidst the carnality of some of the public debate it was no small encouragement to him that his wife believed as he did in the mystery of God's sovereign and overruling providence. And there were others who shared that conviction, among them the Reverend William Jones of Cardiff who wrote a letter which appeared in the correspondence columns of one of the South Wales newspapers protesting over those who thought they knew how to plan Dr Lloyd-Jones' career:

'They profess that every other minister in the denomination is "called" by God to a new charge. Why do they deny this to Dr Jones? "Man proposes, God disposes." Neither a chair at Bala College, nor the superintendency of the Forward Movement would suit this preacher of the Word; he would be a caged bird in either office.

'The removal of Dr Jones from Wales to England is no loss to the church universally. Methodism and Congregationalism count for nothing save in the councils of sectarians.'

The Welsh correspondent of *The British Weekly* took a similar view:

'The acceptance of the call to become co-pastor of Dr Campbell Morgan at Westminster settles, for the present, the career of Dr Martyn Lloyd-Jones in spite of great efforts to lure him back to his native land. One feels that a man of his calibre and spiritual vision could not fail to do the right thing for the Kingdom, whatever his decision might be.

'Wales is naturally disappointed to some extent, and yet we know that his love for Wales will still ensure us his services as often as he can render such, without sacrificing the claims of his historic church to his ministry. Neither church nor country can set boundaries to the ministry of such a man as he is'.

'Our dreadful weakness is religious. We are not declaring the Gospel with power to a dispirited and disillusioned age; we are not living in the discipline of Gospel fellowship; only in a very imperfect degree are our churches God's resting place and holy habitation. The depressing and alarming thing about our churches is not their tiny congregations, their shabby buildings, their social insignificance, their political impotence. If our churches are in peril it is not because they are less crowded than cinemas, less powerful than the promoters of dog-racing, less correct than the Sunday golf, less fashionable even than Romanism or Christian Science. If our churches are in peril, it is because they have forgotten what they are.'

> From a 'Fraternal Letter' by eight professors and ministers of the Congregational Union, published in *The British Weekly*, March 23, 1939

'There is the widespread indifference of today. Men do not challenge Christianity – they simply ignore it. This indifference to Christianity reveals itself in the neglect of the ordinances of religion – what our fathers called the means of grace.

'Speaking broadly, churches are not half-full; in some cases the congregation is a mere handful. Wales has been a church-going country, but a census taken in a town of 25,000 people revealed that not 5,000 darkened the door of a church. The truth is, this age of ours is infected by the secular temper and is in danger of lapsing into sheer paganism.'

> DR J. D. JONES
> speaking on 'the special difficulties of the present time' at the Annual Meetings of the Congregational Union, 1939.

18

The First Year's Work in England

The sight of Westminster Chapel looming ahead as one rounds the bend of one of the city's narrow streets – its tower rising above the surrounding roofs of apartment blocks, shops and houses – has hastened the steps of many generations of worshippers. Yet it may be doubted whether the external appearance of the building alone ever really contributed to that sense of attraction. Probably most people pass by – as Martyn Lloyd-Jones on his milk deliveries in 1915 – without its making any impression. The truth is that the Congregationalists who between 1863 and 1865 took down their former building and rebuilt, never had enough room on their site at the corner of Buckingham Gate and Castle Lane to give their Victorian 'cathedral' the setting which it needed. Even two centuries before the original Westminster Hospital had stood on that same corner, those historic streets and lanes were already crowded with buildings. The new church of 1865 was inevitably hemmed in. Nor had the fog and grime of seventy winters improved its appearance by the mid-1930's. John Harries, who published his biography *G. Campbell Morgan, The Man and His Ministry*, in 1930, mentions that despite these factors the building still held a certain magnetism for Dr Morgan. In his Prologue to that biography, speaking of his first sight of the building, he says, 'He was instantly enamoured of the dull red brick of the exterior – the grim, doughty character of the place.' In his case also, the exterior was not the real attraction.

From within, however, the tall, comparatively slender building supplies a different story. If its cavernous size reminded Dr Jowett of Charing Cross Station, few others would have thought of such a comparison. Given his possibly mistaken instructions that the church must hold 2,500 worshippers, the architect had designed it with two galleries – finely fronted with curved wrought iron and held in position by slender supporting pillars – and although both galleries, one above the other, almost entirely encircle the building, the mass of the congregation below are not overshadowed. Despite the woodwork of so many pews, the impression given is one of balance, height and light, the last named being conveyed from the circular windows beneath and between the galleries, or from the many clerestory ones which rise towards the high, moulded ceiling. From almost all the seats the central pulpit desk is clearly visible.

Campbell Morgan had set his mark on the building in more ways than one. Such was the enthusiasm of his reception on his first settlement in 1904 that he had even succeeded in obtaining the removal of the old pulpit – used by such figures as C. H. Spurgeon – and had replaced it by a large circular rostrum which was an ideal pulpit. But in a more important sense Campbell Morgan had influenced Westminster, and not least since his return in 1932. When he had been asked to join Dr Hubert Simpson in that year, it was not as associate minister: he would only be a pulpit supply 'co-operating' with Dr Simpson who remained the minister and who, as the Minutes of the Church Meeting record, asked him to preach 'for a period, or periods, amounting in the aggregate to six months in any one year'. It is clear that a number in the church membership never envisaged the man who had fulfilled his 'threescore years and ten' undertaking the ministerial office again at Westminster.

With Simpson gone, however, in 1934 a new situation arose and Morgan's future position was in doubt. Some, who considered that his pulpit supply for Sunday services should be terminated, moved a resolution in a church meeting of October 31, 1935, that the Deacons 'take the necessary steps forthwith to find a suitable man to fill the pulpit as Minister and Preacher.' An amendment to this resolution proposed that, in accordance with the requirements of the Trust Deed, another meeting be called 'for the purpose of considering a call to Dr. G. Campbell Morgan to the Ministerial office of the church'. This amendment was carried, with 171 for and 71 against. At an ensuing meeting on November 21,1935, when 311 members were present, 256 voted to extend a call to Dr Morgan.

Morgan did not accept at once. In the near-twenty years since he was last officially minister at Westminster Chapel there had been changes in the church and in himself. While the three ministers who had followed him – Jowett, Hutton and Simpson – were to varying degrees broadly evangelical, none of them had distinctly upheld the unique inspiration of the Scriptures. As a result, Westminster

Chapel, along with the general trend in Nonconformity, had become a congregation in which the Bible was less vitally believed and followed. Left to themselves, there would have been nothing to stop the majority in the congregation from calling any preacher who impressed them, irrespective of his position on Scripture. It was precisely in this area that Campbell Morgan's own belief had stiffened. A quarter-century of religious decline in the United Kingdom had caused him to see spiritual conditions which he had not dreamed of when he had gone to his first pastoral charge in Staffordshire in the far-off summer of 1889. The change, he was convinced, was connected with the popular error that Christianity could prosper amidst a variety of 'theories' on the inspiration of Scripture. Accordingly, when the offer of leadership at Westminster came to him again late in 1935, it was not so much his future ministry which concerned him – for that must necessarily be short – but rather the need to secure that the pulpit and church, by firm adherence to Scripture, would be committed to biblical Christianity.

Thus when Morgan, after five days' deliberation, did write his acceptance of the call on November 28, 1935, he was careful in his letter to the Members to indicate certain implications which he 'trusted were involved in the invitation' and which, he wrote, 'govern my acceptance of the same'. He continued:

'In 1904, when with my colleague Albert Swift, we came to Westminster, we came to make it a centre for Bible interpretation and application. . . . All its work from the beginning was based upon the belief in the full and final authority of the Bible in all matters of Faith and Practice. In that outlook upon our work we recognised the unity of the Church, and that the whole of its activities would be governed thereby.'

In his future ministry, Morgan went on to say, Westminster must be controlled by 'the authority of the Bible, not as amended by the thinking of man. . . . Other views of the Bible may be honestly held by perfectly sincere people, but these are those which must govern my own work, and that of any church over which I thus accept oversight.'[1]

---

[1] Here, and in earlier quotations in this chapter, I am quoting from the MS. Minutes of the Westminster Chapel Church Meetings. Morgan was making the same point in sermons of this period. In a sermon from Amos on 'Famine for the Word of God' he spoke of a change 'discoverable within organised

Morgan rightly sensed that the providence which had brought him back to Westminster was in order to settle the church's direction for years to come, and there is no doubt that even when Lloyd-Jones joined him as a 'pulpit supply' in September 1938 he was already convinced that this was the man for whom he had been enabled to prepare the way.

Some others among the older generation of Nonconformist leaders were definitely of the same opinion. Dr J. D. Jones, President of the Free Church Council in 1938, may have come to the conviction before Morgan: the two men were certainly close in friendship and in consultation. Also closely sympathetic was Dr S. W. Hughes, a prominent Baptist, who was the general secretary of the National Free Church Council. Being at Westminster Chapel the day that the news of Dr Lloyd-Jones' acceptance of the call to be Associate Minister was announced in 1939, Morgan asked Hughes to speak 'as representing the Free Churches of the land'. Hughes did so and referred to the 'spirit of general gratification' which this news was going to produce. This was an exaggeration, for time was to show that the real sympathies of the Nonconformist ministry already lay elsewhere. Men such as J. D. Jones, S. W. Hughes and Campbell Morgan himself were the rear-guard of a generation which was passing away.

The truth is that by 1938, with very few exceptions, the Free Church pulpits of central London were committed to views widely different from those of the newcomer to Westminster Chapel. That year, in fact, saw changes in several London pulpits. At near-by Westminster Central Hall, Dinsdale T. Young ended his evangelical ministry of fifty years. Dr A. D. Belden also concluded a ministry at Whitefield's Chapel, where he had preached a very different message from that of the eighteenth-century evangelist whose biography he had attempted to write.[1] Some years earlier, Belden, while on a preaching visit to Port Talbot for the Free Church Federal Council, had been keen to meet Lloyd-Jones who was ill with influenza at the time and confined to bed. Undeterred, Belden visited him and explained his plans for a new 'Holy Club', with men chosen

---

Church life. . . . The calf of Samaria is put up where God ought to be. Something mean, paltry, vanishing and destructive, is where God ought to be; and the result is that there is a famine of hearing the Word of the Lord' (*The Westminster Record*, August 1937).

[1] *George Whitefield – The Awakener*, 1930.

for membership from different parts of Britain, and the minister of Sandfields invited to be the Welsh representative. Lloyd-Jones declined to give Belden any response until he had read his biography of Whitefield. This was duly sent and when he discovered that Belden credited Whitefield with little understanding of theology and of the Bible – for the evangelist had been unfortunate to live before the age of Higher Criticism – he wrote to say that he 'was in entire agreement with Whitefield's theology'! If the new Holy Club ever began, it failed as dismally as did the originator's own ministry at Whitefield's Tabernacle.

The 1930's had brought a new generation of preachers to London, the last of whom, R. F. V. Scott at St. Columba's Church of Scotland, Pont Street, and W. E. Sangster at Westminster Central Hall, arrived almost simultaneously with Lloyd-Jones. Prominent pace-setters among these new men were Donald Soper at the Methodist Kingsway Hall and Leslie D. Weatherhead who, although a Methodist, was now minister of the historic Congregational cause, The City Temple. Unlike men of an older generation, who while rejecting the full inspiration of the Scriptures yet thought it the part of wisdom to say nothing on that subject from the pulpit, Soper[1] and Weatherhead were ready to speak plainly of the 'errors' of the Bible and to decry making the Bible the starting point for religious belief. People needed deliverance, they declared, from the narrowness of the old doctrines if 'Christianity' was to progress in modern times.[2] As though to illustrate in practical terms what this 'deliverance' would mean for the churches, the City Temple led the way in appointing a woman assistant minister in 1938.

[1] A relative of Mrs Lloyd-Jones, meeting Soper on one occasion in the U.S.A., asked him if he knew M.L.-J. He did, and after some kind and respectful remarks the Methodist leader concluded: 'He's right up his own street. Mind you, it isn't *my* street, but he's right up his *own* street'!
[2] 'The Bible,' Weatherhead claimed, 'was to be judged by the life and character of Christ Jesus', and yet not the biblical Christ, for he rejected both Christ's miracles and his atoning death. To speak of Christ's cleansing blood was 'repulsive sentiment and antiquated theology'. The breadth of Weatherhead's views is revealed in his words: 'To my mind we do not yet know what Christianity really is, for we have never adequately seen it in the perspective of the truth which other religions undoubtedly reveal. The Christianity we know now cannot be the final religion ... which will include the truth of every religion.'

David Martyn Lloyd-Jones

The church-life into which the Lloyd-Joneses came at Westminster Chapel requires some comment. Although in principle ruled by the church-meeting (according to Congregational church polity), the long-established custom gave the minister almost sole power of the church as long as he remained in office. In part this was due to Victorian conceptions of ministerial autocracy, which lingered far into the twentieth century, and yet it was also inevitable in large congregations where the church meeting was necessarily ineffective as a means of control and leadership. Although Campbell Morgan, in approaching Lloyd-Jones in 1938, had spoken of 'red-tape' within the Chapel, there was little of it to trammel him. For Morgan to propose a 'pulpit supply' or a colleague was virtually enough to make such an appointment highly probable.

By the use of deaconesses, and other workers, Westminster Chapel had long sought to reach the local population, and the poor in particular, and none had organised this more efficiently than Morgan and Swift before the First World War. Generally speaking, however, this outreach, hindered as it was by the absence of church members living in the Westminster area, seems to have contributed very little to the strength of the church. Far more significant in the life of the church was 'the Institute', introduced by Morgan in his early period to overcome problems associated with down-town churches. The Sunday School was only one department of the Institute, for once children left that age group they passed into Sunday-afternoon Bible classes. The Institute also catered for missionary and recreational interests. Its chief meeting, however, was intended to be 'the Friday Evening Bible School' which Morgan himself conducted weekly at 7.30 p.m. This Friday night was so much Morgan's brain-child that even after Lloyd-Jones became co-pastor in 1939 the older man continued it entirely by himself. One Sunday each year was appointed as an 'Institute Anniversary' and every issue of the Chapel's magazine, *The Westminster Record*, carried 'Sunday School and Institute Notes'.

Though the Institute was still continued in the late 1930's – the Friday night meeting being strongly attended – Campbell Morgan had come to doubt its value, and he was subsequently to tell his colleague that if he had his time over again he would never have started it. When Lloyd-Jones asked, 'Why?' the older man replied, 'Well, it produced a church within a church'. This was indeed true. Whereas the Sunday congregation usually filled the ground-floor and the first gallery – perhaps 1,500 or 1,800 people – as already noted, the number of members (311) present at the church meeting which re-called Morgan in 1935 was only a fraction of that congregation. Many people came to Westminster Chapel who had no actual church commitment and, except for the Friday nights, the Institute only catered for a relatively small proportion of those people.

Certainly the Lloyd-Joneses, after their experience at Aberavon, felt that there was little sense of unity in Westminster Chapel and little close spiritual fellowship among the people. Too much attention was given to organisations at the expense of spiritual life, the most striking omission of all from the weekly activities of the Church being a prayer meeting. Those who only knew Dr Lloyd-Jones at Westminster in later years could scarcely imagine him as chairman at a display of 'the gymnastic classes' but with such things he was to be occasionally involved in his first year at Westminster. Branches of the Girl Covenanters and the Boys' Brigade, also to be found at the Chapel, looked to him for aid, assuming that he – as everyone else – regarded their existence as vital.

*　　*　　*

As time was to prove, there was one miscalculation in Dr Lloyd-Jones' assessment of the situation outside Wales. He had supposed that mid-week religious services were so comparatively unusual that, were he to settle in England, invitations to such services would be far less frequent! His surmise proved wrong. Through unofficial reports of his sermons, his name was becoming well known in England, and after the Bournemouth Assembly of March 1938 the leaders of the Free Church Council were freely recommending him for inter-denominational services in different parts of the country. As a result he had a number of engagements settled for different parts of Britain even before his move to London in September 1938. The part-time nature of his work at Westminster – which, at that date, he only looked upon as temporary – also encouraged him to accept more engagements than he would otherwise have done.

The result was that, almost from the outset of his return to London, Dr Lloyd-Jones had quite as many mid-week engagements and often with longer distances to travel. During October 1938 the places in England where he preached included Eastbourne, Ilford, Kettering, Wellingborough (three nights for the Free Church Coun-

David Martyn Lloyd-Jones

cil), Willesden Green and Bromley, while in Wales, the same month, he was in Newcastle Emlyn, Neath, Llanelly, and Pencoed. Also in October he was the main speaker at the Annual Convention of the Newcastle-upon-Tyne and District Free Church Council in the north-east of England. These meetings began with a United service held in Newcastle City Hall on Sunday evening October 16. That night was his first memorable experience of the large gatherings – mainly from Methodist churches – which could be counted on to support evangelical Christianity in that part of England. The next day he preached at Brunswick Methodist church and in the evening at another great meeting in the City Hall. 'Dr Lloyd-Jones is a newcomer to Tyneside,' a reporter of the Convention noted in *The British Weekly*, 'but his fame has gone before him and his visit created an extraordinary amount of interest.'

For November 1938 his programme was similar[1] except that another country now came into his itinerary for the first time. It was a Welshman, G. Nantlais Williams, United Free minister of North Woodside church, Glasgow, who first introduced him to Scotland with an invitation to preach to his congregation for four week-nights, November 15–18, 1938. Prominence was given to this visit by one of Glasgow's most respected religious journalists, Alexander Gammie, in his columns in the *Evening Citizen* for November 12. Urging attendance at the North Woodside meetings, Gammie wrote of how he was personally looking forward to seeing and hearing 'this new figure in our religious life', and he went on to quote the words of Dr John Short written after the Free Church Council in Bournemouth.

The following Saturday, Gammie gave two columns to the 'mission' at North Woodside which he personally attended on the first night only. He was impressed, as was the crowd, which, he reports, gathered from all quarters and filled the church to overflowing 'some time before the hour of service'. Yet perhaps there was an element of hesitation in Gammie's tribute. Possibly the visitor was not all that he expected. He wrote:

'There was nothing clerical or ecclesiastical about him. In the jacket

---

[1] Two of his most important engagements in November were at the Central Hall Mid-day Service in Manchester, when his subject, 'The Nature of the Christian church' (1 Cor. 12:27), was one to which he was often to return, and three nights for the Free Church Council in Llandudno.

suit which he wore in the pulpit, Dr Jones still looked like what we would have expected him to be in his consulting room. He made no immediate impression by anything arresting or dominating about his personality. But one liked the quiet, modest way in which he bore himself in the earlier part of the service. He seldom even glanced at the congregation, but seemed held as in some air of absorption. There was nothing striking about his reading of the Scripture Lesson, and his prayer, while certainly very comprehensive, seemed long for such an occasion.

'It was in the sermon that the man stood fully revealed. After a little time – but it took him a little time – he began to get his grip on his hearers. I am not to attempt any analysis of the sermon itself. It was on a familiar text on which I have heard many preachers. Dr Jones may have shed no fresh light on the passage by way of exposition. There may have been nothing strikingly original in what he said. But he took his own way in handling it with great effect. He made it alive with new meaning, and drove home the practical application with impressive power.

'A prominent layman remarked to me afterwards that what specially impressed him was that Dr Jones was free from the conventional attitude and outlook and mode of expression of the average minister. Can this be accounted for by the fact that he had been trained elsewhere than in the Divinity Halls, and is all the more able to think and speak on spiritual things in a way which appeals to the people?

'But let this not be misunderstood. He never says anything outré; there is not a trace of sentimentality or sensationalism in his preaching. He works out his theme logically and consecutively, quite in the Scottish tradition, proceeding from point to point until his case is complete. His sermon on Tuesday lasted 40 minutes – a proof that he does not feed his hearers on snippets. He does not adopt the methods of the professional evangelist, but is content to proclaim his message without calling for immediate public professions of faith or attempting any counting of converts.'

After Glasgow, Dr Lloyd-Jones went on to spend a first week-end in Edinburgh, preaching on the Sunday at the Congregational Church in Leith. One of his hearers was a leader in the committee of the 'Edinburgh Recall to Religion Campaign' and this committee promptly urged Dr Lloyd-Jones to return to the Scottish capital the following Spring to take a week's united mission in the city's largest auditorium, the Usher Hall. This he agreed to do, provided that the Sunday meetings at the start and close of the proposed week were taken by other speakers. As it happened, the Sunday on which the Mission began, April 23, 1939, was the day when Dr Lloyd-Jones' permanent settlement was announced at Westminster. Early next morning he travelled to Scotland again for what was to prove perhaps the most important series of evangelistic services which he had yet taken. The Edinburgh press reported that after the first two nights the Usher Hall was filled to capacity: 'The general impression of his address was that nothing weightier or more impressive, spiritually as well as intellectually, had been heard in Edinburgh for a long time.' The same paper also drew attention to the interest which the University's medical fraternity showed in the meetings. The President of the College of Surgeons presided at the Monday evening meeting, and, at a special students' meeting, which crowded the Pollock Memorial Hall on the Tuesday afternoon, the chair was taken by Professor John Fraser. No record of the spiritual results of this week was attempted, but one individual who first spoke to the preacher thirty-five years later must have been a representative of others. He sought out Dr Lloyd-Jones during a visit to Edinburgh in 1974 to tell him that he had gone to the Usher Hall meetings of 1939 as 'a self-satisfied, self-righteous, elder in the Church of Scotland, and there God had met with him'.[1]

In London itself Dr Lloyd-Jones was now faced in a new way with his relationship to the inter-denominational evangelical movements which were under no church control. All these organisations had their headquarters in the capital and a number of them soon invited him to speak at meetings. He did not hide the difficulties he experienced in giving them his enthusiastic support. At a joint meeting of leaders of the Inter-Varsity Fellowship and the boys' and girls' branches of the Crusaders' Union, held at Syon House, he began his address – half seriously – by saying: 'I have been trying to find your organisations in the Bible, but you are not to be found in the New Testament. I did find you, however, in the Old – in the Book of Judges, chapter 17, verse 6, "In those days there was no king in Israel, but every man did that which was right in his own eyes"!'

[1] The present writer happened to be present on that occasion in 1974 and heard Dr Lloyd-Jones' comment, 'It was worth coming from London just to hear the testimony of that man.'

The First Year's Work in England

Due to the persistence of Dr Douglas Johnson, its General Secretary, Dr Lloyd-Jones had reconsidered his relationship to the Inter-Varsity Fellowship, for whom he had not spoken since the Swanwick Conference of 1935. Though still troubled at the poverty of doctrinal understanding within English evangelicalism, he came to see that, given the I.V.F.'s adherence to Scripture as the inerrant Word of God, he owed it his support. Another fact also impressed him. Since 1935 I.V.F. had noticeably strengthened its international links, particularly with Scotland and Holland. Such Free Church of Scotland figures as Professor Donald Maclean, first known to Lloyd-Jones through the pages of *The Evangelical Quarterly*, were now speaking for Inter-Varsity and contributing the same kind of deepening influence as was also coming from the new ties with the Calvinist Student Movement of Holland. Dr Lloyd-Jones began to believe that he would not be a lone voice in I.V.F. and that there was a real possibility of a broader restoration of stronger, God-centred convictions.

Accordingly he had agreed to speak at the Annual Meeting of I.V.F. held in the Great Hall of University College, London, in September 1938, shortly after his arrival in the capital. It was an engagement which, through no fault of his own, he was unable to fulfil. By that date fears of war were widespread. In the churches a 'Gas Mask Sunday' had alerted the population to the necessity of acquiring gas masks at once. But it happened that the I.V.F.'s Annual Meeting was held on the same day that Neville Chamberlain, the Prime Minister, had arrived back from his talks with Hitler in Munich. The scrap of paper which Chamberlain flourished triumphantly on his return, exclaiming, 'I believe it is peace for our time', produced such excitement and relief in central London that all traffic was forced to a halt. After a fruitless hour or more in a taxi, Dr Lloyd-Jones abandoned his attempt to get from Vincent Square, Westminster, to University College.

Four months later there was not the same euphoria in the air when he preached at a New Year United Meeting, held at the Mansion House on January 2, 1939, as part of the Universal Week of Prayer of the World's Evangelical Alliance. 'I think 1939 will be a more tranquil year than 1938,' Chamberlain professed. Not all who met that week to pray shared his confidence.

Week by week during this period Westminster Chapel remained Dr Lloyd-Jones' first commitment. In September 1938 he had taken the Sunday evening services,[1] changing to the mornings in October, and thereafter the two co-pastors continued to alternate every month. Campbell Morgan and Lloyd-Jones were so different that the harmony of their association was notable. Curiously, Morgan had spent most of his own childhood in the Roath District of Cardiff, but he was born in England and in temperament and outlook he owed far more to that country than to Wales. It was not Welshness which drew the two men together. Nor was it a common theology. Morgan, while evangelical in his loyalty to the Bible had little precise doctrinal structure to his thinking which was Arminian in its affinities. The older man could not miss the difference in Lloyd-Jones' position, and yet if this had caused him to hesitate before issuing the invitation to Westminster, it had been overcome by his certainty that Lloyd-Jones' preaching strikingly fulfilled the three pre-requisites of truth, clarity and passion which he had always regarded as the essentials of real preaching.[2] Above all else, Morgan was a preacher and he was willing to overlook much in a man who shared his own vision of what preaching ought to be.

This is not to say that the style and form of their sermons was similar, for the differences were not inconsiderable. Morgan's preoccupation was with the explanation of the meaning of verses of Scripture; the words and their exegesis were his chief interest. His associate, however, while making the technical explanation the starting point, was intent upon the need to formulate doctrinal principles which he would then unfold in practical terms and in relation to the needs of his hearers.

One of the younger members of Westminster Chapel at this date, Geoffrey T. Thomas, recalls the difference between the two men. He was fourteen when Lloyd-Jones first visited the Chapel to preach in December 1935. The preceding Sunday Morgan had told the congregation, 'Dr Lloyd-Jones' message is vital' and they must be sure to be there. Of that first Sunday, and of their subsequent ministry together, Thomas writes:

'I strongly recollect a man of slight stature, pale face, fine forehead and ascetic appearance. He wore a black gown but no academic hood. . . . I distinctly remember the packed congregation and my

[1] His texts on these four Sunday nights were: Matthew 21:28-32; John 3:19; Mark 5:17-18a; Genesis 26:17-18.
[2] Morgan's views are well presented in his volume, *Preaching*, 1937.

father – himself a Chelsea Physician – pointing out to my mother and myself distinguished members of the medical profession whom he recognised . . . I had never heard a preacher so intense, so serious, so terribly in earnest. Not until I met him personally some years later did I realise how calm he was outside the pulpit.

'Dr Campbell Morgan and Dr Lloyd-Jones became good colleagues; each complemented the other in pulpit style. Morgan gave close exegesis, close exposition, and then became imaginative – as Dr Sydney Berry once said, "like an aeroplane proceeding along the runway, then taking off and you see the glint of the sun on the wings". Lloyd-Jones was more doctrinal and applied the message more vigorously. Both worked very well together and admired each other's gifts despite their different styles. In language Morgan was briefer and more beautiful. Lloyd-Jones was discursive and unconcerned about the actual vocabulary of his sentences though he had a great gift of words.'

It is certainly true that Dr Lloyd-Jones was uninterested in the 'literary' form of sermons. He did not prepare in order to print, which was almost certainly a reason why, even when he was formally associate minister, Morgan provided more for *The Westminster Record*. Dr Lloyd-Jones considered the preparation of sermons for the press a very different thing from preparation for the pulpit and it never appealed to him. Nor did he use sermon titles. The great majority of his sermons printed in a number of Christian papers at this period were little more than notes of a hearer with a title invented by an editor.

Had Morgan been a lesser man he might have moderated his generous esteem and praise for his colleague, thirty-six years his junior, when the younger man's sermons at Westminster received the degree of newspaper attention which they attracted in 1938–39. One reporter, under the heading 'A New Pulpit Power' described at length a visit which he made to the Chapel in December 1938, and in the manner of other writers already quoted, explored 'the secret of his popularity'. A brief quotation will suffice:

'It was a bitterly cold Sunday morning. The very wind seemed to carry the tidings of snow on the mountains and moorlands of the North country. Central London appeared deserted. "Thin congregations in all the churches this morning," I said to my wife. But when I reached Westminster Chapel there was a stream of people going in, and by the time the service commenced there was a surprisingly large number present.

'Dr Martyn Lloyd-Jones has undoubtedly risen to the front rank of "popular" preachers. . . . He does not preach to the sinners who are not present, but to those in the pews before him. He has the wooing note – but one can also hear the rumble of the distant thunder of the Judgment Day. The divine imperative is in his message: he will, if I mistake not, go far.'[1]

Winter had turned to Spring by the time Alexander Gammie came down from Glasgow and wrote a lengthy account of the new preacher at Westminster Chapel:

'Easter in London is very different from Easter in Glasgow. This year it has been different even in the matter of weather. After a spell of varied and unsatisfactory conditions there came a welcome change on Good Friday, and over the week-end there was bright sunshine with a real warmth in the atmosphere that was sometimes more like summer than spring.

'On Good Friday, as on Christmas Day, London is at its quietest. Business is entirely suspended, all the shops are closed, and the streets are more deserted than on an average Sunday. The churches are open everywhere. Glasgow and Scotland as a whole are still far behind London and England in the religious observance of Easter.

'On Saturday the Sabbatic calm of the Friday still continued. London Bridge is said to be the busiest bridge in London, but when I crossed it on Saturday afternoon there was scarcely any traffic at all and the policemen on point duty were for the time being among the unemployed.

'On scanning the church service announcements for Easter Sunday, I decided to go to Westminster Chapel where the preacher was to be Dr D. Martyn Lloyd-Jones, who made so great an impression on the occasion of his week's visit to Glasgow some months ago.

'The attendance on Sunday forenoon was remarkably good in view of the fact that so many of the regular congregation must have been out of town. The whole of the area was practically filled – and it is not easily filled, for Westminster Chapel is a vast building – while

---

[1] Kenneth Woodfleet in *The Christian World*, December 29, 1938.

the first gallery was very largely occupied. The choir, however, was mostly conspicuous by its absence, only five ladies putting in an appearance.

'Dr Lloyd-Jones might still be a medical man as far as appearance and dress are concerned. He wears a pulpit gown but it is his only concession to clerical custom. With the exception of making the intimations, which are always in the hands of Mr A. E. Marsh, the well-known secretary, he conducted the entire service. Everything was quietly, reverently done, but there was nothing particularly striking or impressive until the time came for the sermon. Then Dr Lloyd-Jones seemed to throw off his reserve and to become vibrant in every fibre of his being. His delivery was marked by a freedom, a vigour, and an impassioned eloquence such as he never displayed on his Glasgow visit.[1]

'His sermon was based on the text, "Remember that Jesus Christ of the seed of David was raised from the dead according to my gospel" (2 Tim. 2:8). Even the reiteration of these words held his hearers. They must have burned themselves into the memories and hearts of every worshipper as they were presented and repeated from one angle after another. It was a closely-reasoned discourse without a single illustration except from the Bible. But I never heard the Easter message more powerfully or more effectively proclaimed.

'I do not think the word crisis was ever used; there was certainly no reference to the international situation, and yet everything he said was intensely applicable to the problems facing us in these days. The preacher proclaimed the eternal and unchallengeable supremacy of the risen Christ. He sounded a note of triumph over all the forces of evil, and in the closing hymn, "Rejoice! The Lord is King", the feelings of the worshippers found vent.

'Although it was in no sense a topical sermon, and, as I have said, there was no direct reference to present-day affairs, one found, in mixing with the people as the congregation dispersed, how many of them were making the application themselves. "That's the kind of thing we need to hear today"; "How this would have heartened Mr Chamberlain, who carries so heavy a burden of care"; "I feel better after hearing that and fitter to face life in days of war and rumours of war" – these were among the grateful expressions of deeply moved

[1] Perhaps Gammie was forgetting that he had only been present for one of the four services in Glasgow!

hearers. It made one feel anew that preaching is still worth-while when preachers are alive to the opportunity and the responsibility of their calling.'¹

Not to be outdone by Scotland, leading London papers now took up the same subject. A correspondent for the *Evening Standard*, April 24, 1939, headed his column, 'Harley-street Man Draws Thousands to His Church', and the next Sunday *The People* diverged from its usually different content to provide a 'special' article on the man who, they announced, 'Left Riches and Fame to Become Poor Pastor'. Despite the celebrity of their papers neither reporter had managed to secure an interview with the preacher, though the *Evening Standard* writer was able to quote one personal sentence: '"Why did you give up medicine for preaching?" I asked him. He looked at me searchingly, and, after a second's hesitation, replied: "Because I became more interested in people than in their diseases."' Of the service itself the same reporter wrote:

'I went to discover why people travel from distant towns and suburbs to hear this man; how this chapel attracts thousands. . . .

'The service is simple and severe. There is no choir even. The appeal is that of Dr Jones.

'One gets a hint of his secret and power in his eyes and in his pulpit demeanour. He hardly moves at all. His eyes do not rove all over his congregation. He looks straight ahead. He gives the impression of a man who moves in a world of his own.

'The Scripture reading gave one the feeling that he was reading from a current book.

'His sermon was on the text, "God is our refuge and strength, a very present help in trouble. Therefore will we not fear, though the earth do change. . . ." He treated it symbolically as a description of the reaction of the Christian to the challenge and confusion of our time.'

May 1939 brought the annual meetings of the Congregational Union of England and Wales in London, with evening gatherings in the large City Temple and daily business meetings held in Memorial Hall. One special morning service was also held in the City Temple for the reception of ministers into the Union and, as the *Western Mail*

¹ *The Evening Citizen*, Glasgow, April 15, 1939.

reported, 'there was a good deal of interest' as to whether Dr Lloyd-Jones would be found among that number. 'Dr Lloyd-Jones was not at the morning meeting, and his name was not mentioned. Afterwards one of the leaders explained that there was no need to expedite the admission of Dr. Lloyd-Jones to the Union. That formality could be carried through at any time when he himself decided to ask for it.'[1] But he never did so formally, and his name was thereafter to remain on the roll of the Calvinistic Methodist Association.

Apart from an address by Dr J. D. Jones on the completion of his fifty years in the Congregational ministry, the business of the Annual Assembly was largely occupied with the usual denominational machinery, together with questions considered relevant to the hour–the Military Training Bill, Reunion among the Denominations, Education, Temperance, Unemployment and kindred concerns. It is improbable that Dr Lloyd-Jones was present to share in them. His one duty during the Meetings was to be the chief speaker on behalf of the Colonial Missionary Society which filled the City Temple for Thursday evening, May 11. Since the end of the eighteenth century, missionary sermons had been a high-point of the Nonconformist May gatherings. William Jay, Matthew Wilkes, John Angell James, C. H. Spurgeon and many other leading preachers urged missionary endeavour forward on such occasions. In contrast with the subjects occupying the earlier meetings of the day, and in even greater contrast with the messages normally delivered from the City Temple pulpit every Sunday, Dr Lloyd-Jones presented and applied the implications of the Apostolic gospel from 1 Corinthians 9:22, 'I am made all things to all men, that I might by all means save some.' Christianity has a unique message and objective:

'It is to "gain" men, to "save" men. St Paul went out and travelled day and night across continents and seas, and laboured without ceasing, for that reason and that reason only. Men had become lost, they had become slaves of darkness and of sin, they were alienated from God, rebels against Him and His law, and therefore under condemnation and under wrath. Their position was desperate, though they did not realise it. They must be roused, they must be warned, they must be brought to repentance; and what is still more important, they must be shown the one and only way to escape, which was to be found in Jesus Christ and Him crucified. Here was a

[1] *Western Mail*, May 10, 1939.

David Martyn Lloyd-Jones

message from God Himself, offering pardon and forgiveness and a new life in Christ. Men must be saved from the dominion of Satan and translated into the Kingdom of the Son of God.'

Whatever some thought of 'the Colonial Sermon' there could be no doubt concerning the interest which it aroused. Nor could any critic dismiss the speaker as a mere advocate for one of the religious parties observable on the British scene. While his opposition to those who 'tampered' with the 'deposit of truth' was evident, he was equally critical of the man 'who is so conscious of his own orthodoxy, and so proud of it, that he becomes a stumbling block to his weaker brother, and altogether forgets the lost souls that are round about him.' The *Christian World* published the sermon in full two weeks later.[1]

The British Weekly commented:

'Dr Lloyd-Jones delivered a remarkably effective missionary sermon. He treated his subject under three heads: The missionary objective, the missionary method, the missionary passion; and we carried away the impression that a preacher of unusual power has arisen in our midst.'

Not surprisingly after such a year, by the summer of 1939 Dr Lloyd-Jones was as tired as he had been twelve months before, and was glad to be able to turn to his old chief, Lord Horder, for advice on his health. His last Sunday in Westminster Chapel pulpit before the summer vacation was on June 25. This was followed by an International Conference of Evangelical Students, convened by I.V.F. at Cambridge from June 27 to July 3 at which he was to play a prominent part. The same year he had been elected to the presidency of the I.V.F. – a post normally held for twelve months – for the first time.

Three previous international conferences had been held by Inter-Varsity in Europe, but this, attended by nearly 800 students, and requiring the use of six Cambridge Colleges, was the first in Britain and was a major development. Norway alone provided over 200 delegates and others came from as far afield as China, Japan, India and Africa. Speakers included O. Hallesby from Norway, Daniel Lamont from New College, Edinburgh, Clarence Bouma from Grand Rapids and F. W. Grosheide from Holland.

[1] *The Christian World Pulpit*, published as an inset to *The Christian World*, May 25, 1939.

To these students, gathered from twenty-one countries, Lloyd-Jones spoke three times, giving an address based on Hosea 14:2, another on 'Christ our Sanctification' from 1 Corinthians 1:30, and finally an evangelistic sermon, 'The One Essential'. It was probably the second of these, on sanctification, delivered in the large Examination Hall on the morning of Friday June 30, which was most influential and certainly the longest to be remembered in its published form.[1] In addition to a closely-knit statement of the biblical teaching of sanctification, the address contained a polemic against 'the victorious life' teaching of the holiness movements, a teaching which so many of his hearers until that moment had equated with evangelical orthodoxy. What was involved, he demonstrated, was not only the meaning of sanctification but the whole definition of what it means to be a Christian. There were not a few startled and thoughtful hearers who for the first time heard such assertions as the following:

'You cannot receive Christ as your justification only, and then, later, decide to refuse or to accept Him as your sanctification. He is one and indivisible, and if you receive Him at all, at once He is made unto you "wisdom and righteousness and sanctification and redemption." You cannot receive Him as your Saviour only, and later decide to accept or refuse Him as your Lord; for the Saviour is the Lord who by His death has bought us and therefore owns us. Sanctification is nowhere taught or offered in the New Testament as some additional experience possible to the believer. It is represented rather as something which is already within the believer, something which he must realise more and more and in which he must grow increasingly.'

The Cambridge Conference was Lloyd-Jones' first introduction to work among international students. Daniel Lamont, reporting the occasion for *The British Weekly*, wrote of Lloyd-Jones speaking 'with his customary insight and power' and, despite the interference of world upheaval which was so soon to follow, comment later received from various lands indicated that Lamont's sense of the significance of the conference was correct: 'Here was an assembly of young people, prospective leaders of the thought and life of many lands, many of them already pledged to witness for Christ among

---

[1] It first appeared along with other conference addresses in *Christ Our Freedom*, I.V.F., 1939, and in booklet form from 1948 onwards.

their fellows and all of them eager for more knowledge in the deep things of life and more power to help to rescue the world from its present sorrowful plight.'

After Cambridge Dr Lloyd-Jones was more than ready for nearly two months' break – mostly for holiday and the usual reading – in Wales. On August 31, vacation over, he was in Llanelly for a preaching engagement (with Mrs Lloyd-Jones and Ann) when the radio, speaking of the imminent possibility of War, announced plans for the evacuation of children from London and other major cities, commencing the following day. It was hard to believe. The same day he closed a letter to his mother in Cardiganshire – she had Elizabeth with her – 'I am still hopeful about the general position'.

Nonetheless, Dr Lloyd-Jones took the precaution of leaving the family in South Wales, and went back alone to London for Sunday, September 3; he was expecting to preach at Westminster in the evening. By that hour, however, Britain was already at War. At eleven o'clock that same morning Campbell Morgan had climbed the pulpit stairs to announce that owing to the fear of immediate enemy bombing all services for the day were cancelled. So also was the formal public service of Induction planned for Dr Lloyd-Jones as co-Pastor with Campbell Morgan for the following evening, September 4. Unregretted by Dr Lloyd-Jones, it was never to take place.

John A. Hutton who, with Eliseus Howells, was to have shared the speaking on the occasion, gave his readers in *The British Weekly* what he had intended to say to the new minister at Westminster Chapel. He began with his own testimony to the help of God which he had known in that pulpit:

'When my dear and almost life-long friend, Campbell Morgan, first invited me to take his place here, I hesitatingly consented. The date was Sunday, July 10, 1916. On the Friday, less than 48 hours earlier, I stood on a shivered universe. We had had a telegram from the War Office that our eldest son had been killed on a ridge at Thiepval in the Somme. I decided to wire Mr Marsh, excusing myself. Preaching seemed impossible; preaching also seemed a preposterous proceeding; as St Paul declared, it frequently seems to be sheer foolishness.

'The wire, however, which should have excused me from such a trial was never sent. We set out from Scotland. The journey seemed to be a thousand miles. It was a lovely Sunday morning. I knew later that loving hands were supporting me. But I had not whispered or muttered or mumbled "Let us Worship God!" when my secret issue of blood was staunched at its source and the tide became spirit and power.

'You are a doctor of medicine. You have had the training and must always have had the aptitude to see the *essential*, the *vital*, the *threatening* thing, or the thing *threatened* in the human system. It is this faculty which has made so many doctors supreme in their knowledge of the soul – from St Luke, the beloved physician, to Sir Thomas Browne, to come no nearer to our day.

'I congratulate you on coming at the height of your natural powers, to this great and demanding opportunity. I envy you your prospects, God willing, of a long career. You come at a time when the world needs thinking, responsible men, humble and diffident indeed in view of their own poor wisdom and the present hazardousness, but strong and confident, knowing Him in whom they have believed. We who know the Bible and accept it, are prepared for anything.'

That confidence was to be tested at its foundations in the years of trial immediately ahead. The next time the thirty-nine-year-old co-Pastor entered the pulpit, on Sunday evening, September 10, 1939, there was only one text from which he could preach,

'For here we have no continuing city, but we seek one to come' (Heb. 13:14).

He would have preached it no less urgently had he known that for himself another forty years of ministry lay ahead.

Appendix

In Memoriam – A Tribute to Henry Lloyd-Jones[1]

By Ieuan Phillips

It was with very heavy hearts that London Welshmen gathered together on Paddington Station that Monday evening, to bid farewell to one, who, although he had not lived amongst us very long, had endeared himself to all who had the privilege of knowing him.

Mr Lloyd-Jones was an exceptional man in every way. One could not see him in a crowd without making enquiries as to his identity. Well-built of medium height, he carried himself like a young man, and his face gave indications of the nature of his inner character.

There is some trait predominant in every man, and whatever that may be – whether noble, indifferent or actually base – this trait will colour and influence his every thought and action. The predominating trait in Mr Lloyd-Jones' character was his true gentleness of spirit, and from this sprang the many other traits which so endeared him to us. Many men have, by keen observation and continual contact with gentlefolk, acquired a certain polish which passes in the world for gentlemanliness – but at best this is but a feeble veneer which knows nothing of the gentle heart – here one found a true spring of love and consideration for his fellow-man welling from the heart. One heartily acquiesced in the title applied to him by a friend, 'One of nature's gentlemen.'

How this spring gushed could be related by many secret hearts. No one defeated by the buffets of the storms of life ever appealed to him in vain – indeed his gentle spirit was many times imposed upon and his generosity abused.

[1] From *Y Gorlan*, the magazine of Charing Cross Road Chapel, London, October 1922.

David Martyn Lloyd-Jones

He himself had seen more of the bitter side of life than falls to the lot of most men, and when the storms of adversity and sorrow occasionally eased a little, his thoughts and practical sympathy were ever with those who had failed to find the haven. Many instances of his kindness could be enumerated, but lack of space forbids – their record is sure with Him who saw the widow's action.

You might meet Mr Lloyd-Jones in many places, and he always proved an interesting and entertaining companion. He was well informed on many aspects of life, and an inimitable raconteur, but one never really knew him unless one had seen and heard him in his favourite chair on his own hearth – there you got his very best, as many of us young Welsh people know.

He had elderly friends – lifelong friends and newly-made ones – but I think that the ones he really loved to have about him were the young ones. He was young to the end, and his sympathy with our aspirations, and his concern as to the progress of our careers, never failed. He had the heart of a child, and his power of enjoying gentle and innocent fun at our expense was keen and deep. He had reduced the process of gentle teasing to a fine art, but his darts never hurt and his victim could never fail to laugh with him if his heart was in the right place. There was no room in his circle for the braggart or the snob, these did not usually come a second time.

He carried Wales in his heart, and for that reason you entered Wales as soon as you crossed the threshold of his home. The Welsh tongue, the Welsh spirit and Welsh hospitality greeted you like a breeze from the hills, and amid tale, debate and joke how many pleasant hours have passed there!

As a teller of tales of the Welsh hills and villages I have never met his master. There is the born story-teller and the imitator. I have many times tried to reproduce some of Mr Lloyd-Jones' stories, and I am very conscious of the distinction, but it was not in the raconteur that you discovered the real Mr Lloyd-Jones, for he lost his own identity as he threw himself heart and soul into the departed worthy he was depicting.

It was as a citizen – in the widest sense of the word – that he revealed the depths of his character. A liberal of the old school for a lifetime, he had fought and suffered for his political conscience. He had taken part in the tithe war (*Rhyfel y Degwm*), and Oh! that now I could recall his vivid accounts of those stirring times! Who can forget the leonine aspect of his face and the flash of his eye as he defended some cherished principle or personality against some modern iconoclast?

He was at his very best in a political argument. I have often witnessed the defeat at his hands of wary and experienced political debaters, and I attribute this entirely to his tremendous grip of first principles together with his own innate gentleness, which made him keenly sensitive to anything that savoured of injustice.

I often heard him mention with regret that he never had the advantages which he would have wished in early life, and I am driven to ask myself whether we, the product of the Secondary Schools and Colleges, have after all so rich an equipment for the battle of life as our fathers. These quiet heroes having to cut and hew and build from the raw material of life a creed and a policy for themselves, gained amazing power through the exercise of some spiritual muscles, which in us have atrophied, because we are never forced to use them. We are spoon-fed, and our moral fibre is weaker.

Such men as Mr Lloyd-Jones are rare, and in his passing our loss is great, and we can but dimly and inadequately realise the loss in his own home. We can but extend our tenderest sympathy to Mrs Lloyd-Jones, Dr Martyn Lloyd-Jones, and Mr Vincent Lloyd-Jones, B.A., and pray that they may be given strength and comfort by Him who calls himself *Barnwr y weddw a Thad yr amddifad.*[1]

---

[1] A Judge of the widows and a Father of the fatherless (Psa. 68:5).

Index

Aberavon (Calvinistic Methodist
   Mission Church) 110, 281
   (Calvinistic Methodist Welsh-
   speaking Church) 157–8
   D. M. Lloyd-Jones becomes
   pastor 113 *et seq*
   its church life 157 *et seq.*, 229 *et
   seq.*
   its manse 153 *et seq.*, 280–1
   sermons in 135–43, 144–5
   conversions in 209 *et seq.*
   Brotherhood 134–5, 231–4
   church finance 264–5
   links with inter-denominational
   Societies 292
   D. M. Lloyd-Jones resigns
   pastorate 337
Aberdare 183
Abergavenny 9, 183
Aberkenfig 183
Abermeurig 10
Abernethy, John 43, 51
Aberystwyth 16, 44, 183, 184, 186,
   290
   Calvinistic Methodist Theological
   College 85, 107, 149, 168, 189,
   335, 348
Albert Hall *see* London
Aldis, W. H. 295
America *see* North America
Ammanford 183
Anglesey 249
Anxious Inquirer Directed, The
   (James) 166
Arminian Theology 295, 368
Arnold, Matthew 20, 132
Ashford Chace 54

Asquith, Herbert H. 31, 38, 39, 46,
   47, 48
Atherstone 321
Augustine 206, 284
Aylesbury 147

Bala (Calvinistic Methodist
   Theological College) 167, 168,
   288, 335, 346, 348, 349, 351
Baldwin, Stanley 278
Bampton Lectures 254
Band of Hope 166
Baptists (in Wales) 180, 192
Barry 183
Barth, Karl 191, 291
Bart's *see* St Bartholomew's
   Hospital
Baxter, Richard 97, 99, 100, 155,
   156
B.B.C. (Welsh): broadcast addresses
   314–15
Beaverbrook, Lord 63
Beddow, Morgan 213–14, 235–6,
   244
Belden, A. D. 360–1
Berry, Sidney M. 369
Bethany (Wales) 183
Bethlehem Forward Movement 109,
   115, 116–17, 126
Bevan, Aneurin 307, 324
Bible, The, its authority and
   inspiration 147–8, 293, 301,
   359, 367
Bible Testimony Fellowship 301
Birchill 26
Blackwood 183

[383]

Blaenavon 183, 200
Boer War (2nd) 1, 33
Bonar, Andrew 62
Booth, William (Genl.) 204
Borth 197
Bouma, Clarence 374
Bournemouth 333, 336, 363, 364
Brainerd, David 289
Brandon, Miss 35
Brecon 183, 191
Brethren *see* Plymouth Brethren
Bridgend 172, 181, 183, 189, 191,
    199, 220, 266, 318, 348
British Weekly 89 *et seq.*, 96, 97
Bristol 293
Briton Ferry 183, 235
Bromley 364
Brongest 77
Browne, Thomas (Sir) 377
Browning, Robert 132
Bruce, Robert 95
Brunner, Emil 254, 291
Bryn 211
Brynamman 183, 191
Brynmawr 319
Buchman, Frank 289, 290
Buffalo 275
Bunyan, John 97, 98, 99
Burke, Edmund 59
Burns, J. Golder 333
Bwlch 9
Bwlchyllan 10

Cadifor (Prince) 4
Caernarfon (& Boroughs) 2
Caerphilly 183
Calvin, John 189, 190, 206, 234,
    291
Calvinism 329
Calvinistic Methodism *see*
    Methodism, Calvinistic
Cambridge 293, 374, 375
Campbell, R. J. 4
Canada 28, 29, 268 *et seq.*
Capel Gwynfil 2
Capper, W. Melville 293, 294
Cardi, The 11

Cardiff 1, 26, 77, 106, 118, 138,
    183, 184, 199, 253, 287, 292,
    298, 303, 308, 309, 317, 318,
    368
Cardiganshire, farmers of 70
Carlyle, Thomas 55
Carmarthen 187, 251
Carmel Chapel, Aberavon 157, 180,
    183, 258
Carson, Edward (Sir) 38, 39, 46
Cefn-Ceirw 2
Chadwick, Samuel 148
Chamberlain, Neville 367, 371
Charles, Thomas 352
Chester 348, 349
Chilvers, H. Tydeman 304
Chautauqua Institution 274–6
China Inland Mission 292, 293
Christian Commonwealth, The 4
Christian Directory, The (Baxter)
    156
Christian Science (cult) 151
Christian Sanity (Schofield) 161
Church History 231–2
Clow, W. M. 148
Clydach 290
Cole, F. W. 199
Colonial Missionary Society 373,
    374
Columbus (Ohio) 327, 328
Congregationalists (in Wales) 4,
    132, 180
Congregational Union 372–3
Conwil Elvet 350
Craig-las 308
Craven Arms 60
Crickhowell 178, 183
Cross Hands 183
Cruciality of the Cross, The
    (Forsyth) 191
Crusaders' Union 366
Crydd, Ianto 12n, 183
Cwmavon 183
Cwmbran 210
Cwmbwrla 183

Dale, R. W. 191
Dalton, A. E. 199

Index

Lloyd-Jones—*cont.*
Bethan (*wife*)—*cont.*
rejoicing over converts 287n
describes preaching in sheep-
farming area of Wales 322–4
birth of second daughter (Ann)
327
reflects on her husband's
Aberavon pastorate 340
moves with family to London
341–2
describes her husband's
understanding of guidance
344
reflects on the Bala-
Aberystwyth contention 353
Elizabeth (*daughter*) 170, 171,
172, 254, 269, 274, 275, 282,
329, 377
Ann (*daughter*) 327, 329, 376
DAVID MARTYN LLOYD-JONES:
born in Cardiff 1
parents move to Llangeitho
(Cards.) 1
'I'm a Welshman now!' 5
boyhood 6 *et seq.*
first visit to London 8
rescued from fire in home 16–
17
at Llangeitho School
at Tregaron County School 18,
21 *et seq.*
first hears open-air preaching
26
becomes communicant in
Calvinistic Methodist Church
(1914) 57, 169
influence of Calvinistic
Association Meetings 26, 27
family moves to London 32–3
helps in milk deliveries 33, 34
school examination results
(1914) 34
first visit to Westminster
Chapel 35, 36
views on war 37
prepares for London 'Matric'
38

passes London University
Senior School Examination 39
listens to debates in Parliament
38–9
his first sight of Bethan Phillips
46
joins Dr Tom Phillips' Sunday-
school class (1917) 46
accepts doctrine of
predestination 60
first public address 47
becomes Sunday-school
superintendent (1918) 57
his earliest surviving letter (July
1919) 49
awarded degrees of M.R.C.S.,
L.R.C.P., and M.B., B.S.
(1921) 50
begins to work under Sir
Thomas Horder 50
becomes Horder's Junior
House Physician (1921) 52
chief Clinical Assistant to
Horder (1923–4) 52
awarded Research Scholarship
in Medicine (1924) 52
engages in research on
endocarditis 52
becomes M.R.C.P. (1925) 54
a music lover 55
becomes deeply concerned
about his Christian
profession 57–8
gives address on 'The Signs of
the Times' 65–9
is attracted by J. A. Hutton's
ministry at Westminster
Chapel 61, 96
deeply impressed by the fact of
sin 61
his conversion 64, 78
addresses at Literary and
Debating Society 65–72
called to the ministry of the
Word of God 81 *et seq.*
preaches first sermon 84
considers entering Aberystwyth
Theological College 84

Index

Lloyd-Jones—*cont.*
DAVID MARTYN LLOYD-JONES—
cont.
studies Greek 82, 85
gives his first address in Wales
on 'The Problem of Modern
Wales' 86–92
an inner struggle: Medicine or
Ministry? 92–5
Sunday-school teaching at
Charing Cross Chapel 95
gives address on Puritanism
97–101
preaches first sermon in Wales
109
his first sermon at Aberavon
118–20
becomes pastor at Aberavon
(1926) 120, 125, 128–9
marriage to Bethan Phillips
(1927) 125, 126
specimens of sermons at
Aberavon 135–7, 137–9,
140–3, 144–6
his style of preaching 146–7,
148–50
sermon preparation 154–5
the question of ordination 167–
70
gives address at Tregaron
County School 174
a 'fisher of men' 176
ministry in Wales away from
Aberavon 179 *et seq.*
'Hyper-Calvinist or Quaker'
191
two firm and important
principles 195
revival at Aberavon 203 *et seq.*
evangelistic sermons 214 *et seq.*
the 'Church Family' at
Aberavon 229 *et seq.*
restoring the erring 242
a wide correspondence 244–6
preaching in North Wales 251–
3
'Farewell to Medicine' 257–8
difficult medical cases 258–63

gives up smoking 263–4
views on mental illness 265–7
first visit to North America
(1932) 269 *et seq.*
an a-millennialist 271
at Chautauqua Institution
(U.S.A.) 274–6
'This Chrysostom man' 276
a new Aberavon manse 281–2
revels in writings of B. B.
Warfield 285–6
the Pauline note appears 286–
7, 294
speaks on the minister as man,
pastor, and in private 288–9
first reactions to Inter-Varsity
Fellowship 293–8
'The new John Elias' 298
services at Llangeitho (1935)
299–300
speaks in Albert Hall, London
301–2
preaches in Westminster
Chapel for first time (1935)
303–4
as seen through Welsh eyes 307
et seq.
broadcast addresses (Welsh
B.B.C.) 314–15
questions of language (Welsh,
English) 320–1
preaching to Welsh rural
gatherings 321–4
'The modern Moody' 326, 335
second visit to North America
(1937) 327 *et seq.*
becomes conscious that
Aberavon ministry is about
to close 331
vocal trials 331
receives call from Marylebone
Presbyterian Church 331 *et
seq.*
resigns Aberavon pastorate 337
accepts call for part-service at
Westminster Chapel (1938)
339–40
begins Westminster Chapel

[389]

Index

[393]

OTHER TITLES BY DR MARTYN LLOYD-JONES
AVAILABLE FROM THE
BANNER OF TRUTH
TRUST

ROMANS SERIES:
The Gospel of God (1:1–32)
ISBN 978 0 85151 467 3, 408 pp.
The Righteous Judgment of God (2:1–3:20)
ISBN 978 0 85151 545 8, 240 pp.
Atonement and Justification (3:20–4:25)
ISBN 978 0 85151 034 7, 272 pp.
Assurance (5:1–21)
ISBN 978 0 85151 050 7, 384 pp.
The New Man (6:1–23)
ISBN 978 0 85151 158 0, 328 pp.
The Law (7:1–8:4)
ISBN 978 0 85151 180 1, 372 pp.
The Sons of God (8:5–17)
ISBN 978 0 85151 207 5, 400 pp.
Final Perseverance (8:17–39)
ISBN 978 0 85151 231 0, 460 pp.
God's Sovereign Purpose (9:1–33)
ISBN 978 0 85151 579 3, 344 pp.
Saving Faith (10:1–21)
ISBN 978 0 85151 737 7, 411 pp.
To God's Glory (11:1–36)
ISBN 978 0 85151 748 3, 304 pp.
Christian Conduct (12:1–21)
ISBN 978 0 85151 794 0, 528 pp.
Life in Two Kingdoms (13:1–14)
ISBN 978 0 85151 824 4, 336 pp.
Liberty and Conscience (14:1–17)
ISBN 978 0 85151 849 7, 288 pp.

'Dr Lloyd-Jones' expository sermons on Romans are thorough, magisterial, warm-hearted, earnest and energetic.'

Church of England Newspaper

'Dr Lloyd-Jones is a great biblical theologian but the reader will be impressed afresh by the strong experimental note in his theology.'

Evangelical Quarterly

EPHESIANS SERIES:
God's Ultimate Purpose (1:1–23)
ISBN 978 0 85151 272 3, 448 pp.
God's Way of Reconciliation (2:1–22)
ISBN 978 0 85151 299 0, 480 pp.
The Unsearchable Riches of Christ (3:1–21)
ISBN 978 0 85151 293 8, 320 pp.
Christian Unity (4:1–16)
ISBN 978 0 85151 312 6, 280 pp.
Darkness and Light (4:17–5:17)
ISBN 978 0 85151 343 0, 464 pp.
Life in the Spirit (5:18–6:9)
ISBN 978 0 85151 194 8, 372 pp.
The Christian Warfare (6:10–13)
ISBN 978 0 85151 243 3, 376 pp.
The Christian Soldier (6:10–20)
ISBN 978 0 85151 258 7, 368 pp.

(Series not available in the USA)

'Good old-fashioned theological preaching of this kind is a healthy antidote to the superficiality of many modern sermons.'

Scottish Journal of Theology

ACTS SERIES:
Authentic Christianity, Vol. 1 (1–3)
ISBN 978 0 85151 776 6, 336 pp.
Authentic Christianity, Vol. 2 (4–5)
ISBN 978 0 85151 807 7, 336 pp.
Authentic Christianity, Vol. 3 (5–6)
ISBN 978 0 85151 832 9, 352 pp.
Authentic Christianity, Vol. 4 (7:1–29)
ISBN 978 0 85151 869 5, 336 pp.
Authentic Christianity, Vol. 5 (4–5)
ISBN 978 0 85151 922 7, 320 pp.
Authentic Christianity, Vol. 6 (8:1–35)
ISBN 978 0 85151 943 2, 320 pp.

2 PETER
ISBN 978 0 85151 379 9
272 pp. Cloth-bound; and
ISBN 978 0 85151 771 1
272 pp. Paperback

'A masterly example of the kind of expository preaching in popular vein that can result in the building up of a congregation in the Christian faith.'

Reformed Theological Review

'A model for preaching and . . . a storehouse of spiritual benefit.'

Ministry

OLD TESTAMENT
EVANGELISTIC SERMONS
ISBN 978 0 85151 683 7
304 pp. Cloth-bound

'It is vintage wine indeed, and one could have wished for a volume twice the size. Can we expect more?'

Evangelical Presbyterian

'Nearly fifty years on, and the words are in cold print, yet they fire the soul! And surely that is why the book has been published . . . buy it! You will not be disappointed.'

Evangelical Action

EVANGELISTIC SERMONS
AT ABERAVON
ISBN 978 0 85151 362 1
308 pp. Large Paperback

'Early examples of that "logic-on-fire" which the author desired and commended to others. To me their abiding value lies in the intense seriousness of the preacher. They are worlds apart from the triviality of so much evangelism today.'

Dick Lucas in *Churchman*

AUTHORITY
ISBN 978 0 85151 386 7
96 pp. Paperback

'These addresses given at a conference of students in 1957 are still of superb value for students and young Christians . . .'
Vox Reformata

'This is a splendid introduction to the whole question of authority and may be studied with profit by the specialist or layman alike.'
The Gospel Magazine

WHAT IS AN EVANGELICAL?
ISBN 978 0 85151 626 4
80 pp. Paperback

'In characteristic style, Dr Lloyd-Jones offers a clear and succinct analysis of the theological trends within Evangelicalism . . . This must surely be one of the most useful books ever to come from Lloyd-Jones.'
Scottish Bulletin of Evangelical Theology

KNOWING THE TIMES
Addresses delivered on Various Occasions
1942–1977
ISBN 978 0 85151 556 4
400 pp. Case-bound

'Probably one of the most significant of all the Lloyd-Jones works that has ever been published . . . it will give both encouragement and vision to those who are concerned with the cause of the gospel.'
Churchman

THE PURITANS: THEIR ORIGINS & SUCCESSORS
ISBN 978 0 85151 496 3
436 pp. Case-bound

'This book is hard to put down; it grips the reader, and to it he will want to return again and again. None can read it without immense profit.'
Evangelical Times

D. MARTYN LLOYD-JONES: LETTERS 1919–1981
Selected with Notes by Iain H. Murray
ISBN 978 0 85151 674 5
270 pp. Cloth-bound

'Read this book to be enriched by the depth of spiritual insight and understanding which God graciously gave to his servant . . . well-produced, lovely to handle, full of meaty subjects, with a good photograph of M.L.-J. on the dust-cover . . . worth consideration as a "gift to a friend", but put one on your own shelf first!'

Reformed Theological Journal

GOD'S WAY NOT OURS:
Sermons on Isaiah 1:1–18
ISBN 978 0 85151 753 7
168 pp. Paperback

'Both faithful to the text and powerfully applicable to the present situation . . . [These sermons] were preached in 1963, but reading them you would think they had been delivered last Sunday . . . They show how the prophet's word to Israel can be legitimately applied to the whole human race.'

Foundations

THE ALL-SUFFICIENT GOD
Sermons on Isaiah 40
ISBN 978 0 85151 908 1
160 pp. Paperback

'Lloyd-Jones's razor-sharp, verse-by-verse exposition and relentless application are like taking a pin out of a grenade and planting it unbeknown in the pocket of a non-Christian (or sleepy Christian?) – and then waiting for the inevitable, devastating effects!'

Evangelicals Now

For free illustrated catalogue please write to
THE BANNER OF TRUTH TRUST

3 Murrayfield Road,
Edinburgh EH12 6EL
UK

P O Box 621, Carlisle,
PA 17013,
USA